VICKY
Princess Royal of England
and German Empress

Victoria, Princess Royal
from a painting by Winterhalter, 1857

VICKY

Princess Royal of England
and German Empress

DAPHNE BENNETT

Collins and Harvill Press
LONDON

© Daphne Bennett 1971
Reprinted 1971
Reprinted 1972
ISBN 0 00 262883 X
Set in Monotype Garamond
Made and Printed in Great Britain by
Wm Collins Sons & Co Ltd, Glasgow

To Ralph

Contents

Illustrations

All illustrations are reproduced by gracious permission of Her Majesty Queen Elizabeth II, with the exception of photographs No 16, 17, 27 and 28 which are reproduced by permission of the Radio Times Hulton Picture Library.

Endpapers: The Kronprinzenpalais, Berlin

Foreword

For over a hundred years the name of Victoria, Princess Royal of England, the eldest child of Queen Victoria, has lain under a shadow. It is a shadow placed over her not by accident, but quite deliberately by one man: Bismarck. Her life was already darkened by it in the middle 1860's, soon after she married the heir to the Prussian throne, for Bismarck feared and hated her almost from the moment when, in 1862, her father-in-law appointed him Minister-President of the kingdom which was within a few years to become the German Empire. It is the object of this book to dispel the shadow and to show Vicky in a truer light.

Until 1929, when Sir Frederick Ponsonby published the (mainly political) letters* which the dying Empress-Dowager had asked him to place for safe-keeping in the Royal Archives at Windsor, historians had little material for her biography except contemporary articles in the press which Bismarck controlled and accounts written by his followers. This meant that the unkind allegations against her (and, to a lesser degree, against her husband) could not be checked and therefore remained uncontradicted. Count Corti's attempt to give a more balanced picture nearly thirty years later was cut short by his untimely death: the large volume published under the title *Wenn . . .†* is little more than a working draft of the narrative and of the quotations which he intended to use in preparing the edited version which he did not live to write. More light was let into dark places by Mr Roger Fulford's *Dearest Child* (1964) and *Dearest Mama* (1968), which printed a selection of her private correspondence between 1858 and 1864, and revealed Vicky as tender and affectionate, and by no means the cold creature she had hitherto seemed. Although this new evidence suggested that she was occasionally naïve, yet it also showed the touches of worldly wisdom which made her so appealing even when she spoke out of turn now and again, and made her seem all the more lovable because of it.

*Letters of the Empress Frederick, ed. by Sir F. Ponsonby, London, 1929.
†Egon Caesar, Count Corti: *Wenn. . . .* Berlin 1955. A shortened English translation was published as *The English Empress* in 1957.

Although she lived continuously in England for only the first seventeen years of her life, part of Vicky always remained English— 'My country which I shall love so passionately until my dying day', she wrote in 1858.* Bismarck recognised this, but he made the mistake of thinking that her love for England would always prevent her from being a loyal Prussian. The truth was the exact opposite, for she became devoted to her husband's country and felt it her duty to prefer the German loyalty when conflict between the two was unavoidable. Yet of course, as she herself said, it was the Englishwoman in her which made her speak out against injustice, oppression and cruelty— things which 'I shall fight while I have breath in my body'. She deserves to stand alongside such reformers as Florence Nightingale and Elizabeth Fry. Like them, she was touched to the heart by pain and suffering, and all the vigour and persistence of her nature was directed to projects of social amelioration, towards which England was advancing faster than Prussia at the time of her marriage.

Her story is not the sad one of a woman who could have been great if she had been given the chance, but that of a woman who was great because she achieved so much against impossible odds. The words which Martin Luther King made the theme of his last sermon—'I refuse to accept . . .'—might equally have been hers.

She always refused to accept that wrongdoing could be justified by political advantage, but she could not prevent the vast political changes which transformed the face of Germany in her lifetime, nor the ambitions which made its rulers so powerful for ill. If her early and middle married years were clouded by Bismarck's hostility, most of her widowhood was darkened by her son's unkindness. Both saddened her; far worse, both frustrated her immense capacity to do good. It was ironical that the child of a marriage between the most liberal and modern-minded English princess who had yet lived and the only Hohenzollern who was not cast in the mould of Frederick the Great should prove to be the last autocrat of Europe's nineteenth century *ancien régime* – the man who, more than any other single individual, by his own actions caused the destruction of the society which, with an arrogance from which both his parents were entirely free, he felt himself divinely chosen to dominate. His mother had faintly foreseen what might be the consequences.

*

I am most grateful to Dr Ronald Hyam of Magdalene College for sparing me time which he could ill afford from his own writing, for guiding me through the mazes of nineteenth century diplomatic history,

*Dearest Child, p. 137.

and for long and helpful discussions of Bismarck's character and policy. He patiently read the whole manuscript and I have benefited enormously from his detailed criticisms, although I am of course alone responsible for any mistakes that remain. Dr Hyam gave me encouragement when I most needed it, and for this I thank him very warmly.

My thanks are due to my typist, Mrs G. V. Woolrich, for the skill with which she deciphered my abominable handwriting and uncomplainingly re-typed successive drafts of my work.

My husband has made many valuable critical suggestions from which I have profited greatly, and has encouraged and supported me throughout.

I am grateful to the following authors, editors and publishers for permission to quote from their books: *The Prince Consort and His Brother* and *Further Letters of Queen Victoria* edited by Hector Bolitho; Macmillan, London and Basingstoke for *Letters of the Empress Frederick* edited by Sir Frederick Ponsonby; John Murray Ltd for *Letters of the Prince Consort, 1831-1861* edited by K. Jagow and *Queen Victoria Letters: A Selection from Her Majesty's Correspondence*, series I edited by A. C. Benson and Viscount Esher, series II and III edited by G. E. Buckle; Cambridge University Press for *Recollections and Reminiscences* by Prince Otto von Bismarck, edited by A. M. Gibson, *The Holstein Papers* edited by N. B. Rich and M. R. Fisher, *Friedrich von Holstein: Politics and Diplomacy in the era of Bismarck and Wilhelm II* by N. B. Rich; Stanley Paul & Co Ltd for *War Diary 1870-1871* by Emperor Frederick III, edited by A. R. Allison; Evans Brothers Ltd for *Dearest Child* and *Dearest Mama* both edited by Roger Fulford; Cassel & Co Ltd for *The English Empress* by Egon Caesar Conte Corti; *The Empress Frederick writes to Sophie ... Letters 1889-1901* edited by Arthur Gould Lee.

CAMBRIDGE
September 1970

DAPHNE BENNETT

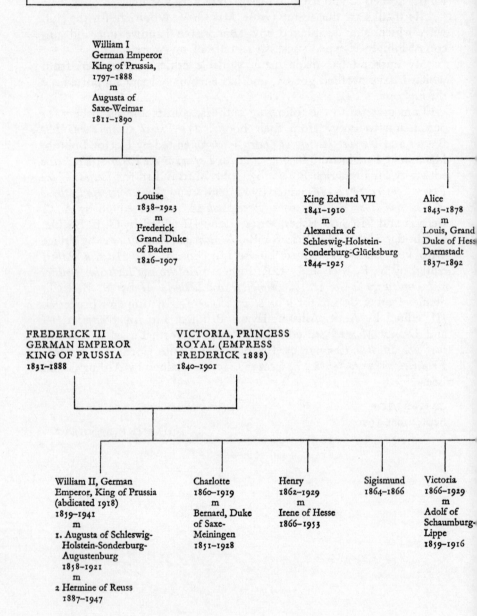

The Family Tree of the

Emperor and Empress Frederick III

William I
German Emperor
King of Prussia,
1797–1888
m
Augusta of
Saxe-Weimar
1811–1890

Louise
1838–1923
m
Frederick
Grand Duke
of Baden
1826–1907

King Edward VII
1841–1910
m
Alexandra of
Schleswig-Holstein-
Sonderburg-Glücksburg
1844–1925

Alice
1843–1878
m
Louis, Grand
Duke of Hess
Darmstadt
1837–1892

FREDERICK III
GERMAN EMPEROR
KING OF PRUSSIA
1831–1888

VICTORIA, PRINCESS
ROYAL (EMPRESS
FREDERICK 1888)
1840–1901

William II, German
Emperor, King of Prussia
(abdicated 1918)
1859–1941
m
1. Augusta of Schleswig-
Holstein-Sonderburg-
Augustenburg
1858–1921
m
2 Hermine of Reuss
1887–1947

Charlotte
1860–1919
m
Bernard, Duke
of Saxe-
Meiningen
1851–1928

Henry
1862–1929
m
Irene of Hesse
1866–1953

Sigismund
1864–1866

Victoria
1866–1929
m
Adolf of
Schaumburg-
Lippe
1859–1916

Queen Victoria
1819–1901
m
Albert of Saxe-Coburg
& Gotha, Prince Consort
1819–1861

...red, Duke of
...inburgh, Duke
...Saxe-Coburg
...4–1900
m
...and Duchess
...rie of Russia
...3–1920

Helena
1846–1923
m
Christian of
Schleswig-
Holstein
1831–1917

Louise
1848–1939
m
Marquis of Lorne,
Duke of Argyll
1845–1914

Arthur, Duke
of Connaught
1850–1942
m
Louise of
Prussia
1860–1917

Leopold,
Duke of
Albany
1853–1884
m
Helen
of Waldeck
1861–1922

Beatrice
1857–1944
m
Henry of
Battenberg
1858–1896

...demar
...–1879

Sophie
1870–1932
m
King Constantine
of Greece
1868–1923

Margaret
1872–1954
m
Frederick Charles
Landgrave of Hesse
1868–1940

CHAPTER I

'Albert, Father of a Daughter'

THE Prince Consort always felt that he only became an Englishman after the birth of his first child, the Princess Royal, on the 21st of November 1840, and that in consequence he enjoyed an affinity with her which he never had with any of his other children.

At first he had been disappointed when, waiting with the Queen's mother, the Duchess of Kent, behind a screen in the bedroom at Buckingham Palace, he heard Dr Locock say that it was 'a fine healthy princess'; but this disappointment vanished, never to return, when Mrs Lilley the midwife brought him the child wrapped in a piece of flannel. 'All is well', he wrote delightedly to his brother Ernest, 'Albert, father of a daughter, you will laugh at me.'[1] But perhaps the most remarkable event of a crowded day was still to come: because of the baby's birth, he had to represent the Queen at a Privy Council, rushing straight off from the confinement to do so. In her first moments of life, the child thus gave him a standing which he had never had before. Confirmation of it came at once. On his way back from the Council, he met Baron Stockmar, who told him that, 'as the wish the Queen has most at heart at the moment', he had asked Lord Melbourne to arrange for his name to be introduced into the liturgy.[2] This meant that for the first time the Queen's subjects would pray for him: the heiress to the throne naturally had to be included at once, and she was carrying her father with her into the wording of the prayer.

Despite his happiness with the Queen, in the nine months of his marriage to her he had found many things he longed to alter. The Queen had been almost too quick in handing over to him everything to do with the running of her homes and the management of her servants, a tiresome and boring job that did not interest her in the least. It never occurred to her that it might bore Albert too and that his talents would be better employed helping her with state affairs, for which he thought himself more fitted than a woman could be. If the Queen thought this too, she did not show it by asking his opinion on a single thing.

Albert ought to have known what to expect, for before their marriage the Queen had told him, a little tactlessly, that the English disliked foreigners interfering in their affairs. He had taken this literally, assuming that it applied to him only before Parliament had naturalised him. This belief was strengthened when, on their brief honeymoon at Windsor, the Queen had suggested that their desks should be placed side by side in the Blue Closet so that they could work together. But the Prince soon saw that this meant nothing; for he sat disconsolate and idle, his desk quite bare, watching the Queen struggle alone with her papers, while all he was expected to do was to blot her signature until it was dry.

There were other things to make him depressed. His household was not even of his own choosing. It was – somewhat heartlessly, he considered – entirely English, and not a single member of it had been known to him before. He did not take much comfort from the Queen's assurances that this was done for his own good and that he must trust her and believe this.[3] It pained him deeply, too, that his rank had not been settled. The Queen had never told him that she had asked Lord Melbourne's opinion about 'King Consort' as a title for him, and that he had rejected it as too high for the English to swallow at a gulp. His uncle King Leopold of the Belgians suggested a peerage as a way to get rid of the 'foreignship' of his name. This was too low for the Queen's taste, for it would mean that her uncles, the dukes of Sussex, Hanover and Cambridge (who were still smarting because she had not married one or the other of her Hanover or Cambridge cousins and so kept the throne in the family) would then be able to take precedence over her own husband – which would never do. Too high, too low; they could think of nothing. But Lord Melbourne said 'Never mind, in any case the Consort of a Queen will receive the highest precedence without difficulty.' The matter was therefore shelved, and although he was dismayed Prince Albert was too proud to bring the subject up again.

This was not all. Not long after the announcement of his engagement 'stupid people' began to assert that the Queen was marrying a Roman Catholic, producing a story that was perfectly true to prove their point – when on a tour of Italy in 1836, Albert had on one occasion attended mass in St Peter's, Rome. They also tried to make out that he was not the son of Duke Ernest, on evidence even flimsier: that he did not look in the least like his father or his brother, who were two of a kind in appearance and behaviour. If the 'old' royal family did not actually start this gossip, they certainly spread it, for they were only too glad to bring the lucky suitor down a peg. As though this were not enough to bear, Parliament meanly cut his allowance from £50,000 to £30,000. Hurt pride kept Albert silent, but King Leopold voiced the opinions of the whole Coburg family when he cried 'shame, shame'.[4]

All this trickled through to Albert in ingenuous letters from the Queen as he was preparing, at Christmas 1839, to leave his home in central Germany and travel to England for his marriage. The Rosenau in Thuringia was a mock medieval manor-house situated in glorious country just outside Coburg, a hundred and fifty miles east of Frankfurt. He was passionately attached to 'the paradise of my childhood', and it had bred in him an undying love for everything to do with the countryside, yet paradoxically he had been so unhappy there that he once told his daughter that he had seriously considered suicide.[5]

As every letter brought disquieting news, Prince Albert wondered very much what would happen to him in England. 'While I possess your love they cannot make me unhappy'[6] he told the Queen, but unhappy they made him all the same. Something of his real feelings breaks through in a letter to a friend in Germany: 'my future life is high and brilliant, but plentifully strewn with thorns.'[7] The Queen had told him in an unguarded moment that although the marriage was well enough liked in England, there was no enthusiasm for it; yet Albert was desperately in need of a little enthusiasm. All his suggestions for the wedding, the honeymoon and their future life had been brushed aside. Even the harmless little engagement ceremony he had set his heart on was dismissed as 'too foreign', until his self-confidence, never very strong when it came to personal relationships, was badly shaken. He became very depressed. He needed to be liked, he knew when he was not, and then his protective visor shut down and he became cold, formal and unbending and the amiable disposition which King Leopold praised so highly in his nephew completely disappeared. His home, his family and his old associations had never been so dear as, angry and exasperated, Albert buried himself in the *Commentaries on the Laws of England*, trying to discover what Blackstone had to say on the Consort of a Queen.

*

Prince Albert's character was not an easy one to understand. Outwardly he was very much a man of his time. He was never afraid of showing emotion – tears came easily to his eyes and rolled unashamedly down his cheeks. He often gave way to sentimentality – the mention of his home in Thuringia or the sound of an old German tune would make him start and grow pale. This kind of external display was then thought right and natural, and Albert did no more than conform to convention. But most of his real feelings remained hidden; when deeply moved there was only a tightening of the heart-strings and a frozen look. As a child his health was poor and he suffered from fits of depression and, though maturity brought better health, the depression never left him. This made him a prey to anxiety and set up a vicious circle of worry about himself and those he loved, which lowered his resistance and gave him a lack of confidence which made him sensitive to criticism and set up a barrier to plain speaking. In later life he buried himself in work, piling it on relentlessly and often unnecessarily. This eventually took the edge off the pleasure in living which had been so characteristic of him when he was an athletic young man excelling in outdoor sports. Even as a child he showed unnatural control over his temper and took excessive pains with his lessons. He never knew childhood tantrums or the sweet pleasure of defiance, and as a boy he recorded in his diary his intention to 'train myself to be a good and useful man'.[8] It is disturbing to read, however, that his 'little naughtinesses' were stopped merely by a 'grave look' and that the lifting of a finger was enough of a reproof.[9]

It has been said that Albert's moodiness was due to an imbalance in his life. When he was four and his brother Ernest five, his beautiful unhappy young mother, unable to put up any longer with her aged husband's infidelities, ran away with an officer in the Coburg army. The children never saw her again and in 1826 Duke Ernest divorced her. Albert never forgot his mother. He idolised her memory and romanticised her going away, but he did not miss her. At first the Duke's mother cared for the children and on her death in 1831 two other relations briefly took her place until the Duke remarried in 1832 and the new Duchess took charge of the boys. She doted on the little Albert with golden curls, bright blue eyes and a delicate air which gave him the look of a 'little angel' who was not long for this world. Indeed the one thing this gifted man never lacked was affection. He left the tender care of a stepmother for the arms of a wife who adored him and who gave him children who worshipped him as 'an oracle'. The Queen's adoration is not difficult to understand when it is remembered that during the Princess Royal's childhood, before he was bowed down with work and worry, Albert was a very attractive man. Slender, broad-shouldered with long legs, a well-shaped head, fair hair, very blue eyes and a becoming military moustache, he was full of fun and gaiety, 'bounding' from place to place, showing his children how to turn somersaults, helping them to fly their kites or to build brick houses on the nursery floor.[10] Music was the absorbing relaxation of his life and he would play to his wife and children for hours on the organ specially built for him at Windsor, or sing duets with the Queen, happy and natural only in the company of his family. Outside this close circle the picture is not so kindly or perhaps so true. Mary Bulteel, a young lady-in-waiting, said that the Prince aroused the fiercest antagonisms in her mind and that there was not one spark of spontaneity in his make-up. She thought his humour cruel because he would laugh out loud if someone fell into the fire or out of a window.[11] She refused to accept shyness as an excuse, to understand that Prince Albert's laughter could equally well have been his way of expressing alarm as mirth, or to realise that it might be sheer unease in the unaccustomed company of a young woman. Mary Bulteel forgot that she was not only young but intellectually formidable (a combination Prince Albert at that time found unattractive in females) and that she herself may have been the cause of his discomfiture. Ironically, under his guidance his own daughter was soon to develop into something very similar and to delight his heart with her erudition.

Indeed the baby delighted his heart instantly, turning him overnight into an adoring but anxious parent, so anxious indeed that for the first few months of her life he was haunted by the fear that she would not survive. Before her birth he had made a point of asking Queen Adelaide, William IV's widow, the reason why her three little girls had died in infancy. The dowager Queen had told him that her children had been weakly from the start, slow to gain weight and uninterested in food, and he had watched apprehensively for similar signs in his own daughter. It was a wonderful relief to see his child thrive and to get a favourable report from Mrs Parker, the Scottish wet-nurse. He became a nuisance in the nursery, running there several times a day, undeterred by black looks from Mrs Roberts the nurse or gentle teasing from the Queen.

One fear was no sooner resolved than his nervous imagination replaced it by another – suppose the child were to be killed in a carriage accident, so common in those days of bad roads? It was unfortunate for his peace of mind that Prince Albert had an almost obsessional fear of accidents after having seen a young Coburg cousin killed by a bolting horse. And so when the court returned to Windsor for Christmas he held the baby himself, anxiously warning the coachman to look out for ice or pot-holes in the roads. All the same, Prince Albert had not been so happy for months. He was filled with 'quiet satisfaction' as he looked at the radiant Queen (her ordeal over she felt 'better than ever', she said) and at his child sleeping peacefully in his arms.

Like many reserved people Albert was given to understating his feelings. 'Quiet satisfaction' were the words he used to express deep emotion. He had been deeply moved by the first sight of his child. She was more beautiful than he ever expected; he had seen nothing 'frog-like' in the first ungainly movements the Queen had warned him he would find so ugly in a new-born infant. Alone with his child he could give free vent to that German sentimentality he was so careful to hide from the mocking glances of what the Queen called the 'fashionables' and laughed at as 'so foreign'.

Prince Albert and his daughter had their first English Christmas together. With his gift for an occasion, nothing was too much trouble for his 'own dear Festival time'. This was why the Princess Royal enjoyed as a child the kind of Christmas which was unforgettable. Christmas to her meant trees gay with tinsel and candles, present-tables – one for each member of the family – decorated with laurel and holly, and above all it meant music and dancing, laughter and fun without end. As no other Christmas quite matched those at Windsor for the Princess Royal, so for Prince Albert no Christmas could quite compare with those he had spent in his native Coburg, no tree could be so beautiful as those which he had pranced round with his father, his brother Ernest and his tutor Herr Florschütz, in the hall of the Rosenau with the stags' heads on the wall and the huge log fire which smelt so deliciously of the pine-woods outside.

*

Perhaps because of Albert's overflowing affection, the Queen prided herself on being matter-of-fact about her child. Yet she was not so indifferent as she pretended, for as early as the 15th of December 1840, when the Princess Royal was not yet a month old and still in her estimation 'quite frightful', she wrote to her uncle Leopold that his little great-niece 'grows daily in health, strength and I may add beauty',[12] giving herself away completely when she paid her the highest compliment she could think of: 'Pussy shows a marvellous likeness to her dearest papa.'

The baby gave King Leopold his first chance for four years to come to England without laying himself open to the charge of 'interference' from the 'old' royal family (who were against him because he had been behind Victoria's match with Albert) and reminding the English tax-payers that he was still receiving an allowance of £50,000 a year granted him on his marriage to the late Princess Charlotte of Wales.* He was delighted to be godfather to his great-niece when she was christened in the throne-room at Buckingham Palace on the 10th of February 1841 (the anniversary of 'our dear marriage day'), with Jordan water from a golden font. The christening was another land-mark in Prince Albert's life. He introduced a daring innovation when he broke away from long-established tradition and used the elegant

---

*Daughter of George IV, and heiress presumptive to the throne until her death in 1817. She married Leopold in 1816. If she had lived, Victoria would not have succeeded to the throne in 1837, and Leopold would have been in the position held later by Albert. Leopold became King of the Belgians in 1831.

picture-gallery for the dinner after the ceremony. Perhaps the christen-ing-cake was the most endearing touch of all. It was meant as a tribute to his wife and child, and showed Neptune with Britannia holding the infant princess in her arms. Albert did not know it, but he had sym-bolised in transient form his own happiness, which was to reach its peak during his daughter's childhood; like the cake itself, it was slowly to disappear.

Nothing was lacking except that the Prince's cantankerous old father Duke Ernest had not bothered to answer his son's invitation to be godfather. This was deliberate because he wanted to rub in the fact of his pique at Albert's refusal of his request to demand a handsome allowance for him from the Queen so that he could carry on his dissipated life in the style his rank required. Despite offensive letters Albert still loved his father dearly and up to the very last moment kept hoping he would come. When it was plain that he would not, the Duke of Wellington was hurriedly asked to stand proxy. According to a *Times* reporter, invited by Prince Albert so that there would be an accurate account of the christening, the Duke ruined one of the high-lights of the day. The Prince had arranged for the ceremonial entrance of the baby in the arms of Queen Adelaide, who was to walk down the improvised aisle to the music of a solemn chorale which he had specially composed for the occasion. By mischance, the doors were suddenly flung open to reveal the tiny figure of the Duke of Wellington at the exact moment when the dowager Queen began to move towards the font; whereupon the band instantly broke off in the middle of the Prince's chorale and burst into 'See the conquering hero comes', ending up with three rousing cheers.[13]

The baptism over, little 'Pussy' – now Victoria Adelaide Mary Louise – was whipped out of sight. For some reason the young parents had got it into their heads that the 'fawning and flattery' of court life would ruin her character. At least that is what they told each other. But Prince Albert had another reason which he was not fully aware of himself: he did not want to share his child with anyone, not even very much with the Queen. Putting his foot down about this paid hand-somely, for he was so often in the nursery that he caught his daughter's first smile, discovered her first tooth and heard her first word, which was of course a barely recognisable 'Papa'. Since no one saw the child, however, there were bound to be rumours. The gossips recalled the madness of the Queen's grandfather, George III, the oddities of her uncles and the licentiousness of her father-in-law Duke Ernest – who, it was alleged, was more than half crazy too – while the superstitious pointed to the terrible storm which had suddenly arisen just as the Queen entered her carriage for her confinement in London, and had torn the flag from its pole on the Round Tower at Windsor.[14] This was taken as a bad omen, and the little princess was thought to be blind, misshapen or backward.

Fortunately no child can be hidden for long. Strolling in the grounds of the castle one hot June day, Lady Lyttelton, the Queen's elderly Woman of the Bedchamber, came across the Princess Royal in her pram. She knew her at once, for she was 'absurdly like the Queen'; far from being a monster, the little girl was particularly beautiful, very fair with huge intelligent blue eyes that gazed unblinkingly at the inquisitive stranger who had disturbed her play.[15] Lady Lyttelton, who had half believed the stories, was overcome. Her lavish praise opened up a new train of thought in Prince Albert's mind. He was no more willing to share his child than before, but he also longed for everybody to sing the praises of this perfection of babyhood. By August half London had seen her. Every morning she took a drive in a carriage with the windows open, clapping her hands and screaming with delight as the crowds pressed close and tried to touch the little morsel of royalty in her white muslin dress and Quaker bonnet – simple clothes for such an important child – while Mrs Roberts did her best to beat them off. 'She will soon have seen every pair of teeth in the kingdom', Lady Lyttelton wrote to her daughter, describing the scene as she saw it from the carriage behind.

Prince Albert's possessive nature made an exception of Baron Stockmar. It was in Stockmar's role as physician that he wanted the old philosopher near at hand during the first dangerous year of the baby's life. He had pressed him to stay on in the suite of rooms the Queen had allocated him in Buckingham Palace on her accession. For Stockmar – who like himself was a native of Coburg – had started his career as a doctor of medicine, and it was in this capacity that he had joined the household of Prince Leopold of Saxe-Coburg-Gotha (later King Leopold of the Belgians) in 1816 just before his marriage to Princess Charlotte of Wales. He soon became Leopold's friend, confidant and trusted adviser, a position he continued with Victoria and Albert, and to some extent (through his son Ernest) with their daughter and son-in-law. He always kept himself in the background, for he had no personal ambition, but was no less powerful for that. There was nothing he did not know about those he served, and little of importance that happened to them in which he did not have a hand, for he managed their lives much better than they did themselves; when he negotiated Prince Leopold's marriage settlement with Parliament, for instance, he got much more favourable terms than Lord Melbourne did later for Prince Albert.

If Stockmar had a fault, it was to make Albert too dependent on him

('If you want me, write and I will come', in a letter of December 1842,[16] is typical) and to drive him too hard, a mistake the Prince repeated with his eldest daughter. Until his death in 1863 Stockmar flitted between England and Coburg like a kindly will-o'-the-wisp, often unheralded but never unwelcomed. His spare frame, sallow gnome-like features, piercing blue eyes that missed nothing and thin bony legs often made him an object of mirth to the more lively members of Queen Victoria's household, who were in reality more than a little afraid of him. Many of his ideas on pre- and post-natal care were surprisingly modern. A great believer in sun and fresh air for children, he urged Queen Victoria to scrap the gloomy old nurseries and to choose instead light airy rooms on the sunny side of Buckingham Palace and Windsor Castle. He drew up diet-sheets which are not so very different from those in use today, and refused to allow the tender-hearted Albert (who could not bear to see his child suffer all over again) to believe that a vaccination which did not take meant immunity.[17]

It was Stockmar who convinced the Queen and Prince Albert that there is no substitute for a child's parents, and who helped the Queen to compose a simple memorandum as a guide for bringing up the royal children: 'That they should be brought up as simply as possible and that they should be as often as possible with their parents (without interfering with their lessons) and place their greatest confidence in them in all things.'[18] Stockmar did not dandle the Princess Royal on his knee and so earn (like Prince Albert) the Queen's praise that he made a 'capital nurse'. But he fussed just as much about coughs and colds and other childish ailments, and was nearly as often in the nursery as the father himself.

In this charmed circle Pussy grew apace, lapping up adulation as her right, happy, loved and secure.

*

Lady Lyttelton was Pussy's first governess. Cultivated, devout, and with a great sense of humour, she was a daughter of Lord Spencer of Reform Ministry fame and had married the second Lord Lyttelton in 1813, entering the Queen's service when she was widowed in 1836. All her life she had cherished a secret ambition to teach, a dream which was to be fulfilled in middle age. Walking with this intelligent woman on the slopes at Windsor Castle one summer evening, Stockmar learned of her admiration for Froebel's methods of teaching young children and her sadness that it was too late for her to try them out. From that moment he watched her covertly and noticed her tolerant and good-humoured handling of the young and often silly ladies-in-waiting, her admiration for Prince Albert, her consideration for the Queen and above all her understanding of children, and said to himself 'this is the one'. At first her deep-seated humility made her hard to persuade. But this humility did nothing to lessen her ability to deal wisely with a high-spirited and lovable child. She tried to believe that her son was right when he told her that she had been 'called to it',[19] and that her years of study had been a preparation for the task of moulding so important a life and fitting a princess to withstand the hard knocks which she might have to take.

An intimate note was immediately struck between governess and pupil when Pussy promptly christened her 'Laddle' and soon became 'Princessy' in return. With great skill Lady Lyttelton started to teach through play, stimulating the child's curiosity and never allowing her to become bored. She admitted that the Princess was spoiled but felt that it did her no harm, for she was all gracefulness and prettiness, talking fluently in English, French and German, lively and intelligent, mercurial and easily distracted, getting her own way by devious clever wiles, holding her face up to be kissed when she sensed a rebuke coming, affectionate even when scolded. The child was much given to hot temper (and remained so for years) which she found difficulty in controlling. But she was sensitive too, and easily hurt. She could be sorry, crying piteously with remorse when she saw the red marks of her sharp little teeth on Lady Lyttelton's hand. Honest to a fault, she never hesitated to admit her naughtinesses and would not ask to be forgiven 'for I mean to be just as naughty another time'. The Queen (for whom no letter was complete without at least one anecdote of her child) called her 'a sly little rogue' and 'so obstinate',[20] and by so doing almost seemed to turn these qualities into virtues to be boasted about; perhaps this is why the 'improvement' which all Victorian parents looked for was rather slow in coming.

Improvement in the Prince's status kept pace with his child's education and was as rapid as her comic repartee. Her very existence had done wonders for his self-confidence, which now increased so fast that he began to feel that there was little he could not do. He successfully championed the Duchess of Kent's cause against the Queen's former governess Baroness Lehzen. The removal of Lehzen in September 1842 brought mother and daughter closer together than ever before and lifted the last barrier between Albert and the Queen. When Lord Melbourne's government fell, Prince Albert cut short her lamentations at the loss of this dear old friend and showed her where her constitutional duty lay. He did this so well that within eighteen months she was writing to tell King Leopold that her new Prime Minister (Sir Robert Peel) was undoubtedly a great statesman,[21] and Cabinet Ministers began to treat this new confident Albert with deference and respect. Their changed attitude encouraged him to take the initiative himself and he started to clean up the Regency manners and morals of the court, which Victoria had left untouched. What had so recently been contempt for the Queen's 'foreign husband' changed overnight into awe, and the courtiers learned to be more careful of their words.

But however much there was to be put right, Albert always made time for his child. Every stage was taken with great seriousness. In 1842, not long after her second birthday, with his help the Queen drew up a most enlightened document on religion as a guide for the Princess Royal. 'I am quite clear she should have great reverence for God and for religion and that she should show that devotion and love our Heavenly Father encourages his earthly children to have for him, and not one of fear and trembling, and that the thoughts of death and an after-life should not be represented in an alarming and forbidding way and that she should be made to know as yet no difference of creeds and not think that she can only pray on her knees and that those who do not kneel are less devout in their prayers.'[22] To kneel or not to kneel in prayer caused the only difference of opinion between Lady Lyttelton and her royal employers. Whenever possible the Queen and Prince Albert heard Pussy say her prayers, which she would do sitting up in bed. When it was Lady Lyttelton's turn she always insisted that the child kneel, but it made the conscientious governess very unhappy to differ from the child's parents on this vital issue until one day the little girl showed that she could accept without question two different points of view if they were held by people she loved and trusted. As she ran along the great corridor at Windsor one day Pussy trod on a large nail which almost penetrated the thin sole of her satin shoe. As she removed the nail, Lady Lyttelton seized the chance to point the moral – God had seen fit to spare Princessy pain. The answer came quick as a flash: 'Shall we kneel down?'[23]

*

Before she could walk alone the Princess Royal was meeting everyone who came to Windsor and Buckingham Palace. Ministers would find her sitting on the Queen's knee when they came for an audience, or holding up business while she crawled over their papers. Both parents gloried in the praise of amazed statesmen and guests alike as they listened spellbound to the sophisticated conversation pouring out from this comical little figure in a blue velvet dress and yellow kid mittens who quickly showed she did not intend to be ignored as she thrust out a diminutive hand for the expected kiss.

Very early on she showed a great penchant for the bizarre. She at once took to the lumbering figure of the King of Prussia, Frederick William IV, who was hideously ugly, with a head like an egg and a high falsetto voice. (The kind-hearted Lady Lyttelton said he looked like a 'good-natured farmer', but the Queen, nearer the mark, described him to her uncle Leopold as 'very fat, with small features and not much hair'.)[24] The King had come to England in 1842 to be godfather to the Prince of Wales. Pussy sat on his knee and played with a huge blood-stone hanging from a heavy gold watch-chain stretched across his protruding stomach. This performance was not repeated two years later when the King's brother and heir, the Prince of Prussia (Prince William) came to be sponsor to another son, Alfred ('Affie'). Albert had taken the little girl to the white drawing-room at Windsor to meet the man who thirteen years later was to become her father-in-law. Unlike his brother, Prince William was a fine looking man, tall and dignified with a shock of hair like a lion's mane and a deep sonorous voice, and he had none of those personal idiosyncrasies that made the King so trying. But Pussy shrank from him, hiding her head against her father's knee and vexing him very much by refusing to say a word.

Albert, however, was much taken with Prince William's frank manner and bluff soldier's ways[25] – a dangerous cover-up for the complexities beneath. Without giving himself time to look below the surface, Albert deluded himself into thinking that he understood this man thoroughly. But there was much he did not know. In his youth William had fallen in love with Princess Elise Radziwill, whom his father forbade him to marry because she was not 'of the blood'. He obediently gave her up, but he never forgot her or his sacrifice, and the affair left a deep scar. Princess Augusta of Saxe-Weimar became his wife instead. She was the kind of woman he could not tolerate, and he quarrelled with her incessantly. Because of this he developed an inhibition: he could not bear to see people in love or to hear endearments of any kind. After his own fashion, he was quite fond of his two children Frederick William ('Fritz') and Louise ('Wiwy'), although he often treated them roughly and with scant consideration. The kindly and gracious manner he adopted towards strangers was sadly lacking in his dealings with his family, with whom he was hard, tyrannical and sometimes even cruel.

The Queen and Prince Albert had met the Prince and Princess of Prussia for the first time in 1845 during an idyllic holiday in Coburg which coloured their view of Prussia for many years to come. When Princess Augusta appeared on the Windsor scene in 1846, two years after her husband's visit, Queen Victoria therefore received her with open arms, believing her to be amiability itself and her character an 'open book'. A week's close proximity did not change her mind, although she had been warned – probably by Queen Adelaide – that she must not be taken in and that Augusta could be 'false'.[26]

Queen Victoria would have found her a very different person in her own home. There Princess Augusta was filled with self-destroying nervous energy, and her chief interest in life was the pursuit of pleasure. She thought nothing of staying up all night at a ball or a reception, going without sleep and expecting her ladies to do the same, so that they looked on their periods of waiting with dread. Clever, well-educated and interested in politics, Augusta often acted so foolishly that few thought her half as intelligent as she really was.

At Windsor, on those chill autumn evenings in September 1846 when the first fires were lit and Albert was at his desk immersed in affairs of state, the two women had cosy talks in which everything was discussed with great freedom, a rare treat for the Queen, who never since her marriage had been so open with another woman.

The Prince found Augusta just as congenial. They discussed politics and discovered a common bond in their liberal ideas and belief in constitutional government. Augusta was not afraid of criticising Russia (despite a Russian mother) and she had little good to say about France, calling Louis Philippe 'weak and vacillating', a man with no fight in him who in an emergency would 'crumble at a touch'. While they were talking, the strange idea came into Albert's head that somehow, through this clever and high-principled woman, he might be able to influence the future of Germany and so bring about a dream that had been with him since he first discussed it with Stockmar in 1836: the unification of Germany under Prussia.

CHAPTER 2

'A Child with very strong Feelings'

WITH his interest in human nature Stockmar spent a great deal of time observing the Princess Royal's mental progress. What he saw filled him with joy. He expected that, with the good fortune which attended everything he set his hand to, her future would be as high and glorious as her father's, for she possessed, as he did, all the qualities of kingship.

But unlike her father, Pussy was a rebellious child with turbulent feelings that led her into a tangle of bewildering emotions which she could not understand and which all too often ended in storms of tears. Stockmar guessed that at the root of her tempers were those strong feelings the Queen had often remarked, so that she was already (as she was all her life) too easily torn with pity, anxiety, or sheer terror for those in distress. By his rare insight into the reasons why these feelings ruled her, Stockmar went a long way towards helping her to learn control. 'Know thyself' was to him a maxim of the first importance. In those early lessons in self-analysis he taught the growing child how to conserve her energies, teaching her not to waste them on needless distress – and to recognise when distress was needless. Yet a great part of her charm and fascination for everyone – even on occasions for her enemies – was the different shades and depths of the emotions she was capable of experiencing. The very sensitivity that left her open to hurts and bruises made her greatly coveted as a friend.

Formal education began at seven with a change of name: Pussy became Vicky and remained so for the rest of her life. Lady Lyttelton still gave her lessons, although she could see that her usefulness to the little girl was coming to an end. A talent for drawing, quite marked even at the age of three, was encouraged by the Queen who let the child sketch by her side and gave her simple lessons in mixing paints. Vicky sat on a pile of cushions (and once outdoors disastrously on a wasps' nest) in front of a miniature easel and discovered how to make recognisable shapes. Painting was to become to her what music was to Prince Albert.

Her father supervised her piano playing, although the drudgery was left to Mrs Anderson, a gifted widow who had once been a concert pianist. Vicky hated scales and five-finger exercises but she loved to sit at one end of the long organ stool and turn the pages of the music her father played so beautifully. She heard Mendelssohn play on that very organ, but was too young at the time to appreciate him, although by a curious trick of memory she could remember her father showing the great musician how to work the stops and could even recall the tune of the few chords he played before he relinquished the instrument to his guest. Later she came to enjoy Mendelssohn's oratorios as much as her father.

In the forties and fifties London was full of continental musicians who performed nightly at Covent Garden and Drury Lane. Italian opera was especially popular and with musical parents Vicky soon became familiar with singers like the tenor Mario and the sopranos Grisi and Garcia who were asked to sing at Windsor. It was Vicky who arranged for Jenny Lind to perform at the wedding of the Prince of Wales in 1862, because Prince Albert had once said how much he admired her voice.

The arrival of Miss Hildyard, a clergyman's daughter, marked a great change in Vicky's life. The new governess was well-educated, intelligent and an inspired teacher, a fit successor to Lady Lyttelton. Without wasting time she briskly started Vicky on an invigorating course of study which captured her imagination. Vicky's temper improved overnight because she was taken out of herself and into the world of real learning where she belonged and which she was never to leave again. Out went the improving books by Mrs Sarah Trimmer, Miss Edgeworth and Hannah Moore that cast such a shadow over the lives of Victorian youth. Instead Miss Hildyard revealed the delights of history, literature and science. Vicky learned Latin declensions for fun before breakfast and worked out mathematical problems before going to sleep. Pupil and teacher read Gibbon's *Decline and Fall* together and Macaulay's *History of England* as each volume was published. For relaxation there was Dickens, the Brontës and George Eliot and above all, Shakespeare, who was made unforgettable by the sight of the great Macready in some of her favourite plays.

Stockmar encouraged her bent for politics, which according to him was so remarkable that it almost amounted to genius. Stockmar had a nose for discerning talent – Prince Albert himself was one of his brightest discoveries. There is no doubt that he was right when he said that Vicky was born with a natural aptitude for politics and a grasp of political situations that would have made her name had she been a man and a commoner. In his eagerness to nurture this rare gift he was too inclined to give everything a political twist and sometimes overdid things. He used the revolutions of 1848 to illustrate to the little girl the advantages of constitutional government over autocracy when trouble came, pointing to England and Belgium as two democratic countries which had stood firm in the midst of chaos.

But Vicky was more affected by what she learned from a polyglot mixture of young refugees than from any amount of impersonal theory. These children arrived in a bedraggled state with only the clothes they stood up in and with horrible stories of kidnappings and brutalities. Vicky had never realised before that thrones could fall and monarchs be deposed overnight and that nothing was secure, not even her own home. She was perfectly aware of the Chartist riots and the seriousness of her father's grim-faced order that no one was to leave the palace. She experienced all the terror of an imaginative child when she thought of her mother, unable to move because she had just given birth to another daughter, Louise ('caught in a trap' was the way she described this kind of situation in later life, and it never failed to fill her with horror). It was as much a relief to Vicky as it was to Prince Albert to be given an excuse to leave London with dignity and without the slightest hint of running away. Princess Sophia of Gloucester died in April, and Albert seized the excuse to take them with all speed to Osborne – 'court mourning', he called it.[1]

Vicky was deeply attached to Osborne, above all because it was her father's creation. Seeking a suitable country refuge where their children could be brought up as simply as possible, Victoria and Albert bought a thousand-acre estate in the Isle of Wight in 1845, demolished the existing mansion and built a house to Albert's design. The mild climate, the sea, the sands and the grounds in which they could ride at will made Osborne a paradise for Vicky and her brothers and sisters. In a corner of the gardens Albert had placed a Swiss chalet, where they all played 'house' and where Vicky baked her first cake. After she went to live in Prussia, Osborne became a haven of rest, a place where she could regain sense and sanity.

With parents who loved the open air and whose systems required constant refreshment by frequent changes of scene, holidays became an integral part of Vicky's life. To the dismay of Stockmar and Lady Lyttelton, but to their own delight, the children were often snatched away from lessons for what Stockmar and Lady Lyttelton disapprovingly called 'treats', which the royal parents justified by the benefits that would accrue from lungfuls of 'pure air' – perhaps for a sail down the Solent in the *Fairy*, or round the Isle of Wight. Dressed in smart sailor suits and yachting caps, they would have fun chasing their gay uncle Charles of Leiningen (the Queen's half-brother) round the deck in some game he had invented for their amusement. There were other 'treats' just as thrilling. All the children loved to travel through the night in a train at the reckless speed of thirty miles an hour to the Highlands, breaking the journey at Edinburgh to see the historic sights.

It was perhaps significant that Vicky's sailor suit was a boy's. In *tableaux vivants* – very popular for celebrating birthdays and other anniversaries – charades or anything that required dressing up, Vicky was always given the boys' parts in which she excelled. The Queen took great pride in this small swaggering figure that made such a 'splendid' or 'fine' boy. Vicky could not help overshadowing the slower, less versatile Prince of Wales, a year her junior, who was always being compared with his clever, quick-witted sister to his own disadvantage. It says much for his good nature that he adored her through all the normal squabbles of childhood. In her turn, she was devoted to him. But the Queen and Prince Albert (Stockmar too, is not blameless) made it plain that they never ceased regretting that this 'splendid boy' was not heir to the throne. However, Vicky's often repeated cry 'I wish I were a man' was not – as some have alleged – a desire to be masculine, but merely a longing to share masculine status and to throw off the shackles which hindered a woman from doing what she wanted.

*

Vicky's destiny was shaped by a mere accident – that Frederick William, the only son of the Prince and Princess of Prussia, was a liberal in politics.

The importance of this boy in Albert's schemes for Germany was not at first self-evident. Until he met Fritz in 1851, Albert had taken Princess Augusta's list of her son's virtues as maternal exaggeration. It was too much to expect a youth of twenty to be as ardent a liberal as his mother and to share her hopes for a united Germany. How could he be sure the Princess had not grossly overrated her son's idealism? Thus for the moment Albert was not ready to take up Augusta's suggestion that Fritz should come to England for a week or two. After all that had happened he preferred to wait and see how matters shaped.

Albert's caution was the result of bitter disappointment. For some time past he had been corresponding with Fritz's uncle, the Prussian king, on the subject of German unity. He drew up long memoranda (rivalling Stockmar's in length and complexity) which he changed and developed as the months went by to suit the altering mood on the continent. To his delight his schemes seemed to touch a chord in the heart of Frederick William IV, who wrote that he had not only studied them carefully but had sent copies to all his fellow monarchs with added notes of his own.[2] But the King soon lost interest, and all that came of this painstaking work were some disconcerting howls of amusement from Albert's brother Ernest, who returned his copy with the jocular marginal comment that the 'conception of the King of

Prussia . . . rivalled the draft of my brother . . . in the doctrinaire statement of improbabilities and impossibilities'.[3]

When revolution broke out in Germany in 1848 Albert took it for granted that unification would follow as a matter of course. He was wrong. Instead, the unpredictable Frederick William's extraordinary behaviour dashed these hopes. At the height of the street-fighting in Berlin the King emerged from his palace swathed in the black, red and yellow colours of the Democratic party; mounting his horse, he then spouted a 'lot of nonsense'[4] to a wildly cheering crowd. Stockmar's philosophical dismissal of the whole business as a 'sad mess' found no echo in Prince Albert's mind; he was contemptuous of such conduct, and for once words failed him.

A fortnight later Prince William of Prussia redeemed his brother's shocking behaviour by a dignified flight to England,[5] although he was forced to leave Augusta and his children behind in Potsdam. Without a moment's delay Albert had called at the Prussian Embassy in Carlton House Terrace, where William had taken refuge, to pay his respects and to show his pleasure that the Prince had chosen England for his exile.

It was a chance not to be missed. Before the week was out William was an honoured guest at Windsor, where an enthusiastic Albert showered him with the 'best advice'. The royal refugee's taciturnity would have been disconcerting to anyone less consumed with his subject than Albert. Unwillingness to listen had not been one of William's vices, but Albert forgot that silence often goes with a stubborn nature. In Prussia the Prince had a reputation for being as immovable as a rock. Albert did not know this, and mistook silence for acquiescence. Day after day he expounded his reasons for thinking that it was only a matter of time before Germany was unified – 'it must come'.[6] He tried to ensure that Prince William understood that 'Germany must be first in importance, although of course it shall be led by Prussia', warning him not to expect too much all at once; the change might be gradual. Thinking of his own Coburg, Albert stressed the need for the smaller states to keep their individuality, although of course they must not be an obstacle to progress. There was only one way for Prussia to settle her difficulties; a form of constitutional government, possibly after the English pattern.[7]

There is no doubt that Albert was impressed by his guest. He sent an account of the visit to King Leopold, praising the Prussian Prince to the skies – 'Men like him Germany cannot do without'.[8]

Events soon proved to Albert that he was right in thinking how well Prince William compared with his unstable brother. In June King Frederick William was offered the imperial crown by the National

Assembly. He haughtily refused to accept it from the hands of the people, a gesture which drew some caustic comments from Windsor. But it did not surprise Victoria and Albert. In February 1848 the Queen had received a letter from Frederick William signed 'King by the Grace of God'. This style was always used by the Hohenzollerns, as they knew, but it seemed hopelessly at variance with the temper of 1848 and in a mere private letter to a fellow-sovereign. But they excused it to each other because the King's ailment – softening of the brain – was steadily getting worse, so that he hardly knew any more what went on in a world he would not inhabit for much longer. Albert remembered how Prince William had referred more than once to his own advancing years and had said gloomily that his reign was bound to be short. The future lay with his son Fritz, who would rule for a very long time.

Suddenly Albert saw in this boy the doorkeeper of the German unity which he had been seeking. If he was to get his foot inside the door – and after Princess Augusta's visit it was already slightly ajar – Fritz must come to England and see the happy result of a freely-elected parliament on trade and commerce. But how to get him to England naturally?

Not for the first time Stockmar's practical common sense solved the problem. Why not invite the whole Prussian royal family to the opening of Prince Albert's great Exhibition on the 1st of May 1851? In order that no mistaken inference should be drawn from the visit (the Baron had already thought of one that might spring to people's minds) Stockmar suggested sending wholesale invitations to all the crowned heads of Europe – the more the merrier. There was not one who would not profit from a sight of Prince Albert's hard-won achievement. Alas, the response was poor: 1848 was still too green a memory and the crowned heads felt safer at home. It was a blow when the King of Prussia refused to allow his brother and his family to come. But his resistance collapsed – just as that of the opponents of the Exhibition had done – after a scathing letter from Prince Albert.

When Prince William, his wife and children at last set foot in England on the 31st of April they had nothing to complain of in the warmth of their reception, despite the fact that there was no love lost between the two countries (the fault of the newspapers, led by the most powerful of all, *The Times*). London was packed for the Exhibition, and the sight of the pale but triumphant Albert driving away from the station in an open carriage with his guests was the signal for loud cheering. It was a beautiful warm spring evening, much too good to waste indoors. So as soon as she decently could the Queen whisked her guests off to have their eyes opened by an educational tour of the glass

house in Hyde Park, which although not exactly in the fresh air looked
amazingly like it with trees and shrubs cleverly enclosed within the
dome. The Prussians were gratifyingly thunderstruck.

That night, on her way to bed, the Queen dropped in on Stockmar
to have a quick gossip while she took the weight off her swollen feet.
She wanted him to know how delighted she was with young Fritz. He
was good-looking and friendly, the children were quite taken with
him. Stockmar had not been idle. He had managed a few words alone
with Prince William. He wanted Prince Albert to know all was well in
that quarter. The Prince was 'firm as ever' in his constitutional views,
and highly indignant with his brother's foolish behaviour.[9]

*

It was generally accepted that, although he was twenty years old and
nominally belonged to the adult world, Fritz would prefer to tour the
Exhibition in the lively company of 'our children'. This pleased Vicky,
who was never happier than with an audience. Fritz was astonished
that such a child could know so much. His own sister Louise, although
nearly five years older, compared very unfavourably with her and was
already, even in that dazzling Aladdin's cave, showing signs of boredom. Perhaps even at ten there was a certain coquetry in Vicky's
manner towards one whom she immediately sensed was an admirer.
But the real pleasure she got from Fritz's presence came more from the
chance it gave her to instruct – there was always something of the
school-marm hidden away in Vicky that did not take much tempting
to emerge. Fritz's English was imperfect, Vicky's German faultless.
Fritz could not make out what half the exhibits were meant for; Vicky
had been round the stands several times before the Exhibition was
opened and had all her answers pat. He noticed that for one so young
she showed remarkable tact. Whenever she saw from the corner of her
eye that the Prince and Princess of Prussia were starting to bicker
about some trifling matter they had blown up to outsize proportions,
she skilfully steered him in the opposite direction out of earshot so that
he should not be embarrassed. She was indefatigable in answering
questions, never complaining of the heat or the dust which gave Fritz
a headache. But when she was told that she was too young to go with
the royal party to the opera or a play, she was furiously angry and
marched off to bed too sulky to say goodnight.

Before the end of the second day there was little about Fritz which
Vicky did not know. Like her dear papa he had been at the university
of Bonn, he was a lonely person although he had many acquaintances,
he loved animals and had a horse called 'Firefly' who could go like the
wind, but had never kept a pet. He loved reading as she did, and as

much time as he could spare from soldiering he spent in his uncle the King's huge library – which to Vicky's amazement held not one single novel. He enjoyed poetry but preferred history, and unlike Vicky herself he did not like mathematics, chemistry and science. She extracted some information of which he was ashamed – he had never before been abroad, but he was glad his first trip was to England. Fritz was having his eyes opened as wide as his host and hostess could wish, and not only by the marvels of the Exhibition. To begin with, he could not get over the freedom enjoyed by the royal children, who were on the best of terms with their parents although full of respect towards them. The open affection between the Queen and her husband amazed him no less. The Queen seemed to take a pride in being 'Albert's wife'; indeed all the children looked up to their father as head of the family. Most surprising of all, there was never a cross word between husband and wife, nor even the suggestion of a quarrel.

Up to the time of his engagement, Fritz's ideas on matrimony were thoroughly cynical. He knew that he had to marry to provide an heir to the throne, but he had been made to understand that it was not the girl herself who mattered, but the concessions, bargains and advantages which his wife brought with her. Love, such a vital ingredient to the English royal family, was never mentioned. To Fritz, love meant the illicit extra-marital affairs of his uncles and cousins or the brief amorous adventures of his contemporaries, and had nothing to do with marriage. Never before in his life had he seen married love like this between the Queen and Prince Albert. He did not know what to make of it, but he did know that he had never been so happy before and that it was all because of the jolly atmosphere created by this kind, close-knit family.

Years later Fritz confessed to Vicky that he had dreaded going to England. He knew only too well that in the unaccustomed company of people of his own age he was shy, tongue-tied and easily embarrassed. But with these cheerful unselfconscious children he did not feel awkward or uncomfortable. The days flew by, and the frightening four weeks had suddenly become the last precious day.

What was Fritz really like? Legend has it that he was an unprepossessing youth, but portraits of him at this period tell a different story. These show him to have been tall and thin with fair hair that curled slightly, blue eyes whose direct gaze Queen Victoria described as 'innocent', and a Hohenzollern nose which became less prominent as his face filled out. He held himself well, the result of the military training which he had started at the age of ten, like all Prussian princes. The Empress Eugénie, a good judge of men's looks, called him 'exactly her idea of Hamlet' when he stayed in Paris on his way back to Prussia in 1855.

In the short time at his disposal Prince Albert succeeded in convincing Fritz how imperfectly he was being prepared for kingship.
Although Fritz believed that liberalism was the answer to the world's
problems, ignorant and short-sighted people had been trying to convince him that the absolutist principles of his uncle Frederick William
IV were the only right and proper ones for Prussia. They were so
persuasive that sometimes he did not know what to think.[10] Albert
soon put that right. Fritz's confidence in himself increased by leaps and
bounds when he heard this clever and distinguished man produce
arguments which put an end to his doubts once and for all. Even his
mother's theoretical schemes for unification became a possibility when
Albert explained them. The whole idea (and his own share in it) was
stupendous enough to make his heart beat fast with excitement. But
he would have to re-educate himself, painful though it was. Although
it would hurt his father, he knew that this could not be done if he were
still treated like a child and kept ignorant of state affairs. Fritz had also
long suspected that the old man feared that if he saw too much of his
mother she might indoctrinate him with the liberalism which was
abhorrent to him. But this Prince Albert did not know.

Eagerly Fritz asked Prince Albert if he would help him – perhaps, if
it was not too much to ask, with an occasional letter or memorandum.*
And he gazed on his host with devotion, vowing that in future no one
else should guide him.

By the time he left England at the end of the month his head was
reeling with the plans Prince Albert had made to broaden his mind.
Not one word had been said about his parents' quarrels, how they
heartlessly made their son an issue between them, and the terrible
effect of this on a sensitive boy. Fritz was grateful to the Prince for
sparing his feelings.

Albert decided that something must be said to Augusta, as the more
responsive parent. In June he helped the Queen to compose a straight-
forward letter to her friend: 'I beg you to show more confidence in your
dear son, so that he may likewise have more confidence in himself. I
am always afraid in his case of the consequences of a moral clash should
his father strongly recommend something and his mother warn against
it. He will wish to please both and the fear of not succeeding will make
him uncertain and hesitant, two of the greatest evils that can befall a
prince.'[11] They were both shocked to discover, eighteen months later,
that Fritz had still not done even a little travelling on the continent.

*Albert took immediate advantage of the suggestion. Instead of simply writing
his name in the autograph album which Fritz asked him to sign at the end of the
visit, he sought to impress his views on Fritz succinctly by writing 'May Prussia
be merged in Germany, and not Germany in Prussia'.

Another frank letter was sent to Coblenz, where Augusta spent spring and summer and as much of the winter as her husband would allow: Augusta must insist on Fritz seeing the world and must see that he was given a chance to meet distinguished people, who were not to be found in the barracks of Berlin or the dull provincialism of Potsdam.[12]

Even so, all that happened was a flying visit to Warsaw, arranged on most economical lines by Prince William, who saw no advantage in travel for its own sake and had given in only to stop Augusta nagging. He grumbled endlessly at the expense, since the boy would have to go in a certain style – needless to say cut to the bone by a miserly William. He argued that as Fritz would be king before long he ought to wait until he could go in state at the taxpayer's expense. Until this happened he could get on with his soldiering.

Although outwardly nothing was changed by the holiday in England, in fact things were very different. Fritz tried to keep Prince Albert's advice in mind, and in order not to lose contact with England he wrote long though intermittent letters to Vicky all about 'my very dull life', which he gloomily thought could not interest her in the least.

*

Their correspondence lapsed during the Crimean War as Prussia's popularity in England dropped to rock-bottom, taking the innocent Fritz down with it. Prussia's neutrality had been a shock after the warmth of the friendship between the royal houses of Guelph and Hohenzollern – sealed (at least on one side) by the Garter, invitations to be sponsor to the Queen's growing family, lavish hospitality and endless free advice, not to mention the hours spent writing reams on politics (Prince Albert) and pages on every aspect of family news (the Queen). Now it seemed that all this was wasted.

In the tense and dramatic months following the declaration of war on the 28th of February 1854, the memory of Fritz faded in the one and only enjoyable war of Vicky's life. How she enjoyed it! Something in Vicky always responded to the thrill of the pageantry of war. It was part of the mysterious ambivalence of her nature that the fire of patriotism could burn fiercely at the sight of soldiers marching to their death in defence of their country, while her heart rejected with loathing the barbaric idea of men killing each other and calling it honour and glory.

While Fritz stayed in Berlin and drilled his men, or sat lonely in the king's library at Charlottenburg, Vicky's horizons were widening in the magical world of the sophisticated French court. She had fallen instantly in love with the ugly but charming Napoleon III with his great waxed moustaches, and with his glamorous wife Eugénie, when the Emperor and Empress came to Windsor in the spring of 1855 to discuss the problems of the war with the Queen and Prince Albert. A return visit to Paris in August with her parents and the Prince of Wales added a new dimension to Vicky's growing sophistication. A whole week in the fairy-tale palace of St Cloud took her breath away. She was old enough (nearly fifteen) in 1855 to recognise that the décor, the furniture and the pictures were perfection itself, and everything the last word in elegance and luxury. She had her own bedroom (at home she shared one with Alice) which the Empress Eugénie had herself arranged. A little door curtained in white satin opened on to a miniature garden scented with orange trees and with a glorious panoramic view of Paris that sent Vicky flying for her sketch book. She was in raptures the whole time and barely noticed the suffocating heat, the dust, the eager crowds, not even the ache in her legs from hours of sightseeing.

It was while waltzing with Napoleon during a ball in the Salle des Glaces at Versailles that Vicky caught a glimpse of herself and saw with surprise that she was pretty.

In the months that followed, the war naturally took on less and less glamour as bad news came from the front. Vicky was allowed to read all the newspapers – she never remembered any censorship as a child or growing girl – but she only half believed what they said. The delights of Paris and the feeling that she was growing up occupied most of her thoughts. It was the famous Florence Nightingale herself who brought her down to earth, when she came to Balmoral shortly after returning from the Crimea in January 1856. To everyone's surprise she was not at all formidable, but a very simple person, 'quiet, gentle and modest in the extreme', with short hair, mild blue eyes and a sweet smile. She was dressed plainly in black, her only ornament the brooch the Queen had given her 'to commemorate your great and blessed work'.[13] Vicky asked her eagerly if it was true about the fever, the cholera and the cold which froze the men's moustaches and was more deadly than disease, questions which Miss Nightingale answered plainly and directly, in no way glossing over the facts because she was talking to a child, so that Prince Albert was much impressed. She told them that the Scots bore pain best, then the English and last the Irish, but all wonderfully. 'But when did you sleep?' 'Oh, that first winter we did not feel as though we needed much sleep.'[14]

The friendship with Prussia's royal family was gradually renewed although Queen Victoria and Princess Augusta had never lost touch completely. Both knew the bonds between them to have been strengthened through having survived the mud smeared on their countries during the war. Both women were anxious to forgive and forget. They shared a common interest in their growing daughters, and

H.R.H. PRINCE ALBERT & THE PRINCESS ROYAL.

E. LANDSEER.

Prince Albert with the Princess Royal, *from a drawing by Landseer, 1842*

Queen Victoria and Prince
Albert with their children,
left to right: the Princes
Alfred and Edward, the
Princesses Alice, Helena and
Victoria, *from a painting by
Winterhalter, 1846*

Victoria, Princess Royal,
detail from the above painting

The Princess Royal
as 'Summer', in a
tableau with Prince
Arthur, 1854

Victoria, Princess
Royal, about 1856

left to right: The Princess Royal, Princess Alice, Queen Victoria and the Prince of Wales, 1857

left to right: Prince Alfred, the Prince Consort, Princesses Helena and Alice, Prince Arthur (in kilt), Queen Victoria holding Princess Beatrice, the Princess Royal, Princess Louise, Prince Leopold and the Prince of Wales, 1857

this made a useful non-controversial subject to start the ball rolling again. Lack of maternal feeling did not stop Princess Augusta endlessly singing her daughter's praises. Wiwy was obedient, docile, helpful, sweet-tempered and confiding, and had never given her mother a day's trouble. The Queen knew only too well that her own eldest daughter possessed none of these virtues, although she had some good points, and she tried to make the most of them in her reply: 'She has made much progress with her music, and has a great talent for drawing. She has a genuine love of art, and expresses opinions about it like a grown-up person with rare good sense.'[15] Augusta had noticed with disapproval in 1851 this freedom to express opinions. It had been a surprise to see the Queen and Prince Albert draw a ten-year-old girl into the conversation, a shock to hear them take her views seriously. Augusta had been forced to swallow her resentment at having to treat Vicky like a grown-up person. Nevertheless, she saw that, for reasons of her own, she could not afford to disregard Vicky.

By 1856 Augusta was seriously considering Fritz's marriage prospects and had come to the conclusion that a Princess Royal of England would not be a bad match. But Vicky as a person did not appeal to her, and had it not been for her position Augusta would not for a moment have thought her suitable for Fritz. As she saw it, the marriage would join two great countries together for the benefit of one – her own. England was great and powerful and much respected abroad. Only that summer a curious cartoon had appeared in journals all over the continent. It showed the sovereigns of Europe huddled together high in the air in one pan of a pair of scales. In the other, outweighing them all, stood the slight figure of Queen Victoria. Under the cartoon were the words 'Light-weight sovereigns'.[16] Augusta had seen this, and it had given her food for thought. More than anything in the world she hoped to see Germany united under Prussia in her life-time – and she was no longer young. This dream was her chief point of contact with Prince Albert. But it never occurred to either that there was no bond between them except that they shared a common short-coming; neither took the human element into account. To them people were merely pawns in a game played with ideas. After fifteen years in England, Prince Albert was convinced that a constitutional government on British lines was best for Germany. Princess Augusta agreed. As far as she saw, the only stumbling block was her husband's reactionary outlook – which he had so skilfully hidden from the Prince. In the soothsayer's language he sometimes used, Albert had told her that although he 'saw' Prince William's future as 'dark and misty' so long as he kept before him certain 'fixed principles' 'the clouds will clear away revealing the sun in all its glory'.[17]

On the marriage question Prince Albert was quite ready to meet Princess Augusta half-way. In the years between 1851 and 1855 he had come to see that his talented daughter's marriage to the son of the heir to the Prussian throne might open the road to German unity, and he used her for that purpose without hesitation. Lost in lofty day-dreaming, he did not realise that this was to treat a human life exactly as he treated ideas in the long and detailed memoranda which he sent to Princess Augusta. It would be quite wrong, however, to think of him as sacrificing the child whom he adored. He would never have coerced an unwilling girl into a distasteful marriage. There must be love. To him and the Queen, love, which had come to them both so suddenly and unexpectedly, was an absolute essential.

CHAPTER 3

A Sprig of White Heather

THE ash from the bonfire which celebrated the fall of Sebastopol on the 9th of September 1855 was still smouldering when Fritz arrived at Balmoral a week later. He was shy and apprehensive, and heartily wished he had never allowed his mother to persuade him into coming. But he thawed rapidly in a welcome as warm as the blaze of tartan that covered the floors, windows and furniture, even the occupants of the house itself, who instantly put him at his ease.

No one had told Vicky the reason for the visit, so she greeted Fritz unselfconsciously, shaking hands in a friendly way and beaming with pleasure, so delighted was she to see him again.[1] She sat next to him at dinner that night and chattered away as though she had known him all her life, while Fritz looked amused and laughed at her jokes. The Queen and Prince Albert, quite aware of what was going on, tried to look unconcerned.

Next day Albert took his young guest out stag-hunting, but Fritz could not keep his mind on the sport. Vicky had been a surprise. She had changed: she was prettier, and at almost fifteen had grown up more than he thought possible in only four years. He had forgotten how big and blue her eyes were, and how they sparkled with humour and fun, and her gay light laugh was like music in his ears. She moved in a quick graceful way that he loved to watch. At first it had seemed the same as before, but he soon perceived a subtle difference. Instinctively he sensed that she was aware of him in a way that had been impossible in 1851. But more than anything he enjoyed talking to her about himself, something that had never happened to him before. By the time he went to bed on the second day his head was in a whirl and he hardly slept a wink. Next morning he missed stag after stag and it it was only Prince Albert who returned with a sprig in his cap.

Fritz was not the only one whose feelings were upside down. The Queen had been greatly surprised at the change in her guest. The callow tongue-tied youth of twenty had been replaced by a mature young man of twenty-four, with more charm and attractive qualities than she had ever expected. It was most provoking to have to stand aside, a helpless onlooker, while Vicky behaved all too naturally. It

43

dismayed the Queen to see her not at all at her best, laughing loudly, stooping over a book and waddling when she walked. Like most mothers of marriageable daughters with an unhooked suitor hovering but undecided, she enlarged her daughter's faults to outsize proportions – unless Vicky took herself in hand, Fritz would be 'snapped up' by somebody else. Prince Albert was no help. He had got soaked to the skin while out hunting with Fritz and was tortured with rheumatism and very much taken up with his own sufferings.[2]

How comforted the Queen would have been if she had known that Fritz was deeply attracted and that he looked dejected only because the more his heart was stirred the more hopeless he felt his chances to be. How could such a girl see anything in a dull fellow like himself? And looking at Vicky, on whose face he saw fresh charms each day, he did not dare speak for fear of a rebuff. At the end of four days he was given a hopeful sign: when he was alone with Vicky for a moment she suddenly seized his hand and squeezed it. The touch of her fingers was electrifying. In an instant he knew – this was love. That night he was so happy that he slept soundly for the first time since coming to Scotland.

The next morning – it was the 20th of September, a date he was never to forget – as soon as breakfast was over he followed the Queen out; blushing and stammering he asked if he might speak to her and Prince Albert alone. Then all in a rush he said that he longed to 'belong to our family' more than anything in the world and that the king and his parents wished it too.[3] The Queen had been hoping for something of the sort and was so on edge with waiting that she could only squeeze Fritz's hand and say in a voice choked with tears how happy she was.

It was agreed that Vicky was too young to be told, and that Fritz should return in a year and a half's time and propose to her himself after her confirmation, when it was felt she would be old enough to know her own mind. But looking at her mother's flushed face and her father's abstracted air, Vicky guessed there was something going on. Fritz was no good at hiding his feelings and now that his own mind was made up he was impatient to know how Vicky felt. He was allowed to give her a bracelet, the Queen relenting so far as to say that 'something' should be said to the child and that he had better be the one to do it.[4] Fritz's chance came a few days later on a clear bright morning sharp with autumn frost as they all set out on ponies for Craig-na-Ban. Vicky rode next to Fritz and looked quite ravishing in her plaid. Half-way up they spurred their horses on and before the others could catch up with them, Fritz had dismounted, picked a sprig of white heather, and given it to Vicky with his first kiss. As they rode down side by side Fritz told her his hopes and plans for the future.

When they reached Glen Girnoch, where the carriage was waiting, Fritz gave the Queen a meaning look which told her he had spoken. Afterwards Vicky poured everything out to her mother – yes, she had suspected something and she really did love Fritz – with an indescribably happy look.

The Queen was thankful that it was to be a love-match like her own, and not one of those loveless arranged marriages which so horrified her. But her assertion to Leopold that 'I experience all she feels' was not strictly true; in her delight, she was reliving her own courtship, and so experienced far more.

The feelings Fritz awakened in Vicky caught the child unprepared and not mature enough to cope with them. She confided everything to the Queen, surprising herself that she could do so, while the Queen was struck by her simplicity and candour. 'They are ardently in love', Prince Albert wrote to Stockmar, sentimentality overcoming common sense. This may have been true of Fritz, whose passionate nature had never before had anything on which to bestow his affection. At fourteen Vicky was too young to love deeply, but she was delighted to be the centre of attention and to be adored by the handsome young Prince from Prussia. 'The purity, innocence and unselfishness of the young man are touching',[5] Albert told Stockmar in one of his more unworldly letters. But supposing he had not been willing to wait? What then? Albert had forgotten that Fritz was already four years older than he himself had been when he married the Queen, and that even at the tender age of twenty he had made up his mind not to wait three years for his bride.[6]

Since the Prince was determined that nothing should spoil what he coyly called the 'unconstraint of girlhood', it was lucky that Fritz was not only devoted but – as Albert had noticed – quite selfless in his attitude to Vicky. Her father was getting the best of both worlds in securing a 'clean living young man' (in an age when every continental prince was supposed to be ruining his health with 'excesses' – hence the stress in so many of Prince Albert's letters of that period on Fritz's 'innocence') and one, moreover, who was willing to be patient.

Two days later Fritz returned to Prussia an engaged man. When he had gone mother and daughter enjoyed a good cry together, the Queen treating Vicky like a grown-up woman. The engagement drew them closer together. It drew the Queen even closer to Princess Augusta, so close indeed that she threw off all restraint as she happily discussed Vicky with one who had become overnight 'my dearest darling Augusta'. She described Vicky as 'grown visibly' (her eldest's slow growth was a sore spot), and how she found her 'very good company and this important event in her life has now brought us even closer . . .

her health is excellent. Early this year she went through a critical time and did not suffer even the slightest indisposition. But she is half a child and has to develop herself both physically and morally before the marriage takes place in two years' time.'[7] Although no one outside the family was to know of the engagement, nevertheless Prince Albert felt that 'certain persons' should be told. So Lords Palmerston and Clarendon were let into the secret. But the Prince took a risk when he told his brother Ernest – a man never known to keep a secret in his life. Ernest mocked at this 'exalted position' for his niece, but although a cynic, he had to admit that Albert loved his favourite child deeply and was anxious to make her 'truly happy'.[8]

Of course the secret leaked out and the Queen and Prince Albert were startled into surprised outrage. A biting leading article in *The Times* followed: the engagement was 'unfortunate', Prussia was nothing more than a 'wretched German state' and the Hohenzollerns a 'paltry German dynasty'. The royal parents had to read a lurid description of their child returning to England an 'exile and a fugitive'.[9] With singular lack of flair for public relations Albert made an answering statement which he hoped would clarify the position and silence criticism: 'that . . . no consideration . . . would have induced the Queen or himself to imperil the happiness of their child by a marriage in which she could not have scope to practise the constitutional principles in which she has been reared.'[10]

*

Vicky must be trained for her new life; Fritz must be trained to be king. In each case the instruction was to be undertaken by Prince Albert. The moment Fritz had gone, the Prince kept two hours each evening free to teach Vicky although he was overwhelmed with work, while Vicky would prepare an historical essay or a short compendium of Roman history to discuss with him. Politics were not forgotten. The Prince went thoroughly into the question of Prussia's special difficulties after the débâcle of the 1848 revolution, since Vicky had read the recent newspaper accounts of what they unkindly called the 'King's cowardice' and 'Prussia's craven behaviour in the Crimean war'.[11] Every Wednesday morning Miss Hildyard accompanied Vicky to the South Kensington Museum to hear a lecture on chemistry by Professor Hofmann (when Vicky showed a real scientific bent the Professor came to Buckingham Palace to teach her). The Queen kept Princess Augusta informed of the curriculum Vicky was following, mistakenly going out of her way to explain with uncharacteristic humility that it was all done so that 'Vicky may prove herself worthy of her great good fortune'.[12] The Prince had to instruct Fritz by correspondence, but he was no less exigent for that. If he had ever had any illusions about the country over which he was one day to rule, Fritz had few left after Prince Albert had opened his eyes to the deplorable state of Prussian politics which, he said, were 'most critical'. Fritz did his part. He sent Vicky a diary describing incidents he had witnessed during the 1848 revolution, so that she should know 'all the secret events of my life'. In return Vicky wrote him long letters every day, but they are very much the outpourings of a school-girl to an affectionate friend. 'From dear papa I learn more than from anyone else in the world' – 'the hours I spend with my parents are the happiest in the day.'[13]

Six months later Vicky was confirmed on Maundy Thursday, the 20th of March 1856, in the private chapel at Windsor Castle. She looked touchingly young as, wearing a simple white dress, she walked to the altar between her father and her godfather King Leopold, and knelt on the faldstool, an affianced bride at fifteen. Her religious views were already formed and were Lutheran in sympathy but also remarkably elastic and unbigoted; she was never willing to condone tyranny in religious matters in any form at either end of the scale.

The confirmation was the end of childhood; an act of faith that was expected to turn Vicky overnight into a woman.[14] It did a great deal more than that, for it triggered off a series of vulgar wrangles with the Prussian royal family – with the newspapers on both sides as able seconds – that nearly wrecked the match. That controversial subject, the Prussian engagement ceremony, was the first of them. Prince Albert was now so anglicised that he wanted nothing of the sort for Vicky, although in 1840 he had set his heart on it for himself. Not only would it mean handing the initiative to Prussia ('which would never do'), but it would be putting the cart before the horse. The Queen and Prince Albert had planned to make an official announcement as soon as the tricky question of Vicky's dowry had been settled by Parliament. Albert was firm, therefore, but it was some time before the Prussians gave in and stopped insisting on their 'rights'.[15] Similarly, the Queen and Prince Albert were determined to keep politics out of the marriage, while the Prussians were determined to bring them in. When England refused to allow the King a seat at the conference table to settle the peace terms after the Crimean War he said some nasty things about the marriage and the newspapers of both countries promptly came out into the open with the cry 'the marriage is a mistake'.

Everything seemed to be going wrong. Vicky's new household had been chosen for her by the Queen of Prussia and Princess Augusta. Not only was it entirely German, but it consisted of women as elderly as themselves. It was only after a great deal of persuasion on Prince Albert's part that they could be induced to include two girls of Vicky's own age. The Queen went further and insisted that Vicky's ladies must come to Windsor for Vicky to get to know them. Her new physician, Dr Wegner, was invited to attend the Queen's own confinement in April 1857 (for her last child, Beatrice) 'to see how these things are managed here'. The Prussians were showing an insensitivity that shocked the Queen and Prince Albert and set up a train of thought which they hardly dared face. The climax was reached in October 1857 with the insulting request for the marriage to take place in Berlin. Furious and in no mood for compromise, the Queen crushed the idea in masterly fashion in a letter the gist of which Lord Clarendon was to transmit to Prussia: 'the assumption that it is too much for a Prince Royal of Prussia to come over to marry a Princess Royal of Great Britain in England is too absurd to say the least . . . Whatever may be the usual practice of Prussian princes, it is not every day that one marries the eldest daughter of a Queen of England. The question therefore must be considered settled and closed.'[16]

These distasteful disputes did not help the Queen to overcome her misery at the thought of her child going so far away, nor her feeling of guilt that they were wrong in allowing Vicky to marry so young and to go alone and unprotected into the 'labyrinth of Berlin'. Her letters to Princess Augusta are filled with piteous references to the effect of the parting on an emotional child who had never known anything but her parents' tender care. She beseeched Augusta to be a second mother to Vicky in her loneliness and Prince William to be a second father'.

*

In May 1857 Fritz arrived at Osborne for a short visit with the confidence of a man with an established position, only to be made instantly jealous by Vicky's preparations for her first season. So much talk of antique moiré for ball-dresses, and whether to put cornflowers or roses in her hair, when she should be thinking of her trousseau and her wedding dress!

Vicky was delighted to see Fritz again and to be openly engaged. In Fritz's eyes she had not only grown in height, but in beauty too. A portrait by Winterhalter of this period is however not very different from one by Ross when she was a child. The features are much the same, the large, slightly hooded eyes and the upward curve of the lips giving the face a most pleasing expression. Only the hair style is changed. In 1857 she wore it parted in the middle, slightly bouffant at the sides and drawn back from her face.

An atmosphere of gloom brought on by thoughts of the coming separation from her parents made the visit not quite the success it should have been. Fourteen-year-old Alice had only recently been told of the engagement and could hardly look at Fritz without bursting into tears. Fritz too was showing a new side. He wanted to have Vicky to himself for at least an hour a day, and the Queen had to be chaperone (sitting in the next room with the door open), a role she found distasteful and boring. He was possessive, and terribly jealous when at a ball Vicky danced with others. Her mother was astonished that a child could inspire such passionate feelings.

For the first time in his life Fritz was living at close quarters with two lively and affectionate women, and it was showing up the gaps in his experience. Used as he was to a family that was cold and formal when not engaged in heated arguments, he was amazed at the way the children were encouraged to show their feelings. He therefore did not guess that Vicky's prostration at the sudden death of Prince Charles of Leiningen from a stroke had a deeper significance than shock at the loss of a beloved uncle, and that it was the spark that set off the barrel of gunpowder that comprised her feelings at that time. A new terror was added to the fear of separation: 'anything' could happen when she was far away. As she cried for her uncle, Fritz felt ill-used and neglected when he knew he should only feel compassion. He complained to the Queen – who took Vicky's side – that she wept so much it put an end to conversation. So Vicky wept all the more because Fritz did not understand what she only half understood herself. But court mourning brought one blessing. Living quietly in their own apartments at Windsor, the family got to know Fritz much better. 'Serious conversation' took place every day, and Prince Albert was in his element discussing plans for German unity with two such responsive young people.

Two days before leaving for Prussia Fritz realised afresh how precious Vicky had become to him. She was sealing a letter by an open window when a sudden draught made the lighted taper flare up and set fire to the sleeves of her muslin dress. Fortunately she was not alone, and Miss Hildyard and Mrs Anderson put the fire out with the hearth-rug. Vicky's right arm was badly burned from below the elbow to the shoulder. She took it all with great coolness and the arm was soon on the mend, but Fritz was horrified and looked white and shaken for hours.

*

Vicky's last few months as an unmarried girl were rapidly drawing to an end, but the future in Prussia as Fritz's wife still seemed unreal and far away.

The spring of 1857 had brought much to be thankful for. Vicky's grant passed smoothly through Parliament with only one dissident vote. She was given a dowry of £40,000 and £8,000 a year income: not a fortune, not as much as they had hoped, but it was not mean. It was to prove a life-saver to Vicky in the years to come. In April Stockmar came to Windsor (as it happened, for the last time) bringing his son Ernest to meet Vicky, whose private secretary he was to become. Fritz did not think that a Coburger was the best person to cope with Berliners who despised people from that part of Germany, but in Prince Albert's opinion Ernest's Coburg origin was counter-balanced by a character which he could not distinguish from that of his father.[17]

On the 10th of May the public announcement of the marriage passed without incident. There were no celebrations, for the family were in mourning for 'Aunt Gloucester', the last of the formidable old royal family which had been so unkind to Prince Albert. With the old royals gone and his own children growing up, the time had come to put right a long-standing omission: Prince Albert had been the Queen's foreign husband long enough. On the 25th of June she created him 'Prince Consort' by Letters Patent – 'But I should have preferred it by act of Parliament'. As Albert told his brother Ernest 'Wicked people might succeed in bringing up the Prince of Wales against his father to tell him that he could not allow a foreign prince to take precedence before him.'[18] Albert knew to his cost just how far 'wicked people' could go.

When the leaves changed colour and began to fall, Vicky went to Balmoral. It was her last visit before her marriage, which had been fixed for the 25th of January 1858 in the Chapel Royal of St James's, where eighteen years before the Queen had been married to Prince Albert. She rode her pony over the heather, loving every sprig because she was going to leave it, forgetting that not long ago she loved it because it was here that Fritz had asked her to be his wife. When she went round the cottages the 'good simple Highlanders' broke down, saying 'we shall never see you again', as though Prussia were at the other end of the earth – which Vicky was beginning to fear it was. In her fierce affection for her home, the thought of Fritz had no place. He was forgotten in the pain of the coming separation which at times threatened to overwhelm her so that she felt quite ill, though she bore it all with courage and self-control.[19]

In between fittings for her elaborate trousseau, Vicky spent her time strangely for a bride. She translated Droysen's *Karl August**, an abstruse book made all the more difficult by the author's peculiar style. Getting down to hard work had been the Prince Consort's antidote for

---

*The historian J. G. Droysen's liberal pamphlet *Karl August und die deutsche Politik* had appeared on the occasion of the Goethe and Schiller festival at Weimar in September 1857.

homesickness. He tried the same remedy with Vicky, with what seemed equally good results. It was all the more disconcerting to find her mind wandering when they were going through a difficult passage together, to see a lost look come over her face and to hear her say sadly 'the little sister will never have known me in the house'. Through incidents like this the Prince Consort guessed something of the enormous strain Vicky was undergoing, the dread she felt at leaving the known and her fear of the unknown. He drew comfort from the knowledge that he had prepared her well for her future life.

As January approached all was 'bustle and excitement' for the Queen and Vicky but a headache for the Prince, who had to find rooms for the large number of guests, many of whom arrived a week early and were promptly despatched to Scotland for some health-giving field sports in the Prince Consort's care. All too soon, eighty or ninety people were dining nightly at Buckingham Palace. Vicky moved informally among them, having a word with each, a duty she performed with dignity and composure. The Queen took her guests to *Macbeth* and they made an imposing row of royalties. Vicky sat next to her father, who had never been so dear. The Prussians were quite startled by the cheers, the hand-waving, the emotional rendering of the National Anthem and the respect showed for the monarchy. There was a state dinner, brilliant with gold plate and sparkling with jewels, a footman behind every chair. The Queen, gay as a lark, was in blue and looked too young – as her brother-in-law Ernest told her gallantly – to be the mother of the bride. Vicky was in blue too, but with lace flounces and cornflowers in her hair, just a little subdued and thinking how her wonderfully handsome father outshone all the other men in the room. But he was pale and told Stockmar that he was 'torn to pieces' by 'many little details that had gone wrong'.

On the 23rd of January Fritz arrived, wan and tired after a rough crossing, nervous at meeting Vicky again and showing the strain. But dancing with her that night at a splendid state ball – 'packed with more princes than the Congress of Vienna' – his doubts and fears evaporated, never to return. Everyone remarked on his tender consideration for his bride, which 'excelled everything'. He seemed to love her all the more for the pain she felt on leaving home. As he watched her calm and serious face following every move of Mr Rarey's demonstration in the riding school of the method he used to train wild horses – a show the ingenious Prince Consort had arranged to entertain his guests[20] – he guessed the hidden anguish beneath her composed appearance and vowed that he would do all in his power to make her happy.

*

On 'poor Vicky's last unmarried day', the Queen led her into the present-room and showed her Fritz's pearls – 'the largest I ever saw' – which quite startled Vicky by their size and beauty, while Fritz looked on delighted. It needed three large tables to hold the Queen and Prince Albert's present to Fritz – a magnificent set of crystal candelabra, so large and fine that everything else was dwarfed. Before they left for church, Vicky went to the Queen's sitting-room to give her a brooch containing her hair. Clinging to her mother she said in a voice choked with emotion 'I hope to be worthy to be your child'.[21]

At the end of this exciting, tiring Sunday, when the Queen and Vicky had been interrupted and disturbed every instant, the forlorn parents walked with their child to her room where they kissed her and gave her their blessing, whereupon Vicky broke down, clinging to her 'truly adored papa' with much tenderness.

*

Monday, the 25th of January 1858 – that dreaded yet longed-for day dawned at last. Vicky went in her dressing-gown to her mother's room, looking quite cheerful. The Queen gave her a 'pretty book', *The Bridal Offering*, then they dressed together like two girls, the Queen watching critically as Vicky was helped into her wedding dress of white moiré silk trimmed with Honiton lace, her hair dressed flat to take the bridal veil with its topknot of white roses. The Queen had chosen lilac and silver for her dress with a tiara and necklace of diamonds. When they were ready the Prince Consort was called so that they could be daguerreotyped together, but the Queen was so nervous and trembled so much that her likeness came out blurred.

It was time to be off. Vicky drove the short distance in a carriage alone with her mother, then joined her father and her eight white-clad bridesmaids in an ante-room while the Queen walked down the aisle to her pew, escorted by her two youngest sons in Highland dress. She was scarcely seated before 'our darling flower' entered, walking, as she had done at her confirmation, between her father and King Leopold of the Belgians, her veil thrown back in the custom of royal brides and with such an 'innocent, confident, serious expression' that the Queen's nervousness vanished. Vicky knelt in exactly the same spot as her mother had done before her, listening to the archbishop bungling the service (as he had done at her confirmation). Vicky and Fritz spoke the responses clearly; the Prince Consort, standing a little behind the bride, stared straight in front of him, his face white and withdrawn.

As the bride and bridegroom walked hand-in-hand to the vestry, Fritz looked just as he described himself – 'the happiest of the happy' – while Vicky smiled at everyone as she hugged her mother lovingly.

There were hand-squeezings and choked words of congratulation as both royal families signed the register. Then Vicky and Fritz led the procession out to Mendelssohn's wedding march.

There were tremendous cheers as first the bride and bridegroom and then both sets of parents appeared on the balcony at Buckingham Palace, and again after the wedding breakfast and just before Vicky, a ravishing little figure in white velvet and fur, left with Fritz for their two-day honeymoon.

There was more excitement at Windsor when over-enthusiastic Eton boys unhitched the horses and dragged the carriage from the station to the castle gates, while huge crowds cheered. It was past one o'clock when the Queen and Prince Consort got to bed, rather the worse for wear, after a concert where no one had listened to the music but discussed the wedding in whispers behind their fans instead. The Prussians were especially impressed, and referred to the ceremony as 'the event of the year'. The Prince Consort had snatched a moment from this long day to write a line to his 'dear old friend' Stockmar, whose spare figure had been much missed, to let him know that everything had gone off without the slightest hitch. If Vicky had not been going so far away, the Prince could have quite enjoyed himself.

*

After dining quietly together the bride and bridegroom sat in the red drawing-room doing nothing. They were both strangely tongue-tied. Now that Vicky was alone with Fritz for the first time in her life she felt miserably shy and embarrassed, with a dry throat and tears not far off as she vainly struggled for something to say. But nothing would come. Without her bonnet and cloak she looked younger and smaller than ever as she sat dejectedly on the sofa, her white velvet dress clinging to her figure here and there showing all her childish roundness. In a minute or two Fritz came and sat next to her and taking her hand with its brand-new wedding ring, he gently kissed it.[22]

*

On the 27th of January the court returned to Windsor and the brief honeymoon was over. From then on events moved fast. Fritz was invested with the Garter before a magnificent state dinner (where 'the ceremony' was still the chief topic of conversation). There was an exciting Drawing Room, at which the bride was the centre of attention. But as the dreaded day of departure approached Vicky felt sick at heart; alone with her mother, in an unguarded moment, she broke down and sobbed 'I think it will kill me to take leave of papa'.

Tuesday, the 2nd of February was a wretched day of cold winds and an overcast sky. Vicky had slept badly and awoke depressed. She went at once to her mother's room and sobbed bitterly, but tried to calm herself when her father joined them with a few last-minute instructions for the journey. Sadly they went to the Audience Room where the Duchess of Kent – with all the children clinging to her skirts and wailing dismally – and the Duchess of Cambridge and her daughter Mary waited to say good-bye. Then through another barrage of sobs in the hall, where the household and servants had collected to watch the little bride leave, her face swollen with tears but trying to be brave as Fritz wrapped her tenderly in a thick shawl. In a daze she walked to the door, a quick kiss, a feeling of faintness, then she was lifted into the carriage – an open one despite the bitter weather – the band struck up a march and they moved slowly off.

It had started to snow, and as though in a dream Vicky felt the icy flakes sting her cheeks and heard the cheers of the people as they wished her good luck. Outside Barclay and Perkins' brewery some cockney draymen shouted loudly to Fritz 'be good to her, or we'll have her back'.

At Gravesend, where young girls had scattered flowers on a snow-covered pier, the *Victoria and Albert* waited to take them across a windswept channel. Fritz led Vicky down to her cabin, where she clung to her father in a last embrace.

As the *Victoria and Albert* slowly drew away, the Prince Consort stood on the quay with her brothers Bertie and Affie, but Vicky did not come on deck. Sadly they returned to London. That night the Prince wrote his child an anguished letter: 'My heart was very full when yesterday in the saloon you laid your forehead on my breast to give free vent to your tears. I am not of a demonstrative nature and therefore you can hardly know how dear you have always been to me and what a void you have left in my heart.'[23]

CHAPTER 4

'That Cruel Moment'

By seven o'clock the *Victoria and Albert* was on her way. Until the moment Vicky had kissed her father good-bye, her new country with its different customs and habits held no fears for her. She spoke its language fluently, she had read its literature widely and she had discussed Prussia's peculiar political responsibilities to the Confederation over and over again with her father.* She had married Prussia's future king and this had opened up to her endless possibilities to 'do good' where, she had been told, it was very much needed. The serene mood that had almost deserted her before the wedding, and which she had recaptured just in time to sail through the ceremony unruffled and with 'a demeanour so childlike, so dignified and firm',[1] seemed now to melt away with each mile and to take her self-confidence with it. Her calmness had deceived them all. She had even taken herself in. She had made her father believe that she had come to terms with the parting, whereas her inexperience was such that to imagine it was beyond her. The break with childhood was too abrupt. Because of her extreme youth the two-year engagement had done nothing to prepare her for married life in a foreign country with a husband who was kind and loving, it is true, and whom she loved in return, but whom she hardly knew.

Prince Albert was not altogether blind to his daughter's mixed feelings, for he had told Fritz with some pride that Vicky had a 'man's head and a child's heart'.[2] He had overlooked the fact that in times of stress and strain the child's heart with all its doubts and fears would

*After the Napoleonic wars, the enormous number (over 300) of states in the Germany of the *ancien régime* had been reduced to thirty-eight at the Congress of Vienna in 1815. They were loosely federated in the German Confederation, but each retained its independence. Austria was perpetual president of the Confederation, and Prussia (the next largest state) was her chief rival. The 1848 revolution had unsuccessfully tried to draw the Confederation closer together, so that Germany should have one policy and not several; during the short period when he supported the revolution, Frederick William IV, the King of Prussia, had expressed this by proclaiming 'Prussia will henceforth be merged in Germany', but he had soon welcomed the return of the old divisions. Inside Prussia (as in most of the other states) the government was an absolute monarchy.

take charge, while the man's head would only aggravate the situation by deepening her capacity for suffering. When the separation came it left her more cruelly bereft than she had ever expected. But she was mature enough to know that she could not yet discuss these strange feelings with a new husband, who might misunderstand. Somehow or other she must get through the next few days without showing her feelings, otherwise Fritz might think she was sorry she had married him.

In those first hours alone with Fritz, Vicky learned a useful lesson in self-control. It helped to still trembling nerves and stifle tears to do as usual the ordinary everyday things she had always done at this time of night at home. She opened her desk, just as she had done only a week ago; but instead of writing her weekly essay, she picked up the little red-leather pocket diary Alice had thrust at her as she walked down the stairs to the carriage. In the clear white space under the 2nd of February she wrote in her neat legible hand 'Today I left England for ever'. Many years later when flicking through the pages of this little book she amended this entry, deleting 'for ever' and substituting 'for Prussia'. It brought back to her, in a way nothing else could, her stricken state of mind that night.

She could not leave her desk without writing a word to her father: 'once more before this dreadful day ends, let your child thank you for all your kindness, for all your love, once more let me repeat that dreadful word good-bye which twice today had well-nigh broke my heart – and hardest of all that last dreadful farewell here on board.'[3]

The temptation to write on and on must be resisted. Determinedly she wound the little tortoiseshell clock the Duchess of Kent had given her on her eighth birthday in 1848. Fritz had remarked on it particularly during their honeymoon because that was the year he had stood at the window of the King's palace in the Unter den Linden in Berlin and watched the fighting in the street. It was the first time he had ever seen bloodshed and he had been very frightened although he had been a year older than she was now. In a strange way the thought of Fritz overcoming his fears was a comfort to her tonight. She undressed rapidly, and laid her folded clothes neatly on a chair; then pouring a few drops of chloroform on a lump of sugar – the Queen's remedy for seasickness – she sucked it sitting up in bed, as she said her prayers. They were very short: simply that Fritz would never guess how much she wished she were at home.

*

Not unnaturally Vicky slept badly. She was frightened by the howling wind, by the sound of the hail and sleet beating against the port-hole and by the thunder of the waves as they broke against the ship's side. Nothing could have been worse than the weather that night.

She awoke to a cheerless day. At dawn they anchored at Antwerp, where even before it was light hundreds of people were drenched by the torrential rain as they waited to wave the young bride on her way. At nine o'clock they were to leave the ship to start the long and tedious journey to Prussia. But Vicky could not go before writing to papa to tell him what she knew he too felt as keenly, that the 'pain of parting from you yesterday was greater than I can describe. I thought my heart was going to break when you shut the cabin door and were gone – that cruel moment which I had been dreading even to think of for two years and a half was past – it was more painful than I ever pictured to myself.'[4]

Lady Churchill, the Queen's Woman of the Bedchamber, was travelling with Vicky to Prussia. As they came on deck she noticed with approval Vicky's quick response to the exacting demands of public life. The pale set little face broke into a smile as she stepped off the boat on Fritz's arm. Remembering her father's telling homily that the true way to happiness was to think of others and not of herself, she acknowledged the cheers with a gay wave, an effort that was amply rewarded when she read in the papers next day of the pleasure her 'happy smiling face' had given the waiting crowds.

How she had dreaded that seven days' journey to Berlin! Nothing in the programme for her entertainment along the route appealed to her. All she wanted was to get to Prussia as quickly as possible and begin her idyllic life with Fritz, their desks side by side like her parents', cantering together in the early morning; at night, after Fritz had finished his military duties and she her studies, she pictured herself singing and playing to him or Fritz reading aloud to her, either constitutional history (for 'history is the best guide for royalties'[5]), or the latest George Eliot or other novel from the parcel sent weekly by Mudie's in London.

It was a surprise to find it inexpressible joy to dance with Fritz at a ball in Brussels, a delight to visit the cathedrals of Cologne and Magdeburg with Fritz as guide and historian. With his strong arm to protect her, she was not at all put out when crowds surrounded them and tore her new green tartan travelling dress. She had understood at once that they were only eager to make her welcome. Her father had prepared her for this (but he had called it curiosity), and also for the frigid welcome she might get from the anti-English Queen Elizabeth,[6] who was waiting with the ailing King to greet them outside Berlin at the Palace of Bellevue which she had considerately lent them so that they should have some proper rest before the trying ride into the capital next day.

No one had prepared her however for the welcome the Berliners gave her. She was so transported by their enthusiasm that she did not feel the icy air on her bare skin as she rode next to Fritz in the open state coach without a wrap of any sort over her low-cut dress. 'Your dear people' she called them to Fritz, grateful for so much affection to a complete stranger. When the coach drew up at the Schloss, Vicky was so bemused by the cheers and so eager to meet Fritz's family that she impulsively jumped down unaided and, seizing her voluminous skirts in both hands, ran lightly up the steps.[7] She never forgot the first sight of her father-in-law, the Prince of Prussia, who stood a little apart from a large group of relations at the top of the grand staircase. More kingly than the King himself, he looked magnificent in his white and gold uniform with its order of the Black Eagle. A surge of pride went through her at the thought that this splendid figure was the person who was to be – after Fritz – her closest male relation in Prussia. She swept to the floor in a deep curtsy, then shyly lifted her face for the expected kiss. But Prince William had already moved on to speak to Fritz. There is a story that Queen Elizabeth was so startled by the snub to the shivering little bride that she dropped her cold manner and asked anxiously 'Are you not frozen?' Vicky answered with a radiant smile 'I have only one warm place and that is my heart'.[8]

*

Vicky's first home had been chosen for her by Princess Augusta. The Berlin Schloss was a large, decaying, dreary palace which had not been lived in since Frederick William III had died there in 1840, although balls and receptions were frequently held in its spacious state rooms. Vicky and Fritz were to live on the second floor, in the same suite that had been used by the dead king and his wife. On that first night, even to Vicky's tired eyes, a swift glance revealed many surprises: threadbare and dusty carpets, torn and tattered brocades black with cobwebs, old-fashioned stoves that over the years had darkened the portraits of dead Hohenzollerns with smoke – everything struck a chill in her heart. As for her own apartments, she looked round her in amazement. Where were the cupboards to hang her clothes – beautiful dresses of the finest material, which at home were placed in muslin bags before being hung in a large airy closet? Where was the tub for her daily bath? Or one of those 'little rooms' so unobtrusively but liberally scattered throughout her mother's palaces? Where were the lights to dress by, to read and write by? A flickering candle would hurt her eyes and make them smart. And where, oh where, was kindly comforting warmth? The wind that blew straight from Arctic Russia made the ill-fitting windows rattle and so lowered the temperature that Vicky had to wrap herself in thick shawls and blow on her hands to keep the circulation going – for to her dismay, in less than a week she could see the first signs of chilblains on her fingers. There was not one warm spot in the place. To get up in the morning and find a mere inch of tepid water in her bath was not a good start to the day. Yet complaining about it improved nothing and only made her cross. She had to face the grumbles of her maids as they bewailed the lack of cupboards whenever they had to search through boxes to find a particular dress and then found it so crumpled that it took hours to get the creases out. This sort of thing revealed another irritating shortcoming. There was no maids' pantry close at hand, equipped with iron, sewing-machine and curling-tongs, as there was at home. Instead everything had to be carried to the kitchen quarters at the other end of the Schloss, and Vicky's maids did not endure the long walk along dark and draughty corridors many times a day with good humour.

If Fritz did not turn a deaf ear to Vicky's entreaties to make the Hofmarschälle* order the servants to sweep the chimneys so that the stoves would give more heat, and to the carpenters to build cupboards for her clothes, it was because he was very much in love and not because he thought any good would come of it. Fritz was used to going without. He cheerfully washed in cold water, ate cold food and lived in a cold house – and thought nothing of it. It never occurred to him to emulate the luxuries of Queen Victoria's homes in his Prussian palaces. Secretly he thought such fal-lals a lot of nonsense.

Breakfast with Fritz always restored Vicky's good temper. It was the only time in the day when they were alone. Soon after Fritz's return the Prince of Prussia callously ordered Fritz to undergo an intensive course of training of the kind he had found so enjoyable as a young man. This meant that Fritz was out all day, leaving the inexperienced Vicky to cope with the household and the servants as best she could. The Hofmarschälle who should have done this for her were too superior to do any work – they were almost royalty themselves. Large numbers of them were attached to every royal palace, and it was their duty to see that all repairs and alterations were properly carried out and that the servants did their work efficiently. But they were often lazy and corrupt. It made the energetic Vicky furious to see them so idle when there was so much to be done. Yet how could the Hofmarschälle control the servants when they were so out of hand themselves? It suited them to connive at petty pilfering or a back answer. The lower

*Major-domos.

servants would only stay if they could fill their pockets unchecked – it was a recognised way of augmenting their wages.

Countess Perponcher, her Woman of the Bedchamber, managed the household no better. Though devoted and kind to her young mistress, she lacked humour and tolerance and took offence too easily, bridling with hurt pride at the most innocent remarks. So the household quarrelled among themselves like a pack of spoilt children, angling to get Vicky alone in order to complain and vilify each other, making her life a torment with their sulks and vendettas. Ernest Stockmar – the young Baron, her secretary – could have taken charge if he had possessed a more forceful character, but he was shy and timid and kept aloof. Indeed, the whole household loathed him because he spent more time with the young couple than they did. The charge of favouritism may have been unfair; it was his duty to read the papers and discuss many private and personal matters with Vicky, but this would not have mattered if he had also taken a hand at whist occasionally or sat round the huge table in the household sitting-room and joined in the popular craze for telling fortunes with tea leaves.

Fortunately there was a lighter side to Vicky's new life. When Fritz was out she often had a great deal of fun with her young ladies-in-waiting, Walpurga ('Wally') Hohenthal and Marie Lynar. They painted, played the piano and sang, read aloud or embroidered kneelers for the English church that was being built in Berlin. They challenged each other to nursery games like quoits, ludo or draughts, which Vicky had brought with her from England, or chased each other along the corridors in a game of hide-and-seek. Wally mischievously frightened them with stories of the 'lady in white' who walked along these very corridors moaning and groaning. She was so good at this that when one night while she was reading to Vicky the door behind the sofa on which she was sitting slowly opened by itself, both girls nearly screamed with terror. The Hofmarschälle's explanation of traffic vibrations and crooked hinges did something to calm their nerves, but Vicky was more frightened than ever of walking through the death-chamber of Frederick William III, which separated her room from Fritz's and which had been left exactly as it was and still smelt of death and decay.

In these warm friendships – the nearest thing to her life with her brothers and sisters – her parents' warnings not to give her confidence to anyone but the Prince and Princess of Prussia were forgotten. She was often indiscreet, telling her ladies how much better things were done 'at home', forgetting that these young girls were Prussians and that in their hearts they very much resented criticism of their country. They could not help loving her, though, and were captivated by her charm and simplicity. But they did not understand her. She had a direct way of going about things which was very different from the devious methods of the aristocratic Prussian mind, and her changeable moods were never moodiness. She could be headstrong and stubborn, refusing to listen when they begged her not to do what they thought unwise, reminding her that she would not be incognito for long when the broad ribbon on the coachman's hat told everyone that a member of the royal family was in the neighbourhood. In those intractable moods she led them a terrible dance, and they would wring their hands in despair, frightened out of their wits, for they were answerable to the Princess of Prussia for her conduct.

In those first few months her restless eye was everywhere, uncovering things they never knew existed and commenting on them with an alarming frankness. She thought nothing of walking all over Berlin, covering more ground as her confidence increased, dragging her weary and protesting ladies after her. There was no rule against this, because no one had ever imagined that a royal princess would want to do such a thing. When they told her this she laughed and said, very well, if they did not want to come she would go alone.

She asked questions all the time. Why has Berlin not got a museum? Or an art gallery? Where is the public library? Where is the hospital? Where do the poor live? When they could not tell her, a note of severity would creep into her voice and they would hang their heads as she said impatiently 'Never mind, I will find out.'

Sometimes, without any reason, she would be sensible and pliable and they would congratulate themselves that they were learning to manage this wilful princess. But they spoke too soon, for the next moment she would be off, walking rapidly down some dirty side-street, with the two girls in hot pursuit, for they dared not let her out of their sight. Instead of taking notice of Wally's pleading cries 'please, Ma'am, take care', she called them to come and look at the green and evil-smelling filth overflowing from the gutters after a shower of rain, or made a face as she held up her skirts for them to see the slime on the hem. She drew their attention to a sight they had seen many times and thought nothing of – poor women forced, because there was no pavement, to press up against the walls of the houses so as not to be trampled on when the cavalry rode by. With a sharp note in her voice she ordered them to look at their terrified faces, saying it was significant that the only well-kept building was the barracks. Alone together, they vowed this was the last time they would shield her, but they never stuck to their resolution. Vicky beckoned, speaking to them in her gentle voice that had the ring of authority despite its softness, and they came running. When they were most angry she could melt them without knowing it by being unexpectedly kind – arranging for Marie Lynar to see her old father who was ailing, or sending Wally off in the carriage to spend an evening with a favourite aunt.

*

Vicky took it for granted that after her marriage a bond of mutual affection would grow as a matter of course between herself and Fritz's relations. She had seen the whole royal family together for the first time only a few hours after her arrival in Berlin. When Fritz had led her into the Weisser Saal for a ball that first night,[9] he had taken her straight to where they sat on a velvet-covered dais to present her to them as his wife. It had been difficult even for one of her stout heart not to quail before such an unsmiling array of faces. She had known at once that they would be hard to please, for they reminded her all too vividly of her mother's descriptions of the 'old' royal family whose spleen and spite towards dearest papa had been so shocking. How could she know that they were scrutinising her so hard because the newspapers had made much of her diminutive size? They had read that it had taken three cushions to raise her high enough to be seen in the state coach (a piece of reporting that had made Vicky indignant, for she had used only one not very thick cushion). Was she deformed? It was a poor prospect for the throne if she was. All the Hohenzollern princesses were very tall and sometimes very fat as well; there was not one below five feet ten inches. When Princess Charles, Prince William's sister-in-law, pointed out that Augusta had only two children (and one of them a daughter), she was brushed aside as talking treasonable nonsense – Augusta could have done better if 'things' had been different. What they did not understand was that Vicky's small features created the illusion that she was tiny. But she was not really short. Her height at the time of her marriage was five feet two inches, slightly more than the Queen who had read the same account and wrote to Vicky that 'you are taller than I am and I am not a dwarf'.[10] It is important to remember that although her lack of height was a considerable talking-point in Berlin she felt neither small nor insignificant. Later, when she had acquired a reputation for strength of character and strong will, nobody ever referred to her as small again.

*

Vicky found some of the family customs absurd. She was astonished to learn that she and Fritz were expected to join all the old aunts, uncles and cousins every Sunday for dinner in a room on the ground floor of the Berlin Schloss. Ever since the King had been too ill to attend, this meal was at any time between two and five according to the whim of the Prince of Prussia. Full evening dress with decorations was worn. In the beginning Vicky was highly amused by the antics of her new relations, then disconcerted as, the ice broken, they bickered and quarrelled, the women jealous and spiteful, the men teasing a girl they felt to be only a child by pinching her legs under the table or tickling her bare arms, so that she did not know where to look, though it was all she could do not to burst out laughing. They used her mercilessly as a buffer, demanding her opinion, appealing to her to arbitrate, which at first she was rash enough to do. If what she said did not please them, they forgot their original dispute and turned on her, refusing to allow her to defend herself, her family or her country, but criticising all three with a freedom that quite took her breath away. She tried to make the best of it, for the family did not mean to be unkind. 'All the family receive me very kindly and it makes it doubly painful for me to see them together with only the mere outward appearance of mutual affection.'[11] Quickly the Prince Consort told Vicky how to deal with such familiarities – she must show a 'stiff' attitude, which would at once make them realise they had gone too far. In this way she would not be drawn into the current. The Queen, remembering past faults, had a bit to add. There must be 'no familiarity, no loud laughter – be very civil but keep your position'.[12]

Vicky tried to explain to her mother, who had little idea of her dilemma, that however guarded her tongue tittle-tattle was spread by what she called 'a sort of spy' – a poor relation or a dependant – which every household had in its midst, but who on the whole was harmless, and whose duty it was to give information to the person who paid her. Vicky was not only newly-married but English, and the family were full of curiosity about what went on in her home, including much that Vicky would have told them freely if they had asked. But it was not 'done' to be inquisitive, and anyway this method was more thorough.

Vicky tried hard to please Fritz's relations, but sooner or later with her temperament there were bound to be clashes – neither side could understand the other at all. Vicky was the least to blame: she was young, quick-witted, quick-tempered, open, intolerant, lively and affectionate – and much cleverer than they were. Indeed she possessed all the qualities guaranteed to irritate jealous pigheaded old people who were also intensely proud. Allowances were never made for her youth, nor for the fact that sometimes – even in the midst of laughter – she would suddenly break down because something had reminded her of her own family, whom she confessed she never stopped missing. This unexpected childishness and longing for affection was part of her charm. Her young ladies-in-waiting forgave her trying moods over and over again because of it. It was a source of wonder to them that everyone was not captivated by her. They could see that some were not. The King's sister the Grand Duchess of Schwerin went out of her way to be rude, and so did the Crown Princess Olga of Württemberg (she was born a Russian Grand Duchess, and blamed Vicky for the Crimean War), who had turned her back on her new relation after asking Vicky if she was yet sixteen.[13]

But the Prince of Prussia was another matter. It must be the fault of the Princess that she was not on better terms with her father-in-law. Wally had noticed that Vicky was shy and uneasy in the Prince's presence. She herself got on splendidly with him, indeed he made 'quite a pet' of her. From this she deduced that the Prince was open to the influence of women and would have been wax in the hands of his charming daughter-in-law if she had treated him like a 'loving child with a doting father'.[14] Vicky would have liked nothing better than to be on these easy terms with Prince William: had she not gone to Prussia expecting him to be that 'second father' the Queen and Prince Albert had begged him to be to their child? The Queen herself was only too delighted to be a 'kind of mama' to the German princesses who passed through England en route to some foreign marriage-market or who fled to her country as refugees. But Vicky was now 'family', and because of this Prince William could not treat her kindly. Like all weak men with defenceless dependants, he was hard with his own flesh and blood. Moreover, there is not one scrap of evidence that Prince William was open to the influence of women – rather the reverse. The only woman who kept his affection and therefore perhaps could be said to have influenced him was a ghost – the long-dead Elise Radziwill.

If Vicky's relations with Prince William lacked warmth, those with the 'dear, dear Princess' lacked nothing. It grieved her very much that husband and wife behaved so badly to each other. They quarrelled bitterly all the time, saying the most hurtful things without caring in the least who heard. Vicky had noticed that the old prince in his sly way knew just how to make Augusta lose her temper, maddening her beyond endurance by his refusal to answer back, or indeed to say a single word. In the end he always won by saying nothing; a cheap triumph that gave him much pleasure. One day after a particularly bad row Augusta had taken Vicky aside and begged her 'not to think ill of her if I saw her lose her command over herself'.[15] Vicky had been indignant that Prince William so often mistook his wife's intentions – which he might not have done 'if only she set the right way about it'. After the wedding celebrations were over Augusta had gone back to Coblenz. Vicky had driven with her to the railway station to see her off, kissing her with great affection, for she was saddened that the princess was so misunderstood and had so little gratitude shown her. She hoped her mother-in-law would see by the warmth of her manner that she knew 'what sacrifices she bears and in how noble a way'.[16]

*

It did not take Vicky long to understand why her father had warned her so often not to waste time in what she herself graphically called 'busy idleness',[17] a vice that had all the Prussian princesses in its grip. She was too aware of the gaps in her education to allow this to happen to her. Each day was going to be filled from morning till night with some improving task, she told herself severely. But she had not been in Prussia long enough to have any idea how her zeal for knowledge could complicate her life with Fritz's relations. A weekly essay for her father was all right – only Fritz knew of it. It was a very different matter when she began to create a scholarly world of scientists, historians, painters and literary people of all kinds from whom she could learn, who began by teaching her and ended up staying to a meal at which they laughed and talked as equals. Vicky had not understood how class-conscious the family were, nor that they had a horror (in some cases amounting to abnormality) of mixing with any one below the rank of prince.

After two months in Prussia Vicky had met no one who was not of royal blood. Their ignorance appalled her. Not only did they know little of what went on in the world, but they were quite unaware of even the simplest things. The women were interested only in gossip and fashion, the men only in women and military affairs. Prince William – who looked a most cultivated and intelligent man – actually boasted in Vicky's hearing that his only interest in life was soldiering. And he was their future king! Princess Augusta, who was a really clever woman, was so narrow-minded that she had ordered everything that was 'not nice' to be expunged from her daughter's history books – with the result that Wiwy believed that Louis XIV had three wives and asked 'Why did the pope allow it?'

This sort of thing was the consequence of being too proud to learn. These people were so conscious of their superiority that they genuinely believed nobody had anything to teach them. Vicky wondered how many of them could read or write. It was dreadful that they depended on an accident of birth to shield them from the day-to-day hazards of life – if pushed out into the world, how many of them would last a day? Such a frightening thought stiffened Vicky's determination to break out of this suffocating enclosed circle straight away. But how to begin?

A chance meeting in a Berlin street gave her an opening. Fritz bumped into Professor Schellbach, who had taught him mathematics at Bonn. This cultivated, congenial man was widely travelled and knew England well. Fritz invited him to meet Vicky, certain she would like him. The professor went to the Schloss with some misgivings. He had heard that the English princess was 'difficult', which to him meant haughty and (since he had heard that she was supposed to be clever) intellectually arrogant – a combination he could not stand in men, let alone in a woman. What he found was a simple unaffected young girl, intelligent but modest and – what appealed to him at once – tremendously eager to learn. She came running down the stairs to greet him, looking incredibly young ('almost a child') wearing a simple plaid dress and black slippers, her unbound hair streaming behind her. She took his hand and said in a breathless voice, whose clear silver tones struck him as most pleasing, 'I love mathematics, physics and chemistry'[18] and immediately plunged into a discussion of Faraday and Hofmann, both of whom had taught her. After such a good start, the rest was simple. Through Professor Schellbach she met Ernst Curtius, another tutor of Fritz's, and the historian Droysen – one of whose articles Vicky had translated only a few months before – the classical scholar Christian August Brandis and Kurt Werder, professor of philosophy at the University of Berlin. All these men (who were joined later by the historian Ranke) took a hand in Vicky's further education. Apart from that, they talked politics with her freely – 'which is not the fashion here now-a-days' – giving voice to the same kind of nineteenth-century liberalism as she had heard from her father. She was in her element, sparring with clever men from whom she could learn much, back in the school-room from which she had been so precipitously ejected.

If tongues began to wag, what of it? If the family pulled long faces, it was their affair. Vicky was scornful of their contempt. It never occurred to her that it might have been better if she had not moved quite so fast and perhaps allowed the family to get used to the idea of the professors gradually. But it was not in her nature to do things slowly; she had to plunge in at once. She was too young to understand that they were genuinely puzzled and upset. The story had leaked out that these men actually taught her! Was it really true? School at her age and a married woman too! Preposterous!

When Princess Marianne, the wife of Prince Fritz Karl and daughter-in-law of the King's brother Prince Charles of Prussia, who had become friendly with Vicky, was questioned about these goings on, she inadvertently let out not only stories about the professors but also the fact that Vicky had been walking in a disreputable part of Berlin and making disparaging remarks about the wretched conditions in the slums. The family were up in arms at once. How dare she! So Prussia wasn't good enough for her? They had all noticed how she complained about everything, comparing their country to her own – of course to Prussia's disadvantage. Princess Charles had something to say about that. She had been in England and told them the Thames was like a sewer and stank horribly and that she had been made quite ill by the food, the dust and the weather and had been thankful to get back alive.

Vicky was quite oblivious of the talk that went on behind her back. She was happy because she had taken a step her father had urged before she left home. A full account of the course she was following together with a time-table had gone to Windsor for comments. She could not believe it would not meet with approval, and longed to see her father's face when he read how well she had followed his advice in planning her day.

CHAPTER 5

'The Pull of Home'

WHEN the novelty and excitement of her new life had worn off and the long hard winter showed little sign of turning into spring, Vicky sometimes felt overwhelmed with longing for her home and family and she would creep away to be alone to think of them all at 'dear Osborne' without her.

In England her 'mission' had a glamour it sadly lacked in Prussia; in these moods it weighed heavily on her and she referred too often to the 'responsibility we are under'.[1] She suffered from contradictory feelings – over-confidence one moment, hesitancy and doubt the next. Sometimes nothing would deflect her from her purpose if she imagined it was 'what dearest papa wished'. At others she was so tossed about in the bewildering new world that she was unsure of herself when decisive action was called for, and created fears and difficulties that did not exist. Simple matters took on undue importance and brought on a nervous headache if there was no ready-made answer previously supplied by her father.

Vicky had always enjoyed the theatre, and when she heard that the Théâtre Paré was having a season of French plays she longed to go. But ought she? Everything French was tainted in Prussia since the Napoleonic wars, and moreover the French had such a habit of glossing wickedness over and making it appear attractive[2] that she was doubtful if it was proper for her to show an interest. This was easily answered, and a letter came by return of post from Windsor: 'dearest papa used to delight in going to the French play.'[3]

Much more important, because the Prussian royal family set much store by it, was the delicate question of Vicky's married title, which was still unsettled. What should she be called? Vicky herself was quite happy with 'Princess Frederick William', but the Queen indignantly rejected this, saying it would give Vicky too low a rank and precedence after the Crown Princess Olga of Württemberg – which would never do, particularly because Olga regularly used her Russian title of Grand Duchess. 'I think this distinction is one that cannot be accepted by anyone . . . our princesses never admitted the Grand Dukes of Russia having precedence over them.'[4] The Queen suggested she sign herself

'V., Princess Royal, Princess Frederick William of Prussia', and sent Vicky a scrap of paper to be signed in this manner and pasted into her own visitors' book at Buckingham Palace – which Vicky had forgotten to sign when she stayed there for three days as a married woman. The Prince Consort could not understand the confusion. He thought he had made this perfectly clear to Vicky when he told her ambiguously 'your place is as your husband's wife, as your mother's daughter, you must not expect anything else, but you must not give up anything which you owe to your husband and your mother'.[5] Moreover he had told Princess Augusta after the marriage that he wished Vicky to be known as the 'English Princess'.[6] Yet when he first came to England the last thing the Prince Consort wanted to be called was 'the Coburg Prince'. He had bitterly resented being known as the Queen's foreign husband and suffered greatly from not being accepted in society because his title was German. He had considered the stress on his 'foreignship' a grave source of weakness for the Crown. Eighteen years later he had forgotten this. Thinking to strengthen his argument, the Prince wrote to Vicky that 'much as you should avoid every appearance of your new home not being sufficient for you, you must not, on the other hand, give the impression that you wish to discard your native country or let it drop'.[7] The Prince sent Vicky an article on this very point which he had cut out of *The Times* for the 9th of February 1858; it expressed the hope that she would keep her English title 'and never forget the land that gave her birth'. Vicky made haste to assure her parents that she perfectly understood that 'if I were to lose sight of my English title and dignity I should be doing myself and my husband much harm'.[8]

The Prince Consort was proud of the confidence Vicky placed in his advice and directives, mistaking her uncharacteristic lack of self-reliance for trust in himself. Neither he nor the Queen saw that in refusing to cut the cord that bound her to them (indeed in pulling it even tighter) they weakened her confidence and destroyed her judgement. Their attitude did not, as they supposed, help her to stand on her own feet.

The pulpit was used as well as the pen to make her feel the 'pull of home'. Dr Macleod, the Queen's favourite preacher, prayed in his sovereign's presence 'May the Princess Royal never forget the early lessons she has received.' The Queen breathed a fervent 'Amen', and sent Vicky that very night a copy in the minister's own hand, at the same time telling her that this was a hope echoed by all the English people: 'never, dear child, let go what you owe to your country . . . and happily there is nothing in these two-fold affections and duties which need ever clash; the interests are so much the same and will in time get more and more united.'[9] How surprised Queen Victoria would have been if she had been told that she was talking nonsense.

Mother and daughter had never been further apart. Fortunately this lack of understanding was not to last. The Queen's longing for her child made her inquisitive about even the most trivial things. She had to know everything at once. Her insatiable curiosity gave Vicky the impression that her mother wanted to live her life for her – which she did, but only because of her deep love. What was Vicky doing at such an hour on such a day? What 'toilettes' did she wear for this and that reception? What did she eat (send a menu), whom did she meet and what did she say? How had she placed her furniture (send a sketch). 'You must try and answer my questions . . . else we can never replace conversation.'[10]

The Queen was disappointed that Vicky did not wish to exchange confidences as one married woman to another. She failed to see that Vicky needed to be reassured, that she was in constant dread of forfeiting her family's affection by something she might do or say. The strain of separation made her unnaturally humble and contrite and gave her a feeling of unworthiness that was most uncharacteristic – 'I feel ashamed of myself' – 'I often tremble' – 'I am unworthy of so much love'. She was afraid that youthful bouts of bad temper might have hidden from her parents how much she loved them. If she said how happy she was with Fritz, would they take it to mean she loved them less? She missed the security, steady affection and understanding, and the freedom to discuss openly whatever came into her head – for this was thought strange and forward in Prussia. She had no doubt that marriage would draw her closer to her mother, but she needed time and peace of mind to sort out her emotions and to adjust to the strange people who now made up her family. Above all, she longed for them to know at home how she had changed for the better in a few short weeks. If they could only see the good effect of their teaching, they must surely love her more. 'My reform is complete, I hope you would not find me the same.'[11]

*

Since Vicky's arrival in Prussia political affairs had taken a turn for the better. She wrote in delighted terms to tell her father that it was all 'on account of the marriage'. Count Perponcher, acting that first winter as special political equerry to Fritz, had brought her the Prussian Year Book for March 1858. In it was an article by an anonymous author, drawing attention to the 'overwhelming enthusiasm' shown by the German people for the marriage. There were many outspoken references to the 'rise' of Prussia, to the 'setting of the sun' on the old régime and the 'bright hopes' of the new one. Vicky was so excited that she sent it off at once to her father, who read it with a thankful

'God be praised'. Here must surely be the first link in the chain that could end in German unity, the acceptance by the people of the future heir to the throne and his English wife, both of whom were known to have liberal and constitutional opinions. His life's dream was taking shape at last in the exhilarating welcome of a normally cold and un-demonstrative nation. 'All is going splendidly' he wrote in a quick encouraging line to his fellow conspirator in Coblenz.[12]

This flattering article sparked off leaders in the *Kölnische Zeitung* and the *Allgemeine Zeitung*, the two foremost liberal papers; they were full of praise for the marriage, Queen Victoria, the Prince Consort and everything English. Vicky read these papers through with Ernest Stockmar, and both were speechless with triumph as they solemnly marked special passages with a red pencil. If Ernest had taken the trouble to consult his father, the old baron would have warned his son not to draw conclusions from too little evidence. No one knew better than the elder Stockmar that the Prussian liberal newspapers were as idealistic in outlook as the Prince Consort. They had been stressing the need for a closer union with England for years. Now that it had come about they were jumping over the moon, taking the Prince Consort and Vicky with them. They all believed that the 'blighted hopes of the people were again rising high'.[13]

Yet Prince Albert saw the necessity for caution. As he saw it, events were moving too fast for Vicky's good. In this way they might soon be dangerously out of control. A firm foundation was preferable to a shaky one built in the full flush of popularity. From Windsor the leading reins were given a sharp tug. Vicky must have patience, prudence and a cool head. To this the Prince added a dire warning – Vicky must not read the *Kreuz Zeitung* (the paper of the extreme Right), nor the *Herald* (the Catholic paper) 'for they might give you a false impression'.[14]

All the same, after this Vicky looked upon herself as a symbol of hope for the future and saw a special meaning in every smile and every cheer. Her professors encouraged her in this, talking expansively of 'big changes' and of Prussia's 'need to be roused'. They told her how morality, conscience and patriotism had been asleep since the débâcle of 1848, but could be awakened by a 'touch' which was to come from the gentle but firm fingers of the Princess Royal – it was the moral of the plum-stone which, planted in healthy soil, grew into a strong and beautiful tree. Vicky was so affected that she allowed her mind to leap ahead into all kinds of plans for the future. Her court should be modelled on her mother's and in this way regain the 'good opinions' and the 'respect' the family had so lamentably allowed to slip away. 'They look to England, to mama's court, then at the bright character

I am thankful to say my husband bears and expect good results from this alliance.'[15]

*

As early as the summer of 1858 many people in England and Prussia expected that Fritz would be on the throne before many months. Prince Albert took it for a certainty and redoubled his efforts to educate 'our Prussian children' for the golden future. This was not mere wishful thinking. He had noticed at the wedding that Prince William was a bad colour and had aged considerably since 1851. Vicky had written to say that he had crippling pains in his arms and legs and walked very bent with the help of two sticks. William himself believed he would never be king. It was a sore point that his brother was only three years older, making the chance of the throne very slight. Added to that, Frederick William's particular illness increased this belief since it was well known that once the mind had gone the body was relieved of the stresses and strains of an active brain and could go on indefinitely. Very reasonably therefore, the Prince Consort wanted to be told what steps were being taken to initiate Fritz into the intricacies of statecraft. His idea was simple: once he knew what was being done he could himself fill in the gaps by correspondence – a type of instruction at which he had become an expert.

In the Prince Consort's opinion Fritz was still in some respects immature although he possessed many of the right ideas. This he put down to 'army mania', which had every Prussian prince enmeshed.[16] But it was not Fritz's fault that it had held him back. He had never received a proper education. He had the misfortune to live in a country where guns were prized above books. Marriage had altered nothing. It distressed the Prince that Fritz still had a tutor at an age when the Prince Consort himself had been mentor to much older men – Prince William amongst them. Paradoxically, Fritz spent many hours a day with his regiment – despite the tutor – drilling and marching and all the rest of it. 'Hints' had gone to the right quarters that instead of wasting time playing soldiers, Fritz should be invited as heir presumptive to sit on the council, should be given state papers to study and should help to take the burden of governing off his sick and ageing uncle's shoulders – a task for which he was better equipped mentally than Prince William. The Prince Consort asked Vicky to support him at her end. He urged her to speak to her father-in-law and to explain to him (what he only imperfectly understood) the difference between 'learning' which sapped energy and 'work' which toughened the character and enriched the soul. Trembling a little, Vicky did her best; she came away crestfallen, snubbed and told not to interfere.

She knew only too well that she was in the worst possible position. She could see all the dangers that could befall a young and ignorant king, and yet her opinions (like those of her father) were not listened to or even given a moment's polite consideration. Soon after their marriage Fritz had told her how he had been longing for years to be given some useful work to do and had frequently begged for his father's permission to read state papers. But Prince William had procrastinated over and over again, and had never bothered to discuss the question with the King.

Princess Augusta believed she did her share in spurring Fritz on to greater things. She meant well, but her way of doing it only increased Fritz's lack of confidence. Vicky had seen her criticising, scolding and harping on Fritz's faults, driving him into his shell, so that even Vicky could do nothing with him. Yet she could sympathise, for she knew Fritz felt his degrading position keenly and complained bitterly of being kept back by his mother and ignored by his father, while Vicky knew that he was too shy and timid to approach either parent.[17]

Vicky had first seen this diffidence when she and Fritz spent a few days with Princess Augusta in her native state of Weimar in April. This visit was to mean everything, and Vicky had looked forward to it for weeks. It was a poor start to be given separate rooms which were not even on the same floor. The atmosphere was anything but cosy. Princess Augusta never noticed her surroundings and ate what was put before her without relish, so her servants were slovenly and did as little as possible. The food was atrocious and roughly served, the castle cold and the washing arrangements archaic – Vicky was expected to bathe in a huge old-fashioned tub made for Queen Victoria's visit in 1845 and not used since.[18] Augusta was bored. Since boredom made her irritable she was in a scolding mood, so that everything Vicky and Fritz had intended to discuss with her went unsaid and all they took back with them were terrible colds.

Vicky had to relieve her feelings by pouring it all out to her father who, in a rare fit of irritation against the whole Prussian royal family, in his turn unwisely unburdened himself to his brother Ernest in Coburg. 'Fritz has absolutely nothing to do . . . travelling and hearing lectures does not suffice for a young man in his twenty-seventh year. So there remains nothing but the military parade ground for his physical strength.'[19] The indiscreet Ernest was so amused at the idea of brother Albert falling out with his chums that he could not resist the temptation of passing it on (in strictest confidence) to various friends and relations abroad. It emerged, as gossip always does, in garbled form: a story was soon going the rounds of Berlin that the Princess Royal was being ill-treated by her husband and that a furious Prince

Consort was even then on his way to take her home.[20] Hidden in the mass of falsehood was a grain of truth; Vicky had fallen down some steps and sprained her ankle. She had just returned from attending the proxy marriage of Princess Stephanie, daughter of Prince Hohenzollern-Sigmaringen, to King Pedro of Portugal. The horror she felt at the barbaric custom that tied an innocent girl to a man she had never seen, and the intense heat of the crowded room, had made her feel sick and faint. When it was over she had hurried upstairs to remove her heavy court dress and, with her mind on the marriage and her own very different good fortune, she had forgotten the three treacherous steps that led to her dressing-room and had fallen headlong. Dr Wegner took a grave view of the accident; although not in itself serious it could have serious results, for there was a chance that Vicky was pregnant.

*

It seemed hard to Vicky that no one was pleased that she was to have a child. Princess Augusta had thrown up her hands in dismayed surprise. The Queen called it 'horrid news' which she had hoped might be postponed indefinitely, while the Prince Consort worried about Vicky's youth and health and the inadequacy of German doctors. At the same time he saw a gleam of hope. The pregnancy gave him an excuse for an early visit to his daughter. Although Vicky had said all the right things about her marriage ('When we are together all seems joy and peace'), both parents had sensed that all was not as it should be between the young husband and wife. This, they suspected, was at the root of Vicky's inability to settle down, her restlessness, homesickness and general dissatisfaction about everything in Prussia. Partly because Vicky had not been quite frank in her letters and partly because they thought she exaggerated, it never occurred to them that she was suffering from nervous tension caused by family rows and worry about Fritz's enforced idleness, or that she was utterly worn out with coping with unruly servants, the dirt, the terrible cold of the Schloss, fear of child-birth and not least the commands and advice showered on her in every letter from home.

An enigmatic and almost illegible scribble from Stockmar – who was suffering from fibrositis in his fingers – hinting at 'trouble', followed by one from Vicky talking excitedly of a 'plot' to remove Ernest Stockmar, put a stop to the Prince Consort's waverings. He telegraphed to Vicky to expect him early in May.

Was someone trying to get rid of Ernest Stockmar? He certainly behaved as if he thought so himself. But the mistake he made was to look on the attempts to remove him as political, a dastardly scheme of the Manteuffel government who wanted him out of the way because of his liberal opinions. If there ever really was a plot, however (and it has never been proved), it was nothing more than a longing by the household to have this dour private secretary replaced by someone more congenial to themselves.[21] But if Ernest was right, it was highly dangerous (as old Stockmar saw at once) to allow himself to be befuddled by doubt and held back by the fear of making a mistake. Ernest Stockmar was a loyal and devoted private secretary, but this was not enough. Vicky needed an older and wiser man – similar to the old Baron in his prime – to sort out the many problems that daily confronted a young girl in her position. Ernest never pretended to be like his father except in his honest upright character and his willingness to serve. The fault was the Prince Consort's, who imagined it would be easy to advise from a distance and who saw the young Stockmar in the mirror of the old one.

At about the time Vicky discovered she was pregnant, she was in particular need of such a person to fight her battles for her. Like many women carrying their first child, her feelings were in an upheaval and she was uncharacteristically peevish and fretful – bad temper which she mistakenly attributed to the pain in her ankle and Dr Wegner's 'weakening' treatment, against which she rebelled. He made her lie on a sofa all day, which bored her to tears; she became lethargic, fell into unnatural dozes and awoke with a headache so that she lost her appetite. She refused to have her hair arranged, complaining that the pulling hurt her; nor could she be bothered to let her maids change her dress. Books – for which there had never been enough time since coming to Prussia – lost their charm, and Vicky passed the time staring at the ceiling and thinking how ill-used she was, and was cross with her maids and ladies alike, so that they fled in fright out of reach of her bad temper.

Fresh air was an absolute necessity to Vicky; without it she drooped. She begged Dr Wegner to let her go for a drive, to be carried on a chair into the garden or just to have the windows open: requests he blandly ignored, making Vicky feel like a prisoner. Dr Wegner was perfectly aware of Queen Victoria's advanced views on pre-natal care, and knew that Vicky shared them. On the other hand, he owed his position in her household to Princess Augusta, and her orders were very different. Dr Wegner was an ambitious man; Princess Augusta could make or break him. Queen Victoria was far away in England, Princess Augusta was on the spot. It was inevitable that Augusta should win.

Suddenly everything was changed. Into this house of gloom a letter from the Prince Consort came as a reprieve. He would meet Vicky in Coburg. She was radiant at once, seeing beauty in things that had irritated her before, excitedly making plans for the visit, reading and re-reading the letter in which her father told her how much he longed 'to see you and to hear from you those impressions which your first entrance from childhood into life must have made upon your heart and mind'.[22] The 'blessed meeting' was all she could talk about, and she began to sing to herself as she called the maids to do her hair and help her change her dress. She was in no mood to accept the unpleasant surprise which Dr Wegner gave her. In his blunt officious way he told her he could not allow her to travel to Coburg. At first Vicky was so furious she could not speak. Then, in a voice that shook despite efforts to control it, she said coldly that she could not put her father off and that was an end of the matter.[23] When she liked she had an air of authority which could not be ignored. Used to taking orders and to being put in his place, Dr Wegner gave up the argument, but not his firm intention that Vicky should not leave Berlin. Without another word he went straight to Fritz and asked him to impress on Vicky the need for the greatest care. Certain that she would see things in a reasonable light, Fritz explained the importance of a healthy heir and gently begged her to be sensible.

Vicky could hardly believe her ears. She listened with mounting indignation; then, covering her face with her hands, she burst into tears. Between sobs she said that she did not want this child if her body belonged to the state.[24] Refusing to listen to another word, and no better than other young wives when it came to a quarrel, she said brokenly that she would never speak to him again and that she wished she had never married, so that Fritz, now as furious as she was, marched straight out of the room banging the door behind him.

What had he done? What had he said? He had only repeated Dr Wegner's orders, which had seemed very right and proper. As he tramped through the grounds to cool off he felt hard done by and misunderstood. He had not meant to be cruel, yet he had taken a pleasure in being unkind: was the reason that deep inside him there was a feeling of jealousy, so deep and so suppressed that he had not been fully aware of it himself? Vicky's smiles, her warmth, her endless excited talk and her references to times he had never shared with her, were all because of her father. Ever since she had known of the Prince Consort's visit, Vicky's mind had fled to Coburg as she made endless plans 'to please papa', shutting Fritz out as completely as though he did not exist. He was dreadfully hurt that Vicky's pleasure at the prospect of seeing her father again was far greater than her joy at the idea of their child. Was the child to come between them? Fritz felt that he did not come first with Vicky as it was, and this he could not accept. He was old enough to know – what Vicky did not – that this was no mere lover's tiff and that their marriage was more in the balance than she knew.

Because she was artless and open herself, Vicky had no idea that the real cause of Fritz's anger was her own father. It was Fritz's admiration for her father that had drawn her to him in the first place, and she had always taken it for granted that he loved him almost as much as she did. He had certainly said he looked forward to having him with them in Prussia. They had agreed that they needed his wise advice and guidance more than ever. It never occurred to her – partly because it did not affect her own love for Fritz – that her complete dependence on her father made her husband feel inadequate. Because Fritz had never said it in so many words, Vicky had not guessed how much he longed for her to lean on him a little, and ask his advice occasionally, or that it hurt him to hear her say, whenever a problem arose which she could not solve herself, 'I shall write and ask papa – he will know what to do'.

Fritz had innocently imagined that once they were married Vicky would turn to him as a matter of course. It had been a shock when nothing of the sort happened. Without fully realising it, he had borne both father-in-law and wife a grudge. When Vicky told him how happy it made her to know they shared everything – even their thoughts – he had felt guilty. She had gone on to say that this complete frankness between them must be cherished at all costs. It was because she did not want this closeness to be spoilt that she was against Fritz's becoming patron of the Masonic Lodges of Prussia, for it would mean he would have secrets she could not share. If that happened their marriage would no longer be perfect.[25] It made Fritz miserable to hear her say this when he remembered how much he already hid from her. The failure of communication on his side was due to his shyness in showing affection; he still had difficulty in revealing to her the true depths of his own love. It did not help matters that he understood the reasons for Vicky's adoration of her father. He had himself been immediately attracted to the older man when he first met him in 1851. No one before had bothered to talk to him as an equal while keeping that position of authority a young man can respond to. From that time he had hero-worshipped the Prince and he was overcome with shame that he had wanted to deny Vicky her happiness with her father and had positively enjoyed doing it.

Perhaps the root of the trouble with Fritz was the knowledge that his love was the greater. Vicky was perfectly sincere when she repeated over and over again that she loved him and was blissfully happy. But she was too young to love completely, and too insecure in her new life to cast off the chains that bound her to her familiar and carefree childhood. Because she could rely on it, she clung with all her might to the past. The passionate love Vicky was to develop for Fritz – and which was to help ease many a rough patch – had its beginnings seven months after her marriage when Fritz was sent to Posen in August for a short spell of military duty. It was their first parting. When Fritz had ridden out of sight, Vicky realised with a shock how empty life without him would be. It was the longest five days she ever remembered. As she wandered through the empty rooms, so ugly and cold without Fritz's warm personality, she pondered the awful possibility that she might never have met Fritz. What would have happened to her then?

The parting brought one blessed discovery, however, she could write love letters. She no longer found difficulty in saying 'I cannot live without you' – 'Now I belong to you, you are my own and we are one' – 'I would give my life for you if that would help you' – 'You are my protector, my dearest and best friend'.[26]

CHAPTER 6

'Not the Conqueror, perhaps the Great'

THEY moved to Babelsberg outside Potsdam at the end of May 1858. It was to be their home for the summer and it was here the Prince Consort came on the 4th of June, a month later than expected. Vicky said good-bye to the Berlin Schloss, 'that dark and dreadful prison', without regret. She expected a great deal from the move. Would a change of home bring with it a change of feelings? For with characteristic insight she knew that she was too young for motherhood.[1]

There had been no emotional reconciliation between husband and wife. To the relief of both the quarrel blew over because neither wished to prolong it. Years of listening to his parents' bickering about nothing forced Fritz to control his feelings, while Vicky, overcome by all the unjust things she had flung at Fritz in the heat of the moment, was only too glad to forgive and forget.

Fritz did his best to overcome his jealousy by doing all in his power to make the Prince Consort's visit a success; getting up at dawn to fetch him from Grossbeeren, so that the Prince would not have to wait over an hour for a connection to the Wildpark station and Vicky could then see him sooner. For the first few hours afterwards, he kept in the background as much as possible, so that Vicky could have her father to herself – indeed, he effaced himself as much as politeness allowed all through the visit.

Vicky was wild with joy. It was a delight to walk round the garden, her arm tucked affectionately into her father's, chatting to him in the same old companionable way, as though they had never been apart.

Next day the King and Queen drove over from Charlottenburg, bringing the Prince and Princess of Prussia with them. All four made a great fuss of the Prince Consort, telling him how much better he looked than at the wedding, while the Prince Consort – unable to return the compliment – could hardly hide his shock at the deterioration in the King. When he described this scene to the Queen, he would not call Frederick William 'mad', but referred to him rather mawkishly as a 'man just out of sleep', whom it was heart-rending to see, for he still had the 'feelings of a King'.[2]

The Prince of Prussia, too, was in worse shape than Vicky had described him. He no longer stood upright, his once ruddy complexion was as sallow as old parchment and he was thin and hardly spoke. But to an observer the party drinking tea on the terrace and admiring the glorious view of the River Havel and the little wooded hill that gave such charm to the surroundings, looked the picture of family content-ment. Albert too felt this, and was again convinced of the 'rightness' of the match. There was so little amiss that he wondered why he had ever been troubled. As soon as he could get away he wrote to the Queen to let her know that 'the relation between the young people is all that can be desired. I have had long talks with them both separately and together which gave me the greatest satisfaction.'[3]

What had happened? Was the Prince Consort insensitive or blind? Or was the family unnaturally good-tempered, so that the ripples of discontent and disharmony did not show? Vicky had not seen her mother-in-law since the disastrous Weimar visit in April. In common with the rest of the family, Princess Augusta was more than a little in awe of the Prince Consort and when confronted with him face to face, as on this occasion, she was affability itself. Vicky said little, because she saw at once how unwell her father looked. The visit had been delayed in the first place to give the Prince time to recover from a bout of influenza. A bad crossing on the *Vivid*, followed by an emotional two days in Coburg, had left their mark. The Queen had warned Vicky not to 'plague papa with visits'; therefore to plague him with worries would have been, in the circumstances, unthinkable. Moreover, in her father's company Vicky's troubles resolved so that she wondered if she had made too much of them before. It was unfortunate that for the first time in her life her doubts meant that she was not open with the one person of whom she boasted that she could 'say anything I thought to you rather than anyone else'.[4]

It was the same when both parents came to Babelsberg in August. Their presence brought about such changes that Vicky was again hesitant and doubtful. Although the visit was supposed to be private, Vicky had arranged for her parents to meet some of Prussia's important figures. They plodded up the steep hill to Babelsberg to pay their respects, but equal effort did not mean equal treatment. The seventy-eight-year-old Field Marshal Wrangel (talking of Vicky as his 'angel' and the marriage as a 'blessing to the whole country') was greeted effusively. The Prince Consort thought he had a surprisingly 'acute' conversation with Alexander Humboldt, shouting into the ear-trumpet of the nonagenarian who was now stone deaf. (When Humboldt's diaries were published after his death, however, it was plain that he had completely misunderstood the Prince.) But both Queen Victoria and the Prince Consort were 'very stiff' with the reactionary Prime Minister

Otto von Manteuffel, and made it plain that they did not care for his politics. Every time the Queen drove in an open carriage with Vicky, she was recognised and cheered, and she mistook this for a sign of 'great respect' for the Prussian monarchy and especially for Vicky herself.

Ceremony was whittled down to nothing. 'Gemütlich' dinners replaced the large receptions Princess Augusta had wanted to arrange. The family evenings at Windsor were recreated instead, Vicky and her father singing together and playing duets while Fritz leaned on the piano and turned the music. The Queen sat on a sofa with old Stockmar, over from Coburg for a few days, reviving her memories (and his too) of days gone by with photographs of dead Hohenzollerns.[5]

On the last night of all Vicky went to her mother's room to give her a gold locket with her hair, to mark the visit. The moment for confidences came as Vicky fastened the chain round her mother's neck. Before she could say a word the Queen remarked emotionally that she had a strange feeling that she had 'always been here'.[6] Vicky was 'so grateful' for all the happiness their presence had brought her that she was glad she had not spoilt things by complaints against the family or Prussia.

By a lucky chance Prince Albert's love for old buildings brought his daughter a permanent source of happiness in the Neue Palais in Potsdam. Vicky had taken her father on a tour of the royal palaces, and the Prince had been much struck with Frederick the Great's masterpiece. It was in a poor state, running to seed as only a place of great grandeur can. But it was not empty, as he supposed; hidden within its crumbling walls retired old ladies-in-waiting spent their last days like so many forgotten and unloved tabby cats, solitary and lonely.[7] The place was so huge that the Prince was certain there was room enough for Vicky and her family. He had been horrified by the conditions at Babelsberg. Although it was modern – it had been built by Prince William – Vicky's bedroom was over the huge kitchen-range which never went out and made her apartments unbearably stuffy and hot. On a sultry June day the Prince had felt quite faint even with the windows wide open. He had been appalled when Vicky told him cheerfully that it was a hundred times better than the Schloss. But she confessed that she did not want to stay in Babelsberg, explaining why it was impossible to feel at home there. The personality of the Prince of Prussia pervaded the rooms to such an extent that no souvenirs from Windsor or Buckingham Palace, no photographs of the English royal family nor pictures painted by Vicky herself could make it hers. The heavy furniture, the hot-house plants which Princess Augusta had trained to climb over looking-glasses and screens (and which the

Queen thought so pretty) were a daily reminder to Vicky of her father-in-law's increasing tyranny and her mother-in-law's demanding character. Nothing could be altered. Vicky and Fritz lived there and were expected to call it home, but they had no rights in the place at all.

*

The royal visit to Prussia had done nothing to clear up those small irritating misunderstandings that all too often now caused the Queen and her eldest daughter to be at odds with each other. Neither realised the effect a careless word could have at a distance. Vicky was too absorbed with her own problems to see that her mother was anxious at the thought of a first confinement so far away from home and under conditions of which she did not approve. She knew nothing of her mother's feeling of guilt that she had allowed Vicky to marry so young and did not realise that her condition reawakened this old bogey. The Queen was wretched too, since because Parliament would be sitting at the time she could not be with Vicky when the child was born. Her feelings broke through all her efforts to keep them hidden, and the brunt of her irritation and disappointment was borne by the innocent cause of it all – Vicky herself.[8]

This took the form of 'fidgetty' letters, filled with rebukes and warnings not to do what the Queen considered unwise or improper. Vicky could do nothing right. When Affie returned from a visit to his sister in the early autumn full of his aquatic exploits Vicky could not think what she had done to make mama so angry. She soon knew. How dare she allow Affie to 'play the sailor' on the Havel, instead of sending him off with the young Baron on a tour of the palaces 'to improve himself'.[9] The Prince of Wales's visit the following month brought more trouble upon her head. Why had Vicky failed to speak openly to Colonel Bruce of Bertie's 'faults'? It did not soften the Queen to be told that Vicky found nothing to criticise and that she had enjoyed the jolly company of her affectionate brother. It was unfair to be told that she was 'making too much' of a natural condition and that she exaggerated her discomforts, 'as you always do'. The Queen scolded because she did not write often enough; the Prince warned her she would make herself ill if she wrote too often. By the end of September Vicky was complaining to Fritz that contradictory commands from home were making her confused and upset. What was she to do? For the first time she turned to Fritz for help – here was his chance to be 'guardian and protector'. Taken by surprise, Fritz could think of nothing until by a lucky chance he remembered that Stockmar was still in Berlin. Did Vicky think it a good idea to consult this old friend? It was a stroke of genius. To talk things over with Stockmar was the most natural thing in the world. Had not papa always done so when he wanted advice?[10] In a moment Vicky looked happier than she had done for weeks. Indeed she was so light-hearted that she was able to carry on with Fritz's musical education – which she had begun when she had discovered the only tune he recognised was the Prussian National Anthem, and which had lapsed through her inertia.[11]

*

The upshot of consulting Stockmar was not quite what Vicky and Fritz intended. He made more of Vicky's complaints than she did herself. She was used to talking to him without reserve; she knew he had both her parents' confidence and she asked him to intercede for her, so that she and her mother could get on to a more comfortable footing, never dreaming he would read so much into her words. Stockmar called on Lord Clarendon, who happened to be in Berlin, and told him that the Queen was behaving badly 'to this poor child', and that unless the angry letters ceased the Princess Royal might become very ill, for she was 'worried and frightened to death'. He asked Lord Clarendon to speak to the Prince Consort on the matter, while he paved the way for the interview by a letter advocating 'more consideration, moderation, calm and passivity' towards the Princess.[12]

More than anyone else, Stockmar should have been aware of the many factors that caused strain. Not the least of these was the weekly essay for her father. But she was certainly not frightened to death. If there were no other evidence, the letter Vicky wrote on the 9th of October in answer to one from the Queen which had warned her against doing 'so improper and indecorous a thing as to be lying on a sofa in a dressing-gown at a christening'[13] is proof enough that Vicky was not in the least in awe of her mother. Showing remarkable common sense and commendable maturity Vicky replied without the slightest trace of fear that 'as to the possibility of being like other Princesses on a sofa in the event of a christening . . . I can give no promise against . . . it would seem strange if a German Princess married in England insisted on having a christening here with the same customs observed as in her home. I fear I would make myself disliked if I showed contempt for a custom which is after all an innocent one.'[14]

The Queen was not, as Greville made out,[15] 'in a towering passion' with Stockmar for interfering. If she had been angry, her honesty would have compelled her to say as much to Vicky. She was vexed perhaps, even probably hurt, that her love and natural anxiety should have been so misunderstood, but she wrote Vicky a tender letter.

Vicky knew too how distressed the Queen was that her twelve-year-old son Affie was being sent to sea so young and how this irritated her nerves. To lose two children in one year was indeed 'horrible'. 'Altogether I feel so sad' were words to wring the heart of any daughter.

*

Vicky had a bad pregnancy. In normal circumstances she would soon have been well again. Instead she was pale and low, and much given to bursts of unaccountable weeping. She complained daily of dizziness, exhaustion and sickness, in the hope that someone would rescue her from her misery. It distressed her to feel so ill and look so pinched. Remembering her mother's excellent health in a similar condition (Lady Lyttelton had told her that the Queen was so well before the birth of the Prince of Wales that she could run round the Great Park at Windsor[16]), Vicky told Dr Wegner that she was sure all was not right with her, a remark he dismissed as the foolish fancy of a pregnant woman. But by August the Queen was so worried that she asked her own physician, Dr Clark, to examine Vicky. Clark found nothing amiss, however, and assured the Queen that the tears and low spirits would disappear as soon as the baby was born. It was the same in December, when the Queen sent her doctor to Potsdam for a first-hand report on Vicky's condition. Dr Clark, using a favourite phrase, was certain that there was no cause for alarm. Yet when soon after Christmas Mrs Innocent, the Queen's midwife, arrived to be at hand should the child come early, she was horrified by the change in the young expectant mother and guessed at once they were 'in for trouble'.

The Queen's faith in her old physician was not shaken even when on the 27th of January 1859, a son was born to Vicky at Babelsberg, after a long and dangerous labour in which both mother and child nearly died. It was a breech-birth complicated by the (often fatal) *placenta previa*. Vicky's sufferings are described as 'terrible', so that one marvels at the resilience of a girl who was able to bear seven more children after such a calamitous birth. 'My precious darling', the anguished Queen wrote, 'you suffered much more than I ever did.'[17] Vicky's life was saved by a lucky chance: the Queen's distrust of German obstetricians and her insistence on sending the Scottish Dr Martin, who had attended her at her last confinement.

There are still too many unsolved mysteries surrounding William II's birth, which time and the discovery of new material have not helped to clear up. In the first place, no one has attempted to explain why it was necessary to put a key doctor (Dr Martin) in lodgings in Berlin, instead of close at hand in Potsdam. Dr Wegner had apartments at Babelsberg as one of the household. Therefore the excuse given in early biographies that court etiquette was the reason for excluding

Dr Martin cannot apply. There was nothing to make Dr Wegner exempt from this strange rule – if rule it was. The mystery deepens when one learns that Dr Martin was at least one hour's fast driving away – possibly longer at night or in bad weather. This means that at least two hours would elapse between a summons and his arrival. There is no doubt – as later events showed – that an English doctor in attendance on Prussian royalty was unwelcome to German doctors. Was Dr Martin kept out of the way on purpose?

When labour began at 1 a.m. on the 26th of January, Dr Wegner wrote a note asking Dr Martin to come at once. The letter was given to a servant who put it in the post-box by mistake instead of delivering it at once by hand. Dr Martin received it at 1 p.m. next day, just thirty-six hours later. What had happened in those lost hours? Dr Martin, who hurried to Potsdam at once, soon found out. The scene that met his gaze was horrifying. The German doctors, hope abandoned, were huddled together in a corner of the room, while a distraught Fritz knelt at the head of the bed, holding a semi-conscious Vicky in his arms. As Dr Martin rolled up his sleeves one of the German doctors said in English 'It is no use, the Princess and her child are dying'. At the sound of voices Vicky opened her eyes and Dr Martin saw by the look in them that she had understood what had been said. That Vicky did not die was due to the skill of the Scottish doctor, who with determination and chloroform produced a living child and saved both mother and infant.

The undelivered letter poses many questions. Was it deliberately put into the post-box? If so, whoever ordered this could not possibly have expected such a difficult confinement and might later have been too frightened to confess to a mistake. When Dr Martin did not turn up in a reasonable time, why did not Dr Wegner send for him again? When he did not come even after several hours, why did Dr Wegner not fetch him himself or send a special messenger? There were so many doctors round the patient that he could well have been spared. Indeed Dr Wegner's thoughts are the biggest mystery of all. What did he imagine had happened to Dr Martin when he did not appear after what amounted to one and a half days? Did he think there had been an accident? Did he question the footman to whom he gave the letter in the first place? He should have done so if it was a genuine mistake. Above all, why were Dr Wegner's orders not absolutely explicit in the first place – why was he careless about the delivery of such an important message? What part did the other German doctors play in the confusion? No doubt they were furious that Dr Martin had come at all, for it cast a slur on their skill. They had been very angry in the summer when Dr Saunders, the Queen's dentist, who 'happened' to be in Potsdam,

called and examined Vicky's teeth.[18] They would never have heard of
this incident in the first place if Dr Wegner had not disloyally disclosed
it. He was not a strong character, and could easily be intimidated –
hence the wish to throw his weight about at every opportunity to save
his face. In the general rejoicings at Vicky's safe delivery, Dr Wegner's
part in this bad business was overlooked. It was certainly black,
whether it proceeded from inefficiency or deliberate intent. Even if he
was merely careless and not the instigator of a plot this is enough to
condemn him.

One more question remains. Did Vicky herself think him culpable?
Did she suspect anything? At first she was too weak to do more than
be thankful that she was alive and the baby thriving. When she was
strong again, it was too late to probe. It is worth noting that there was
a deterioration in Vicky's relations with the doctor as the years went
by – they ultimately disagreed on almost everything. But he was never
dismissed. Nor was anything ever discovered about the servant who
posted the letter. We shall never know now whether he was bribed or
not: frightened to death, he kept his mouth shut.

*

Next day, Mrs Innocent drew the doctor's attention to the baby's left
arm. It was in a horrid state, hanging loose from the socket and quite
blue. Fritz was told at once but Vicky was not to know until she was
stronger. When the anxious young father questioned the doctors about
the exact extent of the injury, they were reassuring, implying rather
than stating that the damage was not permanent. They glossed over the
truth when they said that the paralysis – for that is what they called it –
would improve with special exercises, which the child could have when
he was older. Meanwhile a little gentle massage could begin at once.
They said enough to make Fritz believe that nothing was wrong with
his son which time and exercise could not cure. Even so, it was a little
difficult to answer the Queen's telegram 'Is it a fine boy?' with perfect
truth. For the moment all that mattered was that mother and child were
recovering. When Vicky was told a few days later, the doctors again
made light of the injury. She accepted what they said without comment,
a piece of misplaced tact which only increased their concern later on
when the arm did not respond to treatment. At the time, all the doctors
were really worried about was to extricate themselves without having
to admit their ignorance. Not one of them gave a thought to the
feelings of the young parents.

'Baby worship', which the Queen had warned Vicky against, went
on unchecked at Babelsberg. Fritz carried his son about in his arms,
beaming at everyone. He wrote to the Queen and Prince Consort
describing the child's beauty at great length, displaying the same kind

of passionate possessiveness he had shown towards Vicky and which should have touched a sympathetic chord in the Prince Consort's heart when he recalled his own unbridled adoration of the child's mother. The Queen wrote to say 'Papa cannot quite enter into Fritz's ecstasy about him', adding with her usual honesty 'I never cared for you half as much as you seem to about baby'.[19]

Vicky was sublimely happy with her child, for despite the arm he was perfection in her eyes. She had wanted her first to be a boy so much that she had scarcely dared to hope for it, explaining her feelings to her mother by citing the fable of the fox and the grapes.[20]

She was soon to find out that her son was not really to be her own, even though his birth had almost cost her her life. The long arm of Prussian royal prejudice reached out and touched her before the baby was a week old. Princess Augusta happened to call one day when Vicky was breast-feeding her child. She was disgusted, and at once sent an appeal to Queen Victoria – whose views she knew to be like her own – asking for help to put a stop to this natural instinct. To both women it was an 'odious habit', but 'we princesses have other duties to perform'[21] was cold comfort to Vicky, who had to hand her son over to a wet-nurse. This was not the end of the matter. Many years later the Empress Augusta – as she had by then become – told this same baby the ludicrous and cruel story that his mother could not face feeding him herself because his injured arm was repugnant to her.

No child was ever more wanted or welcomed with more warmth by his young parents than Prince William of Prussia. The agony of the birth and the thought that they had nearly lost him made him doubly precious, while the injury made them more protective. For this there is abundant and unassailable evidence. Yet in later years William II preferred to believe that he was unwanted and reviled because of an accident he could not help. It suited his irritable nature to turn this into a convenient stick with which to beat his parents from time to time.

'Frederick William Albert Victor' were the names chosen for the boy, who had forty-two god-parents at his christening – a number which Queen Victoria found 'most alarming'. To be one of such a motley crowd was not an honour, but the Queen consoled herself that the four grandparents had a special function as 'peculiar sponsors'.[22] He was to be known as William (it soon became Willy) to lessen the confusion with legions of Fritzes. The Prince Consort began at once to look into the future. 'What epitaph history will attach to his name is in the lap of the Gods', the Prince wrote to Fritz, 'not Rufus . . . not "the Conqueror", perhaps "the Great". There is none with this designation.'[23]

It was the custom in Prussia to christen a royal child two weeks after birth. On this occasion the ceremony was postponed for a week to allow Vicky time to recover enough to be present. Because the Queen and Prince Albert could not make the journey, Vicky had to promise to take baby Willy to England in the spring. When the time came Dr Wegner forbade it, and Vicky had to go alone.

It was her first visit since her marriage. When she arrived at Windsor Castle in May 1859 her brothers and sisters greeted her with delight, almost smothering her with kisses. Their demonstrative affection combined with the 'sameness' of everything satisfied her craving for reassurance and wiped out her deep-seated fears that in going so far away she had become an outcast. Behind her laconic words to Fritz, 'nothing here is changed, all is the same',[24] lay a world of healing balm.

The terrible shared experience of Willy's birth had deepened Vicky's need for Fritz's love and had revealed to her his true place in her life. The sight of the rooms where she and Fritz had spent their short honeymoon brought him nearer and at the same time increased her longing to be with him again: 'In this room I experienced the happiest moment of my life when you took me in your arms as your wife and pressed me to your heart',[25] but she only realised that it was the 'happiest moment' sixteen months afterwards.

CHAPTER 7

'Between two Fires'

By the spring of 1859 Vicky and Fritz were living in the Neue Palais in Potsdam, which was to be their home for nearly thirty years.

What was there in this vast rococo building that appealed so much to Vicky that she came to cherish every stick and stone? In the first place she was prepared to like it because it was hallowed by her father's blessing and was where Fritz had been born. It awakened her sense of history and showed up her own importance as the wife of a descendant of Frederick the Great. Perhaps most important of all it cried out for improvement – a cry, wherever it came from, which never failed to find an answering call in Vicky.

It was very grand. Nearly all the rooms were vast (one of the few exceptions became a replica of the Blue Closet at Windsor), and there were so many of them that to visit them all was a day's work. It was not easy to run, although at first Vicky and Fritz only lived in a small part of it (they took over more as each old lady-in-waiting died). It was as difficult to heat as the Berlin Schloss, yet Vicky never felt the cold there in the same way. When Vicky was first shown round she felt that it would be impossible to get it clean enough to live in at all. The shabby walls were covered with huge tapestries, blackened with age and dust like those in the Schloss; the priceless Aubusson and Savonnerie carpets were rotting, faded by the sun and here and there eaten by mice. In one room alone Vicky found 'thousands of dead bats', while all the beds crawled with lice.[1] There were no lavatories (William I, who had lived there for a time, having vetoed these as a needless extravagance) and not a single bathroom. All the water came from a pump in the courtyard. The silver furniture so beloved by Frederick the Great was tarnished, the beautiful workmanship obliterated by the filth of years. It could not have looked more unpromising, yet Vicky recognised what she could do with its painted ceilings, elegant columns, richly carved chimney-pieces and perfect proportions. Whenever the sun shone, the rooms were filled with a golden glow which enhanced their beauty and lit up every corner, so that even after sunset the warmth remained. Everything was worth restoring. If there were ghosts they were kindly ones, so that Vicky came to understand why

Frederick William III and Queen Louise had been so happy there; she instinctively felt that she could recreate their happiness.

On that summer's day in 1858 when she and the Prince Consort had walked in the overgrown gardens, the Prince had shown her what could be done, pointing out where he thought the paths must have been, making practical suggestions for clearing the once impressive drive, plucking handfuls of dock, dandelion and grass and revealing to Vicky's startled gaze the flower-beds and stunted shrubs beneath. Nothing was dead, everything could be reclaimed, and was only waiting for the gardener's hand to spring to radiant life.

Restoring the Neue Palais brought out a side of Vicky she did not know she possessed – a refusal to admit defeat. Many surviving letters – some to her daughter Sophie, who showed a tendency to be 'knocked under' too easily by similar conditions in Greece – reveal the woman whom the girl was to grow into. With her father's encouragement, but very little else, and in a comparatively short time, she transformed her apartments in the Neue Palais into a comfortable and beautiful home. Nothing was easy. As each old lady died she had by sheer force of character to wrench more and more rooms from a reluctant father-in-law, until the whole palace was theirs: no mean task when it is remembered that, at the time she moved in, Vicky was only eighteen years old.

*

Vicky needed the challenge of the Neue Palais to take her mind off her worries. A bad summer with Fritz had set off a train of alarming thoughts. Had Princess Charles been right when she had told Vicky in a resigned voice to make the most of those first idyllic weeks of marriage, for 'nothing lasts' – cynical talk Vicky dismissed as quite shocking? Good manners had stopped her bursting out with a hundred valid reasons why her life would be different.

Vicky had at once sensed something ominous in a letter which King Leopold of the Belgians wrote to Queen Victoria while she was still at Windsor in May 1859, warning his niece that France was about to take advantage of Italian national aspirations to go to war with Austria.[2] Vicky knew very well that her uncle had no reason to love the French Emperor who was occupying (and much more royally) the throne that rightly belonged to his father-in-law Louis Philippe, and she divined that Leopold's somewhat strident tone was caused as much by personal feelings as by fears for the safety of his Coburg relations attached to the Austrian army. Vicky had been in Prussia long enough to realise that nothing French must ever be praised, and that nobody had a good word to say for Napoleon III, whose misdeeds were so enlarged that even Vicky began to think back on her childish admiration for the

French Emperor with a certain shame. However, the criticism increased her belief in her father's good judgement, when she recalled that there had always been 'something' about the Emperor which Papa had not quite taken to. It never occurred to Vicky that this 'something' could be put down to the enormous attraction the man of sin had for mother and daughter.

The first signs of trouble came soon after her return to Berlin. The Manteuffel government had fallen in October 1858 and had been replaced by a liberal government under the peace-loving Prince Karl Anton Hohenzollern-Sigmaringen. This, together with the anti-war views of Prince William (who had formally accepted the Regency in the autumn), gave Vicky reason to hope that as long as the French left Prussia alone, all would be well. Even as Napoleon III was marching his soldiers south the Regent declared that Prussia would mobilise but remain neutral.

Vicky's thankfulness for her father-in-law's 'calm and reasoned views'[3] was short-lived. She had reckoned without Fritz, who said grimly that to sit back and do nothing while a friend and neighbour was being butchered was more than he could stand, and sent Vicky half out of her mind with his calculations of the number of men and horses he would need for a long campaign. When Vicky burst into tears he was astonished by her failure to understand that he was only doing his duty as a soldier, 'which you have always known I must do'. Nothing could deflect Fritz from his purpose, not even Vicky's pathetic plea – what would happen to her and baby Willy if he did not return from a war to which he had gone alone and unsupported by the Regent? Fritz remained unmoved, and the ring of exasperation as well as of despair can be heard clearly in the letter Vicky dashed off to her parents in the full flush of her quarrel with Fritz: 'It breaks my heart he will not understand.'[4] This blind spot was not new to her. She had first encountered it soon after her arrival in Prussia, when despite her fears for his safety Fritz had taken a nightly walk alone in the streets of Berlin. It was as though he shut a door in her face through which he could not hear her frantic cries, which would have been much less wild if he had listened calmly instead of dismissing her fears as so much feminine silliness. Many years of coping with his mother's nagging had taught him to close his mind to women's entreaties. He needed to learn that the tone was not the same in every case.

The moment the fighting had started in June 1859, Fritz rushed impulsively to help the Austrians, to the sound of Vicky's wails. He was soon back again, furious with friend and foe alike. The Austrians had not needed him. After a disastrous defeat at Solferino on the 24th of June, they had been only too glad to sign the peace of Villa Franca on the 11th of July. Almost before Fritz had reached the front, the war was over. He had not been called upon to fire one shot and his failure to be 'of use' put him into a very black mood. Depressed and upset, he blamed Austria's conduct of the war, calling it 'bad beyond belief' and muttering that there were lessons to be learned from her defeat – and that he was going to put one of them into operation without delay, in order that the 'same does not happen here'.[5] Vicky was alarmed when a set-faced Fritz rose at dawn to spend the day drilling and marching his troops in order to make them the kind of army that would be ready to meet 'what might come'. He returned at night so exhausted that he fell asleep as soon as his head touched the pillow, and this made her thoroughly cross. When they did have an hour or two to themselves, Vicky tried in vain to coax him into a better mood. She had slipped into the habit of writing about him to the Queen in terms only too familiar to both women – 'fagged and pale', 'worn out and silent', 'yellow and no appetite'. To her cost Vicky was learning what her father meant by 'army mania'. It had caught Fritz in its grip of steel, and he was showing signs of that single-minded purpose which so exhausted the Prince Consort and drove the Queen frantic with worry, although in Fritz's case it was the army boot and not the scholar's lamp that called before daybreak.

Quite at a loss to know how to deal with this strange new Fritz, a little unwisely Vicky unburdened herself to her father and soon came to regret her moment of weakness. An anxious Prince bombarded her with letters, doubling her trouble, for now she had two men to contend with where one had been too much. The Prince begged Vicky to remind Fritz that Prussia was less important than Germany; with this in mind Fritz must 'be courageous and act like a German', for he was behaving in a parochial fashion unseemly in the heir to the Prussian throne. The Prince Consort angrily called Fritz 'deplorably childish', telling Vicky (the unhappy go-between) that it was crazy to act as though Prussia was expecting to be soon at war: behaviour like this might be all that was needed to start such a conflagration as might set the whole of Europe on fire.[6] Fritz refused to listen. Another war was exactly what he wanted. Nothing but another war could wipe out his humiliation, which was no less hurtful for being imaginary. In his heart he knew that all he really wanted was honourable occupation, but that as matters stood at present he had only the battle-field on which to prove himself. If he did well, his standing with everyone would rise. He was sick of having the other princes tease him about his easy life, a joke he found hard to bear with good humour. Above all, he longed for Vicky to be proud of him. But he found it difficult to tell her this, especially when he saw how upset she was at the gulf that was widening daily between the Prince Consort and himself, a gulf Vicky mistakenly tried to bridge by doing all she could to win Fritz's sympathy for her father. Papa was tired out with overwork and worry; it was galling for him to see unity going from strength to strength in Italy under Cavour while it was at a standstill in Prussia.[7] How sad it had made her to hear her father say, not without bitterness, that he wondered if he was the only German who cared.[8] But Fritz was not to be won over. He told Vicky bluntly that the Prince was attempting more than mortal man could achieve – governing England through the Queen and trying to govern Prussia through the Regent: no wonder he was tired. Vicky refused to listen to such talk; and because he felt even his own wife to be against him, Fritz's frustration and sense of isolation increased. With it grew Vicky's determination to save her marriage, which she imagined was in grave danger.

She had got it into her head that the reason for so much infidelity in Prussian society was simply the amount of frivolity that went on – nothing was taken seriously. There was no time for home life nor for those peaceful evenings when husband and wife could relax together, read aloud or talk. Again and again she had seen princesses fritter away their time (and 'to waste time is a sin') in a round of gaiety or – what was just as bad – in doing nothing while they waited for more fun to begin. The tempo of life in Berlin society had become faster since the regency. There were balls or receptions every night, and a revived interest in the opera and the theatre, moribund for so long, while the Prince Regent indulged his taste for reviews that showed off his magnificent army in spectacles which drew crowds from all over Germany. Out of tune with this mood, Vicky wrote disparagingly of these delights to her parents. Everything came under fire: the princesses for flirting outrageously, the conversation for its banality, the food, the heat, even the same old faces that turned up (as Vicky did herself) night after night, to bore and be bored. Suddenly Vicky was as difficult to please as Fritz. She did not know how to deal with the situation except by going to the opposite extreme, and this made her uncharacteristically prudish, not to say priggish. In reality she loved dancing, especially with Fritz. It had been a great disappointment that on account of the King's illness there had been practically no balls when she first came to Prussia. Now that they had started again, her longing for them had vanished, removed by the complexities of Fritz's character, which was more devious and less open than she had realised. He was not really secretive – as Vicky was soon to learn – simply unused to discussing his feelings, a thing which to Vicky was natural and easy. Yet a glimmer of hope was contained in her instinctive feeling that she must learn to sympathise before she could expect to understand. She did not yet know how to do this, because so much of her nervous energy was used up in under-standing, sympathising with and bracing her father. Besides, her own problems were not yet by any means all resolved.

Moving into the Neue Palais had opened up fresh possibilities for Vicky, but it did not open them wide enough. She had tremendous energy which she longed to use, especially in 'doing good'. She was oppressed by the narrow boundaries of her royal existence because they restricted her scope for this. She often asked herself what went on in the real world outside closed court circles. No one could tell her, because all were too concerned with their own narrow lives. It was even difficult to discover exactly what was happening in the political world. Count Perponcher was supposed to provide information, but his reports were a mass of words – none strictly untrue, yet none revealing the truth. Perponcher might have done better had he been less of a courtier and more of a politician, and it did not help that he was a bit of a dandy and spent more time in front of his looking-glass than at his desk.

With his flair for managing other people's lives, the Prince Consort should have been the one to help Vicky – correspondence courses were his particular forte. But he was bowed down with work, his desk piled high with boxes marked 'urgent'. The green German lamp burned long after midnight and was lit again before dawn. He wrote to Vicky as regularly as ever, but these letters are the least understanding of any he sent her. All work and no play had affected his spirits, and the unhappy result was a joylessness that did nothing to brace his daughter. When she complained, he offered a draught of his own medicine – she should lose herself in hard unremitting work. If the remaking of the Neue Palais gardens was not solace enough, she must enlarge her range of occupations. Architecture might do as an escape from the 'treadmill of life'.[9] Pathetically blind, this loving father failed to see that the only escape Vicky needed was from her present barren existence into a swiftly moving world – for which he himself had equipped her well and from which her marriage into the Prussian royal family had cut her off. During the period 1860–61 there is no mention in the Prince's letters of leisure, relaxation or fun of any kind – a remarkable fact since the recipient was still under twenty. There was no lack, on the other hand, of grim exhortations to work, more work and greater and greater effort; 'for only in this way will you succeed'.[10]

The lesson sank in. Vicky's reply to her father took the form of a long and learned essay on 'Ministerial Responsibility'. Writing this had kept her indoors in beautiful spring weather, a sacrifice she made cheerfully if the result gave dearest papa pleasure – which of course it did. Its erudition convinced the Prince once again how right he had been to urge Vicky to set her sights high. Did ever a father have such a daughter? The Prince Consort thought not, and in his pride at her achievement he sent copies of her essay to Lords Clarendon and Granville, basking in the reflected glory of their astonishment that this statesmanlike document was the work of a young girl. The melancholy that had settled on him more or less permanently was lifted for a short time, and he experienced the 'quiet satisfaction' his daughter was still able to give him. In this frame of mind he wrote confidently to Ernest Stockmar 'she is the right person to be in her difficult position'.[11]

Father and daughter were slowly but surely changing places. Unconsciously Vicky was adopting a protective attitude, telling her father only what was good for him to know, assuming an optimistic tone she did not always feel. The Prince asked for news of the Regent, who no longer answered letters. Vicky disliked being evasive, yet how could she tell him the truth, which would mean hurting him deeply? Prince William was putting all the Prince's letters in the fire and was developing a power-complex, cracking the whip with the assurance of an eastern potentate over the heads of all who opposed him.

During the winter of 1860 the Regent published his first programme. It included some startling 'reforms': an increase in conscription from two to three years, a heavy increase in taxation (to pay for it) and the abolition of the *Landwehr* (a body resembling a modern territorial army) because in William's opinion it was not worth its keep. Fritz was in bed with influenza at the time, but he was so incensed that he got up too soon, and weak as he was, confronted his father, demanding an explanation. All the Regent would do was to say angrily that he was 'sick and tired of amateurs who were neither disciplined nor reliable'.[12] There was a row; both soon descended to personalities, the Regent calling Fritz lazy and incompetent, while Fritz accused his father of treating him like a child and deliberately keeping him out of things. High words gained Fritz nothing, and he had disregarded Vicky's advice. More than once she had urged him to thrash out with his father the vexed question of his anomalous position, a question which had become more urgent since the Regency, but she meant him to do so with a cool head and irrefutable arguments, not in the heat of the moment.

Early in 1859, shamed into it by the Prince Consort, the Regent had taken a few hesitant steps to improve Fritz's position. Fritz was allowed to sit on the Council, but there were conditions: he could neither speak nor take part in discussions, but was to learn by observing, one of the most unrewarding ways of acquiring knowledge and accepted by Fritz only because he hoped it was merely the first rung of a promising ladder. But the Prince Consort did not care for the concession and warned Vicky and Fritz that conditions like these could have insidious side-effects and could even be dangerous. Who outside the walls of the council chamber would know of Fritz's passive role? Had it occurred to them that if the Regent behaved unconstitutionally, the mud thrown at the father would also stick to the son?

With the succession in mind, the Prince Consort had read the list of the Regent's reforms with mounting concern. As a result, the wires between Windsor and the Neue Palais vibrated with cypher telegrams. How far, the Prince wanted to know, would the Regent go to achieve his ends? Would there be a clash with the Chamber? Would Fritz be involved? With a sinking heart and little hope of keeping 'the worst' from papa, Vicky was forced to answer with the truth.

With an instinct for the preservation of her skin and Fritz's too, Vicky saw the gravity of a conflict with the Regent at a time when Fritz was in no fit state to do himself justice, nor his father to be tolerant. She did her best to persuade Fritz to go with her to England in order to give the Regent time to cool off. But Fritz said that it was his duty to stay even if it killed him, to which Vicky replied that it would soon do so if he did not listen to reason.

Fritz was full of aches and pains, plagued by indigestion and its consequence – insomnia. He had formed the irritating habit of getting up in the night when he could not sleep and sitting in a chair with a book until he was overcome by exhaustion, only to wake stiff and tired to what he called 'another hopeless day'. Vicky blamed the Regent for Fritz's nerves. Neither of them realised that Fritz's 'lowness' was simply the aftermath of a bad bout of influenza which would soon clear up, given time and a change of air. Similarly, they had not divined that the Regent's bad temper was not really directed at Fritz, but was caused by the fear that his so-called reforms were unwelcome and that he would be forced to drop them.

When in November Vicky did manage to get Fritz to England, far from Prussia's lowering skies, he improved at once in the mild rural air of Windsor. Vicky was pregnant again, but she was well and in the highest spirits as soon as she stepped on to English soil. She loved the sound of English voices, the strong English tea served to them as their train rushed towards London, and even the grey fog of a typical English autumn day. During the long peaceful evenings at Windsor, Vicky sat happily at her father's feet, discussing the state of Prussia. But Fritz could not bring himself to criticise his father. Instead he enjoyed domestic chit-chat with the Queen, who told Vicky 'you have an excellent husband'.

CHAPTER 8

'Goodness can provide a Purpose in Life'

THE New Year of 1860 began inauspiciously. By tradition Christmas was always spent with Fritz's parents in Berlin and was a joyless affair. Princess Augusta had not inherited the German gift of making the most of an occasion. There was no tree, the present-tables were badly arranged, the food unfestive and Vicky's carefully chosen presents – a sketch of Babelsberg and a paper-weight of Scottish deers' teeth – were coldly received.

Vicky and Fritz arrived on Christmas Eve to find Prince William and Princess Augusta having a quarrel about a little matter of a green tea-service the Prince had given his wife on her birthday and which she disliked and would not use.[1] They continued the quarrel for the whole four days, and this so poisoned the atmosphere that Vicky and Fritz could not wait to go home. In any case it was a strain for one of Vicky's demonstrative nature to have to take care not to speak affectionately to Fritz. If she forgot and used an endearment, the Regent would glower and Princess Augusta snap. Music was forbidden as it gave Prince William a headache and set Princess Augusta's nerves on edge. Vicky told Fritz crossly that the only sound they liked to hear was that of their own voices raised in dispute. Altogether it was as unpleasant a Christmas as Vicky had ever lived through.

In January their fortunes took another beating. During the autumn session the Chamber had thrown out the Regent's reforms. When Parliament reassembled, he nevertheless brought the subject up again and met stalwart opposition for the second time – the Chamber remained firm to a man. In no mood to be crossed, William lost his temper and shouted that he would get his own way or they could take the consequences – he would abdicate. It was to be all or nothing, they could take it or leave it.

Next morning, a black day of sleet and high winds which broke the branches of the young trees in the Neue Palais gardens, Fritz, his heart as bitter as the weather, was about to enter the barracks when he was handed a mysterious message – would he go at once to the ante-room in the Council chamber? There he found some of the bolder members of the Conservative and Liberal parties waiting for him. They came to the point at once. They had decided that an army dictatorship under a man they trusted would be preferable to the rule of a Regent as difficult as the mad King himself. They had a plan to overthrow the Regent and put Fritz on the throne in his father's place.

Fritz could hardly believe his ears. How right the Prince Consort had been! – Prussia was full of traitors. White and shaken at this 'foul plot', and unwilling to listen to another word, Fritz turned on his heel and fled.[2] He then made a fatal mistake. Boiling with rage and unable to think coherently, and forgetting the promise he had given Vicky – never to speak to his father on an important matter without first talking it over with her – he marched straight to the Regent and blurted out the whole story. Prince William listened in silence, then the storm broke. Scarlet with rage he rounded on the astonished Fritz, shouting that he had always suspected he wanted him dead. He was a Judas and had only confessed because the miserable plot had failed and he feared the consequences. What had he done to deserve such a son?[3]

Fritz was so miserable that Vicky was forbearing with him when, head in hands, he told her what had happened. She did not for one moment believe the Regent distrusted Fritz. Why then had he railed at him? Why did he attribute horrible things to his own son whom he knew to be the soul of honour? The Regent's atrocious temper did not frighten her in the least, but she was worried by the effect such scenes had on Fritz – and in the long run on herself. Surrounded by dishonest people, would they be caught in the net and smothered?[4]

Vicky understood the Regent very much better than Fritz. But her feelings towards her difficult father-in-law were not as ambivalent as her letters make them appear. Brought up to have respect for her elders, she was distressed at feeling so little for a man who should have been so close to her. It was this that made her stress his good qualities and the occasional kindnesses he showed them; because they were so rare, they never went unremarked. She suspected that his trumpetings at Fritz on this occasion were nothing more than a cover for his realisation that what he called his 'reforms' were unwelcome to many in Prussia and that he was creating a serious internal crisis by insisting on them. William was absolutist by temperament and a soldier by training, and the brief mobilisation during the summer of 1859 had revealed shortcomings in the Prussian army which no doubt called for firm remedies; but his ministers were more liberal than he, and memories of 1848 ensured them a good deal of popular support. Tension began to build up between two opposing points of view. The proposal to replace William by his son was one of the first signs of this tension, but of course did nothing to relieve it. The Regent refused to withdraw his schemes, and the resultant crisis dominated Prussian internal affairs for another eighteen months, until the advent of Bismarck in September 1862. But these were also anxious, indeed tragic months for Vicky in more personal ways.

*

The nursery which should have been a haven of peace and quiet was the very opposite. Mrs Hobbs, Willy's English nurse, was always bewailing the fact that the baby's arm would not respond to the oil massage which she rubbed on day and night with fervent prayers for success. In every other way Willy was a robust child. Wrapped in a shawl, clasped in his mother's arms he looked a perfect specimen. In his bath and when he began to walk, it was another matter. In her heart Vicky was as anxious as Mrs Hobbs about the injury, but she knew that she must control her worry or it would overwhelm her. When after a year the arm showed no improvement and Vicky began to show signs of despair, Mrs Hobbs took a different line; she now said doggedly that it was better and that her massage was working. Queen Victoria adopted the same attitude of self-deception and refused to give up seeking specialist advice.[5] Using her own doctor Sir James Clark as go-between, she consulted Sir Benjamin Brodie. Very quickly he sent the Queen a lengthy report to the effect that the arm was gradually improving and that it would ultimately reach the normal length. The Queen asked Sir James Clark's new assistant, Dr Baly, to find out the views of Mr Cesar Hawkins and Mr Paget, two men of wide experience with a high reputation in orthopaedic surgery. Both gave favourable answers, and both used hypothetical cases to illustrate their points, which they wrote down at great length for the Queen. But the only good they did was to themselves – Her Majesty was impressed. The Queen spent many hours and reams of paper explaining exactly what they meant to Vicky, who tried not to delude herself that it was any use. Not as gullible as the Queen, she could not see how these doctors could know what they were talking about, since they had never seen the child and had only Sir James's description to guide them, 'and we know how much that can be depended on'.[6]

On the 24th of July 1860 Vicky's second child, a daughter, was born in the Neue Palais after an easy labour, and given the names Victoria Elizabeth Augusta Charlotte. She was to be called Charlotte (soon shortened to 'Ditta') but Vicky was not without a certain fear that mama would disapprove and think it a housemaid's name – she did, but was prepared to overlook it since Vicky was so well and the baby perfect. Fritz's family were quite disappointed to find Vicky smiling and well and the baby thriving, indeed nothing wrong anywhere; deprived of the chance to condole and to gossip about it afterwards, they stayed to criticise – Queen Elizabeth, for instance, finding fault with the 'Englishness' of the bedroom, the wide open windows, and the colour of the baby's hair. Afterwards Fritz explained away their conduct by telling her that the husbands of most of these women were unfaithful and that they were jealous that he loved her alone.

In his heart he recognised that the real trouble began at the top. They would see a change at once if the Regent and Princess Augusta behaved like proper parents to them both instead of encouraging impertinence and slights. Fritz was humiliated by the thought that if he had any authority he would be in a better position to shield his wife from the biting tongues of his family. It had made him furious to be compelled to take Vicky away from the Neue Palais in June, one month before her confinement, so that his relations could celebrate the anniversary of the death of Frederick William III, using Vicky's sitting-room for the purpose because the gruesome ceremony had always been held there. With brutal thoroughness they ousted the living to worship the dead, removing all Vicky's furniture and the pictures which she had arranged with such care, draping black crape over everything and converting the room into a hideous mausoleum. Fritz was terribly distressed, but Vicky made light of being turned out of her home without being consulted – Fritz should not take such absurdities so much to heart. But he could not help doing so and his anger forced him to complain about it to his mother, who shrugged it off as of no consequence. How could it matter since it was only one day in the year?[7]

Princess Augusta's coldness drew Vicky closer to her mother. The steadiness of the Queen's love was a life-line to which Vicky clung for sanity and protection. It awakened in her a sense of her responsibilities as the eldest of a large family. Living, as she did, in a land of uneasy wedlock in which her own 'golden lot' shone like a bright beacon, she understood better than the Prince Consort the reasons for the Queen's anxiety and why she fussed about the right partners for 'our children' before the best were all 'snapped up'. For her second daughter Alice, the Queen had set her heart on a young man she had met as an eight-year-old boy in Coburg in 1845. He was Prince Louis of Hesse-Darmstadt, but it was said (erroneously) that he was in love with Princess Marie of Leuchtenberg, a great-niece of the King of Prussia. If this was the case, would Vicky find someone else? A photograph of Princess Alice, looking demure in her confirmation dress and wearing the family order, a cameo set in diamonds, was sent to Potsdam 'as a help'. Vicky put it on a table where it would catch the eye of a likely suitor. At last Vicky could repay her parents for her own happiness by handling this, as well as the search for a wife for Bertie – both delicate commissions – with maturity and common sense. During the long hot days of summer while she was recovering from her confinement, Vicky lay in the shade of a huge English chestnut-tree (planted years before by her great-great-grandfather George II) and thumbed through the *Almanach de Gotha* to find the paragon who was to be the Prince of Wales's help-mate and salvation. By July she had found her. She was the Danish beauty, sixteen-year-old Princess Alexandra, the eldest daughter of Prince Christian of Sonderburg-Glücksburg, whom Vicky had met when the young princess was staying with her Hessian relations. She knew at once that this charming girl was the 'jewel' they were looking for. But there was a snag – a marriage between England and Denmark would not be good for Prussia. The Prince Consort's naïve solution was that politics could be kept out of it by stressing that it was a love-match brought about by 'our Prussian children' without pressure from anyone – forgetting that although this point of view might appeal to the romantic English it would not move the hard-headed Prussians, who saw politics in everything.

Vicky was to meet her parents in Coburg in September 1860 and show them their grandson Willy for the first time. The Danish princess's possibilities were to be discussed then. It turned out to be a calamitous two weeks that began with a funeral and ended with an accident. The death of the dowager Duchess of Saxe-Coburg-Altenburg, the Prince Consort's step-grandmother, did not in itself affect Vicky closely, but she was very distressed for her father who she knew had longed for a 'last look' at this amiable old lady who adored him.

The Prince's own light was burning low. While Vicky's love for her father sharpened her senses in some directions, paradoxically it also blinded her to much that she should have noticed. Although she was aware of a look of strain on his face and knew that he was too often 'pale and fagged', she did not see how rapidly he was ageing. The handsome young father who had drawn delighted shrieks as he skated effortlessly on the frozen lake at Buckingham Palace, was already an old man at forty. The deterioration in his spirits was even more noticeable: he was always depressed and always pessimistic about everything. It was Vicky, now, who cheered and encouraged him, trying to convince him that the odious newspaper articles which sought to widen the gulf between England and Prussia were of no importance. It was these low feelings that made him handle the horses of a four-in-hand carelessly when he went for a drive alone along a Coburg country road. The animals took fright and bolted when a train whistled at a level-crossing. The Prince had to jump from the carriage and although he suffered only superficial cuts and bruises, he was shocked and badly shaken. The Queen and Vicky found him lying on his valet's bed with Dr Baly and Stockmar ministering to him. He insisted on getting up for dinner, when he talked excitedly but ate nothing.

In public, Stockmar referred to the accident as a life-insurance – the Prince would live to be a great age[8] – but Vicky had caught a look of deep concern on his face and for a moment she was thoroughly alarmed. For the first time she wondered if her father was near to collapse. Was the 'treadmill' of never-ending business wearing him down? The thought increased her alarm. The next day her uncle Ernest took her aside and with a grave face told her that when out for a walk with him that morning her father had suddenly broken down and with tears pouring down his cheeks had said that he never expected to see his birth-place again.[9]

The holiday was only saved by the gaiety and amusing sayings of 'darling William', whose intelligence, good looks and sweet disposition had so captivated his grandparents that they were never tired of extolling the virtues of a child who was to be 'a blessing to his country'.

Vicky parted from her father with many misgivings. By December matters had improved again and she was overjoyed to hear that the Prince's spirits had lifted and that he was full of 'quiet satisfaction' at having settled the future of another daughter. Princess Alice had become unofficially engaged to Prince Louis of Hesse-Darmstadt (heir to his uncle the Grand Duke) – 'a dear good fellow who pleases us better and better daily'.[10] The engagement delighted Vicky, whose wish had come true – this favourite sister was to live close to her in Germany.

*

No sooner was the New Year in than the tolling of the mourning bell on the 3rd of January 1861 let Prussia know that her sad King's miserable existence had ended. The last hours of this once charming and cultivated man were long drawn out and not without a fitting touch of drama.

Vicky has left a vivid description of the death-bed scene in a letter to her parents.[11] She and Fritz were roused at midnight by a message ordering them to go at once to Sans Souci. With youthful impetuosity they did not call a carriage or wait for an attendant. In the bitter cold of a Berlin winter, alone and half-awake, they hurried through the deserted streets, and the strangeness of the experience imprinted itself vividly on Vicky's mind. The special train was so slow that they wondered if they would be in time. But Frederick William III was in no hurry to leave the world. They had to wait for him to die – standing all the time – until one o'clock the next morning. A dream-like quality enhanced by the quiet that enveloped Sans Souci at that late hour, hung over everything in the death-chamber. The dimmed light, the shadows cast by the glowing embers in the grate, the family – already in black – huddled together in a corner, the stillness, broken only by the death-rattle of the dying man, 'that dreadful sound which goes to one's heart and which tells plainly that life is ebbing'. Queen Elizabeth sat near the head of the bed, her arm under her husband's shoulders. Vicky was so touched by the sight of her silent grief that she went to her at once and kneeling down took her hand and kissed it. This act of tenderness from a girl she had not treated well won the Queen's heart completely.* The idea of death had always terrified Vicky. No one guessed what an effort it cost her to witness such a scene. Yet again her father's words of wisdom were proved right. Her struggle to overcome her terror (in no way unusual in a young girl) brought its reward. The 'look' on the dead man's face, so peaceful after his terrible sufferings, removed the fear that had haunted her so long. 'I could not bring myself to believe that this was really death about which I had so often shuddered and felt afraid.'[12]

The Grand Duchess of Mecklenburg-Schwerin, the King's sister, had noticed Vicky's trembling hands and scared eyes as soon as she entered the room, and slyly decided to play a joke on her. That bottomless pit – Prussian royal etiquette – gave her the chance she was looking for. In order to show 'respect', it was the custom to walk past the corpse on its death-bed three times a day, until the coffin was closed just before the funeral. On the last day of all, as Vicky took her place at the head of the line of mourners, the Duchess, who was immediately behind gave her a sudden hard push which forced her to bend forward so that her face almost touched that of the dead king, which had started to decompose. Vicky's involuntary backward movement of dismay was cut short by the Duchess's stout body which she purposely pressed against her victim. With a great effort at self-control Vicky did not cry out and after a minute she was able to move on with the same measured dignified tread, giving no sign that anything untoward had happened.[13]

*

The new reign began well with the King and Queen in excellent spirits, affable to everyone – even to each other. For the moment nothing ruffled William. He was even unmoved by the quarrels that arose after the funeral between the old and the new courts on the

*To make amends and to show her affection she bequeathed to Vicky her own wonderful collection of jewels, instead of allowing them to become part of the Crown Jewels as former queens had done.

tangled question of protocol and precedence at the coming coronation, because he was too busy enjoying the unexpected pleasure of being king. Vicky was touched to see his delight when foreign ambassadors paid congratulatory calls (they all praised the new monarch's dignity and composure) and was quite sincere when she said 'May their reign be long and happy'.[14] But with a man of such uncertain moods the ice was thin at times. Vicky had grown in common sense and tact, and although – through no fault of her own – she was never able to handle her father-in-law, she had learned from past experience what to avoid.[15]

Not so the Prince Consort, who with singular clumsiness at once began to bombard the King with good advice, instructing him how to restore Prussia's tottering constitution, attempting in long-winded sentences to kindle a little enthusiasm for German unity. William impatiently threw his former friend's letters into the fire and vented his irritation on that friend's daughter and his own son, saying that they were all 'hand in glove and plotting for my downfall'.[16] He thought he had reason to say this because Fritz had come to him with a most unwelcome suggestion – that he should be crowned in Berlin to mark the beginning of the 'New Era' and not, as other kings before him, at Königsberg. It was a proposal that had won the Prince Consort's instant approval. With misplaced complacency he told Stockmar senior 'our Prussian children know what they are about'.[17]

The King felt he could afford to be high-handed – had he not got the answer to such nonsense in his pocket? This was a letter left him by the late king 'ordering' him not to take the oath to uphold the constitution – a command very much to his taste. It gave him the right to indulge in the outdated dogma of the Divine Right of Kings – 'I do not forget that the crown has come to me from God alone and that I have received it at his hands.'[18] When Fritz protested that Divine Right was a myth which the English had exploded two hundred years ago, the King answered solemnly that out of respect for the dead he had no choice but to follow his brother's commands.[19]

The scene was now set for what the Prince Consort contemptuously called the destruction of Prussia, but he gathered fresh strength from the trump card which he knew he still held – 'Our Prussian children'. The King's conduct was characteristic but pitiable in following the example of an eccentric brother, but the Prince was confident that Vicky and Fritz could keep the new sovereign on the straight and narrow path. This was the reason, he told Ernest Stockmar, why he felt he could afford to take a cool view of the whole business.

The once far-sighted Prince's judgement was already clouded and he no longer saw clearly. Indeed he displayed an astonishing lack of sense

The marriage of the Princess Royal and Prince Frederick William of Prussia at the Chapel Royal, St James's, 25 January 1858, *detail from a painting by John Phillip*

Prince and Princess Frederick William of Prussia at Windsor, a few days after their wedding

Princess Frederick William of Prussia with her children Prince William and Princess Charlotte, 1861

Crown Prince and Princess Frederick William of Prussia, 1863

left to right: Prince Alfred, Princess Alice, Princess Louise, Crown Princess of Prussia, Princess Helena, 1862

Crown Princess of Prussia with her daughter Princess Charlotte, 1863

Crown Princess Frederick William of Prussia

if he believed that a girl of twenty could control an obstinate old man of sixty-four with strong beliefs in his own destiny. Moreover the whole issue was complicated by the King's strong conviction that Fritz wanted him to abdicate and that the people would prefer a younger man, that Fritz knew this and was working to this end. This delusion lay at the root of William's bitter and aggressive feelings towards his subjects and coloured the tone of his early manifestoes, besides causing his cruel behaviour to his son and his fury with the Prince Consort when he had the temerity to try to influence his heir.[20]

*

The death of her mother, the Duchess of Kent, at Frogmore on the 11th of March 1861 gave Queen Victoria a nervous breakdown and considerably increased the Prince Consort's burdens. Anguished by the loss of a beloved friend and aunt – and the only one in England with whom he could talk of the old days in Coburg – he nevertheless uncomplainingly added the Queen's work to his own as well as the Duchess's muddled affairs, which as her sole executor he was left to unravel. A hastily arranged visit by Vicky, herself weighed down with remorse that her grandmother had never seen her children (despite the Queen's exhortations not to delay bringing them to England) did nothing to ease the tension. Her peaceful happy home was in an upheaval. The Queen, prostrate with grief, had shut herself away in her room, the Prince, haggard and worn out with overwork, looked the wreck of her once handsome and energetic father. What could she make of his axiom that life to be fulfilled must be lived for the good of others, if it meant that he sacrificed the very people he slaved for? Vicky was able to bring a little light into this house of mourning by a description of the 'accidental' meeting between the Prince of Wales and Princess Alexandra of Denmark when both were sight-seeing in the cathedral at Speyer, although its effect was offset by the Prince Consort's gloomy prediction that such a pretty girl would never have Bertie.

By the 8th of April Vicky was back in a Berlin agog with rumours: the Queen of England was going mad and had become so violent that she had to be forcibly restrained in a padded cell in the Round Tower at Windsor.[21] Even Queen Augusta believed this story, and took a certain pleasure in relating to Vicky the many oddities the Queen had displayed in the past, among them the 'poor match' she had arranged for her daughter Alice. Vicky found it dreadfully trying, but it would have to be borne, along with the hundred other pin-pricks she had learned to ignore. This particular pin-prick was all the harder to endure because she could not relieve her feelings in a letter home.

*

King William's coronation ceremony at Königsberg on the 18th of October 1861 was unsurpassed for splendour and pomp, and its brilliance was the talk of Europe for months to come. Trivial as it now seems in the light of later events, to William it was the climax of his reign and nothing that came afterwards could compare with it.

The King had dug deep into history – a first excursion into the world of learning that was both profitable and enjoyable – to find the answer to confound the critics who did not want him to revive ancient customs supporting the idea that Prussia was an absolute monarchy. He now produced his 'researches' and cunningly used them to confound his ministers when they sternly ordered him not to demand homage of the Estates of the Realm, adding that they would also prefer him not to crown himself. But William thundered as usual and cowed his ministers, who quaked like schoolboys at the threat of the cane. They were glad to get out of it by accepting what they mistook for a compromise.

The coronation was good for trade. Berlin had never done so much business. The sale of velvet was enormous, far higher than at the dead king's coronation, which was looked on as a poor affair by comparison. Vicky designed her own coronation robes and those of the ladies who were to carry her train. In the long warm days of summer they would gather under Vicky's favourite tree and spend hours poring over different materials and combinations of colours – gold with white, gold with blue, blue with red. What was going to look best in the dim light of the cathedral? Jewels of all kinds were sent to the Neue Palais for Vicky to choose from. There were so many – diamonds, rubies, emeralds, pearls. Which enhanced velvet and miniver most? The weight of the robes was tremendous, and they asked each other if they would ever be able to move at all. Trivial matters took on undue importance. The King was having trouble with his crown, his head was too large, the crown too small. It was alleged that he had pressed it on with such force at the dress rehearsal that it had to be filed off!

In the fuss of preparation the King's reactionary views were forgotten by all but a poor student who felt it his duty to rid the country of such a sovereign. So he took a shot at William when he was out riding, but the glancing bullet did nothing worse than graze the skin on the side of his face. Vicky and Fritz were in England but rushed back to find the King cranky but unhurt, and delighted at the increase in his popularity.

The coronation in the cathedral at Königsberg, hallowed by the past and promising a future which William said he would grasp with an 'ameliorating hand', went far beyond anything Vicky ever imagined.

Beforehand she had been highly critical of what the Prince Consort scathingly referred to as the pantomime William was preparing to put on for Europe's edification. She warned Fritz not to be carried away by the tinsel and the glitter, yet when the day came it was Vicky herself who was so bemused that she was 'swept into the stream and well-nigh drowned'. As she made the long slow walk to her seat near the altar, an unreal world of 'magic tinges', enhanced by soft music and the sun streaming through the high windows like a benediction, opened before her astonished eyes. When the King crowned himself 'von Gottes Gnaden' she accepted it as right and proper, describing William as 'dignified and firm', and the ceremony as 'wonderful beyond description, I shall never forget it all, it was so very fine'.[22]

Vicky was unaware of the hundreds of pairs of eyes that watched her during the ceremony. All Europe knew Prince Albert's views and knew that they were held by his daughter, whom they had heard was a determined young woman who liked having her own way. They were taken aback when she appeared, a tiny graceful figure almost lost in her robes, and made a beautiful and dignified curtsy to the King; the action brought tears to Lord Clarendon's old eyes, and Wally Paget (her former lady-in-waiting who had married Sir Augustus Paget) aptly described it as beauty making obeisance to the beast.[23]

The wonderful day came to an end in fitting fashion with a smiling King fastening a gold locket filled with his rough grey hair round Vicky's slender neck, to mark the occasion. The Prince Consort could not hide his disgust, however (nor could *The Times*), as the last shreds of his respect for this faithless friend vanished for ever: 'the days are past when a single man could expect millions of thoughtful, educated people to entrust their entire welfare and existence to the judgement and hands of one man.'[24]

In the cold sober light cast by her father's letter, Vicky was ready to agree that the King had gone too far. But she guessed that much of the significance of the ceremony would pass over the people's heads. How could they view some of it as retrograde when they did not understand most of it? The real danger was that in their ignorance they might misunderstand something, stubbornly refuse to accept it, and so cause a political convulsion. Vicky was beginning to wonder if Prussia was ready for a constitution after the English pattern. When she remembered the effect of the coronation ceremony on herself and on millions of others, she doubted it. But if all else went in this reign, she and Fritz could still work – in some way still shrouded in darkness – for the good of Prussia. That 'goodness' could in itself provide a purpose in life was the Prince Consort's swan-song: 'and what can mankind desire more? Can anything offer more genuine happiness than this conscious-ness?'25

*

Two days after the coronation Vicky developed a bad cold which turned into bronchitis and kept her in bed for over three weeks.

In England she had been a healthy girl, leading a simple life with plenty of exercise and fresh air. In the hot-house atmosphere of the Berlin winter palaces where evening receptions and balls were held she was hardly ever without some ailment. By the autumn of 1861 she was so ill that Dr Wegner wrote in the gravest terms to the Queen of double pneumonia, and alarmed her with the thought that she was to lose a daughter as well as a mother. Queen Victoria read Dr Wegner's letter with a prick of conscience, for only a few days before she had scoffed at Vicky for taking to her bed in 'approved German fashion' for a mere cold.

Queen Augusta's restless energy and heartless demands were at the root of Vicky's frequent illnesses. As she got into her stride as Queen she took it for granted that Vicky would be dancing attendance on her at every function. She did not hesitate to wake Vicky from a sound sleep, getting her up in the middle of the night to take the place of a lady-in-waiting who had fainted from exhaustion, so that Vicky came to talk of herself as a 'sort of slave'. Fritz could not protect her from this tyranny. As so often in the case of mild men towards the women of the family, he would accept anything for the sake of peace: 'If it keeps mama quiet, it is in everybody's interest.'26 But he suffered too, and was often unwell.

Vicky realised the damage which lack of sleep was doing to her health, and was alarmed. Most of all she dreaded losing contact with Fritz, for by the autumn her fatigue was chronic. She was too tired to walk, too tired to ride, too tired to read. 'Too tired, too tired, too tired' had become her answer to everything. The fun and happiness she and Fritz had once had together were getting less and less, and she had to face the fact that hers would not be the first marriage to be wrecked by a weariness that could (and should) have been prevented.

Vicky's recovery from pneumonia was slow. On the 1st of Novem-ber she was downstairs for the first time when she received a letter from her father written in the most despondent terms. He was thoroughly out of sorts, with a cold and neuralgia, aggravated by severe insomnia, worse than any he had ever experienced, and caused, so he said, by the shock of three tragic deaths in Portugal. King Pedro, who had never recovered from the sudden death of his wife Stephanie in July 1859 scarcely a year after her proxy marriage, had himself succumbed to typhoid fever. He was followed to the grave by his two brothers Louis and Jaco – the whole family wiped out at one stroke. These deaths coincided with an unfortunate love-affair of the Prince of Wales at Cambridge which had upset the Prince Consort and made him irritable, listless and so depressed that he said it would not be long before he too was carried off by typhoid. On the 22nd of November his protective arm stretched out to help Vicky although he was almost too weak to hold a pen; he wrote to Queen Augusta asking very firmly for Vicky's torment to cease: 'without the basis of health it is impossible to rear anything stable.'[27]

It was the last thing he ever did for her.

On the 30th of November the Queen wrote that the 'dear invalid' had amended the draft to the North American States (after the kidnapping of two Confederate envoys from the *Trent* by federal agents while the ship was on its way to English territorial water) making it much more conciliatory, so that the sensitive skins of the Americans would not be offended; this, said the Queen, had averted war. It was his last service to England, but Vicky took it for a good sign especially since the Queen wrote optimistically telling her not to be alarmed: 'you must not expect his getting better for some days.'[28]

Gradually, and unperceived by those around him, the Prince Consort's life ebbed away. From the first he knew that he was going to die, and he gave in without a struggle. Ten days before the end he asked Princess Alice if she had told Vicky that he was ill. She answered that she had; 'you did wrong', he said, 'you should have told her I am dying.'

He mentioned Vicky just once more. On the 12th of December, when the Queen thought he was asleep, he suddenly cried out, half in delirium, 'if only nothing happens to Vicky – I no longer trust anyone'.[29]

On the morning of the 14th of December Vicky was playing the piano in her sitting-room, looking better and more cheerful than she had for weeks, when the door opened and Fritz came in. In his hand he held a telegram from Colonel Phipps, the Prince Consort's private secretary, asking him to prepare Vicky for her father's death. She was not yet fully recovered, and to Fritz she looked so thin and fragile that he did not know how to tell her. As he came slowly towards her she turned and looked at him and something in his face told her what he could not find words to say.

Overwhelmed with grief, Vicky wrote to her mother: 'Why has the earth not swallowed me up? To be separated from you at this moment is a torture which I cannot describe.'[30]

CHAPTER 9

'How terrible to have to say he was'

THE day after her father's death Vicky made a solemn vow: henceforth she would carry out papa's wishes in everything. She was never more like her father than at this moment when grief made her set herself an impossible standard: it was a way of assuaging sorrow and trying to keep alive the special memories she had of him.

She was not always resolute. There were despairing times when the realisation of the magnitude of her self-imposed task made her sleepless for nights on end, and she would quail to think how much she and Fritz had to accomplish alone. It was her bounden duty to forge ahead, yet could she do it without dearest papa? Under his guiding hand Vicky had felt herself capable of anything: strong enough to stand up to the King, to support Fritz along the 'rough road' he had chosen to follow, and to carry out her 'mission' – now a sacred trusteeship. The difficulties and the burdens of her position had been lightened to bearable proportions as long as her father was at her back, encouraging, praising and smoothing a path which like his own was 'plentifully strewn with thorns'. She knew that she did not trust herself to act alone because she was inexperienced, yet who could ever take his place? Who would now tell her when duty should give way to prudence? She lived in a world larger than life; who would now cut it down to size?

It seems never to have occurred to Vicky that some of her difficulties and burdens had been created by the Prince Consort himself through his high idealism, and that she was its victim. Vicky knew that there were many in Berlin who accused the Prince of interfering in their country's affairs, but she was able to justify this to herself because in his plans for Prussia the Prince thought and felt as a German. He could keep his work for the British monarchy and his plans for German unity in separate compartments because his precise and analytical mind prevented any overlap. She did not see the flaw in the argument – that he had no right to concern himself actively with a country to which he no longer belonged, however high-minded and excellent his plans.

After the 14th of December 1861 the Prince's schemes for Germany must not be judged by his daughter's words and actions. For many years Vicky was guided by what she knew of them from the past, and she adhered to them to the letter. But Prince Albert's political vision was perceptive and acute; he might have changed and modified his opinions to suit conditions which Bismarck's appearance altered radically and swiftly. Even those 'fixed principles' for which his brother Ernest mocked him (and which Vicky was said to have inherited) might in due course have become more elastic. Too close to him to see her father's ideas objectively, Vicky apparently never realised how much his plans for unification would have to be pruned to fit a country much less enlightened than her own and that the sudden jump from absolute government to an English-style constitution would have been too much for Prussia.

Vicky was too young to have bothered her head about the future. Leaning trustingly on her father, she had never given a thought to what would happen if she were plunged without preparation into a 'Life responsible to itself alone'[1] – as the Prince Consort called her life with Fritz: it was nothing of the sort, of course, so long as her father lived.

At the time of his death from typhoid fever the Prince was only forty-one and it had not been unreasonable to expect that he might have many more years ahead of him. He must have thought so too, otherwise he would not have made himself chief adviser and confidant to Vicky and Fritz. Although on paper this had little to recommend it – since it meant advising at second-hand and from a distance – it was not wholly unreasonable. His plan had been for Ernest Stockmar to take over gradually, assuming more and more responsibility as he gained experience and knowledge of the difficult people with whom he had to deal. The Prince's fault was to see the young Stockmar in the mirror of the old one, whom in fact he resembled in nothing except his honest and upright character. It was Prince Albert's judgement that was at fault, not his ideas.

With the Prince Consort's death Vicky was left – to use a favourite simile – as bewildered as a child who, learning to swim, has been taken out into the middle of a deep pool which was safe only so long as her father's protective hand was under her chin.[2] This complete dependence on her father was one of the remarkable features of their relationship. Vicky's lively personality, her strong will – remarked on at once in Prussia – her powerful intellect, her fierce championship of freedom, did not lend themselves readily to subservience. It was her high sense of duty and her deeply affectionate nature, combined with the conviction that Prince Albert was no ordinary mortal, but a god-like being (a belief inculcated in her from earliest childhood by the Queen, and which the Prince did nothing to belie) that contributed to her father's mastery over her. Vicky worshipped him and looked up to him as an oracle.[3] That such single-hearted uncritical love could have its dangers never occurred to either father or daughter. It was unfair to delay the development from childhood to maturity of a married woman with her own responsibilities and new loyalties, but neither saw this nor realised that Vicky was unconsciously being forced to suppress many characteristics that were essential to her if she were to survive as an individual and not sink into a mere pale imitation of her father.

It is sad to notice the rapid strides Vicky made in this direction after the Prince Consort's death. Only a few months later she was trying to make the Queen emerge once again into daylight, acting as her mother's 'protector and guide'; Queen Victoria came to rely increasingly upon her 'because you have dearest papa's mind'.[4]

What had Vicky inherited from her father? His idealism certainly, but without the cynicism that sometimes clouded it. It differed from his too in that it was essentially realistic, and related to the world in which she lived, despite the facts that it was a world of extremes (great wealth, great poverty and no middle class) and that her rank was a hindrance rather than a help in carrying out reforms.

Prince Albert had encouraged Vicky's taste for art, infecting her with his own enthusiasm for Italian painters of the fourteenth and fifteenth centuries, nourishing her gift for politics and scientific matters and encouraging her desire to use these talents in social service, stamping them with his own particular imprint, teaching her the self-discipline without which their primary object – to do good – could not be attained. Part of his plan in sending her to Prussia was to give her the opportunity to use these accomplishments where he felt they would be most effective. Above all he impressed on her that she was not only capable of improving herself but also of improving others, and it was to this end that they carried on a lively correspondence about everything from statecraft to religion and even mundane domestic matters, including Vicky's health, which often caused him concern.[5]

After her father's death, his letters became of absorbing interest to Vicky, who read them over and over again. The Prince had left his daughter a rich inheritance of learning mixed with worldly wisdom, but little of it seemed to apply to the pettiness of much that went on around her. It was as though he was arguing from a loftier plane than Vicky could ever reach without him; yet strangely enough this teaching was to help her over many a rough patch.

*

The Prince could not have died at a worse time. Vicky needed help and advice as never before. All the Prince's hopes for Germany were being jeopardised by a headstrong King who had succeeded in winning over the powerful Kreuzzeitung Party, which was now wholly behind him and encouraged him in his unconstitutional ways. The Prince Consort had predicted that if this happened it would be William's undoing.[6] It remained to be seen if he was right.

William's luck had turned. When Fritz saw him soon after the Prince Consort's death, he boasted that a new reign meant a new policy – no knuckling under to England. Fritz knew that his father had always been a little afraid of Queen Victoria and Prince Albert, and that this fear had acted as a brake. Now the brake was off and so was William.

The King never stayed in Berlin in January and February as the winter climate was too cold and damp for his rheumatism. It did not occur to him to change his plans on account of Vicky's bereavement. He left as usual on New Year's Day 1862 after ordering a week's court mourning for the Prince; having done this, he felt he might just as well spend the time drinking the health-giving waters in the pump-room at Ems. He made no pretence at grief and had no time to condole with his daughter-in-law, who received his sympathy by proxy through Queen Augusta in a formal visit. Augusta's friendship with Prince Albert had been as close as any she had ever enjoyed, yet she was incapable of showing his daughter that she was sorry and that she would miss a man with whom she had much in common. Never a reticent woman, she had hoped to further their cause by spreading the good news far and wide. The Prince had looked on their partnership as a boon, whereas she was the worst ally he could have had.

Vicky would not break down in front of her mother-in-law, even when she alluded to the Queen's loneliness – a subject about which Vicky dreaded to think. She had wanted to rush to her mother even before Princess Alice's telegram 'Mama needs you'. But once again Dr Wegner stepped in and said that it was unsafe to travel in her condition. When she protested that she was no longer an invalid and must be with her family, he went over her head to the King, who put his foot down.

Vicky was carrying her third child and this pregnancy was a godsend. She could shut herself away without causing comment, to think, to remember and to marvel at the change in herself in three years. As a child she had hated solitude, but now she welcomed it. In the old days she had loved a good set-to, relying on her quick wit and facile tongue to bring her victory. Since coming to Prussia she had seen so much bad feeling and heard so many verbal pitched battles, that she would now go to any lengths to avoid a row. Only in one respect was she the same: she could not accept what life sent her with meekness and resignation. Lady Lyttelton had tried to teach her rebellious pupil 'God's will be done'. But she could not believe it was God's will to remove from the earth a perfect being, so loved, so needed and doing such useful work. Wisely, however, she tried not to dwell on that side, for it touched the teaching of many fundamental truths which formed the basis of her faith and to which she must now cling.

Fritz went to Windsor for the funeral, but Vicky preferred to spend the day alone. In imagination she followed every step of that heart-breaking last journey, walking in spirit in the procession with her brothers and thinking with pity of her sisters who had gone with the distraught Queen to Osborne. She wondered if her grief would harm her unborn child, if she would die perhaps in giving it birth. At that moment she hardly cared what happened to her. It would have helped during those first awful weeks if there had been something that she could do to assuage her grief. Others could scrutinise plans for memorials and draw sketches for a mausoleum, but she could not even relive the death-bed scene. To dwell on the mechanics of death was not morbid to Vicky's generation. Such thoughts helped healing tears to flow and kept memory alive. The last hand-clasp, the last word, the last look, the burial, were all treasured by the bereaved and discussed again and again. Part of Vicky's unhappiness at that time was caused by the sad fact that she had no one in Prussia with whom she could talk about her dead father once Fritz had returned to his military duties.

When the days lengthened and the weather turned warmer, Vicky went to Osborne and was at last clasped in her mother's arms. All was the same – and yet how different! The sight of her father's hat and coat, hung up as though he had just come in, his walking stick just as he had left it in the umbrella stand, gave Vicky the feeling that her father was still with them; and yet she felt the awful blank too: 'how I miss him whom I worshipped, his step, his dear dear voice, his beloved face.'[7] She sat in his sitting-room, so cold and desolate without the rich personality of the beloved being who had used it. There, it was impossible not to realise he had gone; although nothing was changed – the books, the pink vases on the mantelpiece, even the model of Princess Beatrice's head which Vicky had made while resting before Willy's birth, each was where it had always been – yet the heart had gone out of everything. It was hard to accept that life went on just the same, that the world of nature kept on its eternal course: the primroses were out, the camellia trees already heavy with buds in the mild climate, even the birds were 'filling the air with their sweet song'. But the only real countryman among them was not there to see and to hear.

*

Force of habit made Vicky read the papers every morning. They did not make edifying reading. The Prussian elections took place while she was at Osborne, and the Liberals were returned with an increased majority. After reading the list of new members, Vicky dismissed them with disgust as 'weak and useless', since many – like Fritz's old professor Bethman-Hollweg – were more at home in the classroom than the debating-chamber. Prince Hohenlohe was again Minister-President, a politician of whom Vicky unkindly said that he was 'frightened of his shadow' and that they could not expect great things from him.

Fritz's letters did nothing to put Vicky's mind at rest. The King, he wrote, was antagonising all parties with his foolish favouritism. General Edwin von Manteuffel was chief favourite for the moment and was trying to use his position to reinstate his brother Otto as Minister-President. If this happened it could have disastrous consequences.[8] Ernest Stockmar's letters told much the same tale, with one new addition that quite startled Vicky. He said that the King was hinting that he was looking for a 'strong man' to fill a post of importance[9] and that the War Minister Albrecht von Roon had recommended a man whom the King was considering. Fritz had threatened to speak to the King about this but Vicky begged him not to, for it might be the one thing to tip the scales in the wrong direction if William hesitated. If the reactionary party once got the King into its clutches, he would never escape alive. What would happen then to the 'bright hopes of the future'?[10]

Vicky assumed the rôle of Fritz's adviser, doing her best to take her father's place. She sent him pages of contradictory instructions: 'never miss an opportunity of showing the world by your firmness and decision who you are' – 'Keep away from the sittings of the Chamber' – 'you cannot and must not oppose the King' – 'you cannot sacrifice your Liberal opinions, therefore there is only one way of reconciling the two – silence'.[11]

Back in Berlin at the end of May, Vicky was anything but silent. She told her friends she was unbiased but had to say what she thought, namely, if the conservatives became the King's party and ruled the roost, it would be the end of all her and their hopes for a proper constitution for Prussia: 'I have the example of my dearest father before me – he advocated every true, right and sound principle.'[12] If it achieved nothing else, her indignation provided the therapy she needed and could respond to, because it touched a tender spot – her husband's rights. She became more open in her hostility to the King, calling him 'stupid' to a handful of intimates, an insult he was bound to hear of sooner or later. Yet she would not have condemned his actions half so strongly if he had been kind and affectionate to his son.

When everything looked 'confused', the political future suddenly took a turn for the better. Prince Hohenlohe (who had heard and resented Vicky's slight on his party – 'they are all weak men'), came to the Neue Palais at the end of April to assure her that this was not the case. He felt it only right to tell her that the Liberals were determined that nothing but an earthquake would move them.[13] If he could have looked into the future he would have seen that one was imminent.

*

Vicky realised how easy it was to give way to grief. She made super-human efforts to return to normality with all speed, for only in this way could she carry out her father's commands. In return, the Queen accused her of heartlessness for recovering so quickly from her father's death. If Queen Victoria had reflected, she would have understood that much of Vicky's cheerfulness was assumed and did not spring from the 'good spirits' the Queen taxed her with. Vicky had never had her mother's interests more at heart and she dealt patiently and under-standingly with the Queen's lugubriousness – it was the first sign of her new maturity. At once she recognised her mother's urgent need for male support in domestic matters, and unselfishly she urged Fritz to fill the gap for a time. Fritz was to give Princess Alice away at her marriage to Prince Louis of Hesse-Darmstadt in June, now that the King had given his consent. But when, soon after, the Queen wanted Fritz to take the Prince Consort's place and open the second Great Exhibition in May, William made difficulties. He saw no reason for Fritz to be out of the country twice in two months – three times in five months if he took the Prince Consort's funeral into account. There was, alas, nothing specific to keep Fritz in Prussia, but the King fussed because he felt that Fritz's absence would arouse 'certain suspicions' in some quarters. But Vicky was sure that the real reason was Fritz's great popularity in England. His name was bound to draw huge crowds to the Exhibition, he was certain to have a good press, and this sparked off intense jealousy in his father's heart since he had reason to know how low his own name stood in Britain. In the end he gave way because it had suddenly occurred to him that it might be a pleasant change to address Parliament without having to meet his son's doleful gaze staring at him across the chamber – a sight that always irritated him because it was an uncomfortable reminder that he was spoiling that son's future.

So Fritz left for England to be a bulwark to Queen Victoria while Vicky stayed to watch the King shake Parliament to its foundations with his repeated refusal to accept defeat. He summoned and dissolved the Chamber three times in one week, so that he was in danger of becoming the laughing-stock of Europe. Moral blackmail, which served him so well with the family, had failed to work. Disconcerted, William ranted and raged, shouted insults and threats, grinding his teeth in a way the family dreaded, all without the slightest effect on the stony faces that confronted him from the floor of the Chamber. The Liberals were proving what Prince Hohenlohe had claimed – that they were not so weak as Vicky supposed. They unnerved William and drove him straight to Ems to be revived for the autumn session by his favourite waters, in which he had more faith than in all his ministers put together.

When he returned from England in June, Fritz went immediately to Stettin and from there to open the new university at Königsberg; Vicky kept him fully informed of everything in long letters which described the scenes in Parliament and the King's extraordinary state of mind, and ended with a lengthy directive about Fritz's own conduct, which should be 'circumspect in the extreme'.[14]

On the 14th of August 1862 Vicky's third child and second son was born at the Neue Palais after the easiest labour she had yet had. The boy was to be called Henry; the fact that he was quite healthy showed at once that her grief had done no harm. It was a surprise to find herself recovering quickly, and without any of that dreadful lethargy which had settled on her after her father's death. In ten days she was out of doors. She was not idle. She read the piles of books that had remained unopened all the winter – 'the very worst winter of my life' – delighted to be able to concentrate again. The garden gave her immense pleasure, and she was filled with wonder that so much had been accomplished in so short a time. The trees and shrubs chosen by the Prince Consort were already taller than she was. They were her father's last gift to her, a living testimony to his love and care. Slowly she regained some of the peace that she had lost. A little of what the Prince had meant when he spoke of the real world of nature as opposed to the artificial world of people began to become clear, and for a short time she deceived herself into thinking that this quiet existence was the life which suited her best. She was rudely shaken out of her day-dreams by a few words from the King.

*

On the evening of the 18th of September, after a particularly happy and tranquil day, Vicky was sitting in the garden enjoying the late sunshine and writing to her mother, when a white and shaken Fritz strode rapidly towards her. He brought staggering news: the King wanted to abdicate. It was no empty threat, but a considered decision 'for the sake of the country': 'God and my conscience do not allow me to do any-thing else.'[15] Father and son had held an affecting conversation, quite alone, the King walking up and down with his head 'sunk on his chest', his voice low but strong. Fritz was deeply moved as he described the scene to Vicky, retailing for her benefit his passionate plea to his father to reconsider such a momentous decision, trying to make him believe that it was 'best for the people and the dynasty' for him to remain on a throne he filled with such dignity and for which he had waited so long.[16] Vicky sensed that Fritz had been humbled by what he referred to as an 'unselfish outlook', denigrating himself unduly and making too much of his lack of experience as he protested that he was neither ready nor willing to step into his father's place. He had even wept to see the King so broken.[17] Nevertheless the King repeated that nothing could shake his resolution and he handed Fritz a sheet of paper, explaining as he did so 'this only needs my signature', adding with a sigh the preposterous remark 'I cannot give in any more' – which Fritz well knew was nonsense, since not once in his life had his father yielded on any issue which he considered important. As Vicky read the words which could mean so much to them, Fritz sank into a chair muttering that it was 'appalling'. He was too upset to see that it was not so much the offer that shook him – it had been threatened often enough and thought nothing of – as his own inability to meet the emergency. In his conversation with his father he had unwisely allowed his emotions to get the better of his reason, and the sensible half of him was furious that he had not handled the situation with as much detachment as he would have liked.

The offer could not have come at a worse moment. Fritz's deep concern for Vicky, his own grief for the Prince Consort, the strain of battling against his father's hard disposition – so hard and unyielding that Vicky wondered if he had ever known the affection a father should bear for his son – all had blinded him to the possibility that one day the King would mean what he said. Nor was Vicky any better prepared. Weakened by sorrow and child-birth, her acute sensitivity to the prevailing wind had been dulled. The King had been so strange in the autumn that it had occurred to her that he might be going the same way as his brother, even that he suspected that his mind was softening and would be genuinely glad to abdicate. But in the months that followed she had forgotten this when, sunk into herself, all she cared about was the past. What is more, Vicky did not yet have the confidence to make a snap decision, while Fritz was hampered in taking the lead because he had never acquired the art of opposing his father without becoming agitated – so deep-rooted were his fears of this stern parent.

Nevertheless when Vicky had recovered a little she saw the situation with clearer eyes than Fritz. Instinctively she knew the offer to be a fraud, a tactical move in the war the autocratically-minded King was waging against the liberal resistance of his ministers, and something to be viewed with suspicion. William was playing for high stakes when he told Fritz that he wanted to abdicate, but Vicky sensed that he was sure that Fritz would refuse the offer and that the old man knew his bluff would not be called. By seeming – but only seeming – to yield to the liberal views of those Prussians whose hopes rested on Fritz, he intended perhaps to discredit his son but certainly to advance his own completely contrary plans. The War Minister, Albrecht von Roon, was already pressing him to summon 'a certain strong man' – Bismarck – who would solve all his difficulties by crushing parliamentary opposition.[18] But Fritz did not believe this, and his father knew that he did not. William staked all on the rightness of his guess that, without this knowledge, filial duty would overcome the desire for liberal government in Fritz's mind at the moment of decision. A year later, Fritz would have reacted differently. But William's sense of timing was perfect: a year later he would not have made the offer.

*

That evening Vicky and Fritz paced the terrace of the Neue Palais arm-in-arm, discussing 'the thunderbolt' from every angle. But their thoughts did not run hand-in-hand. Vicky had seen, by Fritz's tender allusions to his father, that he had made up his mind before he reached home, perhaps even before he left the King's presence. His heart overflowed with pity for 'poor father' – 'poor broken old man', 'how could I take his place?' – and he told Vicky of his pride in his father's 'brave and generous gesture, without thought of self'.[19]

All Vicky's fighting spirit was aroused. Why should not she and Fritz take this chance, whether the King was bluffing or not? Why should she not trust to the instinct which told her to push for the throne with all their might? Despite his incurable humility, Fritz was twice the man his father was. Furthermore, it was in the best interests of the country to have a wise and liberal king. But Fritz's laconic 'We must do nothing hastily' had the ring of defeat. Vicky attempted to get round this by changing her tactics and putting the best construction on the King's actions, telling Fritz it was 'wise and honest' to hand over to another those duties which he could no longer perform without going against his conscience. She spoke tentatively, groping for the right words that would find response in him: 'you should make this sacrifice for your country. If you do not accept I believe you will regret it one day. We must not think of ourselves . . . only of the country and our children who will one day have to make good where we have failed.'[20]

Unused to acting alone and to taking decisions, Vicky longed for her father to tell her what to do. When she told Fritz 'I am ready to take what should come, whatever it should be'[21] she thought she meant what she said. Yet she knew that it was essential for Fritz to take the final decision himself. If she took it for him, the throne would be theirs, and with it the chance of fulfilling her father's dream, but their love would be gone with Fritz's self-respect and Fritz as a man would be destroyed for ever.

CHAPTER 10

'A certain strong Man'

VICKY and Fritz lay all night on the rack. Another autumn day broke, was lived through and turned again into night, yet Fritz still hesitated and Vicky was still silent. So time was wasted in fruitless heart-searchings, and suddenly the chance was gone.

Without consulting his son, the King took a step that was to change their lives for ever – he called in Otto von Bismarck, the man Albrecht von Roon had persuaded him would solve all his difficulties. Even as Vicky and Fritz were struggling to find a solution the 'strong man' was already on his way. It gave Vicky no satisfaction to know she had been right all along.

She had seen Bismarck only once before, when he had been presented to the Queen in Paris in August 1855. He had made no impression. Indeed his appearance never seems to have struck her as anything worth talking about, for in those numerous letters in which he figures prominently she never once mentioned it. When she writes about his character, however, the man is before us in the flesh. It was the same with Prince Albert. On a first meeting his reaction had been definite, even violent – Bismarck was a man he could never trust; when his name came up as a possible candidate for the Prussian Embassy in London, the Prince was emphatic – 'not that man'.[1] Apart from his instinctive dislike, the Prince had heard that during the Crimean War the Prussian Junker, his country's representative in Frankfurt, had done everything in his power to foster the antagonism between Prussia and Britain which had proved the major factor in keeping Prussia out of the war.[2] The dislike was mutual, for at the time of Vicky's marriage Bismarck wrote to his friend Leopold von Gerlach, Adjutant-General to King Frederick William, that he 'did not care for the English in the marriage': the only Prussians who would be pleased were the snobbish middle class.[3] By the time Bismarck was made Minister-President of Prussia by King William he could afford to smile at what he was pleased to call 'prejudice'. He had come a long way since those Paris days when as plain Herr von Bismarck he had to endure the humiliation of sitting below the salt.

Otto Edward Leopold von Bismarck-Schönhausen was born on the

1st of April 1815, the third son of Frederick von Bismarck and Wilhelmina Mencken. He grew up at Kniephof in Pomerania. The impressive scenery of this part of Prussia gave him the one and only link with Prince Albert: it became the 'paradise of my boyhood', just as the Rosenau in Thuringia was to the young Albert and for the same reasons. Both men were deeply attached to the country and neither took to town life. But whereas Albert would have been happy to live always in Coburg, tilling the soil of his own estates was not enough for the ambitious Junker. Between 1834 and 1862, after leaving a minor Civil Service post, Bismarck marked time by reading widely, travelling extensively and marrying Johanna von Puttkamer, who was plain but adored him. Advancement was slow, but his colourful personality and striking presence – great height, piercing blue eyes and beetling brows – compelled notice. His character was many-sided: an amusing fellow and a witty raconteur, good value at any social function, he could be all things to all men when it suited him. But he had black moods when his temper was atrocious (one of his staff likened it to thunder and lightning – no one knew where it would strike next) and he saw no good in anything. Few penetrated to the heart of this hard, unrelenting, ambitious man.

From the beginning Vicky thought him vain, arrogant and unscrupulous; she never had reason to change her mind. Yet she felt the fascination of his charm when he cared to exert it, and admitted at times that it was enough to excuse his habit of breaking promises without a blush and lying without blinking an eye. Bismarck's feelings for Vicky were no less cut-and-dried. To begin with she was English, which at once damned her in his eyes. She was also that mysterious thing, a clever woman who was also pretty, charming and very feminine, a combination which made him uneasy. He could not believe that an intelligent woman could also be so guileless, so he was on edge (and showed it) when their conversation took a political turn for fear that she would outwit him and that he would lose face. His intimates knew (and laughed slyly about it behind his back) that he would have liked nothing better than to be on good terms with her, if she could become the only kind of woman he understood – docile, without interest in the man's world of politics and, of course, full of admiration for him. Vicky too deluded herself into believing they could have been friends if it had not been in the interest of so many people to keep them apart. Since this never happened, Bismarck put it down to Vicky's own attitude towards him, white-washing himself when he said it was she who started the enmity between them – 'she was prejudiced against me, she did not trust me'[4] and forgetting that he had given her ample cause not to trust him and that he was far more prejudiced than she was since he condemned her every action because he suspected 'English influence'.[5]

Part of the reason why Vicky did not want Bismarck in Paris was that it was uncomfortably close to Berlin. If Bismarck complained of being 'put on ice' when he was at the Prussian Embassy in St Petersburg, to Vicky the move meant safety – he could not interfere in London or Berlin. Bismarck had made only one trip to Berlin in 1861, travelling for five days in great discomfort and cold to stir up trouble in the British Embassy where a friend of Vicky's, Robert Morier, was attaché. Morier was an Englishman and a confirmed Liberal; Prince Albert had spotted him in 1857, and had arranged to have him sent to the British Embassy in Berlin 'to be a help to Vicky'. Bismarck had been openly hostile to Morier and had so frightened Lord Bloomfield, the Minister, that he acquiesced in everything he said.

Bismarck had been in Paris when he received what he was waiting and hoping for – the telegram from von Roon which changed his life. He did not need to be told 'delay dangerous, make haste'. Almost before he had finished reading the War Minister's summons, he was on his way.

On the 20th of September Bismarck was in Berlin. Two days later he was at Babelsberg face to face with the King. He offered William royal government and no surrender in exchange for the premiership and the Foreign Office. This was all the King wanted to know. Gleefully he tore up the abdication, relief in his heart. With this one act he unloaded all his troubles on to Bismarck's willing shoulders. Next day, the 23rd of September 1862, the Gazette announced the appointment of Herr Otto von Bismarck-Schönhausen as Minister-President of Prussia.

It was still not five days since William's threat to abdicate. But those five days affected the rest of their lives and changed the destinies of Europe.

What of the King's offer now? Vicky's immediate, instinctive reaction had not been wrong. In the hard years ahead it was some comfort to remember that there had never been a real choice. The King had been playing a double game, using Fritz to strengthen his case with Bismarck, should he not find him all that von Roon had claimed him to be. It had been cruel of him to impose on Fritz the agony of an unreal decision simply in order to strike his own bargain. He had gambled on Fritz's refusal. Had Fritz played Prince Hal to William's Henry IV, William would have been quite capable of turning his acceptance into a plot to depose him. When Vicky had penetrated the King's trickery and the infamous way he had treated the husband she loved, she had scarcely a shred of respect for him left.

On the 28th of September the King summoned Fritz to an interview. It was very brief. Making no reference to the events of the past
ten days, he said he was tired of sermons and wanted no more of them.[6]
Fritz was then dismissed from the presence.

Next day at a reception the King behaved so rudely to them both in
full view of everyone, that Vicky urged Fritz to ask permission to join
the Prince of Wales on a Mediterranean cruise. For once William was
delighted to be rid of them. They sailed into the sun for rest and
recuperation, and returned to find Bismarck firmly entrenched after
coining his most famous phrase: 'the great questions of the time
will not be solved by speeches and majority votes, but by iron and
blood.'[7]

Vicky and Fritz have come in for much criticism for leaving Berlin
so soon after Bismarck's appointment, thereby giving him a clear field.
Could they have done anything if they had stayed? Young, inexperienced and without a wise adviser at hand, how could they have
been a match for a man of Bismarck's calibre, especially with the King
behind him?

Bismarck's appointment was not welcomed by everyone. While in
Italy, Vicky took fresh heart from reports in *The Times* and the London
Spectator that the Prussian people as a whole did not like Bismarck,
while the Liberal party positively hated him and took the line that the
rule of the sword at home could only lead to war abroad.[8]

On her return to Berlin Vicky noticed at once that the atmosphere
was changed. It had never been a pleasant town but it was bearable,
and she had cherished the hope that one day she would be in a position
to improve it. Bismarck had transformed it in six weeks, infusing an
air of bustle and excitement it had never had before, and all by warlike
talk of blood and iron and Germany's might. Soon after his return
Fritz went to the barracks; he could hardly credit the smartness and
efficiency. He had been trying for years to instil some discipline into the
princes, to stop the general air of slackness that in peace time hung over
the most blood-thirsty soldiers, and which turned the place into nothing
more than a club for drinking, gossip and gambling. It was galling to
see that Bismarck had achieved in a short time what he had never
managed to do. The King, not without a wish to hurt, slyly remarked
on the change when Vicky and Fritz dined with him, talking of the
transformation as a triumph for a 'mere civilian'. The change in the
barracks was as nothing to the change in William. His gout had
vanished, the weakness in his voice had gone and his cheeks were like
ripe apples from hours in the fresh air with his troops. Vicky was
astonished at his friskiness and his smart appearance. The food,
usually so unappetising, and the weak, watered-down wine, had, like

the master of the house, taken a turn for the better. For once, the King's hospitality was lavish and he even pressed Fritz to a second glass of champagne. Vicky was too vexed to take these signs of grace in good part – it hurt her that her father-in-law should be jovial and carefree at their expense.

When she and Fritz discussed the King together afterwards, Fritz was quick to find excuses for his father – he did not mean to be unkind. He was sure his father had no inkling of the enormity of the mistake he had made in 'selling his soul and that of all of them to an untrustworthy man'.[9] Vicky knew that the fundamental difference between Fritz and herself was the regrettable fact that he had not been born a free Englishman and that 'all Prussians have not the feeling of independence and love of justice and constitutional liberty they ought to have'.[10] Indeed when Vicky thought about all the peculiar circumstances of Fritz's upbringing, she realised that it was a miracle that he was so different from his father and had inherited only his mother's gifts and not her foolishness.

Berlin had become distasteful, and Vicky and Fritz were anxious to get away. Vicky was particularly unhappy. A visit to the theatre to see Harkendon's *Secret Agents* had done nothing to improve matters, for the play turned out to be a parody of the present situation and brought home to her the falseness of Fritz's position. It was all very well to hide themselves away from the sight of the King's 'self-ruin', but they could not do this for ever.

A solution came to her when she was at Windsor for the marriage of the Prince of Wales to Princess Alexandra of Denmark on the 10th of March 1863. Could mama persuade the King to allow them to live half the year in England? It was a suggestion welcomed by Queen Victoria, who made no secret of the fact that she needed her eldest daughter close at hand and was of course willing to provide them with a home. The King made it plain he did not want them: there was no one to welcome them at the Wildpark station when they returned. King William did not summon them for an account of the wedding and Queen Augusta did not send her usual greetings message. But with the return to Prussia came the realisation there could be no escape. It had only been a dream. If she allowed herself to be 'knocked under' so easily, what would happen to her father's hopes? Prussia and its hundred-and-one little pin-pricks would have to be endured.

*

Two things of vital importance to Prussia and the succession happened while Vicky and Fritz were in England. The King began to govern without Parliament and Bismarck seized control of the press. The great majority of the newspapers were Liberal and had opposed the King's and Bismarck's autocratic methods energetically from the beginning.[11] The constitution guaranteed the freedom of the press and Bismarck's act was a breach of the law. In Vicky's eyes it was more than that; it was the realisation of the Prince Consort's worst fears. The Prince had foreseen that if something of the sort were to happen, Fritz's dangerous position would be exposed at once. Who but a mere handful would know that Fritz had nothing to do with it? Vicky saw at once that Fritz must make public the true state of affairs, or run the risk of seeming to be a party to illegal acts. He was due to go on a tour of military inspection in the eastern provinces. On the advice of Herr von Winter, the chief Burgomaster, and with Vicky's full knowledge and backing, Fritz made a speech in the Town Hall of Danzig in which he stated that 'I did not know anything of this order beforehand. I was absent, and not one of those who advised it.'[12]

The speech made a tremendous impact. It was reported fully in the press and reactions to it were most favourable. But the King was furious, and sent Fritz an angry letter in which he treated him 'like a child'.[13] Berlin was ablaze with speculation and everyone asked what the King would do to his son. But still more asked 'Who is behind this?' No one believed that Vicky and Fritz had acted alone. The Prince Consort was dead and Queen Victoria was in a decline, so they could be written off. Bismarck said that he 'detected the hand of Robert Morier', while the King felt certain that Ernest Stockmar (whom he had never liked) was behind it, and probably that crafty old fox his father too. Queen Victoria knew at once that it was the kind of foolhardy act that, without counting the cost, only the young ever do. The speech was too honest and too lacking in subtlety to implicate an older person. Bismarck knew this too, but it suited him to drag Robert Morier's name into the fray. His fear and hatred of this young Englishman, who knew more about Germany and her affairs than any other diplomat of his day, amounted to a phobia and he was doing his best to get rid of him.

An entry in Fritz's diary for the 5th of June records that 'I have openly acknowledged myself an opponent of Bismarck's and his disastrous theories and thereby shown the world that I have not accepted or indeed agreed with his policy.'[14] There is also Vicky's own letter to the Queen of the 8th of June, warning her mother not to be unpleasantly surprised should there be 'awful consequences': 'I did all I could to induce Fritz to do so (speak), knowing how necessary it was that he should at once express his resentment openly and disclaim having any part in the last measures of the government.'[15] Vicky was happy that at last the Liberals knew Fritz was on their side. Indeed she was happy whatever the consequences, for was she not carrying out dearest papa's wishes? Queen Victoria, too, was certain of this: 'you are the best and wisest adviser he could have and the worthy child of your beloved father who will look down approvingly on you.'[16]

But everybody did not approve. King Leopold discerned disobedience and thought it augured badly for the future.[17] Robert Morier (who was in England at the time) considered the speech unwise, despite the backing of the Liberal newspapers and *The Times*'s eulogy of Fritz's part in the Danzig incident, and wrote to his friend Ernest Stockmar in grave terms that his was 'no way to fight Bismarck'.[18] Ernest Stockmar agreed.

It was all too much for Ernest, who had heard *The Times* article was attributed to him because of its 'continentalisms'. Before the end of July 1863 he had asked Vicky to let him go: he was an 'orange squeezed dry' through exhaustion and nervous strain. He could not find strength enough to face the anger of the King who was now beside himself with fury and talked of 'major crimes' and 'punishments', shouting that he would banish Fritz from the council and strike him off the army list. William would not listen to Bismarck, who drily advised his master to ignore the speech 'as I do'. Indeed the new Minister-President went further and urged the King not to make a martyr of his son, quoting one of his favourite texts, 'deal gently with the young man Absalom'.[19]

As June turned into July, Fritz's 'punishment' still hung over his head and he longed to have the affair settled one way or the other. Already up to his neck in trouble, he wrote an explanatory letter to his father in which the words 'heartbroken' – 'laying my military and civil affairs at your feet' – 'willing to retire into the country with all my family' – for a moment hid from the King the awful truth that Fritz would not retract a word.

This brave but reckless refusal took its toll. At first Vicky and Fritz could not sleep for worry and excitement. Later they could not sleep for worry and depression. Soon they both felt quite ill, which was not surprising. Fritz was so emotionally strung up that he prepared himself 'As a soldier who has defied his chief' to be taken under escort to a fortress – a threat the King had hurled at his son in anger.[20] But it broke his heart when he thought of the consequences of this on Vicky and his children. What would become of them?

In cold blood neither wanted to wear the martyr's crown which in hot blood had not been without its attractions. The end of the affair was indeed very tame, for Bismarck had no intention of turning the incident into high drama. On the 29th of July he dictated a conciliatory letter which he made King William copy in his own hand. The suspense was over, but alas, the battle was not won. Although it suited him not to make capital out of the young people's folly for the present, Bismarck never forgave or forgot this first open opposition. It was from this moment that the ruthless isolation of Vicky and Fritz began.[21]

CHAPTER II

'*All the Results that Germany expects*'

IN June 1863, while separated for a short time from Fritz, Vicky wrote to him in language that can only be described as truly Albertian: 'if anyone can do something because it is right, however painful it may be, he can be said to have won a moral victory.'[1]

To Vicky the Danzig affair was such a victory, even if it did make Bismarck sneer, the King furious, draw disapproving frowns from King Leopold and make Fritz and herself miserable with worry and suspense. Indeed opposition only made it more worthwhile. Ideals were never easy to live up to: 'It costs me many a hard struggle' were words uttered with deep feeling. But the knowledge that she was doing what was right made all the hardships endurable. If the results of so much anguish were as yet somewhat nebulous, Vicky comforted herself that it was the long-term effect that mattered and that she was building for the future of their children and their country.

It was as well she felt this, for no one else did. All that autumn and winter Berlin made it plain they thought Fritz's outburst a mistake. Fritz's male relations gossiped about his 'defeat' and what the outcome would be for him. As the weeks went by and nothing happened, Fritz's daring awed but did not silence them; like dogs with a well-loved bone, they had nothing left to chew but could not bring themselves to throw it away. Of course they knew who had put him up to it. Before his marriage Fritz had been a sensible fellow, getting on with his father, enjoying their company and never averse to a bit of a lark in the mess. They had all seen the shameful sight of Fritz driving with his wife on some feminine pursuit – he even took her to the opera or a play, and they were always together at receptions. His father had laughed unkindly when Fritz was found to be wearing an overcoat because the temperature happened to drop a degree.[2]

Vicky heard this unkind gossip and bravely told herself that nothing in the world mattered so long as Fritz understood. But not everything reached her ears, for she did not know that already it was being whispered that she and Bismarck were bitter enemies. Since she was accustomed to getting her own way, it could not be long before the sparks flew; when they did, what fireworks there would be!

Bismarck had the advantage over Vicky, since he was well aware of the gossip and disliked it. It did not suit him. The King was ageing, and the Crown Prince could become his sovereign overnight. If that happened, what was to prevent the new Queen from working on her 'weak' husband to get rid of a Minister-President she did not like? The talk could only do him harm and so it must be stopped; the necessity to work against her harder than ever remained.

By the New Year of 1864 Vicky knew that Bismarck was no fly-by-night royal favourite. He was there to stay and the best must be made of it. There were two courses open to her. One possibility was to swell the number of princesses who, having in the old days turned their backs on a mere Junker, were now falling over each other to invite Prussia's first man to their houses, despite the fact that he was very poor value with his affected, banal conversation and that he was often very rude to those who worshipped. Alternatively, she could take the hard line, remain aloof, a target for criticism and insults but working in some way – she could not yet imagine how – for the good of others. There was no doubt in her mind this was the course she and Fritz must follow, even though it meant doing battle with a formidable foe. In 1864 Vicky had no idea how heavy were the odds against her, but it would have made no difference if she had.

Vicky met Bismarck at every function; it seemed there was nothing to which he was not invited. Possibly because of his straitened early manhood, when he was restricted by lack of money and chafed at the slowness of his career, his capacity for pleasure in middle age amounted almost to a mania. She noticed, not without a certain wry amusement, that he went out of his way to be polite to her, ostentatiously seeking her company, bowing more obsequiously than he ever did to the King, listening attentively to what she had to say, looking as though he asked for nothing more in life than to be with her. Bismarck was a born actor, and this was all an act: Vicky knew it and Bismarck knew she did. She sensed that hidden in his twisted conversation was a longing for her to acknowledge that he was stronger and more powerful than she, and that the game was not worth the candle. He did not say 'give up', but Vicky was made to understand that if she did not capitulate he would take every opportunity to demonstrate his strength and her weakness, while if she was sensible they could live in peace.

Masked balls were just beginning to be popular. Bismarck always attended these, although he never wore a mask. Under cover of her domino Vicky would watch the adulation that went on and marvel at the natural way in which Bismarck accepted it, the cold blue eyes never becoming warmer, the disdainful mouth never breaking into a smile and always that air of arrogance, so blatant that it was offensive.

He never stayed for the unmasking. Vicky guessed this was because etiquette forbade a commoner from sitting on the velvet-covered dais with the royal family to watch the performance of professional dancing that concluded the evening. Vicky enjoyed this most of all. She loved to see the intricate quadrilles and to be bewitched by a ballet of German fairy-tales or exhilarated by the lively Styrian peasant dances which reminded her vividly of Scottish reels as they were danced in her Highland home.[3]

*

It did not take long for Bismarck to show Vicky what he meant by his strength and her weakness, and that he was always going to win. In 1863 Vicky's heart was wrung with pity by accounts in the newspapers of atrocities against the Poles who were trying to throw off a Russian domination that was doing everything to squeeze them out of existence. The insurrection had started in a small way at the end of May with sporadic street fighting; by the autumn it had become a large-scale national rising. Vicky's mounting indignation soon turned to horror at each new brutality. She was not the woman to sit by and do nothing, and she began to devise ways and means of helping a gallant people who were being helplessly ground to dust. She appealed to Fritz – could not Prussia send help? Would he go to the King to ask for money, bandages, food and above all troops? Meanwhile she would organise the despatch of urgent necessities in the quickest possible way.

Fritz was willing, but the King was not. Bismarck had anticipated him. He was greeted with a snarl. Who were the Poles? Since Fritz did not seem to know, he would tell him. They were Prussia's enemies and must be suppressed in the interests of the state. It would not do to antagonise Russia; one day they might be glad of her friendship.[4] Fritz had to return to the Neue Palais empty-handed, and Vicky was beside herself with frustration and despair. His fruitless effort had, however, made one thing clear; the extent of the hold Bismarck had over the King. Now at least they knew where they were.

Three weeks later, when the King was preparing to leave Berlin for the cure at Gastein, in a rare fit of fatherly feeling he invited Fritz, who had been ill with a cold, to go with him. Vicky begged him not to accept. She had heard that Bismarck was to be of the company, and it might do Fritz harm if it was known that he was a willing member of what would look like a friendly triumvirate: 'it might give a wrong impression.' In many ways this was a pity. If Fritz had gone, he might have persuaded his father to follow his inclination and attend the Congress of Princes which the Emperor Franz Joseph had convened at Frankfurt to discuss a scheme for German federal union, for he still had a little influence with his father. Bismarck did not want Prussia to play second fiddle to Austria, but he had his work cut out to find excuses William would accept. In the end he won – he had to – but only through touching a sensitive spot, the King's honour. The invitation had arrived so late that it was an insult.[5]

Vicky saw at once that without the Prussian King the conference would be a fiasco. The King must be made to go. She had a little scheme she hoped might outwit the 'wicked man', as she called Bismarck. It involved Queen Victoria and a letter went post haste to Windsor. Would mama use all her persuasive powers on King William when she met him in Coburg in the autumn? The Queen was making the trip to see the widow of old Baron Stockmar, who had died in July 1863, heartbroken at the loss of that 'perfect being' – Prince Albert – whose character he had helped to mould. Queen Victoria was willing. Vicky prayed that if the mantle of dearest papa was to fall on her mother's shoulders it would be hallowed by guidance from above.

When after much difficulty a meeting was arranged in August 1863, the Queen made no progress at all. William remained firmly of the opinion that the Frankfurt proposals would give Austria the upper hand over Prussia,[6] and played on her sentimental feelings by driving with her to the Festung, which they gazed at with brimming eyes. But they wept for different reasons – she for Albert, and he with self-pity.

*

By 1864 Bismarck's policy was slowly beginning to take shape, and Vicky realised with a shock how far-reaching was his power over them all. There were now two tyrants to contend with, voice and echo, but only one indomitable will. The King had handed the lives of his son and his wife over to Bismarck lock, stock and barrel; he did not care what became of them. The difference in attitude over the Polish question showed clearly how little their feelings were considered. Vicky had not been able to get the Poles out of her mind. They were still suffering horribly and so was she. Through a private source she had sent them all the money she could spare, and if it did nothing else this helped to salve her conscience, although she knew it was dropping pennies into a bottomless pit.

Vicky was soon to feel Bismarck's hard unyielding hand again, this time in a more painful way because it touched her own family. The King of Denmark died on the 15th of November 1863 and was succeeded by his cousin Prince Christian of Schleswig-Holstein-Sonderburg-Glücksburg, father of Princess Alexandra of Wales.

Vicky was 'so glad for dearest Alix's sake', for she loved her like a sister. It never occurred to her that the Danish king's death would be the means of driving a wedge between her and her brother's wife, yet by January 1864 she was already helplessly watching events as they escalated beyond her control.

The duchies of Schleswig and Holstein, the latter with a large German population, had been restive since the London Protocol of 1852 had put them under Danish rule. The legal complexities of the succession question gave rise to Palmerston's famous joke that only three people had ever understood them: the Prince Consort (who was dead), a German professor (who had gone mad) and himself – but he had forgotten all about it. Perhaps no one really did know how to interpret the law of succession correctly, but the opinions of the people were ultimately of greater importance. German national feeling had grown during the last few years, and the populations of the duchies had come to regard themselves as a conquered race and to talk of the 'foreign Danish yoke'. When the king died in 1863, the old cry for self-government was heard again. Matters were complicated still further when another claimant appeared – Duke Frederick of Schleswig-Holstein-Augustenburg* ('Fritz Holstein', the husband of Queen Victoria's niece Adelaide Hohenlohe), who issued a proclamation to the effect that he had assumed the government of the duchies (his father having renounced it in his favour) immediately after the king's death.

How was this difficulty to be solved? Everybody was blaming everybody else. Queen Victoria – who was on the whole pro-Prussian – wrote to tell Vicky that she condemned the 1852 Protocol completely, 'but once signed we cannot upset it without first trying to maintain it . . . where I do however blame Germany is their wanting the two great powers to break their engagements and in not being contented with all the rights of the duchies being obtained'.[7]

The air was laden with suspicion and unrest as each side waited for the other to make the next move. In Berlin Bismarck waited and watched, like a hungry cat with his eye on a sparrow he fancies for his supper, to see which way things would go.

They went the way he wanted them to go.

At first he was discretion itself, not giving the slightest hint of his real intentions – to seize the duchies for Prussia. The fact that Prussia had no claim to them did not disturb him in the least. It was not a question of ethics but of power: Prussia needed the duchies to increase her strength. Unlike Bismarck, Vicky was dreadfully disturbed: she

*Bismark's account of his last meeting with him after the war is worth recording – 'First I called him "Your Royal Highness", then plain "Your Highness", and before he left I was calling him "Your Excellency".'

was pulled in two directions at once, and suffered acutely. She and
Fritz were friends of Fritz Holstein's, and since he was not well off, the
duchies would be a godsend. At the same time she 'felt very much' for
poor King Christian with his kind feelings and good heart. Whatever
happened 'dearest Alix must not fret'. But dearest Alix did fret. Every
night she soaked her pillow with tears and cried out in her sleep.
By day she went about with a woebegone face repeating that 'the
duchies belong to papa'. She was so upset that on the 18th of January
1864 she gave birth prematurely to a son, Albert Victor, Duke of
Clarence.

Vicky had hardly laid down her pen after writing to congratulate
Alix on the birth of an heir when she was thunderstruck to learn that
Bismarck had issued an ultimatum ordering King Christian to evacuate
the duchies within twenty-four hours. On the 1st of February 1864 a
combined force of Prussian and Austrian troops crossed the frontier
into Schleswig.

Fritz was at dinner at the time and knew nothing of the plan. He had
to join his regiment in a hurry. He was furious at being made to look
a fool, hoodwinked as neatly as the Danes (whom Bismarck had
deceived into believing that England would come to their rescue in the
event of war) and his heart was not in the business of fighting a foe
with whom he had no quarrel. There was only time for the briefest of
interviews with the King, who was glad to get rid of his son before he
started asking awkward questions. But Fritz was sorry for his father
who he felt had been as deceived as the rest of them, since 'he sits in
the centre of a web of lies'.[8]

Once Fritz had left for the front, Vicky's loyalties were still more
divided, and her anxiety was intense. She must not be judged too
harshly for the warlike feelings which overwhelmed her despite her
pity for Denmark. Her family entirely failed to understand them.
What, for instance, was Queen Victoria to make of 'I hope and pray
this war may end with honour to our dear troops and attain all the
results that Germany expects . . . it is impossible to blame an Englishman for not understanding the Schleswig-Holstein question – it
remains nevertheless to us Germans plain and simple as daylight and
one for which we would gladly bear any sacrifice'.[9] To the Queen such
violent patriotism could only mean one thing – Vicky had become a
disciple of Bismarck. King Leopold thought so too: 'the poor King of
Prussia wanted war, Vicky and Fritz did the same.'[10] To Queen
Victoria it was a time for plain speaking: 'you all (and God forgive you
for it) would have it.'[11] Vicky was deeply hurt, for the charge was
unjust. In her defence it must be said that neither Queen Victoria nor
King Leopold took into account the effects of living in an overheated

atmosphere. It was difficult enough in peace-time for Vicky to keep a level head in a country where there was no moderation in anything and where it was easy to lose one's sense of proportion. Circumstances were often too much for her, and she was often submerged before she knew she was sinking. The best and more reasonable half of her knew this and tried to act accordingly. When she failed, however, she realised that she was vulnerable and the knowledge was unpleasant.

It was typical of her nature that she swung right round on to the side of the Danes the moment she heard how bravely they faced the huge Prussian army, only to be mown down. Instantly the 'glorious Prussian army' fell in her eyes because it was victorious, and she was bitterly unhappy when in consequence her country did attain 'all the results that Germany expects'. She was just as indignant when she heard the terms of the peace of Vienna. It was 'cruel' since it made the weak bear the brunt. Because he had lost, Vicky was hotly on King Christian's side, not caring how many taunts she earned with her talk of 'injustice' and 'bullying'. He had never needed a champion more, for Bismarck coolly made him hand over the duchies to the Emperor of Austria and the King of Prussia, careless that he appeared greedy.

Like Vicky herself, the English spoke out strongly for the underdog, thereby creating a situation she dreaded – a gulf between England and Prussia, which meant a breach between Vicky and her English family. It was, too, a burden on her conscience to be told how that 'sweet creature' Princess Alix had been half frantic with anxiety for her parents and how the Prince of Wales found Vicky's tactless letters hard to forgive. 'My position is not an easy one', she wrote sorrowfully to Fritz, 'they reprove me here for being too English, at home I am too Prussian. It seems I cannot do anything right.'[12]

Fritz was not happy either. He had been given the order of the Red Eagle with Swords by a King capering with glee, but he burned with shame that he had been rewarded for beating a pitiably small and defenceless country while merely sitting comfortably at headquarters. This experience had stripped him of all illusions about the glory of being a soldier, especially in an unprovoked war and under the orders of a 'most unscrupulous man'. He summed up his feelings in the three words he wrote in his diary: 'I feel ashamed.'[13]

When it was all over there was a brief meeting between Vicky and Fritz and the Waleses at Cologne. The meeting was arranged with reconciliation in mind, but it was not a success. Vicky was ill at ease, even guilty. She struggled to find the right words to wipe out the past, but none would come. Unfortunately she had overlooked one small matter. Fritz was in uniform as usual and wore on his tunic the medal he had won at the battle of Duppel. He possessed no civilian clothes, but the Prince of Wales did not know this and felt insulted. 'Fritz was flaunting before our eyes a most objectionable ribbon.'[14]

Of such small things are family quarrels made.

*

On the 11th of September 1864 a third son and fourth child was born to Vicky at the Neue Palais. They called him Sigismund. Vicky longed for Bertie and Alix to be godparents but she was afraid to risk a snub, and so the Emperor and Empress of Austria were asked instead.

Unhappily the feud looked like continuing despite Queen Victoria's advice to her daughter-in-law to forgive and forget for the sake of family peace.[15] The Convention of Gastein had seen to that. By the peace terms concluded on the 10th of August 1864, the duchies were divided between Prussia and Austria. Even before the ink was dry Bismarck was showing his contempt for Prussia's ally by declaring that he never would have believed that an Austrian diplomat could have signed such a document.[16] Vicky read the English newspapers from cover to cover and found her worst fears confirmed in the black picture they painted of Prussia – who, they asserted, had only gone to war in the first place to seize the duchies for herself. Vicky had suspected from the beginning that Bismarck's 'little game' had not been an open one. What was he after? Where was it all leading to? She was frightened to answer her own question, for she had heard that Bismarck was boasting that 'Austria was only a question of time',[17] and this was something she did not want to believe.

Time had suddenly become a matter of great urgency to Vicky. She wanted time to think, time to plan for the future – which was going to be so different from what she had hoped – and time to find 'a little place of our own', where she and Fritz could escape from a distasteful Berlin and from which they could not be removed at the caprice of the King or Bismarck.

The latter's unseemly celebration of his first big triumph made such a place essential. The King had decreed that the 18th of December 1864 was to be a day of thanksgiving for the Prussian victory; at nine o'clock in the morning church bells would peal and would do so at stated intervals throughout the day, churches were to hold special services and afterwards troops would parade. The day was to end with a mammoth banquet for the privileged princes who had helped to win the war. Vicky said that nothing was lacking but shame. Fritz was not allowed to escape the dinner. With Vicky's backing, however, he made up his mind to make a public protest. When the Minister-

President's health was proposed, he ostentatiously refrained from drinking, a snub Bismarck noted with an enigmatic smile: he could afford to take such nonsense lightly.

Life in Potsdam and Berlin had become so uncomfortable that Vicky redoubled her efforts to find a small estate where they could live as a family, quite informally and far from prying eyes, and yet not so isolated that the chance to 'do good' in a private capacity would be denied them. After several months of searching Vicky found the very thing right on their doorstep, yet so hidden from Potsdam, that straggling suburb of royal palaces, that it might have been in a different world.

She discovered the village of Bornstädt by accident. When she was out driving one afternoon early in September the coachman took a wrong turning. Vicky noticed at once that she was in a part of the country she had never seen before. It was strangely wild, the road no more than a rough track with dark woods on either side. Very soon the trees gave way to untrimmed hedges covered with autumn dog-roses. Behind them was a fast-flowing stream of clear water. A bend in the track revealed a church, a cluster of cottages and a patch of uncut grass doing service as a village green, where two thin-shanked dogs were stretched out fast asleep. Otherwise it was quite deserted. To Vicky's amazed eyes it was exactly like something out of fairy-tale. Bathed in the late autumn sun, everything had a warm and welcoming look, even the broken-down hovels were not untouched with romance.

Excitedly Vicky jumped down from the carriage. Holding her skirts out of the dirt she walked rapidly towards the church. It was in an awful state. She was shocked to see graves trodden over, monuments broken and the whole place a tangled mass of weeds.[18] As she gazed about her she was suddenly seized with a longing to bring life back to this forgotten village. It hurt her to see such chaos. Yet the place had an air of serenity, and when she sat for a few minutes on a fallen tombstone a little of its peace touched her.

The day was not yet done. On the outskirts, half hidden by an avenue of fine poplars and well set back from the road, was a house with peeling paint and broken windows, its garden a tangle of weeds and unpruned trees. It was for sale. By Christmas Vicky had bought it; by the spring, under Fritz's guidance, the work of converting it into a model farm had begun.

The place was to prove a godsend, a refuge from the overcharged atmosphere of a Bismarck-ridden Berlin and a real home where they could live as a family, their children under their eye. In time they rebuilt the school and civilised the inhabitants who had horrified Vicky by never undressing, sleeping on straw in their boots, eating their food with the cattle they were tending, tearing meat with their hands, 'never having heard of knives or forks'.[19]

To watch tumble-down hovels become clean, respectable homes in which a woman could take pride gave them infinite satisfaction, but it was uphill work. It had sickened Vicky to go to these houses before the improvements – they were 'terrible beyond belief'; babies were wrapped in newspaper or dirty rags, and left to lie on straw riddled with lice. Hitherto the lowest point of poverty she had known was in the simple clean Highland cottages where every farthing was counted, but the Highlanders were dignified and proud in their poverty, while at Bornstädt want had degraded and defiled.

The rôle of squire suited Fritz well. Dressed in the clothes of an English country gentleman, he would ride round the village on his quiet cob, talking to the people in the streets, visiting the cottages and the new school, half shocked and half amused to find that the rescued children believed that he came from the Kingdom of God.[20] Trotting home to English tea with Vicky and the family, he never failed to give thanks for this 'small chance to do good'.

At Bornstädt they were changed people. Court and society in Berlin would not have recognised Vicky in the laughing carefree girl who held Tommy the pony's reins while helping young Willy to keep his balance, nor a taciturn Fritz in the companionable father who took his children for walks and encouraged them to hunt for wild flowers, which they took home and pressed in a book. At night he sang to them before they went to bed 'Alle Vögel sind schon da, Alle Vögel alle', in which the high thin voices of the children joined.[21]

Parenthood was bringing out a new side in Fritz. His own sad and lonely childhood had sharpened his understanding, and from the first he had shown a skill in handling little children that delighted Vicky. She encouraged him to go as often as he could to the nursery, where like his father-in-law before him he built brick houses and gave the youngest ones rides on his back. When summer came round he taught them to swim in the Havel, and when it was winter he held their hands while they took their first unsteady steps on the frozen lake. After the Danish war Fritz rearranged his day so that he could see more of his children, who were growing fast and needed a father's discipline. Vicky had a horror of becoming a remote parent like most other Prussian princesses, who hardly knew the way to their own nurseries. No one has ever been able to criticise her for neglecting her children, indeed it has even been said that she spent so much time with them that she neglected her royal duties.

In six years Vicky had borne four children, three of them strong healthy boys, and since she was still so young there would be more.

This alone should have endeared her to the family. On the contrary there was jealousy that she was proving herself capable of reproduction on a scale hitherto unknown among the Hohenzollerns close to the throne. The family had another grievance which they aired whenever they got the chance – they hardly ever saw the children. Why did Vicky keep them away from the Court? Vicky had stated her reasons often enough – the influence of the Court was pernicious for children. She often wondered how much longer she could keep the two apart, and worried about it. Vicky had to put up with many things in her life that Queen Victoria could not understand because she had never known them. Sometimes, for instance, the Queen was too quick to rebuke Vicky for going away so often without the children.[22] But the King's permission had to be given every time she wanted to take them even quite a short distance, to Reinhardsbrunn or Coburg. The King complained too if she took them to their Aunt Alice at Darmstadt without his leave. Moreover Queen Augusta's constant interference was damaging, because although often well-intentioned, it was frequently foolish. When Augusta discovered through a slip of the tongue by a careless governess that Vicky sometimes took the children away from their lessons for a quick look at the dachshunds the farm manager was breeding at Bornstädt, she made a great fuss and complained to the King, who put a stop to it. Vicky was helpless against such tyranny since there was no higher authority to which she could appeal.

She was also helpless to stop Queen Augusta's growing influence over Willy, whose tantrums were getting worse as he grew older. Augusta bought his affection with bribes, and encouraged that 'terrible Prussian pride' (which Queen Victoria told Vicky 'grieved papa so'[23]) believing that a future king should have a sense of his own importance. On the other hand sometimes when alone with his parents, without any outside influence, Willy could be a 'dear interesting charming boy, quick and intelligent, not always in a temper and even affectionate.'[24]

With his grandparents Willy was very ready to show pride and a haughty manner, which would have been funny in so young a child if it had not also been so serious. It made Fritz smile to see his son supplant him in his mother's affections and to watch her, usually so impervious to children's charms, respond to Willy's clever wheedling. Vicky was not amused, but the boy's arm was such a handicap that she had not the heart to interfere.

Treatment for the arm still continued, but with little hope of success. Unfortunately Vicky lacked the courage of her convictions and did not put a stop to more and more specialist treatment. Willy was made to lift heavy weights with fingers that could not grip; he was frightened to death by electric shocks supposed to galvanise dead muscles into life, and he screamed when strapped into a cage for an hour a day to correct the sideways tilt of the head caused by the differing weight of his arms. The reason she did not prevent these things was the faint hope that one day something would be found to do the trick, for she passionately wanted Willy to have every chance. At the back of her mind was a guilty feeling that in some way she might have been to blame. If the deformity could have been accepted and taken naturally, Willy might have been spared years of the unhappiness of strange doctors and useless treatments that did nothing but alarm him, but Vicky could not give up while the doctors refused to admit that it was hopeless. Hopeless she knew it to be, however. By 1865, he could not 'run fast, nor ride, nor climb, nor cut his food'.[25]

Willy first began to overcome his disability in August 1866, when he was seven. One afternoon while staying at Balmoral he wandered into the ghillies' room, where the men were cleaning the guns. He tried to pick up a gun but it was too heavy to lift with one hand and the men burst out laughing to see him so clumsy. Red with fury he was opening his mouth to scream when Grant the head keeper quietly put into his hand the small light rifle that had been his uncle Bertie's first gun. Then Grant began to show him how to use it.

All the same, Vicky sometimes despaired that he would ever be like other boys. She told Queen Victoria in 1862 that she had wanted 'papa's advice on Willy's education'. But would the Prussian royal family have allowed him to interfere? Indeed, would he have been the best person to ask? Prince Albert was hard on his own sons, showing both obstinacy and blindness towards the Prince of Wales and a lack of imagination amounting almost to harshness towards his second son Alfred whom he separated from his devoted elder brother and sent to sea at the age of twelve. Perhaps, however, with a grandson a softer attitude would have prevailed.

Which did Prince William need – the affectionate kiss to cool his fiery temper, or the cane to bring him to heel? Vicky did not know. At seven he passed from the care of women into the hands of a military governor, Captain von Schötte, a pleasant and intelligent Guards officer, who treated Willy with firmness but with sympathetic understanding. They got on very well together.

The same good fortune did not attend the choice of a tutor. Georg Hinzpeter was thirty-eight years old when Vicky first met him. The son of a provincial school-teacher from north Germany, he was a dry, bloodless pedant, entirely devoid of charity, compassion or humour, but with a fanatical belief in himself. Such a man was incapable of understanding any child, let alone a difficult one like Willy. He was picked out from a short list of four. It is difficult to imagine what quality in him, but lacking in the others, can have appealed so strongly to Vicky and Fritz, but among his credentials was a letter from Robert Morier testifying to morals 'of the highest' and to principles and ideals 'not of this world'.[26] If Vicky had not put so much trust in Morier's judgement and had probed further, she would have discovered that his appeal to the diplomat lay in political ideas which were of 'sound sense and great learning' and coincided with Morier's on national economy and social reform, things which had nothing to do with the education of children.

Although he had never conversed before with royalty, Hinzpeter was cool and collected at the interview, displaying far less nervousness than Vicky and showing the egotistical self-possession of a man who has no doubt that he is right. At the time it did not occur to Vicky that this indicated a disturbing lack of balance and normality. He said that if he was chosen he would mould the prince 'on the lines of old Prussian simplicity'.[27]

Simplicity was a magic word to Vicky. It won her over at once. Was it not just this quality that was needed to counteract the bad effects of that 'terrible Prussian pride'? Delighted, she dismissed as 'stupid' the reservations she had felt about the man himself – the insolence of the speckled green eyes which did not match his servile manner, and the general impression of egotism and over-confidence. The mistake she made in appointing this fanatical man – it was to rebound on Vicky herself – was caused by the old trouble; no one was quite open with her. On the basis of a few political talks and nothing more, Morier decided he was the 'right man'. Ernest Stockmar, who also knew Hinzpeter, was held back by the fear of being thought interfering and by trying to see both sides, and said nothing, although he told Morier that while he considered the tutor to be 'a superior man' he had his doubts about his being 'the right man': 'I am afraid he wants heart and is a hard Spartan idealist.'[28]

Georg Hinzpeter went to the Neue Palais as Willy's tutor in 1866 and stayed thirteen disastrous years.

CHAPTER 12

The Waiting Game

IT was in the autumn of 1865 that Vicky first became aware that she was being spied on. To begin with it was little more than instinctive feeling, the consequence of a misplaced letter or a broken lock. Then, six months later when she had forgotten all about it, she returned to the Neue Palais after a brief visit to Reinhardsbrunn, opened her desk and smelled tobacco. Nothing was missing nor disarranged, so she tried to persuade herself it was only foolish imagination, but she knew she was not mistaken. It was a terrible shock.[1]

When she had first come to Prussia it had not taken her long to learn that Fritz's relations were abnormally inquisitive and would go to any lengths to discover what went on in her household. Queen Augusta had been so anxious to know everything that she had forced Vicky to take into her service a meddlesome and quite unnecessary housekeeper before the birth of her second child in 1860.[2] Since Augusta's own cold nature prevented her from getting close to her daughter-in-law, she used an elderly relation who, in return for a 'position', would find out much that Vicky would have told her willingly. Thus the reputation for lack of curiosity on which Augusta prided herself was saved, and the only one who suffered was Vicky. Vicky had become quite accustomed to the family gossiping about her freely – as they did about each other – and to hearing them repeat her own remarks back to her in a twisted form. In a way it meant that they had accepted her as one of themselves. But the incident of the desk suggested something different; something sinister which might discredit her and Fritz. The possibilities were endless and they frightened her badly, but for the next twenty years she had to learn to live with them.

In the beginning fear was replaced by indignation; Fritz must speak to his father. Yet in a calmer frame of mind she knew that this was impossible. No protection could be expected from a king who had become a mere cipher, living in Bismarck's pocket and refusing to listen to a word against his favourite. The situation would have to be accepted. The bad effect of this on Vicky's open temperament was that it made her unnaturally disingenuous. She became guarded and no longer spoke without thinking. At times she was so quiet that the family remarked on it and drew the conclusion that Vicky and Fritz were not getting on well together. But the change pleased Queen Victoria, who took this reserve to be no more than a sign of greater maturity when Vicky was at Osborne shortly before the Austrian war in 1866.[3]

Vicky's brothers and sisters came nearer the mark when they blamed the King's disgraceful treatment of their sister, which made them all furious. If only dearest papa were alive, what short work he would make of such villainy! When the nine of them met in Coburg – all together for the first time since 1858 – where the Queen was to unveil a statue of the Prince Consort, Vicky's heart was warmed by their indignation. It was a relief to know that they saw her difficulties and sympathised. At last they understood that she was not her own mistress; she very much hoped it would smooth her path with them in future.

Vicky had gone to Coburg with a secret romantic plan. She and Fritz had a great friend, Prince Christian of Augustenburg, whom they had invited to the ceremony; Vicky had arranged that if Queen Victoria approved of him, Christian should meet her sister Helena ('Lenchen') 'naturally'. This gay and handsome prince and his elder brother Frederick (one of the claimants to the duchies) had been ruined by Bismarck. At the end of the Danish war he had vindictively stripped the brothers of everything they possessed – land, commissions in the army, even the roof over their heads, so that they were almost paupers. Christian was a frequent visitor to the Bornstädt farm, where only intimate friends were entertained, and it was watching him play with her children that gave Vicky the idea that he would make one of her sisters an excellent husband, if mama could overlook his poverty.[4] In fact, Queen Victoria could, because it would mean that there was nothing to keep him in Germany and England would become his home. What a rebuff it would be for a 'certain nameless person' if the penniless prince married a daughter of the Queen of England! When their engagement was announced shortly before Christmas 1865, it caused quite a stir in Berlin. Queen Augusta was horrified at 'yet another poor match'. Vicky and Fritz were overjoyed, and King Leopold gave them his blessing. But alas, Vicky's favourite uncle did not live to see them married, for he died on the 16th of December.

King William's inability to give a straight answer almost prevented Vicky from seeing her dying uncle for the last time. He procrastinated for so long that Vicky went to see him herself and begged humbly for permission to go to Belgium direct from Coburg with Queen Victoria in the autumn. But Bismarck did not want Vicky to spend so much time in the company of her family – perhaps plotting against Prussia –

and so she had to return to Potsdam. By the time William had given his consent, Vicky and Fritz had to make a long winter journey in an unheated train through country thick with snow. King Leopold was in bed when they arrived, but insisted on getting up for luncheon, although he could eat nothing and had to lie propped up with pillows on a sofa. He was terribly wasted, but his mind was as sharp as ever and his voice quite strong as he warned them of Bismarck's intentions. From his sick-bed he had followed the different stages of the Minister-President's plans, and he explained why he thought the duchies to have been only the beginning and the Convention of Gastein so much waste paper. Where it would end, he could not say. The dying man was heartened and comforted to see Vicky 'very right-minded in everything and Fritz greatly matured'.[5] The visit held an unexpected poignancy for Vicky, as she noticed 'how like dearest papa' were her uncle's voice and manner, though when her father was alive she had never seen the resemblance.

*

Early in 1866, and less than three months after Vicky's first suspicions that they were being watched, Fritz made another alarming discovery that shook them both. In conversation one day with Professor Duncker – who had replaced Count Perponcher as Fritz's political equerry and whose impartiality was essential – it became evident that he too was being sucked into the stream. When Fritz said bluntly that he saw through him, Duncker stopped pretending at once and shamelessly began to unload some 'most unwelcome propaganda' on to Fritz, showing an open admiration for Bismarck that was most unwelcome. Afterwards the professor's manner, once so frank and friendly, was not untinged with insolence.[6]

It was a serious predicament. Duncker could neither be trusted nor dismissed, and Fritz was saddled with a man he regarded as a traitor. The unhappy result of his defection was to place Fritz in a most vulnerable position. He was more or less isolated politically, since Bismarck carried on his work behind closed doors, his secrets hidden in his own mind and shared with no one: Fritz would therefore hear only what Bismarck wanted him to hear. Duncker repeated to him the 'wicked man's' own words and phrases, and these 'quite sickened us both'. Yet the public believed not only that the heir to the throne must be in the centre of affairs but that Minister-President and Crown Prince spoke with one voice. Danzig was forgotten by all but a few, and no one could be expected to realise that Fritz was 'the only one who is not told one iota about political matters'.[7]

In April yet more Bismarckian dirty work came to light. The

Minister-President was doing his utmost to break the last shreds of regard the King still had for his son and daughter-in-law in a way that would touch the old man's pride – by attacking Vicky's influence on his heir. Fritz was under 'English influence'.

Here in 1866 are the first signs of a relentless and cruel campaign to present a false picture of Vicky and Fritz to the King, to Prussia and the whole of Europe, a campaign so successful and lasting that its effects are still apparent even today.

Bismarck's method was simplicity itself. He was a past master in the art of making people look foolish, and he took every opportunity to ridicule Fritz to friends who would be certain to repeat what they had been told. One by one he threw his poisoned darts: the Crown Prince was the tool of England and passed state secrets on to Queen Victoria for the benefit of her own country and Prussia's enemies; he did this because he was weak and completely in the clutches of 'that woman', who sapped his will-power so that he no longer thought for himself; was this to be wondered at, since he was a 'brainless fop who only cared for money, clothes and amusement'.[8] Bismarck unconsciously revealed the reason for his hatred of Vicky when he monotonously repeated that he could never reconcile himself to an Englishwoman on the throne of Prussia. To Bismarck this was tantamount to turning Prussia into an adjunct of England – almost into a conquered country. The very idea was like a canker that ate into his mind, so that he came to believe that Vicky was a thoroughly bad character, difficult, quarrelsome, strong-willed, indeed altogether detestable, although the evidence of his eyes and ears told him otherwise, and that Fritz was so 'hen-pecked' that he had ceased to be a man and had become merely his wife's husband, no longer able to stand up for his children against her.[9]

Albrecht von Stosch, the head of the Prussian Admiralty, was so under Bismarck's domination in the 1860s that he was weak enough to follow Bismarck's lead and tell everybody that the Crown Princess had the most far reaching influence on her husband's thoughts and opinions and that it was all bad:[10] when he broke away from Bismarck in 1877 and became his opponent, he regretted having said this and wanted to make amends, but the damage was done.

Bismarck's disloyalty to the Crown Prince did not meet with quite the same success outside Prussia. Thiers told a friend in 1871 that he was disgusted when Bismarck unblushingly informed him that he was 'in despair about the Crown Prince, who occupies himself with politics which he does not understand, talks of things of which he knows nothing, and opens books which he does not read'.[11] Thiers knew Fritz and had been impressed with his honesty and sense of fair play, as was Jules Favre, who was reported to have turned away when Bismarck began to explain why Prussia's Crown Prince was not fit to take part in the peace negotiations at the end of the Franco-Prussian War.

It is difficult to see what Bismarck hoped to gain from drawing the aged King into the conspiracy to strip Fritz's reputation bare of every virtue and decent instinct – indeed to represent him as no more than a brainless idiot. In his own way William did love his son. To pick quarrels with Fritz on every possible occasion meant little to a man for whom family bickering was as natural as breathing. Bismarck knew this and had been surprised at the success of his denigration of Vicky. William had been quick to respond and had said nothing in his daughter-in-law's defence. But Bismarck dare not let matters rest. Suppose the King and his heir were to join forces against him? Once Bismarck had thought of such a possibility his deep feeling of insecurity goaded him on willy-nilly. If the King still had a shred of paternal feeling left, it must be stamped out. This single-minded approach worked like a charm. Bismarck talked to William of the sorrow of having such a disappointing son, and remarked that it must be dreadful to have to stand back and watch the Crown Prince and his 'power-drunk wife' waiting only to see their King in his grave. With tears of pity slowly trickling down his cheeks Bismarck would murmur 'for such a father to have such a son'.[12] William had never before thought of his irritation with Fritz as disappointment, nor of Vicky as a dangerous woman. Once Bismarck had suggested the idea, however, it took root. William then wished he had not listened to 'soft advice' after Danzig.

The tragedy of this form of attack lay in the knowledge that there was nothing they could do to stop these falsehoods. Vicky and Fritz could never enjoy the satisfaction of redress, but their helplessness deepened their need for each other and brought out all Vicky's protective instincts.

*

Early in 1866 there were signs that relations between Austria and Prussia were becoming strained. Bismarck had lured Austria into a false position in the previous August. By separating Schleswig from Holstein and allotting one to each of the victors in the Danish war, the Convention of Gastein violated the principles for which the war had been fought: this could not harm a Prussia bent on destroying the German Confederation, but was to the disadvantage of a Habsburg Empire which was only kept together by tradition and a respect for agreements. As early as January 1866 Bismarck's policy of stirring up trouble in Holstein had provoked Austria to a sharp rejoinder, while the alliance with Italy in April gave him just three months in which to find a suitable excuse for war if Prussia was to enjoy Italian support in it. Much was being said in Berlin that spring about Austria's 'infamous conduct', but Vicky knew – because her Uncle Leopold had opened her eyes – that all the tension was traceable to Prussia's Minister-President. During the autumn of 1865, they had stayed for several days with the Emperor Franz Joseph in Vienna. They had talked politics freely and found the Emperor very 'right-minded and with a hatred of war', shuddering at the prospect of a conflict with Prussia.

Vicky, too, had a hatred of war and of this one in particular. She wrote to warn Queen Victoria of the possibility of conflict with Austria: 'we are still suspended mid-way between peace and war. Not a day passes without some little incident which might easily be laid hold of to turn the scales on the side of peace, and not a day passes that the wicked man does not with the greatest ability counteract or thwart what is good and drive us towards war, turning and twisting everything to serve his own purpose.'[13]

Queen Victoria disregarded this warning as one of Vicky's exaggerations. If she had lived in Prussia she would have realised how often Vicky played down much that might alarm her mother. Hard as it was not to be believed, it was harder still to watch Bismarck tightening his hold over the King. Yet Bismarck sometimes blundered. If he had used more imagination in small matters the wear and tear on his own nerves would have been considerably less. But his imagination and cunning with the old King never failed when it was a question of the heir to the throne. There Bismarck had to win – or so he believed – and nothing was too much trouble. It was on the larger issues that he slipped up. When he was setting the scene for the war with Austria he was so involved with manufacturing an unreal but thoroughly convincing situation that he left William's neighbourly feelings out of account. The whole project almost came to grief over the King's horror of fighting a friend with whom he had always been on excellent terms. When William told his minister that he had asked Fritz to write to Queen Victoria for help in stopping Austria making war on Prussia,[14] Bismarck had hard work to hide his rage and he cursed William's stupidity. He ought to have cursed his own. But no one was more adroit than Bismarck in retrieving a lost situation. A letter marked 'Secret and Confidential' was hastily despatched to Count Bernstorff in London; in it Bismarck explained his own schemes to his Ambassador, and the extent of his anxiety can be guessed by these uncharacteristic confidences. At the same time he recited a long list of Austria's iniquities against Prussia to the King, who, to Bismarck's relief, became incensed with that 'good neighbour's' perfidious behaviour. Now William was ready for the war and Bismarck had to restrain him – the time was not ripe. Unwittingly, just as Bismarck had got on to the right side of the King, Fritz had the misfortune to do the opposite. When he and his father had discussed the war together, Fritz had said he could never reconcile himself to a fratricidal conflict, and the King had agreed. Later when he believed Austria had betrayed him, he recalled that his own son had sided with the enemy. No wonder that Fritz said in despair that he could never do anything right with his father. Vicky's own position was painful. She had never seen Bismarck's machinations with greater clarity, and to be merely a passive observer was a severe trial for a woman of her fiery yet nervous temperament. Aching to do something, she wrote to her sister Alice assuring her that whatever happened her love would never change. She wrote to her mother, to friends in England, to her blind cousin George of Hanover, warning them to be careful and to remember that if this war should come she and Fritz were dragged into it against their will.

It was a good thing that Bismarck did not see these letters, or he would certainly have used them to brand Vicky as a traitor. As it was, he was preoccupied with preparations for the war, and Vicky's carelessness in not even bothering to send them by messenger went undetected.

*

For several weeks before the war with Austria Vicky could settle at nothing for long, and her lively imagination often took a sombre turn. She was certain that Fritz would be killed in the coming conflict. If that happened, where would she and the children go? After a war of this kind she could not be sure of a welcome in England. She could not tell what effect it would have on a close-knit family like hers. Nearly all her relations seemed to belong, by birth or by marriage, to South German royal houses who were bound to fight for Austria. Alice and George, dear Louis and his brother Heinrich who had come to the Neue Palais in tears when he learned he was to be compelled to 'take up the sword' against Fritz, Uncle Ernest and George of Saxony – they would all be in it but on the opposite side. If Fritz killed Louis, how could she face Alice again? How thin the glory of Prussia would sound to the one who was a widow.

In May Vicky made a brave attempt to write calmly to the Queen, to say she did not despair that the war with Austria might be averted at the eleventh hour. But she had little hope, for 'the chances of peace become smaller every day. Heaven help us, it is a most miserable wretched time'.[15] Touched by this letter, the Queen tried appealing to King William's mythical better nature not to allow brother to be arrayed against brother, and not to trust 'one man'.[16] 'One man' was the only person William did trust, however, and his reply to the Queen was merely a list of Austria's misdeeds which Bismarck had prepared for him, ending with the remarkable statement that his minister had no influence over him.[17] The 'wicked man' smiled as his master signed what his faithful servant had dictated.

For once in his life Duke Ernest was some comfort. He had learned from a secret source in Berlin that no one wanted war: 'neither the King, nor the princes, nor any other mortal, but simply and solely Bismarck, who conceals warning despatches sent by foreign powers so that the King learns nothing of them and knows nothing.'[18] Vicky wanted to send Franz Joseph a copy of the letter, but prudence prevailed. It was nothing new to be told that the King had become so lazy that he handed over everything – even confidential letters from relations – to his minister, who threw those he did not like into the fire.

If the war had to be, Vicky wanted it over and done with, but Bismarck was not ready. He was now seizing every chance to consolidate Prussia's position, and it soon became common knowledge that he was trying to tempt Italy over to Prussia's side. As so often with him, the deed was done before the rumour started. He jumped in and took advantage of Italy's anger with Austria for refusing to give her Venetia, and in April induced her to sign an offensive and defensive alliance with Prussia. Next month the King created Bismarck a count, calling it a reward for a faithful minister who had 'followed his king's governance with such great and distinguished circumspection'.[19]

Bismarck was no less successful at home. He cunningly won Liberal support by promising them, unasked, the universal suffrage for which they had been vainly clamouring. Vicky confronted Prince Hohenlohe and told him plainly that he had been taken in – the Liberals had swallowed the bait and soon Bismarck would be enjoying his fat catch. Why could they not see that he was going to use them for his own ends?

The waiting game was having its effect on Bismarck too. Everybody had a story to tell about him. He was as tempestuous as a prima donna, his nerves at fever pitch from sleeping too little, smoking too much and eating gargantuan meals late at night. The food and wine were so rich and plentiful at the Wilhelmstrasse that people fought for invitations to dinner. Those who wanted to curry favour sent him the pick of their cellars. It was said he would not have to buy a single bottle were he to live to be a hundred. But he had to pay for all this self-indulgence. He was now flatulent in the mornings, his head ached and every clerk in the foreign office felt the lash of his tongue. Vicky had been indignant when she had heard that his behaviour towards his employees was atrocious: he thought nothing of keeping them standing for hours while he smoked and read the papers. She was not surprised when she was told they were more afraid of him than of the King, who was often very kind to those who served him. Yet they licked Bismarck's boots and worshipped him in a way they would never do their sovereign. Moritz Busch said he stood before his master as though he were Jesus Christ.[20]

In Berlin society the stories made the man. The fire at which men loved to warm themselves was all the more exciting if it sometimes burst into a blaze, so long as it did not burn them. Vicky dismissed these people as of no account. But it was another matter when Fritz's father, the King, was among the rabble kneeling at the altar. Then she felt ashamed.

Vicky was pregnant again, and with so much talk of war she looked on her condition as a trap. Alice was in the same unhappy state. If only their children could be born in time! Vicky was far more worried about Alice than about herself. What would happen to this 'sweet sister' if Darmstadt was overrun by Prussian troops? There was no reason to think Bismarck would show mercy to the daughter of the Queen of England. It was a great relief to Vicky when her own baby, another Victoria, arrived too soon on the 12th of April 1866, her labour brought on by anxiety. Necessity forced her to get her strength back quickly; on the second day she insisted on being moved on to her sofa and before the week was out she was dressed and on her feet again. She thanked God that 'whatever should come' she could meet it fully restored to health.

Two months later the blow fell. One morning in the second week of June Vicky woke to the horrifying news that Prussian soldiers had marched overnight into Austrian Holstein without first declaring war. The baby was christened in a hurry. There was no time to wash and starch the fine lawn christening-robe all the others had worn, and so the child went to the font in an ordinary dress.

Next day Fritz left for the front. When he had ridden out of sight Vicky broke down completely. She flung herself on the bed sobbing 'Heaven help us'.[21] She was again in anguish a few days later at the death-bed of Sigismund, 'little Sigi', her twenty-months-old son, 'the apple of his parents' eye, my pride, my joy, my life', the one whom Vicky was certain would be a reincarnation of 'dearest papa', who was struck down with meningitis. Fritz had taken every doctor with him. Distracted, Vicky had the agony of watching her child die while she knelt helplessly by the cot. It was a pain she never forgot. Sigi's illness lasted exactly two and a half days, and on the 18th of June all was over.

Exhausted yet unable to rest, Vicky poured out her heart to the one person she knew would understand – her mother: 'your suffering child turns to you in her grief sure to find sympathy from so tender a heart so versed in sorrow . . . What I suffer none can know, few knew how I loved, it was my own happy secret. The long cry of agony which rises from the inmost depth of my soul reaches Heaven alone.'[22] 'My heart's best treasure was taken,' she wrote a week later, 'and the sorrow seems greater than I can bear.'[23] Yet bear it she had to, though in doing so she reached the brink. Many years later Vicky told her daughter Sophie (who was not born at the time) that she almost lost her reason after the death of this adored child. That she had a nervous breakdown is borne out by some of the extraordinary things she did. Lady Macdonnell, whose husband was at the British Legation in Berlin in 1875, tells a strange story of this period in Vicky's life. Lady Macdonnell became friendly with Vicky, and one day while at the Neue Palais she was shown an extraordinary sight. Acting on impulse Vicky took her guest to a locked room which turned out to be a gay nursery with a cot. Inside the cot was a beautiful baby boy fast asleep. It was the child Sigi in marble, fashioned by the hands of the demented mother whose heart hungered for her baby. Both women stood in silence for a minute looking at the cot that told one woman's tragic story.[24]

The child's death brought out an unexpected kindly streak in Queen Augusta. At nightfall on the 27th of June, after Sigi's funeral, she left Potsdam to make the dangerous journey to the front to tell Fritz that his son was dead.[25] Something in the face of the child's mother touched a chord in her cold heart, for she too had been fond of the little boy. Vicky was deeply grateful.

Stunned and beyond belief, with no one to support her, Vicky knew instinctively that she must try to stifle grief in work of some kind. When she looked at the faces of her children, pale and anxious with distress, she tried to gather her last shreds of courage. Others had endured as much, so must she. It says a great deal for her will-power and her strength of character that in spite of the state of mind into which sorrow had plunged her she pulled herself together sufficiently to undertake strenuous war-work. Hard work had been the Prince Consort's remedy for all ills – now his daughter remembered his words. The exacting jobs she forced herself to do saved her reason. She was pitiably thin, her eyes seemed to burn feverishly in her pale and pinched face, her tightly drawn mouth showed the tension in her nerves as though she was controlling herself only with difficulty. She could not shed a tear, the most unhappy condition of all. They gave her the new baby Victoria to nurse, but she could not enjoy this child for thinking of the other. But work had its effect when she dropped at night exhausted on to her bed, and sleep wiped out for a time the wretchedness of her heart: she no longer crept down the corridor to Sigi's room to press her face against his bed-clothes in agonised yearning to bring him back.

Shock had made her acutely perceptive in some ways, and she asked herself why she had been too blind to see where Bismarck's plans were leading even before King Leopold enlightened her. Blood and iron were bringing her father's dream to reality: '. . . the strong against the weak. Only force counts now, and everything must be achieved by force.'[26] Why was it only she and Fritz who saw the immorality of present-day politics? She had never expected to see the day when she would be glad that her father was dead, and that he had been spared the sorrow of seeing his hopes both achieved and destroyed. With great sadness she wrote to Fritz: 'for me war will ever be a crime, brought on by the irresponsibility and temerity of one man.'[27]

Yet grief had made her insensitive to many things. She felt nothing when Fritz won the battles of Nachod, Skalicz and Schweinschädel on three successive days. Nothing stirred in her heart when one of her dearest wishes was realised and Christian of Augustenburg married her sister Lenchen in the Queen's chapel, Windsor on the 5th of July 1866. The threat of war helped Queen Victoria to make up her mind about this landless and destitute prince – two daughters already on opposite sides showed her that great marriages with heirs to foreign thrones were becoming out of date. Besides, like her subjects, she was beginning to feel that enough British money was being spent abroad.

By the end of June Austria was cracking and on the 3rd of July the battle of Königgrätz brought the war to an end. Fritz's tactics in the battle made him a hero. The King, exultant with success, decorated his son on the field with the order 'Pour le Mérite', giving him the embrace of forgiveness in his delight. Without emotion of any kind, Vicky read the letter in which Fritz bitterly described the scene: 'We have beaten a very brave enemy, but what use are these losses, what use this victory . . . as things are we can only mourn.'[28]

Bismarck would have given him the answer.

Twelve days after the last battle peace was signed at Prague, and on the 24th of January 1867 Schleswig and Holstein were formally joined to Prussia.

*

Fritz came back from the war on a still, warm August day. Vicky knew that in order to reach the Neue Palais he would have to pass through a wood on the outskirts of Potsdam. Taking her children with her, she drove to a clearing and having left her ladies in the carriage walked slowly along a track that led to a bridle-path. She was very quiet, paying no attention to little Charlotte, who talked incessantly of 'papa' and called to her brothers who were running all over the place on some game of their own. So much had happened since she last saw Fritz, so much that was terrible and unforgettable in which she had touched a depth of suffering she had never known before. As a result she was frighteningly changed. Fritz was returning to a home where 'one was missing'. How would it affect him? He had written to say he too was not the same.

Vicky sat on a fallen tree-trunk to rest. Suddenly she heard the sound of horses. Looking up, she saw a thin bearded man riding towards her. At first she did not recognise Fritz, he was so altered. Although not ill, he looked unhappy and this seemed to have aged him. At the sight of his family Fritz sprang from the saddle and ran towards them; as Vicky watched him come she felt the comforting tears pour down her cheeks.

CHAPTER 13

A Patriotic Duty

SEVEN weeks at the front had changed Fritz in more than appearance. He had returned full of admiration for Bismarck's policy. When challenged by an indignant Vicky, horrified to hear him say 'It will make Prussia great', he defended himself by explaining that a united Germany must come before everything: Bismarck was acting very correctly; he felt obliged to support him, 'but I shall not allow myself to be led astray'.[1]

Vicky could hardly believe her ears; Fritz under Bismarck's spell! How effectively the famous charm had worked. Fritz's reiteration that he had 'not been won over' only confirmed her fear that he was more than half-way to the other side already. But if Bismarck had charm, Vicky had persuasion. By nightfall Fritz had realised his peril and was 'determined not to be led astray again'.[2] However, this account of Fritz's rapid change of heart in his wife's company does less than justice to the dilemma in which he found himself. He was liberal by conviction, but he was also a German, and therefore a nationalist. In the conditions of nineteenth-century Germany, liberalism and national unification were difficult to reconcile, and Fritz was torn both ways. Like many Germans then and later,* he found it far harder than a man with an English upbringing would have done to decide between them at critical moments. His seeming indecision played into Bismarck's hands at the time, and still makes it difficult to present him in as favourable a light as his principles deserve. Bismarck believed that his doubts about the war were due to Vicky's influence, and she may even have thought so herself, but their real cause lies much deeper.

Bismarck had returned from the war in triumph, his name on every one's lips. Though a civilian at heart, he was never again seen out of

*Adam von Trott's German Hegelianism, for instance, conflicted with his liking for England and his desire for peace, and he tried to hold on to both in the late 1930s and during the early years of the Second World War. His tragic death as one of those who plotted to murder Hitler on the 20th of July 1944 was in part the product of an indecision comparable to Fritz's (cf. Christopher Sykes: *Troubled Loyalty*). Vicky's 'conversion' of Fritz was not permanent, and in a more nationalist mood Fritz did some of Bismarck's work for him in 1870-71, and also held an ambiguous attitude towards the bombardment of Paris.

uniform, an eccentricity he excused with 'a shabby uniform looks better than a shabby tail-coat'. Yet it was Fritz's excellent generalship that brought the war to a speedy end with victory for Prussia. If he had not reached Königgrätz in time there might have been a different tale to tell, and, as a Prussian general said that night, instead of being hailed as a hero Bismarck would now be the greatest villain.[3]

Fritz had returned with stories of 'awful scenes' between the King and Bismarck after Königgrätz. Bismarck told William that he was not going to take one scrap of Austrian territory. This was not lack of vindictiveness (no one could be more vindictive than Bismarck when he chose) but far-sighted policy. It was essential to exclude Austria from Germany, but it was vital not to close all doors to a reconciliation; her co-operation in a subordinate position was of paramount importance to his schemes.[4] William could not grasp this fact – partly because Bismarck had not taken him into his confidence. To the King victory meant spoils, preferably land. When he heard that he was to have nothing, his face darkened and he closed his lips with the hissing sound which his family knew and dreaded. Bismarck was forced to do something he disliked: he had to ask Fritz's help to explain to his father why it was sensible not to be greedy. Fritz must tell the King that if Prussia were attacked – by France perhaps – Austrian support would become an absolute necessity. Furious with anger at the King's refusal to understand, Bismarck seized the dishes from the table and hurled them against the wall. As he listened, Fritz was reminded of the frequent quarrels between his parents; it amused him to see that the stubborn silence which so exasperated Augusta had the same effect on Bismarck, and that these two old enemies had one thing in common.

When Fritz explained the problem calmly, William capitulated with a bad grace. As a soldier he recognised Fritz's decisive part in the final battle, and because of that he 'swallowed the bitter pill and accepted the shameful peace'.[5]

Bismarck did not want to antagonise his master, however; looking round for a sweetener, his eyes fell on the little states which had sided with Austria in the war. Callously he gave these to William to do what he liked with. The old man was mollified, and when he had finished with them there was nothing left. George of Hanover's huge fortune was seized, ostensibly to form a fund (to be called the Welfen-Fonds) to assist the state. In reality it became a private fund of Bismarck's, used by him for corruption of all sorts and was soon known as the 'reptile fund*'.[6] Queen Victoria told Vicky that it made her hair stand

*Caprivi, Bismarck's successor as Chancellor, abolished the fund and restored the money to George's heirs. For a recent study of the fund see R. Nöll von der Nahmer's *Bismarcks Reptilienfonds* (Mainz 1968).

on end to think of good Hanoverian money being put to such a use. King George was turned out of his country and had to flee to England, a penniless exile. The other states fared no better: 'serves them right', said William. The financial pressure on them was ruthless (Hesse made bankrupt, for instance, and Frankfurt ordered to pay twenty-five million guilders in twenty-four hours, with the result that her distracted mayor hanged himself in despair) and their armies were halved – in future they would have to fight for Prussia. The King's reputation was damaged by such greed. *The Times* gave it great prominence, and the other papers did the same. Queen Victoria sent them all to Vicky to show the 'dear Queen', enclosing a copy of a stinging letter she had sent the King. But William did not care a fig for English newspapers, and dismissed them with a shrug.

Continuing her efforts to decrease Bismarck's influence over him, Vicky appealed to Fritz's feelings for the oppressed and contrasted their bankruptcy with Bismarck's bursting coffers. He was now a very rich man, since a deeply grateful Chamber of Deputies had voted him £60,000. With this money he bought his first large country estate – Varzin in Pomerania. Vicky thought this a monstrous way of making capital out of an unprovoked war.

The end of the war with Austria marked the beginning of a new phase in the persecution of Vicky and Fritz. By the autumn of 1866 Bismarck felt secure enough to infiltrate a large number of spies into the Neue Palais, many of them in menial jobs, and he did this so skilfully that in time he isolated its occupants from almost everybody they could trust in Germany. It was their punishment for Danzig and many other subversive activities, and it all began with the broken lock on Vicky's desk in October 1865. Bismarck's right hand man in this was Moritz Busch, the editor of the *Grenzboten*, who played henceforth a part in their lives which must not be overlooked. Busch found the agents, Bismarck vetted them and persuaded them that their degrading jobs were a patriotic duty. By January 1867 he had managed to place two of them in the accounts department of the Neue Palais. Not only the household bills but Fritz's entire personal expenditure had to pass through their hands. It was a blow to discover that the Prince Consort had made arrangements to keep Vicky's English allowance quite separate – so that no Prussian should lay his hands on it – but although Bismarck knew where it went, and often talked of the amounts Fritz spent at his tailor's, he never mentioned the huge sums of her own money which Vicky gave to Prussian charities. More than anything Bismarck longed to put a man of his own in the one position that would give him the whip-hand – Vicky's private secretary. It was little short of a miracle that he never managed to do this.

There were still a few friends left in the Neue Palais, among them the English-born Countess Blücher and the dry, incorruptible Count Seckendorff, who was just beginning his thirty years of faithful service in the household. Outside court life, Robert Morier and Freiherr von Roggenbach (the Prussian representative at Frankfurt) saw the perils and did their utmost to warn their young friends. Morier may indeed have painted the picture blacker than it really was in 1867, no doubt in order to frighten Vicky and Fritz into being more careful. Robert Morier knew Vicky's trusting nature and how she carelessly left correspondence lying about, and he implored her to be cautious, to write nothing incriminating in a letter or a diary except in cipher, and to put locks on everything – preferably English ones, so that they would not open to German pass-keys. He begged them to be careful what they said to each other when there was a servant in the room (in case he was a spy), and above all to distrust everyone.

But the isolation was a gradual process, and until it was too late Vicky and Fritz believed in the danger only by fits and starts. When Lady Ponsonby, the wife of the Queen's private secretary, visited Potsdam in 1868 she was appalled at what she called espionage and intrigue. She was astonished when Vicky later dismissed their humiliating position as something they had become used to,[7] remarking only that she blessed a kindly providence for providing her with an income of good English money, for 'if all else is taken from us we shall have that to fall back on'.[8] Matthew Arnold's surprise, when he dined at the Neue Palais fifteen years later, that Vicky asked him so many questions about the most commonplace things – so that 'she was like a woman who had been in prison for a number of years' – is evidence that the situation had worsened by then.

The facts were harsher than Matthew Arnold guessed. Vicky was not only isolated but went in constant fear of spreading the enemy's doctrine without knowing what she was doing. In 1867 she wrote a letter of infinite sadness to Robert Morier, the only one in which there is the slightest hint of resignation: 'Bismarck is such a clever man that one day I shall be preaching his gospel and not know it.'

In 1866–7 Bismarck was determined to close every door and guard every escape route. Before long, he had induced the King to tighten his grip, and after 1870 neither Vicky nor Fritz could move – even inside Germany – without the King's leave. This became so tedious that often they preferred to stay at home than be forced through the humiliating rigmarole of question and answer – Why? Where to? To whom? For how long? – as though they were convicts on parole. This not only had the bad effect of cutting them off from their friends (which was after all its purpose), but made special difficulties for Vicky, who refused to stay alone in Berlin or Potsdam when Fritz was away. If the King was taking the cure at some fashionable watering-place and Bismarck was at Varzin, she would risk the King's wrath by slipping away quietly to her aunt Alexandrine in Coburg or to Reinhardsbrunn, where she felt safe. Sometimes she was called to give an account of herself and sometimes Fritz was made to suffer, but it did not restrain her.

Bismarck could not cut them off from all intercourse with the outside world, of course, but his persecution did have the effect of making it more difficult for them to sift right from wrong. Some news trickled in from abroad, from Queen Victoria and the English newspapers. By 1867 she was certain that her letters were being opened and tampered with; only those sent by messenger were safe. Nearly ten years earlier, when Vicky had suspected Otto von Manteuffel's men of doing this sort of thing, she had used the simple device of sending her letters in her banker's mail-bag direct to Rothschild's in London. That method was known, and therefore out of the question.

Next to Vicky herself, Bismarck probably feared Robert Morier more than any one else in Germany. He knew Morier's astuteness, and he knew that Morier disliked his policies. He could not bear the feeling that Morier was always looking over his shoulder and putting obstacles in his way, and the fact that he was an Englishman only made things worse. Almost from the moment when he became Minister-President in 1862, Bismarck determined to break him. He knew that it might take time, but he did not lack patience.

His first chance to give a twist to Morier's fortunes came in September 1867, when the post of Secretary of Embassy became vacant. Morier was the most suitable person for the job. Vicky knew this, and very much wanted him to get it. She asked the Queen to use her influence: but (as over the Polish rising) Bismarck forestalled her. The last thing he wanted was a man of Morier's ability in Berlin, so he brazenly told Lord Stanley that Morier would not do 'because of the way he interfered in the internal politics of Germany'[9] – a piece of bluff which that pompous statesman fell for. Morier was passed over despite Queen Victoria's advocacy: 'the fittest person should always be chosen. Count Bismarck's objections to him are no disadvantage because Count Bismarck dislikes England and does not wish for any intimate relations between the two countries.'[10]

Lord Stanley was more in awe of Prussia's Minister-President than of his Queen – 'the objections are considerable', he could not 'take the risk'. So Morier was sent to servitude in Darmstadt.

*

Up to 1867 Bismarck let it be known at the Neue Palais that he was willing to be friendly – but on his own terms. He was anxious for it to be thought that he got on well with the Crown Prince, and when he remembered the King's great age he wanted to believe it himself. For one so quick and perceptive, he was remarkably slow in learning that the methods he used with the father would not work with the son. Because Fritz was quiet and unassuming, Bismarck underestimated his strength of character, blaming his own failure to master him not on the man himself, but on the determined will of his English wife. Quite aware of this, Vicky never allowed her manner towards the Minister-President to betray her in public. She behaved impeccably, finding a middle way, cordial without being effusive, distant without being stiff. This suited Bismarck, and he responded with outward friendliness, while never being able to hide from Vicky that he was suspicious of everything she said. He did not begin to understand her, yet she fascinated him. Here was a woman who expected to be treated on equal terms, who never let him take the lead in conversation, but attacked every point he made if she disagreed with it. Her grasp of the general principles of politics was extensive, and she could drive Bismarck into a tight corner whenever she cared to exert herself, while keeping perfect control of her temper – which was more than could be said for the Minister-President. When she wanted to wound or hit back, she knew exactly where to find his weakest spot.

Vicky's intellect has made such an impact on history that her charm has suffered in consequence. She was not beautiful – and since she entirely lacked vanity no one knew this better than she did – yet when she was happy and vivacious she could come very near it. Her eyes were always her best feature, and when they sparkled with fun she was irresistible. Bismarck was by no means impervious, and he hated himself for it. This was at the root of much of his behaviour towards her. However, after nearly nine years in Prussia (five of them under Bismarck's domination), few besides her family and close friends saw her gay and animated; she was often subdued in public, and then her expression could sometimes be severe.

A few months after the end of the war with Austria Vicky had sat next to Bismarck at an official dinner. He was very uneasy, for he had been told that she could not bear the sight of him since Prussia had occupied the territories of her relations.[11] Expecting a snub, he could not hide his surprise at Vicky's agreeable manner, and he found himself telling her of the improvements he was making at Varzin. He was astonished by her knowledge of horticulture and he listened attentively to her excellent advice on the right type of trees and crops to grow in that part of Pomerania. She promised to send his wife a list of flowers to plant, and some cuttings of shrubs from the Neue Palais gardens. She even teased him about his reported ambition to be a king or a president; Bismarck replied that he was spoilt for a republic and thanked God he was not destined to live like a king, but that he was 'till death the King's faithful servant'.[12] But in the cheerless light of dawn, when he could not sleep, he was furious that he had allowed Vicky to patronise him, since it meant that he had 'bowed the knee to England'. He had been the victim of Vicky's spell, and he disliked her the more because of it. As for Vicky, she knew exactly how he felt. When discussing Bismarck with a friend in 1869 she said that 'no amount of civilities could bridge the gulf between us'.[13]

*

1867 was a year of reconciliations. A turn for the better in her relations with her family put new heart into Vicky. In September she and Fritz went to the Rosenau in Coburg and there for the first time since the war met her sister Alice and her husband Louis of Hesse. The sisters flew into each other's arms, all differences forgotten. So much had happened since they last met. The war had brought great suffering to Alice. While giving birth to a daughter she had lost touch for a time with her husband; there had not been enough to eat, and when it was all over the Prussians had behaved offensively when they entered Darmstadt as conquerors.[14]

The Coburg visit was in the nature of a pilgrimage – 'Everything of dearest papa's must be seen'. Both sisters had the feeling that his approval hallowed their reunion. In his special shrine, the Ernest-Albert museum, the very stones the two young boys had collected years ago seemed to speak of love and peace. Together they prayed inside the mausoleum of a grandfather they had never known and would not have liked. They went to look at Stockmar's grave, and that most holy spot of all – the statue of the head of the family, 'so like, and so beloved'. All was the same, nothing was changed but themselves.

More trying was the prospect of a meeting with Fritz and Anna of Hesse and Fritz Holstein, all turned out of their homes by Prussia. Yet it passed off very well and Vicky was grateful that they did not hold their misfortunes against her but agreed that she had to do her duty as a Prussian princess.[15]

The courage given her by so much family support made Vicky determined to put an end to the quarrel with the Waleses, otherwise hurt feelings would soon be past mending. The wounds caused by the war over the duchies were healing, but the words of reconciliation were still unsaid. Vicky was afraid of a rebuff because her country had been in the wrong, but she longed to make it up all the same. Then without a parade of any sort the Prince of Wales managed it quite naturally. On the way to Russia for the marriage of his wife's sister Dagmar to the Czarevitch in November 1867, Bertie broke his journey in Berlin. Without a word being said the past was wiped out with Vicky's warm and welcoming kiss.

At last the Prince of Wales saw the helplessness of his sister's position, and how those closest to her only increased her difficulties – the stubborn but changeable King who referred everything (even skeletons in the family cupboard) back to Bismarck, the demanding egotistical Queen, always complaining of her health while doing her best to destroy it, and the incessant rows of the rest of the family. 'Poor Puss has not got a bed of roses' conveyed more compassion than Bertie cared to show. Vicky's explanation went a long way to put matters right: 'In Prussia I always take the part of the Englishman, and in England I stick up for the Germans.'[16]

In her position what else could she do?

CHAPTER 14

'Everyone preaches Peace'

IN the spring of 1867 Berlin society migrated to Paris for the Great Exhibition, sweeping an unwilling Vicky along with them.

Two things had happened to make her reluctant to join in the revelries that marked the pinnacle of Napoleon III's reign. She was pregnant again, and in this over-sensitive state she had heard criticisms of herself as a mother. The injustice cut her to the heart. Everybody knew that she adored her children (though in Berlin it was not felt to be a virtue) and denigrated her for lavishing time and attention on them to the neglect of her royal duties. Indeed she was often laughed at by the more unmaternal Prussian princesses, who could hardly distinguish their own children from those of their friends. Vicky did not care in the least how eccentric she was thought, provided that she managed to do her best for her children under trying conditions, but it was hard to hear that they were pitied for having her for a mother and that because of it 'they could not possibly turn out well'.[1]

If Vicky had been in better health, this story would have gone the way of the others – dismissed as of no importance. But this was her first pregnancy since Sigi's death, and the malaise that comes in the early weeks after conception reminded her poignantly of the way she had felt when she was carrying 'the one who had gone'. All her agonised longings for this adored child came flooding back to take away that common sense she had so much difficulty in preserving in Prussia. Where did these malicious stories start? Princess Catherine Radziwill says that some of them were invented by Queen Augusta's spiteful old maid Fräulein von Neuerndorff to get her own back on little Prince William by spreading vicious stories about his mother. It was Neurndorff who encouraged Augusta in the first place to have William with her as much as possible, in the hope that familiarity would breed irritation and rejection. When quite the opposite happened, and the Queen came to dote more and more on her grandson, her jealousy knew no bounds and she went about spitting venom and made Vicky suffer.[2]

The Paris visit came at a bad time, therefore, and was a penance that had to be endured. Everything fell flat. The magic of the Tuileries, the enchantment of the Seine, the Empress Eugénie's solicitude, Fritz's tenderness and the congenial company of her sister Alice all failed to lift her spirits. She could not fight her depression, and the sight of Bismarck's abundant energy destroyed what was left of hers. Detesting the crowds, the repetitive sound of Offenbach's music, the rich food and the hearty laughter, she entreated Fritz to ask the King for permission to go home. She was dressing listlessly for a ball at the Tuileries when his answer came – she must remain. It was the last straw. Ordering her maids to pack, she tore off her court dress, changed into travelling clothes, and left that night for Potsdam.

The memory of her agony at the loss of Sigi had returned to torment her. In this highly-strung condition she blamed Bismarck for her child's death and asked herself the unanswerable question – if there had been no Bismarck and no war, and therefore no shortage of doctors, would Sigi have lived? It was the knowledge that Sigi had never had a chance which made her savage. As in the days immediately following his death, she paced the rooms in the Neue Palais like a lioness that cannot reconcile herself to the loss of her cub, and in this mood she began feverishly to paint a portrait of her dead child from memory. This painting still hangs in her bedroom at Friedrichshof; it shows Sigi as a big fair-haired boy, holding the favourite ball which she kept for so long afterwards, gazing with large questioning eyes at the world he inhabited for so short a time.

*

Vicky's resentment against Bismarck was mounting. Soon after the end of the war with Austria he began to play a new and heartless game with Fritz: he took to sending him all over Europe on ceremonial duties so that he was seldom at home. At first Vicky was pleased that Fritz should represent the King abroad, because it widened the circles in which his worth would be recognised. But soon, as he was sent more and more often and for longer periods, she began to suspect that Bismarck had a deliberate plan with a two-fold purpose: to banish from Prussia as often as possible a man whose presence was a constant accusation, and to induce Europe to believe that Fritz was fit for nothing better. She was right, but she did not go far enough: there were two other reasons as well. The first – and the cruellest – was to keep husband and wife apart as much as possible in order to diminish the wicked 'English influence'. The second was politically sinister and much more dangerous, since it involved Fritz in actions which he never imagined were anything but innocent, but which were in fact only the reflection of Bismarck's devious intention to use Fritz for his own ends. Fritz's wishes were never considered. Although Bismarck's orders were frequently cloaked in fine words, they were orders and not requests, and Fritz began to resent them. If he looked like objecting, Bismarck would resort to the old trick that never failed – an appeal to Fritz's love for his father.

Bismarck knew that Fritz was delicate – in winter his colds sometimes turned into pneumonia or bronchitis, and Vicky often wrote of him as 'white and drawn' and worried about his coughs and sore throats – and that in spite of his age William was astonishingly robust, although a martyr to the fashionable hypochondria, and hardly ever suffered a day's illness. He was strong himself (in spite of his frequent complaints that he was unwell), and like all strong people he had little pity for those whose health was less good than his own. He showed none towards Fritz. He was barely out of bed after a bout of influenza when Bismarck sent him to Rome for the marriage of Prince Humbert to Princess Margharita of Naples in January 1869. Fritz would have enjoyed the wedding if he could have gone with Vicky, of his own free will and feeling fit, and did not guess that there was a political motive behind Bismarck's unkind insistence that he should go. Prince Napoleon ('Plon-plon') was to be at the wedding. Fritz and the French prince knew each other well and it was therefore likely that they would be seen together. This in fact is what did happen. The two princes had a long talk in which both promised to do all they could to preserve peace. They put it dramatically – one on the left bank, the other on the right bank of the Rhine, holding hands across the water.[3]

Fritz returned to the Neue Palais only just in time to hear his son Waldemar's first cry.

Vicky was unwell that autumn, and Fritz therefore did not want to attend the opening of the Suez Canal in November. William, on the other hand, longed to go, and was only reluctantly deterred when Bismarck pointed out the unwisdom of hob-nobbing with 'the riff-raff of Europe', Napoleon and Eugénie (his real reason being that he did not trust the susceptible William not to compromise Prussia). Fritz went out of a sense of duty when Bismarck dwelt solemnly on the heat of Egypt and the King's age. Bismarck saw in the Suez ceremony another chance of conciliating Austria and in Fritz (who hated feuds) the right person to bring it about, for he knew that Franz Joseph was to be at Suez and that the Emperor was much on Fritz's conscience.

As so often at this period in his life, luck played into Bismarck's hands: the result was more than he dared hope for. After the ceremony, group photographs were taken and one of them happened to include Fritz between Franz Joseph and Eugénie; the Empress, looking ravishing in a naval officer's cap with a blue veil and bright yellow leggings, her skirt looped high to show them off, had one elegant hand resting lightly in Fritz's arm. Bismarck could not have arranged it better himself. Chuckling at the impression of good will and peace it would give, he ordered the press to distribute the photograph to as many newspapers as possible.

Hardest of all to accept was Bismarck's harsh veto upon everything Fritz really wanted to do. Fritz had taken it for granted that he would represent his father at King Leopold's funeral on the 16th of December 1865, for instance, and had been angry and hurt when William had sent instead a member of his entourage without even telling him beforehand. Fritz had protested, saying it was 'right and proper' for one of the family to go, but the King blandly excused his high-handed conduct by saying he had 'reasons' for not wishing his son to leave the country just then, a statement he refused to amplify, since Fritz would 'hear all about it later on'.[4] As Fritz told Vicky angrily 'I shall know the reason when Bismarck has told him what to say'.

*

It was peculiarly frustrating for one of Vicky's temperament not to be able to hit back once in a while, but she refused to accept her lot meekly.

She was not always groping in the dark, however, and when chance offered she was more than a match for Bismarck. She had known for some time that he was determined to keep Robert Morier away from them and that if he thought they were meeting he would have Morier thrown out of Prussia on some trumped-up charge. Morier's friendship with the heir to the throne and his wife had in any case caused jealousy, as Lord Bloomfield (the British Minister) had noticed when Morier was first appointed to Berlin in 1859: Morier was often invited to Babelsberg and the Neue Palais, while the Bloomfields were asked only on official occasions or for formal dinners.

Now, ten years later, Vicky and Fritz had to be very circumspect for Morier's sake. They avoided meeting him when he came to Berlin and stopped inviting him to the Neue Palais; in fact it was thought that the friendship had cooled. The truth was just the opposite. Vicky had devised a plan whereby they could meet as though by chance in some fashionable watering-place. Spas had never been so popular, and in any case Morier was a martyr to gout. Thus when the three friends met by arrangement in Carlsbad in April 1869 they were not at all conspicuous. Every morning Fritz and Morier drank the waters together, and at night they all met in Vicky's sitting-room and talked politics. It was the blind leading the blind. Their conclusions were often mere guesswork, yet by pooling their information and sprinkling it with experience and common sense, one or other of them was often not far from the truth. They were baffled by a recent remark of Bismarck's, made during a chance encounter with Fritz on a railway-train: 'it is time to think again of the Empire.'[5] Morier had noticed how Bismarck had tied the hands of the countries surrounding France, and took the words to mean that he was contemplating war with Napoleon III. Vicky and Fritz, on the other hand, were inclined to believe Bismarck's recent assurance to Fritz that peace was an absolute necessity for Prussia, whose resources had been depleted by two wars. At the end of May they met Morier again, this time in Gastein. Morier was fuming, and feared that his career was in jeopardy. He was not only ignored by Prussia, but insulted by his own country. He had sent Clarendon a résumé of the April talk with Fritz, warning him that Prussia might soon be 'on the move again'. The Foreign Secretary had not even acknowledged the letter, but instead had resurrected the old subject of disarmament – 'a confused humanitarian idea' at which Morier had seen Bismarck smile contemptuously. Vicky sympathised with Morier. She too had suffered the same sort of humiliation. Time and time again her warnings had been laughed at, ignored and called exaggeration. She had become used to it, but when the Foreign Office ignored an envoy's warnings, it was quite a different matter.

Trouble would come soon enough.

Bitter experience had taught Vicky that once war-talk was in the air, war itself was not far away. Bismarck's popularity since his victory over Austria was tremendous. He was now firmly entrenched and sure of support for the first time. Whatever he did, the whole of Prussia would be behind him to a man. He had done nothing for the poor, yet his success had put them on his side. They did not see that the hope of better days was purely ephemeral and that the glory he talked of so freely was insubstantial. Vicky had gone one day incognito into the slum quarters of Berlin and had been astonished to hear the Minister's name shouted up and down the alley ways as little Bismarcks played in the gutter or chased each other in the streets. He had put his stamp on a new generation who had been born in his régime. He ruled Berlin society with a rod of iron, and a word or a gracious smile from him set the seal on success. Madame Charles de Bunsen confessed to Vicky that when she had first arrived in Berlin she was afraid she would not be accepted because Bismarck had disliked her late father-in-law, the Chevalier Charles de Bunsen. She had been introduced to Bismarck at a concert and he had been so pleasant that when she sat down even perfect strangers bowed and smiled at her.[6]

Vicky saw – not without a certain grudging admiration – that a lot of Bismarck's popularity came from his gift of making the most insignificant person feel important and specially needed for some vital part in the new Prussia. In June, when he made an inflammatory speech calling on Prussia to 'crush under a foot of iron every obstacle to the establishment of a German nation in all its splendour and power'[7] he was cheered vociferously, even the Liberals collapsing under the weight of his rhetoric. Vicky had read the account with disgust, calling the speech disgracefully inciting. She had told Fritz so when he returned from the Reichstag deeply moved. He had talked of little else all that evening, but Vicky had been stiff with disapproval. She was fighting her own private war with Bismarck – a war of nerves. She no longer knew whom she could trust in her own household, and this made her suspicious of the most trivial things. At some time since her first suspicions in 1865, she had begun the habit of placing objects on chests, tables and desks in a particular way, so that she could tell at a glance if anything had been touched while she was out. Already isolation was having insidious side effects. What was right, what was wrong? What was true and what was false? Most of the time they could not tell. That is why, when Fritz's cousin Prince Karl Anton of Hohen-zollern-Sigmaringen came to the Neue Palais one night in September 1869 – letting himself in by a secret side-entrance Vicky had once shown him – to ask for advice, they were afraid to give it to him, since they knew so little. The Prince brought startling news, which had perplexed and agitated him. It appeared that Marshal Prim, Prime Minister of Spain, was looking to Prussia for a candidate to replace the dissolute Queen Isabella who had been forced to abdicate in 1868. The Marshal (Karl Anton did not know that he was secretly hand-in-glove with Bismarck) had pinned his hopes on one of the Prince's sons – all of whom were officers in the Prussian army – but Karl Anton had declined the offer first for his younger son Frederick and then for his heir Leopold, whom Prim next approached. Under family law, Prince Leopold could not accept without the King's consent, but King William did not want to see any member of his family on the throne of Spain, and for the present was withholding his permission.

Karl Anton had come to the Neue Palais for help on two points that troubled him. Why had the approaches been made in secret? If his son was acceptable, why keep it quiet? And why was the offer made in such an underhand way? The greatest obstacle – as far as his family were concerned – was the fact that legitimate claimants were still living.

What did his cousins think?

What could they think? Not as much as a hint of what was happening had penetrated the high wall that surrounded them. Vicky considered Leopold and his wife Antoinette highly suitable, yet her reason told her that the Spanish throne was not worth the unpleasantness that must come from those whose place Prince Leopold would take. Her ignorance of the background made her uncharacteristically diffident – she could not 'trust my own feelings'. But talking it over with people whose opinions he could respect cleared Prince Karl Anton's mind of doubts, and by the time he left he wanted nothing to do with Spain.

There the matter might have rested as far as the Hohenzollerns were concerned, had Bismarck not let Prim know that he did not care for the alternative candidate – a member of the Wittelsbach family[8] who would use his position to draw Spain to France and Rome and might afford a remote rallying point for anti-national elements in Germany.[9] If a Hohenzollern sat on the throne of Spain, however, it would provide permanent means of keeping France in check.

Prince Karl Anton was approached again in January 1870. On the 12th of March Vicky wrote a letter marked 'Profoundly Secret' to ask Queen Victoria for her opinion. On Lord Clarendon's advice, the Queen refused to become involved in a matter where no British interest was concerned: 'it was not expedient to meddle.'[10] Vicky herself could see only the complications which would follow acceptance, and was convinced that Karl Anton should refuse to have anything to do with Spain. By the end of March he had in any case done so again, to the delight of Vicky and Fritz.

*

Vicky began to make plans for sending the children to Osborne while she stayed at home and prepared to have yet another baby. Her health had improved rapidly after Waldemar's birth. Her nervousness had disappeared, and it was as though Waldemar filled a little of the gap made by the loss of Sigi. She had enjoyed an untroubled pregnancy and was more cheerful because the Spanish business no longer hung over their heads. She sang light-heartedly to the children, and at night Fritz relaxed while she played or read one of her English novels aloud. She had time and inclination now to encourage Willy's talent for drawing. She began by giving him painting lessons herself, copying the method she remembered the Queen had used many years ago, letting him place his easel next to hers while they both worked at the same subject. One day she was watching him splash paint on to canvas when Fritz rushed in with the unwelcome news that Leopold had accepted the Spanish throne after all. It was another shock. Vicky was indignant when she heard that the negotiations had been going on for days, but that the King had let Fritz wait to hear the news only after it was made public. She knew whose work *that* was! She did not need Karl Anton to tell her either that he only capitulated finally because Prim never stopped putting pressure on him, chicanery of which the King knew nothing.

If the news created turmoil in the Neue Palais, it fell on Paris like a bomb-shell. A German on the Spanish throne, and Bismarck across the Rhine – France seemed encircled. The French went wild with fear and anger, and took up the Duc de Guiche's cry 'Leopold must resign'. Fritz gloomily prophesied war, saying that they might as well mobilise at once and have done with it. Vicky cancelled the holiday in England she had planned for August. For the sake of the younger children – the older ones knew too much already and were becoming frightened – she adopted a cheerful outlook, but talked all the same of 'Prussia turning the other cheek' and the 'horror of war in our own beloved country'.[11]

Fritz went to Berlin to find the King, and found Bismarck instead. He was in one of his most dangerous moods and quite deceived Fritz, as the entry in the latter's diary for the 13th of July 1870 shows plainly. Bismarck, he wrote, was 'right minded, searching for a loop-hole and hoping for the matter to be settled amicably . . . he gave me the impression of being taken completely unawares by the sudden and threatening turn of affairs in France'.[12] He had clearly forgotten something Vicky had remarked on more than once – that Bismarck was always pleasant and conciliatory when things were going right for him, hysterical and depressed only when they were not. Fritz should have remembered this and been on his guard. Before the day was over the clouds were to lift for a second time. Fritz – who had begun to curse his lot as bearer of bad news – had the great joy of telling Vicky that Leopold had resigned the Spanish throne once more, asking that it be given to Prince Ferdinand, father of the King of Portugal.[13] Vicky and Fritz hugged each other with delight.

They dined that night with the King and Queen. William ordered extra champagne, and they all solemnly drank a toast to Prussia and to peace. At last Vicky could enjoy her new baby, a daughter (Sophie) born on the 14th of June. She prayed that the little girl would never know the horror of war or the humiliation of having to flee from her country as an exile, leaving everything she loved in enemy hands. With relief in her heart she wrote in good faith to Queen Victoria 'everyone preaches peace and wishes for peace . . . but if the French are determined to pick a quarrel with us knowing (as they must) that they are well prepared and we are not . . . they cannot choose a better moment for themselves or a worse one for us'.[14]

Bismarck's spies had done their work well. Vicky was convinced (and Fritz had told her so often enough) that Prussia was unprepared for war, that if France should want to fight – and she was threatening it – things would go badly for Prussia. The truth, of course, was the exact opposite. While the scare was at its height Vicky was haunted by visions of herself fleeing to England with the children, as *The Times* had predicted in 1858. What would she have made of a conversation between General Moltke, Prussian Chief of General Staff, and Colonel von Stiehle, Prince Fritz Karl's chief of staff? The Colonel called on Moltke and was astonished to find him lying on a sofa reading a novel. Moltke burst out laughing. 'Everything is ready', he said. 'We have only to press a button.'[15]

*

The danger was apparently over, yet the atmosphere was heavy as though before a thunder-storm; Vicky, however, seemed the only one to be affected. What was the matter with her? Perhaps it was post-natal depression, to which she was prone, for normality seemed to have returned to everyone but herself. Fritz was cheerful again, the Hofmarschälle were back at their job of supervising repairs to some rooms in the Neue Palais where an old lady-in-waiting had just died. Yet Vicky was so uneasy that she persuaded Fritz to write warning the King that 'France has not done with us'. The King did not answer. Vicky was not tenacious for nothing – Fritz must write to Bismarck stressing France's overwhelming superiority in men and arms. The letter struck the Minister-President as very funny, since Fritz was a soldier, but it pleased him to have confirmation that he had successfully thrown dust in Fritz's eyes. Vicky clung to one ray of comfort that June. The Foreign Office in London had at last taken Robert Morier's warnings seriously – not because they thought Morier right, but because Morier's letter had been reinforced by a joint note from Lord Augustus Loftus, the British Minister in Berlin, and his predecessor Lord Bloomfield, who warned Clarendon of 'Bismarck's schemes for unifying Germany'.[16] The question now was – would England do anything?

Having drawn a blank in official quarters, Fritz next went the rounds of the Potsdam summer palaces, crammed with his relations as usual at this time of the year. No one knew anything, but each made it plain that they thought Fritz an alarmist. Next he went to Berlin. It was a city of the dead. The King was at Ems, Queen Augusta was in Coblenz, the Hohenzollern family were in the country and Bismarck had returned to Varzin, preparing – so it was said – for nothing more serious than a bumper harvest.

*

Moritz Busch and Lothar Bucher; who were in Pomerania with their master, have left a graphic picture of those days in the country just before the war. They show Bismarck as the congenial host, the family man, the squire riding over his estate by day and entertaining his guests at night by quoting his favourite passages from the Bible, while

Johanna Bismarck gave a recital of Liszt, Wagner or Brahms, the great man's favourite composers. Busch says that he was playing a waiting game at which no one was more skilful: waiting to see if England's friend Napoleon 'would fall into the trap set for him'.[17] Bismarck made no secret of his knowledge of the French Emperor's reluctance for war. On the 18th of June he told Bucher that if Napoleon had wanted a war any time in the last three years 'a pretext could always be found',[18] adding that he alone had prevented it, because Prussia had not been ready. Now all that was changed.[19] This was not mere boasting on Bismarck's part. He knew that the French people would welcome a war with Prussia and that until recently there had been equal chance of victory for both sides. But a war with equal chances was not what Bismarck wanted. He had to wait until Prussian generals had trained the armies and made them a force to be reckoned with.[20]

Vicky did not take these armies into account when she said that in the circumstances (Prussia's unreadiness) she was loth to believe that Bismarck wanted war. It was the same with Fritz. General Moltke had taken good care that Fritz would only see the unwarlike Bavarians in training. When the 'cruel shock' of war finally hit her, Vicky still believed Bismarck to be innocent. It apparently never dawned on her that if he had really been anxious to avoid war, he would not have stayed so long in Varzin but would have come back to Berlin to control the situation directly it became dangerous. She ingenuously accepted the account of the semi-official newspapers, which declared that he knew nothing.[21] How could she guess that it fitted in well with Bismarck's plans simply to let matters take their course?

In the end, events were hastened through France's blundering and Bismarck's skill in seizing his chance. Prince Leopold's second withdrawal was a diplomatic victory for France, and this at last fetched Bismarck away from Varzin and sent him post-haste to Berlin and into hysterics. But the French now over-reached themselves when they asked King William for a guarantee that Prussia would never repeat the offence.

The King, who was taking the waters at Ems, had already expressed his full approval of the withdrawal to the French Ambassador Benedetti, relief in his heart. He ignored the request for a guarantee. By removing all the civilities Bismarck now turned the King's statement (the Ems telegram) into a grave international snub, as the King immediately recognised when he read the altered version in the newspapers: 'this means war.' But soon, as Bismarck took care he should, he was complaining of French insults which he had not noticed at the time, and when war was declared on the 18th of July he was all for it.[22]

The King had been won over; now Bismarck turned his attention to

Fritz. When Fritz returned to Berlin, Bismarck went out of his way to treat him with great deference. When Fritz called on him, he received him at once (he usually kept Fritz waiting), adopted a paternal air, and in calm sorrowful tones asked Fritz to stay with him until the French reply arrived. Fritz was much impressed with the grave way with which he treated an irresponsible speech by Gramont. When Fritz asked him if he still felt hopeful of avoiding war, Bismarck shook his head, saying with sombre emphasis 'Gramont's speech has really put the fat in the fire. Nothing can be done about it now'.[23] He left Fritz with the strong conviction that here was a calamity he would rather have done without, but Prussian honour was at stake – 'the people would not have it'.[24]

A council of war was held in temporary quarters at Wildpark station. Fritz was summoned to it. By that time he had been so seduced that Bismarck had only to sit back and let Fritz do his work for him. He said to himself 'away from that wife of his, the Crown Prince is a different person. I must see what can be done with him'. The King was in one of his indecisive moods and talked of 'partial mobilisation'. But Fritz insisted on complete mobilisation and war, and when he announced the decision to the waiting crowds they yelled with delight and demonstrated support of Bismarck by lining the route to the palace with 'one unbroken storm of cheers that told more than words their enthusiasm for the coming struggle'.[25]

*

It was 1866 all over again. The baby Sophie was christened in a hurry, and Vicky's despondency made a mockery out of what should have been a happy occasion. Since Fritz was to be in command of the Württemberg and Bavarian troops, he asked the two kings to stand godfather. When the guests had dispersed, husband and wife prayed together in the little chapel over Sigi's grave. Their state of mind was terrible: convinced that they were about to suffer a frightful disaster, and afraid that death might soon separate them for ever.

CHAPTER 15

'The Watch on the Rhine'

WAR was declared on the 18th of July 1870. Unhappy and restless, Vicky found the waiting for news alone in the Neue Palais unbearable. The day had been stiflingly close, and towards evening when it was cooler she drove to Berlin through such dense crowds that she reached the Kronprinzen Palais only with difficulty. Everybody except herself seemed in the gayest mood. Through the open windows of her sitting-room she listened to the people in the street cheering, shouting and singing the familiar 'Die Wacht am Rhein', and marvelled that they were able to rejoice about a war which might, she felt sure, mean the end of Prussia and from which many of them would not return.

She could not bear to contemplate what would happen if Prussia was beaten. Too late she realised that she had pinned all her hopes on England's intervention 'to prevent a war we are forced into against our will'.[1] Now nothing could stop it: matters had gone beyond Queen Victoria's last-ditch appeals to Napoleon III 'to remember former happy days' and to King William's 'better nature'. As far as Vicky could see, there was nothing left but courage and the determination to keep Prussia free.

The danger drew Queen Augusta and Vicky together. Prussia's apparently dangerous plight awakened an unexpected tenderness in Vicky for her mother-in-law, while Augusta understood for the first time that Vicky really did love her adopted country. The two women faced the coming struggle with a solidarity they were surprised to find existing between them. Vicky begged Augusta to go to England 'should the worst happen', but the Queen shook her head: she preferred to die in her own country. They tried to draw the King into the circle of their new understanding, but William wanted none of their nonsense. He was impatient to get rid of them. Fighting was man's work and all he asked of the women was to keep out of the way. Already he looked ten years older, but his quiet dignified manner inspired respect. Generously Vicky added her own love and admiration to that felt for him by his subjects, to whom he had always been a kindly father-figure. She saw him once again before he left for the front. The sight of him, bent and worried, wearing a shabby uniform she had never seen before, went straight to her heart. As he walked shakily towards her, she was so moved by the sight of old age going to war that impulsively she knelt down and kissed his hand.

It was agreed between them that when Fritz knew the date of his departure, he would leave without telling Vicky in order to avoid giving her the pain of parting. At the time it seemed best for both. When it happened, with feminine inconsistency Vicky was distracted and broke down when little Victoria brought her Fritz's letter: 'He has gone without a kiss or a word of farewell and I do not know whether I shall ever see him again.'[2]

Vicky was not the person to waste time in lamentations when there was so much to be done. In the years between the wars, like a squirrel preparing for a long hard winter, she had collected many things that could be used in a hospital. Surgical instruments purchased at the Paris Exhibition in 1867 were used now to save the lives of French and Germans alike; mattresses, pillows, sheets and blankets had been bought on every English holiday, even the beds themselves. Her years in inconvenient palaces had taught Vicky how to put everything to the best use. She had seen enough of the dreadful conditions in the hospitals during the war with Austria to know that the chief obstacle to progress in nursing the sick was the ignorance of the nuns and deaconesses on whose shoulders the care of the wounded fell. Their methods were rough-and-ready, even unkind. In 1866 Vicky had started a training school for nurses in Berlin, and although recruiting had been slow the venture was not without good results. Vicky herself had designed a new type of hospital building ('you must learn architecture'), cheap to build and easy to run. Basically it was nothing more than a bungalow with a roof that rolled back, so that on fine days the patients could enjoy the fresh air without moving from their beds. The walls were to be painted in bright cheerful colours; the floors were to be of wood and each ward was to have a bathroom and drain. Most important of all, these hospitals were to be havens of hope; no longer would a wounded man be brought in and left to lie unattended in his own filth.

If it did nothing else, war developed Vicky's powers of persuasion and determination. It proved that she had a skill in handling people, a skill she had never really had a chance to use before. War enabled her to get to know the wives of the soldiers she met once a year when the Second Regiment of Hussars paraded before its Colonel-in-Chief. For a few shillings a week these women now came to Berlin town hall to cut and roll bandages under Vicky's personal supervision from linen wheedled out of Queen Victoria.

Countess Bismarck also organised a working-party, a band of elegantly dressed lady helpers who were horrified to find they were expected to share a table with 'low class' women, a thing Vicky did without giving it a thought. Every one of these women had a husband or a son (Countess Bismarck had two sons) at the front, but they preferred to gossip in a corner and pass remarks about the Crown Princess fraternising with the common people rather than 'lower themselves', as she did. Vicky was too occupied to notice. She now took difficulties in her stride. Countess Bismarck and her friends were occupying badly needed space, so they were firmly but pleasantly dismissed. This enraged Count Bismarck who felt that his wife had been publicly insulted and he stored it up to deal with another day.

The war brought out a feeling of patriotism in the most unexpected people. Duke Ernest turned up looking like an old and wrinkled toad and very much the worse for wear after an all-night journey from Fiume. He was eager to do his bit, but was too decrepit to be useful. However, Vicky sent for his wife Alexandrine to help in the town hall, as well as for Alice and her children. The Neue Palais was like a fortress, and Alice would be safer there than nearer the front at Darmstadt. Vicky bullied the young married princesses into ransacking their linen-cupboards for old towels, sheets and pillow cases, even persuading Fritz's lackadaisical aunt Princess Charles to give time and money for the wounded. She refused to allow herself to become upset by anything, not even by Countess Bismarck's explosive 'no bandages for the French from me' after she had heard Vicky explain that a wounded man was not an enemy, only a suffering human being.[3] The Countess said she would leave the French to die and good riddance to them.

It is not true to say that jealousy and malicious gossip drove Vicky from Berlin. She never meant to do more than start the work there. She was needed urgently in the hospitals near the front, and before the end of August she had left for Homburg. Her first sight of the town appalled her. It was pouring with rain and she was unprepared for the depressing sight of acres of water and mud. There were men everywhere up to their knees in wet slimy earth, making a railway, digging wells, laying gas mains and telegraph wires, doggedly undeterred by their difficulties, the epitome of German efficiency. After much searching she found several make-shift wooden huts doing duty as an army hospital. The wounded were lying on the floor, still in the uniforms in which they had been shot, waiting for gangrene and dysentery to finish what the *chassepots* had started. Only two of the doctors were qualified. They were helped by ignorant old women from the town, as filthy as the rags they put over the men to keep them warm.[4] These soldiers had been brought in to die and what struck Vicky as so poignant was that they seemed resigned to it.

Working on the assumption that everything is possible, Vicky ruthlessly cut through red tape and protocol, ignorance, prejudice and superstition. How near she came in those days to Stockmar's early assessment of her remarkable talents – 'she is almost inspired'![5] She refused to believe what she was constantly told – 'it can't be done'. Defeat and hopelessness surrounded her, but she would not give way to them.

Prussia was not a country to produce a second Florence Nightingale. There was no eager little woman with mild blue eyes, cropped hair and a will of iron, to appear suddenly at Vicky's side. Vicky would have been astonished to hear herself compared to that idol of her youth, yet the two women had much in common. Paramount in both was the fierce determination to alleviate suffering and save life, together with the belief that they could do it. Prince Albert's ruthlessness was re-born tenfold in his daughter now that she was faced with a task as gargantuan as Florence Nightingale ever had to contend with. Her rank hindered her at every turn: lies, deceit, craven obsequiousness, jealousy, flattery, insolence and broken promises without end were coupled with a longing to get this interfering princess out of the way.

She had no intention of going. Brushing aside anyone who stood in her way, she ordered the rags to be burnt, the men's wounds to be dressed, new beds made up and the walls and floors scrubbed with disinfectant. There was no time to be depressed, and she drew comfort and encouragement from the men themselves as they clung to her hands and skirts with words of gratitude that brought a lump to her throat. A tour of the hospitals on the Rhine – all shocking – did not dim her belief that they could be changed. 'If one has many a painful impression one is also given extra strength to organise the many willing hands that are waiting to be instructed.'[6]

Soon she became too popular. Bismarck had received a full account of Vicky's enterprises from his redoubtable countess. Making use of an artless letter from a proud Fritz, describing in delighted terms Vicky's activities and the people's growing affection for her, Bismarck prevailed on the King to order her back to Berlin. It was an outrage. Vicky angrily told Queen Victoria that she was being treated like a naughty child and punished without reason: 'I never make a plan that is not crossed by the King or Queen and they invariably disapprove of what I do – it is very disheartening.'[7] A possible reason for her recall suggested itself as soon as she reached Berlin, however. The place was in an uproar over an alleged indiscretion by the Prince of Wales, who was supposed to have told the French Ambassador in London that he hoped the French would win. The Berliners did not believe the

Prince's vehement denial of the story, and thought that it might explain why Vicky had been sent home.

*

The enforced rest was in fact a relief to a woman exhausted by long days and short nights. But Vicky was not to be stopped, neither by the King nor by Bismarck. Moreover, she had promised the men she would return. The battle for hospital reform was only joined, not won, and Vicky was not the person to leave a job half finished.

While Vicky rested she made plans for large scale re-organisation of the hospitals, a job that could only be done under peacetime conditions. She was asking herself how soon that would be, when suddenly the future looked bright for Prussia. Fritz had cut through Macmahon's army to win resounding victories at Weissenburg on the 14th of August and at Wörth on the 6th of September 1870. According to the English papers, which Vicky read avidly, Fritz was a hero, his generalship highly praised. The German press, however, ignored his exploits and did not once mention his name. It was the 'old familiar game' which Fritz had become quite used to. Vicky knew he did not care for himself as long as his men got recognition. He abhorred what he called 'blood-stained laurels', and would prefer to 'win recognition in works of peace'.[8]

It puzzled Vicky that even after Wörth Fritz did not once mention peace. In common with many others she took this victory to be the end of the struggle. Yet Fritz did not say so, although he had plenty to say about the King, who was behaving very strangely and was difficult to handle: touchy, depressed, crying bitterly without reason, a mere shadow of what he had been only a few months before. Fritz described for Vicky's benefit the lugubrious scene after Wörth when his father had decorated him with the Iron Cross: his hands had shaken so much that he only just managed to pin the Order on Fritz's tunic, prophesying as he did so the end of his dynasty and doom all round.

Medals were being won right and left – Vicky never remembered a war when they were handed out so freely – but the King could not be persuaded to give the coveted Iron Cross to any Bavarian despite Fritz's pleading that many of them had fought with great bravery. On the other hand, the King of Bavaria, wildly excited by the success of his troops, gave Fritz the unique order 'the Max Joseph medal' – unique because it was only awarded for victories, and the Bavarians had won so few.[9]

Napoleon III was captured and Berlin went mad. But the 'wonderful moment' was ruined for Vicky when she remembered that the Emperor's surrender meant that Eugénie and her son the Prince Imperial were in great danger, alone and unprotected in Paris. The story of the Empress's dignified flight from the capital (she showed no sign of panic when, through the windows of the Tuileries, she saw the crowds storm the Senate, screaming that they had done with Napoleon and his tribe, but coolly stripped off her jewels and left in an ordinary carriage) and her escape to England sent Vicky to her knees 'so thankful' for this old friend's safety.

Compassion drove out triumph when Fritz came face to face with the sick Emperor, who had fought 'honourably if ill-advisedly'. Fritz did his best to keep before him the example of the hard-working Prussians, so much more praiseworthy than the frivolous, immoral, conceited French. Once, however, he had enjoyed to the full the luxurious world created by Napoleon III and this he could not forget. Henceforth he and Vicky successfully managed to separate the imperial pair from the French people in their minds, telling each other that Napoleon was not to blame: ill, racked with pain, hardly able to walk, what chance had he had 'surrounded with bad and deceitful men'?

Some very strange facts were coming to light. Fritz had talked for a long time with Napoleon after his defeat, and had been taken aback to learn that he had 'never wished to have war'.[10] At the same time Queen Victoria had written to Vicky that Colonel Ponsonby had heard on good authority that 'Bismarck alone was responsible for the war', and that a 'trusted man' of the Minister-President's had been in Madrid before the throne was offered to Prince Leopold.[11] Vicky sent the letter to Fritz, who remembered that when he had met Robert Morier briefly and secretly in Speyer, on his way to the front, the latter had said 'this is a war between Bismarck and Napoleon.' Fritz had not wanted to think badly of Bismarck, since it made his job less distasteful if he could work amicably with the man. So far Bismarck's exemplary behaviour had dispelled all uneasiness, but his language grew more brutal as the prolongation of the war increased his impatience: he said that no more prisoners should be taken, exulted in the hanging of *francs-tireurs*, and encouraged the wholesale lynching of Moroccans and Algerians and the shelling of towns even after their inhabitants had hoisted the white flag.[12] Fritz remonstrated with Bismarck, who did not deny his words but remarked casually that such methods were necessary when dealing with people like the French. Then one day in Fritz's presence he ordered a 'handful of shells' to be thrown into towns which were slow to hand over the ransom demanded, to remind them who was master.[13] Fritz was mild and slow to anger, but the thought of such savagery sickened him. Suddenly he saw Bismarck's hard and cruel hand everywhere. He asked Bismarck to put a stop to such brutalities, but Bismarck only smiled and tried to calm him with 'what does it matter cutting off a year or two of life when there is a better one hereafter?'[14]

The foreign press was quick to report these stories* (Bismarck blamed Fritz for this 'treachery', scornfully telling his friends that Prussia's Crown Prince 'opened his doors to anyone who spoke even broken English'), and they created a bad impression in England. *The Times* made much of Napoleon's 'many good qualities' and even Prussia's undoubted champion – Queen Victoria – took up the cudgels on France's behalf: 'The King's name will stand higher if he makes peace now.'[15]

Bismarck would not hear of peace until France was completely crushed. Fritz did not press for it, since it was all he could do to see that Napoleon was treated decently. With great tact he managed to get the King to agree not to humiliate the ex-Emperor by making him surrender in front of his troops. The King, who quite enjoyed entertaining his royal prisoner, asked him with great civility to hand over his sword in private. In this softened mood King William sent Napoleon to a small but charming country house – Bellevue, near Fresnes – letting him know that he could join his family in England after the war was over.

---

*Bismarck's personal responsibility for the treatment of the *francs-tireurs* is difficult to determine. At the beginning of the war, Moltke issued a general order that non-uniformed combatants had no belligerent rights and were to be summarily shot. Both sides later became more brutal, and the conduct of the German troops deteriorated. As his nervous tension grew, Bismarck spoke with increasing ferocity, although he did not usually act as fiercely as he spoke (Howard, 378-381; cf. Richter, 192); Vicky later said of him that although he talked wildly he never acted foolishly. There was also friction between the military and the civil authorities, the former trying to exclude the influence of the latter, even that of Bismarck himself.

Fritz's conduct seems to have been perfectly proper. He enforced Moltke's order and recognised that it was essential, although he deplored the need for it. As early as the 28th of August 1870, he wrote at Ste Ménéhould: 'The arming of the inhabitants of this neighbourhood has already assumed greater proportions, compelling us to take energetic steps to enforce the surrender of all weapons. Single shots are fired, generally in a cunning, cowardly fashion, on patrols, so that *nothing else is left for us to do but to adopt retaliatory measures by burning down the house from which the shots came, or else by help of the lash and forced contributions.* It is horrible, but, to prevent greater mischief, unavoidable, and is consistent with our proclamation of martial law. Fortunately the infliction of such stern penalties does not lie with me, but with the Commanding Generals' (*War Diary*, 75-6). It is unfortunate that Field Marshal Montgomery (*History of Warfare*, 550), by quoting only the section italicised above, has made it appear that Fritz encouraged German brutality, whereas in fact he did his best to restrain it.

CHAPTER 16

'*Prussia's Finest Hour*'

T HE war was over but not won. Bismarck would not make peace until France begged for it on her knees, but Paris refused to surrender and prepared herself for a long siege. Yet as Prussian troops marched towards the French capital through a countryside rich with unharvested corn, there was not a man who did not feel he would soon be turning his horse's head homewards. Even Fritz, usually so inclined to look on the black side when deprived of Vicky's cheerful company, was not untouched by this optimism. As he travelled by easy stages to Versailles his thoughts were full of wife and children from whom each mile took him further and further away.

Ever since the beginning of the war Fritz had kept a careful account of the day's events, with descriptions of places and people, and sent it from time to time to Vicky for safe keeping. From this purely factual diary, written with great honesty and simplicity, Vicky came to have a better understanding of Fritz's difficulties than she had ever had before. From it she learned of the wild rumours that war creates, and how hard it was to tell the true from the false. On his journey to Versailles alone, for instance, Fritz not only heard that Gambetta had floated out of Paris in a balloon, and that consequently some rich Parisians were trying to make or buy their own balloons, but that conditions in the city were so bad that people were shooting each other down;[1] the King of Italy was correctly reported to have taken Rome (empty now of French troops withdrawn to defend the homeland) but the Pope was supposed to have fled to Fulda ('was this the end of that miserable régime of priestly domination?'[2]), while Fritz himself was said to have been taken prisoner.

Vicky felt herself right inside this war. Fritz had made it possible for her to follow each move, and even the military language was no longer a barrier. When she visited the battlefields many years later she was able to identify the exact spot where a manoeuvre or a battle had taken place and to talk about what happened on a given day with knowledge and intelligence.

Above all there was one thing on which husband and wife agreed completely – Paris must not be bombarded.

It was during the long and costly siege of the French capital that Bismarck had to face the fact that Fritz had a will of his own and could sometimes be as stubborn as his father. It enraged the irritable Minister to be thwarted by men he was pleased to call 'mere figureheads'. A blast or two of shell would get the siege over and done with. But Fritz would not hear of it. He insisted that Paris must be starved into surrender not only because this was more humane, but also and mainly because it was the militarily quickest and most effective method and would minimise German losses. Neither would give way, so there was deadlock, in which quarrels abounded. Sides were taken and Teuton was matched against Teuton in a battle of words more destructive than the sword. Everything from the highest to the lowest became the subject of dispute. The servants of the King, the Crown Prince and Bismarck decided with their fists who should have the best lodgings and the freshest meat, so that their masters' comfort depended on the fighting skill of their men. The disagreements at the top were so bad that Fritz even began to wonder whether they might not seriously damage the outcome of the war itself.

Fritz and Bismarck had already clashed over the orders to the troops about looting. Fritz refused to relax the rigid rule – no looting under any circumstances. Bismarck saw no harm in it and was willing to turn a blind eye. The generals followed Fritz, who was a soldier, rather than Bismarck who was not, so Bismarck told his cronies that the 'generals are under the thumb of their future king' because 'if they go against him now, when he is on the throne he may remember how they thwarted him and place his Field Marshals' batons elsewhere'.[3]

The war was being waged in Berlin too. The two wives supported their husbands. Countess Bismarck's caustic tongue spat venom: the war was being carried on from the safety of the Crown Princess's drawing-room, and the King and Crown Prince were so reduced that they allowed themselves to be ruled by their women; the two old hags, Queen Victoria and Queen Augusta, egged on by the young one, would not allow the infidel city to be bombarded and so the men were afraid to act. The Countess's own method of bringing the war to a satisfactory conclusion was simplicity itself – she would shoot every heathen Frenchman, down to the little babies,[4] and she wrote later 'I would gladly have thrown in many thousand fire-bombs, shells and mortars, until this accursed Sodom had been utterly destroyed for ever'.[5]

Vicky's war was being fought on two fronts – against Countess Bismarck in Berlin and against her own family in England. Both sides blamed her for what she could not help. Countess Bismarck 'did not

signify' – indifference which infuriated that matron – but Vicky was
hurt that her mother did not understand. Queen Victoria was angry
when Vicky said that Prussia's misfortunes were due to England's
neutrality – 'If we are annihilated England will be the cause'[6] – and
failed to hear the cry of panic when reason falls by the way. It was
panic which made Vicky write things she was ashamed of in cooler
blood. It was impossible for her family to understand her state of mind
at the outbreak of a war she fully expected would end in defeat for
Prussia. 'It seems all a horrid dream to me – my hand trembles and I
cannot collect my thoughts'[7] were words forgotten at Windsor, while
her more censorious remarks were remembered ('does not Bertie envy
Fritz leading such a useful life?'), discussed and brought up against her
when she was least able to defend herself. The family also forgot
how Vicky's sensitive feelings were anguished when not a day passed
but she had to comfort a newly-made widow or a broken-hearted
parent.

Vicky shirked nothing. Indeed a compelling force drove her to
those hospitals where some of the worst cases were taken, 'to encourage, to comfort and to hold a soldier's hand as he left this world'.
The young girl, who once was terrified at the mere thought of death,
was gone for ever. Death had become an all too familiar sight, as Vicky
closed the eyes of those brave men whose 'last battle was fought and
whose day was done'.

'What would papa do?' was becoming a question harder and harder
to answer, as her work took her increasingly far from Prince Albert's
world of peace and plenty. The stark realities of war left no room for the
academic questions which had obscured so much of importance for him,
and which had made her unaware of the bigger issues. For the first
time she accepted the fact that her mission was no longer a flawless
ideal. This realisation removed the veil that had hidden from her many
of the difficulties of her father's life as the husband of a Queen Regnant.
The pattern could not be quite the same as her own, but there were
similarities. Foremost among them was the prejudice against foreigners
which had inflicted so much pain on them both. In her own case the
prejudice had been all the greater because she had been the first non-
German to marry into the Prussian royal house, whose heirs before had
looked no further afield than their own country for a wife. It might
have made a difference to her handling of Fritz's relations if she had
realised how difficult this novelty was for them to accept. Her heighten-
ed realisation of the extent of her father's difficulties increased her
regard for the saintly patience with which dearest papa had borne his
burdens; but the realisation had been the product of war, and its main
result was to reveal to her how little bearing the dreams and specula-

tions of her father and his friends had on the harsh realities of the world in which she was now living.

*

Versailles soon began to suffer from the Gallic temperament. Vicky could hardly bear to read descriptions in Fritz's diary of the vandalism and stupidity which were devastating a corner of France that she loved and would always associate with her carefree youth. In a futile attempt to stem the enemy advance, terror-stricken soldiers wantonly cut down trees – including the famous avenue of elms – and needlessly burned down the beautiful palace of St Cloud. The stories that came out of Paris were blood-curdling. An English member of Parliament, Lord Ronald Gower, who was allowed into the city with a party of friends, told of wholesale executions and terrible sufferings in the poorer quarters where houses were pulled down without rhyme or reason, the bricks being used for ineffectual barricades, while the homeless families sat in the streets clutching their miserable possessions, exposed to the wind and to the rain which poured down without mercy that autumn. It was said that cats, dogs and even rats were eaten for food. There was dysentery and sickness without end.[8] As always, it was the women who suffered most, especially the women of the lower classes; queueing outside the food shops, scrounging milk for their children, working grimly to keep their families alive in a world which their husbands had so deplorably mismanaged.[9] Vicky begged Lord Gower to help her get food and money to them as quickly as possible. The consequences of such an act of mercy, should it ever be discovered, did not deter her in the least. All that mattered was that they should be saved.

Because the Parisians were starving, Vicky banished all luxuries from the table. The King and Fritz had already done so: they ate mainly bread and cheese, with only a little meat, and Fritz was often hungry. Bismarck, on the other hand, presided over a loaded table – Varzin ham and caviare, washed down with champagne – and when his tongue was loosened by drink he did not spare either Vicky or her husband: Vicky was enriching her relations at Prussia's expense, Fritz was foolish enough to behave 'as though Germany had never possessed a hospital before the Crown Princess arrived on the scene'.[10]

*

The question of the bombardment of Paris came to a head during the winter of 1870–71, when the city was besieged but would not surrender. Bismarck found restraint more intolerable every day, and went about muttering that he would not put up with it for another minute. One evening in late November when his nerves were more on edge than ever, he stalked up to Fritz while he was still dining, bowed ceremoniously, and asked with mock humility for his orders.

Vicky had urged Fritz many times to meet steel with steel, when dealing with the King or Bismarck. Fritz's continued failure to do this had been due to a form of diffidence that attacked him when defending himself or those close to him. Now that he was protecting hundreds of innocent people, many of them children, he found no difficulty in standing 'firm in my resolve', not to be brow-beaten into doing what he knew to be wrong. He met Bismarck's insolence with controlled passion, rose to his feet so that Bismarck should not have the advantage of looking down on him, and said firmly that he would rather give up his command than give the order to fire. Choking with fury Bismarck snarled 'and I am ready to assume it . . . I would then give one command only – commence the bombardment.'[11]

Fritz was a man of sensitive feelings, and humanitarian reasons were undoubtedly prominent in his mind when he first opposed the bombardment of Paris ('I felt a lump rise in my throat as I thought of the innocent folk who have to suffer . . . above all, the children who may possibly be hit', he wrote on the 8th of January 1871[12]). But these were not his main grounds for wanting to delay it. As a soldier, he knew how essential it was not to strike until sufficient guns and ammunition were in position to provide overwhelming force and make quick success likely; and although he wanted to inflict 'the chastisement she deserves' on Paris, the 'modern Babylon', and only 'grieved' about the destruction of art treasures,[13] his attitude was mainly determined by a purely military consideration: a premature and ill-prepared bombardment would mean heavy losses in the subsequent assault, whereas delay would prevent them*.[14] Mere civilians thought that Paris would capitulate at once 'if we just loose off our guns', but they were wrong. Bismarck argued for immediate shelling partly because, like the other civilians, he was both ignorant and blood-thirsty, but perhaps mainly because he feared that neutral intervention might deny Prussia the fruits of victory if Paris did not soon fall: bombardment, he believed, was the only way to ensure speedy capitulation.[15] The accusation that Vicky and Queen Victoria were behind the postponement 'exasperated' Fritz,[16] but his reasons for delay were quite different from theirs.

In the event, Fritz had to give way and open fire sooner than he wished. On the 17th of December 1870 he welcomed the decision for blockade and (later) bombardment of the forts,[17] but on the 31st recorded that, the King having decided on bombardment, he fixed the

*Like most other Germans, he had at first believed that hunger would compel surrender before bombardment became necessary (*War Diary*, 165, 169).

4th of January as the date for it, adding only 'May we not have to repent of our folly.'[18] By the 11th of January a week's shell-fire had had no visible effect on the forts, and he already feared that 'we shall be downright sorry for our mistake'[19] in not making fuller preparations. But Paris capitulated within three more weeks, and an armistice was signed with the French government on the 28th of January. Thus far the civilians turned out to be right.

Meanwhile troubles were multiplying in the Prussian camp. Inaction, over-eating and drinking and too much of one another's company were taking their toll of the staff. The princes in particular were behaving atrociously, and Fritz was at his wits' end to keep them from flying at each other's throats. Every day they rushed to the King with some complaint and were so jealous that they refused to mention others' acts of bravery in despatches. The generals were no better. Personal insults got so entangled in the war that Bismarck – whose temper was notorious – threatened to hang the lot.

When the quarrels overwhelmed him, Fritz would slip away to the great chapel in the palace of Versailles – lent by the heretics to their Lutheran brothers – to seek solace in singing; but even this had to be given up when the boy who pumped the organ fell out with the organist. Indeed the atmosphere was so charged that Fritz found it impossible to mention a subject that was very much on his mind – German unity. Yet he sensed that it was now or never.

He spoke about it to Bismarck one evening when he happened to find him alone. Bismarck did not receive the subject well, indicating, without actually saying so, that a Crown Prince should not interfere in something that was his alone to decide. He parried every question in order to put Fritz off, but Fritz persisted, and when he said 'the German people are more eager than I ever dreamed of' Bismarck feigned incredulity. When he asked if the princes could be persuaded to offer the imperial crown to the King, Bismarck replied indifferently that he had no idea. But the moment Fritz left the room Bismarck burst into a towering rage, shouting that the Crown Prince was obsessed with 'Emperor madness' and that he only wanted unification to aggrandise himself – otherwise why bring it up in the middle of a war?[20]

Fritz suspected Bismarck's real objections sprang from the fear that there had never been a better time for unity to be born of parliamentary action, and that Fritz might persuade the King to allow the Reichstag to take the initiative. His fear was well founded, for Fritz had a long conversation with the President of the Reichstag when he came to Versailles, and wrote that he favoured constitutional monarchy and free elections. If the Reichstag brought about unity, its power and authority would be firmly established.[21] Bismarck, on the other hand, wanted the unification of Germany to increase his own authority and had no desire to promote constitutionalism. He wanted to postpone all action about unity for the moment therefore, calculating that when they all returned to civilian life the King's present admiration for Fritz's military prowess would cool and that with it would disappear the best chance of a parliamentary rather than a dictatorial solution to the 'question of Empire'.

Nothing could remain a secret in the abnormal conditions of the German camp. To proclaim or not to proclaim the Empire became the burning question. Everybody was talking about it. Votes were taken, and immediate proclamation won the day. Bismarck saw he must act at once. Secretly he turned Fritz's plan to his own advantage.[22] His spies had told him that the King of Bavaria was in deep water financially. When Bismarck sounded him, King Ludwig would not commit himself, indeed the last thing he wanted was to elevate the King of Prussia. He did his best to wriggle out of signing the letter which Bismarck had drafted for him, offering William the imperial crown. He invented excuses: he was too ill to hold the pen, his head was too confused to think, he trembled so much he could not stand, he was too this, too that. But Bismarck's hot breath was on the back of his neck. He was deeply in debt and Bismarck had offered him a large sum from the Welfen-Fonds . . . He signed.

King William was thus made to believe a lie – that it really was the German princes who wanted the Empire and not the people, whereas the exact opposite was the case.

The unification of Germany was proclaimed on the 18th of January 1871 in the Salle des Glaces in the Palace of Versailles. The Prince Consort's dream was fulfilled at last, ten years after his death – but with what a difference! Fritz had to make the best of it. He had lost. He had been the first to propose immediate unification, and had planned to use the Reichstag to present it as a popular cause; Bismarck had nipped Fritz's plan in the bud and made unity seem the gift of the princes.

On the day itself the King was irritable, nervous and as changeable as the weather; what he settled one minute he retracted the next, so that no one knew what was happening. He went about spreading gloom and despondency so that the princes were afraid to rejoice when they heard the King mutter brokenly that he 'bade farewell to the old Prussia, to which alone he had clung and would always cling.'[23] Bismarck was as cross-grained as his master and spoiling for a row; he found one in the question of the King's new title. William wished to be styled 'Emperor of Germany' but Bismarck insisted on 'German Emperor' to emphasise the merging of Prussia in something greater.

When Bismarck asked him for details of his new escutcheon, William burst into such a rage that even his Minister was alarmed. The battle was at its height when the King, stalking into the Salle des Glaces with Bismarck at his heels, caught Fritz arranging a mock throne on a dais with the Prussian flag and the flags of all the princes behind. He ordered Fritz to take them down. The tension made Fritz feel so ill that he had to take a 'stiff dose' to get through the ceremony at all.

It was Prussia's finest hour, yet it was ruined by a melancholic King and a bad tempered Minister-President, who read the proclamation in an expressionless voice. When the new Emperor left the hall to the heartening strains of the 'Hohenfriedberg march', he passed Bismarck by without so much as a glance.

*

Vicky and Fritz's thirteenth anniversary fell a few days later, on the 25th of January 1871, and was the first they had spent apart. Vicky felt more tired than she cared to admit. Her work for the hospitals had been arduous and demanding, but it had filled her with a wonderful sense of achievement to know that at last she had done something concrete for 'the people'. But she had been worried that her work had taken her away so often from her children. She was always afraid of losing contact with them. The boys were high-spirited and in Willy's case wilful, and needed a father's discipline to keep them in order and to direct their energies into proper channels. If the war went on much longer they might become out of hand. When would Fritz be able to tell her that the end was in sight?

Queen Augusta was Vicky's only visitor on her anniversary. She turned up unexpectedly with the kindly intention of cheering her daughter-in-law's loneliness. Instead Vicky had to comfort her. She was angry and vexed that the King had not taken the trouble to inform her that Germany was now an Empire. She might never have heard of her elevated position had not her black footman referred to her as 'Empress'. Augusta's complaining tone was hard to bear, but Vicky understood now that it was her unloved and lonely state which made her flare up so easily and spoilt what harmony she could have enjoyed with her children. It was because of the pleasure Augusta took in Willy's affection for her that Vicky let pass many little grandmotherly spoilings that probably harmed an unstable child.

Twelve-year-old Willy was now a very important boy. To show her confidence in him, Vicky had told him of the proclamation while it was still a secret. She read to him that part of Fritz's war diary describing the stages leading up to the 'momentous event', forgivably playing down Bismarck's share and his grandfather's reluctance to accept the imperial crown. At all costs the King's hysteria must be kept from a child already too prone to it himself.

Willy found it difficult to believe that his grandfather's army had beaten the French. During the winter of 1869–70 he had been in Cannes with his parents and had seen French troops for the first time. The men, so strong and grand in their gay uniforms, marching in perfect time to the haunting notes of the buglers, looked invincible to the boy. When war broke out he was scared at the thought of his father fighting them. Wörth was not only a surprise, it was an intense relief. When that battle was over he had shown a remarkably intelligent interest in the war, following his father's movements on a map, measuring with compass and ruler the distance from Versailles to the centre of Paris and calculating the range of the guns accurately. He 'hated the wicked French' so vehemently that Vicky had to remind herself that he was only a child playing a game and that there was nothing to worry about because there was a bond of love and confidence between them that nothing could destroy.[24]

*

Bismarck had said that the Parisians would not survive a single day without strawberries. In fact they had already lasted a long time without bread when the German bombardment started, and yet it was still three more weeks before shell-fire and the despair of relief coming broke their resistance. They asked for an armistice on the 28th of January. Fritz strongly urged Bismarck to be moderate in his demands, but the Imperial Chancellor said nothing. He knew what he wanted and he meant to get it. This time William's thirst for 'spoils' was completely satisfied. Bismarck demanded Alsace, Lorraine and Metz, and France had to concede them to the victors by the Treaty of Frankfurt on the 1st of May 1871.

The war was over at last.

Fritz set foot on German soil for the first time for nine months on a day of pouring rain and howling winds, but nothing could damp his high spirits. At Bingen he caught his first glimpse of the Rhine, which a year before he had expected to be in enemy hands; now, after much suffering and privation, it was doubly dear: 'the watch on the Rhine had been truly kept.'[25]

At the Wildpark station on the 17th of March Vicky and Fritz were together again. Four days later the opening of the Reichstag took place in the White Hall of the Berlin Schloss. The scenes in the capital passed description. From the moment the victorious troops entered Potsdam on the 13th of June the people lost all restraint. Nothing could hold them back. They spat on the tricolour and trampled it under foot. The noise went on day and night without a break, until Vicky felt she could hardly bear another minute of it. She longed to go to England for rest and recuperation. She now had a special reason for getting the children away, which she had not even told Fritz. As she rode through the Brandenburg gate with Fritz at the head of his troops, she had happened to turn and look at Willy, who was following his father on his small dappled pony. The look of complete dedication on his face frightened her.

CHAPTER 17

'The Representatives of the Empire'

THE end of the war did not mean peace at home. Vicky had begun to fear for the King's reason; no one could do anything with him. He had returned from France in a strange mood, with his physical strength waning but his will as inflexible as ever. During the first mad days in Berlin the people expected His Imperial Majesty to show himself and to look happy when he acknowledged the cheers of the crowds. But he would neither appear nor smile. He was painfully touchy, upbraiding his servants for extravagance (the food was too rich and too plentiful) and Vicky for economy (she must drive with four horses and not two). He abused his son-in-law the Duke of Baden for daring to mention the events of 1848, shouting so loudly that his voice could be heard in the streets. When Fritz unthinkingly contradicted his father on some trivial matter, he became so furious that he almost drove himself into a fit. There had been one or two peculiar incidents during the celebrations that had quite worried Vicky. She had been waving to the crowds from a window in the palace when she had been horrified to see the Emperor wandering aimlessly in the street, wearing an ancient mess-jacket with the buttons undone. She had managed to get Fritz to rescue him from being trampled on just in time. Only the day before she had been about to lead her regiment in a grand review when she had noticed that instead of standing on the dais for the march-past, William had taken his place at the head of the troops. (In consequence, she was as confused as the princes, who did not know whom they were to salute, and as the Field Marshals, who were at a loss to know where to collect their batons.) He forgot to unveil the statue of Frederick William III; Fritz had to lead him like a child to the Lustgarten and then help him to raise his sword high enough to cut the cord. The cloths only fell with difficulty, but at last the marble face of the last King of Prussia was revealed looking down as though in amazement at the captured French flags and eagles lying at his feet.[1]

Vicky and Fritz called on the Emperor before leaving for the rest she so much longed for in England. He looked so feeble and acted so oddly that they wondered if they should go. But Vicky yearned to see her family again, and besides she had promised herself a visit to the Empress

Eugénie who was now living quietly with her son at Chislehurst. But would Eugénie receive her after all that had passed? Vicky had a delicate mission to perform: to return to Eugénie a beautiful screen snatched from the flames at St Cloud by a Prussian soldier who had asked that it should be given to the Crown Princess as a souvenir of the war.

So much had happened since she was last in England. There had been the wedding of her sister Louise to Lord Lorne, the son and heir of the Duke of Argyll, a marriage to a subject that had caused adverse comment in Berlin. There had been the birth of another son to Princess Alexandra – Alexander John Charles Albert – who had only survived a few hours. Old servants had died, and the Queen had written to say that she must expect to find everyone looking older. But Vicky noticed with relief that nothing was really changed. Sitting round the table in the Queen's tent at Frogmore they discussed Bismarck from every angle and Vicky had to listen to some 'sound advice' for the future. Fritz was very open with the Queen about his father, telling her frankly that Bismarck was Emperor in all but name and that he would not even be surprised if one day he declared war on England![2] When Vicky tried to persuade her mother to end her seclusion, saying it was a threat to the monarchy, the Queen promptly silenced her with the rejoinder that in Prussia, through weakness (on many sides) and indifference, it was already lost and that she had better take care, for soon it would be Fritz's turn for annihilation.

Queen Augusta wrote consolingly to say that Bismarck was having his troubles – although many were of his own making. He was almost beside himself with anger that the Emperor had allowed them to go to England, and jealous that Fritz was receiving acclaim that he considered rightly belonged to himself. England, he complained, had been pro-French during the war, and the English chose to forget that it was their cartridges and guns which had killed many a fine German.[3] He simply did not understand that one reason why Vicky and Fritz had been anxious to leave Berlin was to escape the celebrations and avoid being acclaimed so often and so extravagantly. They wanted peace and quiet, but naturally could not avoid publicity altogether, and Bismarck took it as a slight upon himself that they were so much praised in the English papers.

Bismarck was not the man to forget a slight, and he waited for an opportunity to retaliate. It soon came. Fritz was very run down after the war, and towards the end of his stay in England he contracted a mild form of pneumonia. On returning to Germany he went straight to·Wiesbaden to convalesce. The Emperor, who was himself taking the cure at Ems, wrote and told Fritz not to hurry home, an unusual and touching piece of magnanimity. When the two of them returned to Potsdam three weeks later the generous and fatherly gesture was explained. Bismarck had used Fritz's absence to throw him out of both the Council of State and the committee of military affairs to which he had recently been elected.

Fritz was quite stunned. Even the little he had gained and guarded so carefully since Danzig was gone. With one devilish stroke of the pen, Bismarck had reduced the future Emperor to nothing. There was no doubt about it now, he really was a 'mere figurehead' representing the Emperor in the drawing-rooms of foreign monarchs, the dilettante Bismarck had set out to make him. Fritz's biographer Philippson summed it up when he said 'Frederick William must appear everywhere as the representative of the Empire in whose existence and power he had less part than the smallest official or the least important officer'.⁴ The final straw for Bismarck had come in an article in *The Times* praising Fritz and referring to him as the 'constant friend of all mild and Liberal administration. When he succeeds the main obstacle to friendship with England will disappear'. Unknown to the writer these were just the words to herald a new wave of persecution against the heir to the throne, of which the expulsion from the Council was the first sign.

Without consulting his son, William made Bismarck a Prince in the summer of 1871, an honour he scoffed at but did not decline. A home fit for a prince went with his new rank, Friedrichsruh in the duchy of Lauenburg – Prussia's first acquisition under Bismarck's rule. It was five times bigger than Varzin, and it grew larger each year as the new prince bought all the land surrounding it. Vicky set foot there only once, during a tour of the area after some heavy winter flooding. She was overcome by the hideousness of the interior: dreary brown paint, massive ugly furniture, every nook and cranny stuffed with elephant's tusks, military caps, war trophies and the like, atrocious presents showered on the Chancellor of which he was inordinately proud. The house had once been an hotel and the numbers were still on the doors. Vicky could not understand how a man who had been inside Versailles and St Cloud could remain so unaffected by these palaces.

Compared with the Imperial Chancellor, the Imperial Crown Prince was a very poor man, since all he had was the allowance granted him by the state – which Bismarck controlled. Without Vicky's English money, they would have found it difficult to live decently, but he could convince no one of this. William, first German Emperor, entirely failed to realise that his heir could hardly make both ends meet.

Vicky noticed a change for the worse in Bismarck after 1871.* He

*It may have begun earlier. A fortune-teller had predicted that he would be

had always been a villain in her eyes, but had been redeemed in some measure hitherto by a charm which had not left her untouched. Since the war the villainy had increased while the charm had dwindled to nothing. Success had rendered its exercise unnecessary. Vicky noticed another change too. Bismarck was becoming more like his master every day in his rigid adherence to a fixed idea. Despite ample proof to the contrary, he refused to admit either that the Crown Prince had a will of his own, or that Vicky did not keep Fritz in chains and that he himself had rendered them powerless. He treated Augusta with less civility than he would have shown to one of his clerks, and the only reason he spared Vicky was the fact that as a pregnant woman she did not go into society after the war but stayed quietly at home awaiting the birth of her eighth and last child – a daughter – Margaret (Mossy) who arrived on the 22nd of April 1872.

While recovering from the birth, Vicky picked up the threads of many old friendships. Professors, painters, politicians and writers were invited to the Neue Palais again, among them a new name, Gustav Freytag the poet, historian and novelist who had been with Fritz in the Franco-Prussian war. She was at her best in the company of some of Germany's cleverest men, living in an intellectual circle far removed from the debilitating world of the Imperial Chancellor.

Vicky had begun to face the fact that the chance for Fritz and herself to 'do good' was becoming smaller: but the old urge to 'be of use' had not diminished. Her mother had come to lean on her increasingly with the years and Vicky was proud that here at least she was needed. The Queen wanted a painter to replace the dying Winterhalter and Vicky was able to recommend Heinrich von Angeli, whom she had met in Vienna in 1873. Von Angeli – who 'did not flatter' – appealed greatly to Queen Victoria since he would rather paint women 'with character in their faces' than their more beautiful sisters. Vicky had learned to handle delicate commissions with tact and discretion. In the summer of 1873 when the Shah of Persia, who was on a European tour, expressed a wish to visit Windsor, the Queen was not at all sure she wanted him to come. Would Vicky entertain him first and let her know what to expect? No one in Prussia had ever met the Shah, but everyone had heard strange stories about him. He was reported to be wonderfully handsome, to wear marvellous jewels and to be 'doing Europe' like a travelling circus, complete with harem. He turned out to be small and insignificant, but the eccentric behaviour was all too

---

murdered at the pinnacle of his career (Busch, i. 350), and his superstitious nature feared assassination from the moment a student shot at him in May 1866 (Eyck, 120).

true. Nevertheless Vicky felt his fascination and was quite captivated by his strange charm. The charm was so potent that her account made light of the wails from the orangery where the harem was housed, and of lambs driven in and supposed to be slaughtered in the bedrooms (a story that set the children wailing louder than the Shah's wives), while the atrocious table manners were hardly mentioned.

Vicky's opinion was needed not only on Persian monarchs but also on Russian princesses. The Queen was doubtful about Alfred, Duke of Edinburgh's choice of a wife. After having been successfully weaned away from his cousin Princess Fredericka of Hanover, he had fallen in love with Princess Marie, only daughter of the Czar of Russia. The Queen had heard that the Czar was anxious to see his daughter settled, since she had compromised herself with Prince Galitzine. But the sailor prince was not untarnished either: he had sowed his wild oats not only too well but too publicly, and if Marie had not fallen from grace, the Czar would never have consented to such a match. But Fritz was against it, saying that it was a poor prospect for Germany if northern Europe became 'populated with anti-German marriages'.[5] However, a romantic match appealed to Vicky, always so sympathetic to true love, and in her delight she telegraphed for von Angeli to come and paint her portrait, as a wedding present for Affie.

*

In 1873 Vicky found herself in the strange position of siding with the Roman Catholics against the Chancellor, who accused her of 'setting the seal of approval' on the centre (Catholic) party by her friendship with its leader Ludwig Windhorst. In fact Bismarck was well aware that her friendship with this charming and talented man had nothing at all to do with religion. She respected Windhorst's moral courage as a politician and his physical courage as a soldier as much as she applauded his loyalty as a Hanoverian to his wronged and deposed King. Eyebrows were raised at this 'strange friendship', yet all that was strange about it was that people of different religions but similar tastes enjoyed each other's company openly and in Prussia.

Vicky was by no means uncompromisingly Lutheran. There was much in Luther's doctrine that she disliked and rejected, as she did certain dogmas of the Roman Catholic Church. Academically, religion interested her profoundly, and she read all the important books of the day as they were published: Darwin's *Origin of Species*, Renan's *Vie de Jésus*, Strauss's *Leben Jesu* and Dr Colenso's (the deposed bishop of Natal) book disproving the literal accuracy of the Old Testament. Nothing in these works changed her conviction that man must be allowed to worship God in his own way and without persecution. She condemned Dr Colenso's critics because they invited scepticism instead of annihilating it. She herself favoured simplicity of worship and she found much in the Presbyterian Church that appealed to her: no bowing, no kneeling in prayer, yet deep reverence and a moving service. Dr Macleod, the head of the Presbyterian Church of Scotland, was among her favourite preachers, as he was among the Queen's. On the other hand, the ceremonial of the Catholic Church 'so full of superstition and prejudice' was abhorrent to her because it seemed to put a barrier between God and man. On a tour of Italy in 1862 she had attended Mass and observed these rituals at close quarters, and had seen nothing to change her mind. She wrote to the Queen: 'those who worshipped a golden calf were more civilised than those . . . Christians who must drag God down to their own wretched level.'[6] These strictures are not as severe as they sound when one remembers the youth of the writer and that she modified these views considerably with increased maturity.

Bismarck's attack on the Catholics – the Kulturkampf – may have begun from irritated nerves and boredom, but it was fed by hatred. He took a very personal view of everything and felt keenly that Vicky's and Fritz's friendship with Windhorst was meant as a snub to himself. With Bismarck little things often led to big ones. Before 1871 he had frequently praised Catholics in public, admitting that he considered the Roman Catholic Church one of the forces for order in the country: 'the Jesuit Order is a solid organisation; under certain circumstances it would be a force you can count on.'[7] At the time, between 1867 and 1870, Bismarck meant this as sincerely as he meant anything, but his opinions depended on the direction of the wind. By 1872 the wind had changed, and Bismarck was saying that Roman Catholicism and love of the Fatherland did not mix – the one turned the other sour.

The Catholics had returned seventy deputies to the first Reichstag in 1871 and were thus the second strongest party. Their success at once put their leader in an exposed position. The Chancellor's argument – that when their loyalties were divided, Catholics always put their religion first – had been disproved by Ludwig Windhorst in particular during the Franco-Prussian War. As Vicky was quick to point out to the Chancellor, the only thing that would drive Roman Catholics to rebellion was persecution; he ought therefore to avoid a policy of repression because it would unite Catholics of different nations as nothing else could.

Bismarck's answer was a series of sharp attacks in the *Grenzboten* on well-known Catholic and pro-Catholic figures, among them the Empress Augusta, who was openly accused of sending money to help refractory priests. In the same article much was made of Vicky's friendship with Windhorst, who, it was hinted, was hiding in cowardly fashion behind them both: 'the old and the young Tartar are hand in glove. The Catholics have nothing to fear while they are alive.'[8]

Unification had not had the effect abroad Vicky had hoped for. Until she went to England in the summer of 1872 she did not think that Bismarck was doing Germany irreparable harm. Vicky was dismayed to find that every hand seemed against her country, though perhaps not so much against the German people as against the German Chancellor, who was making himself a laughing-stock with his cry that France wanted a war of revenge. Indeed these opinions expressed her own fear that the next war would range England and France against Germany. Queen Victoria told Vicky frankly that she too was afraid of this because Germany's overbearing, violent, grasping, unprincipled Chancellor was driving England straight into France's arms.[9] Nor could the Queen forget Hanover – 'the cradle of our family is being swallowed up'. This resentment was behind her refusal to co-operate with Germany on any point: 'it does not mean unification was not right or desired by me and dearest papa . . . but not the dethroning of Princes and taking their private property and palaces.'[10] When Vicky received letters like this from her mother, she wondered what had become of the 'German side' of the family which mama had always been so anxious to keep up. English ministers were now saying openly what their Queen said so forcibly in private, and England's regard for Vicky's adopted country was fast slipping away. It was not until she went to Osborne in May 1874 that Vicky learned how Bismarck was spreading false rumours of France's intention to seize Belgium and how the Foreign Secretary construed this to mean that 'he intends to seize that country for Germany'[11] and saw this as a threat to England. A few days later she read a *Times* report of a speech in which the Prime Minister, Disraeli, likened Bismarck to the first Napoleon 'against whom all Europe had to ally herself'.[12]

*

Vicky had more to cope with than Bismarck. Willy had become very grand and revelled in the 'Empire', his new exalted position, and his beautiful new coat of arms. To Vicky's surprise, Willy's delight did more than anything to reconcile the Emperor to his new status. But Queen Victoria, when she heard of it, deprecated this Prussian pride and told Vicky how wrong it was that a fourteen-year-old boy should live in a palace and hold exaggerated ideas about the position of kings and princes. Willy must not think (but she was sure he did) that princes and princesses were of a different flesh and blood from the poor, the peasants and the working classes![13]

The breach between Willy and his parents had already begun by the summer of 1873. The boy had drifted apart from his mother especially – though as yet she did not realise it. He could not understand her at all, and he was especially bewildered and critical of her generous reactions when the exiled Napoleon III died at Chislehurst on the 9th of January 1873. His parents had been upset, and his mother had talked affectionately of this kind and amiable friend who had borne his misfortunes with such meekness. The teenage Prince was bewildered. He had seen his mother weep when his father had gone to fight this very man whom his mother now mourned with such a woebegone face. How could she regret the passing of this monster? Without the slightest feeling of disloyalty he discussed his mother's odd and inconsistent behaviour with his tutor, Hinzpeter, who in his dry way made Willy believe his mother to be unpatriotic in crying for one of Germany's greatest enemies. The boy now took all his personal problems to the man he called his 'friend', and not to his mother or father. This suited Hinzpeter very well since – through no fault of her own – Vicky always made him feel inferior; this gave him a chance to stand up to a woman he looked on as an enemy.

On the 1st of September 1874 Willy was confirmed in a flower-decked Friedenskirche, kneeling on a carpet Vicky had worked herself, little Sigi's white satin pall with its gold embroidered 'S' draped over the altar. Willy confidently answered forty prepared questions and listened to three long and tedious addresses without showing a trace of boredom – he enjoyed being the centre of attention. Vicky might have been at a funeral with her black dress and coat, only relieved by a white bonnet. Her eyes were red, and she was pale and held her hands together to hide their trembling. She had come straight to the church after a bitter quarrel with the Emperor, who had only that morning heard of her plans to send Willy away to school at Cassel, which had most unwisely been kept from him.

In the four years that had passed since the Franco-Prussian War, Bismarck had done everything possible to widen the breach between Vicky and the Emperor. All point of contact was destroyed, and William was constantly finding fault with his daughter-in-law. In his eyes she could do nothing right. The question of the education of the future heir to the throne was in any case bound to be a contentious one. William felt strongly that however many different points of view were voiced, the final word must come from him. Vicky's so-called effrontery had almost given him a stroke; for he said he knew that the idea of sending Willy to Cassel was hers and hers alone. In fact it had been

Hinzpeter's, but presented with such cunning to Willy's parents that Vicky really did believe that it was she who had thought of it first, and bravely accepted all responsibility.[14]

On the face of it the plan was admirable. The school was the most progressive in Germany; Dr Voigt the head-master was a humane and intelligent man, and his staff highly qualified. Cassel itself was a beautiful little town, not too populous, with a theatre and an interesting museum to both of which the boys were taken frequently. Willy and his brother Henry – who was to attend the Naval Academy nearby – were to live in a castle situated on a hill, with fresh clean air blowing round it. The boys were to be looked after by Hinzpeter and a military governor – whom the tutor loathed and soon got rid of – and to attend the school as day-boys.

Vicky's mistake was in not emulating Bismarck by preparing the aged Emperor well beforehand for such a revolutionary scheme, feeding the idea gradually to him until he believed it his own. But William hardly ever recognised Vicky's presence any more, and if she was disconcerted by his brusqueness he really had only himself to blame.

At first Bismarck was as furious as his master, but soon his annoyance took a philosophical turn: what did it matter which way the pudding was stirred, it would taste the same in the end. The Emperor was too old for philosophy, and he thundered that Willy should not go; he needed the boy to take part in reviews and manoeuvres and to be a prop to him at Ems and Baden-Baden, where his poor health kept him for longer and longer periods each year. This was exactly what Vicky feared, and her resolve was strengthened at once. The Emperor's roars ceased to hurt. She was doing what was right for Willy, and nothing could make her weaken now: 'We shall try our utmost with all duty and respect, but still adhere to what we consider right and necessary for our children', she wrote to her mother.[15] The day was won, but at what a cost!

The Prince of Wales (who had come for the confirmation) took a serious view of his sister's mistake and did what he could to smooth matters over, flattering the Emperor by describing his troops as 'magnificent and unbeatable', so that William became almost genial. To his surprise, the Emperor saw that there was no truth in the saying 'quarrel with one, quarrel with the lot'.

Three days later the boys left for Cassel. Vicky saw them off with tears in her eyes and relief in her heart. Until the last minute she had been afraid something would stop them going. Her confidence in Georg Hinzpeter is difficult to understand. While he had been under her roof she had clashed with him more than once, disagreements which the tutor invariably won; yet strangely enough the fact that he stood his ground only increased her respect if it diminished her liking. Some light is thrown on her reasons for this misplaced trust in a letter she gave the Prince of Wales to take back to the 'Queen. In it she asked for 'some mark of your appreciation for Willy's excellent tutor. . . . you know it has not always been easy for me, nor have I always been in the doctor's good graces, but he has bravely done his duty by the boys and devoted himself heart and soul to their education.'[16]

To use an expression of Queen Victoria's, a 'sort of blindness' seized Vicky where Hinzpeter was concerned. His obstinacy, the tenacity with which he held to his strange and twisted views, his belief that his destiny was to mould a future King of Prussia and thus play an important rôle in Prussian affairs through the ideas he was implanting in Willy's mind, his monk-like asceticism, all helped to confuse Vicky. She rated too highly those who would rather die than stretch a point, mistaking any willingness to compromise for the weakness which she abhorred.

Willy, she knew, was weak. She thought she saw in Hinzpeter all the qualities to counteract this fault.

*

After the two boys left Vicky was lonely, despite five other children at home. The empty bedrooms, the vacant places at the table, the ponies running riderless in the fields, a hundred 'little reminders', all made her heart ache. Strangely enough the Emperor became nicer as soon as the boys left. The reasons for this are obscure. Count Corti says that William 'appeared to sense that he had gone too far',[17] but it is perhaps unlikely that a man as old as the Emperor had suddenly developed a conscience about his behaviour to his daughter-in-law. A more probable explanation is that he thought he saw an advantage in detaching the boys from their mother. Moreover, like Vicky, he had perfect confidence in Hinzpeter. Even so, now and again, when he felt irritable he would remember that he had not been consulted and he would talk of Vicky's 'wanting to be rid' of the two boys. As for Bismarck, the Emperor's mellower mood towards Vicky did not please him. Determined to keep resentment alive, he seized on an incident in St Petersburg at Affie's wedding eight months earlier, in January 1874, which characteristically he had stored up to use on the right occasion. The right occasion had now come. Without a blush he told the Emperor a deliberate lie: that when in Russia Vicky had negotiated a secret alliance between that country and England. As evidence Bismarck pointed to a valuable diamond-and-ruby bracelet the Czar (who had got on excellently with Vicky) had given her to mark the occasion, but which the Chancellor said was for 'services rendered'.[18] The story spread like wild-fire through Berlin. The sight of this badge of sin winking wickedly on Vicky's wrist at a ball or a reception lent substance to the ridiculous story and kept tongues wagging. When the Three Emperors' Conference met for a second time in Berlin in the late autumn of 1875 he used Alexander II's genial behaviour to Vicky as further proof that he had 'got something out of the Englishwoman'.

The 'League of the Three Emperors' had met for the first time in Berlin in September 1872 in order to 'secure peace in Europe while recognising the Frankfurt treaty'.* Vicky had somehow reckoned that the Chancellor was bent on convincing the three ageing monarchs that this could only be done if England were crushed; to her relief the conference ended in nothing more than a repudiation of the clause in the Treaty of Paris (concluded at the end of the Crimean War) which debarred Russia from keeping warships in the Baltic. This was a small price for Prussia to pay for Russia's neutrality in the war with France.

*

In the autumn of 1874 Bismarck tried once more to raise the old spectre of a French menace. By Christmas it was plain that he had failed. The strain of the last few years was beginning to tell on him, he was in poor health and threatened to resign. The thought immediately gave Vicky fresh hope, which however soon faded when nothing more was heard of resignation. She was later to hear the threat so often that it became meaningless, and she soon realised that Emperor and Chancellor played the game of abdication and resignation simply to keep boredom at bay.

*The Treaty of Frankfurt, the 10th of May 1871, ended the Franco-Prussian War.

CHAPTER 18

'If the Emperor died tomorrow'

By 1875 Vicky and Fritz were spending much more time at Bornstädt.
What had begun as an occasional panacea for bruised feelings and
frustrations had become an essential escape from the realities of life in
the fullest sense. After Berlin, the peace, the hours in the fresh air, the
affection of the inhabitants and the simple family life all helped to
restore lost courage and a balanced outlook. Vicky often said that the
times spent on the Bornstädt farm were some of the happiest of her
whole married life. Everything about this compact little estate was of
interest to her and gave scope to the versatility of her talents. When she
taught her daughters to make butter in the model dairy, to skim the
cream and to make butter-milk, she really became for the moment the
farmer's wife she pretended to be. Far away from pernicious influences
she could get close to her sons – even to Willy, who forgot at Bornstädt that he would one day be Emperor and good-humouredly did his
share in grooming the horses and looking after the cats and dogs.

The peace of this rustic existence was roughly shattered when Fritz
returned from a trip to Potsdam one day in the summer of 1875 with
news of disturbances in the Turkish empire. For the next two or three
years, Vicky lived in fear of war and of Germany's participation in it.
Though her alarm was perhaps sometimes exaggerated, her insight
was sound, since with the outbreak of nationalist Slav revolts in
Bosnia and Herzegovina that summer, and in Bulgaria a year later, she
became involved in the Eastern Question for the first time since, as a
child, she had suffered anguish over the Crimean War. At first, it was
her old dread of war itself, combined with a paradoxical fear that
Britain would not act firmly enough ('England has no policy'), which
determined her, but later the fate of her own daughter Moretta became
entangled with Bulgaria's search for independence.

Russia stood to gain by the threatened break-up of Turkey, but
Austria was determined not to be left behind if any of the powers were
to annex Turkish territory. Britain's position in the Middle East, and
her route to India, would be endangered by a Russian advance, above
all by a Russian occupation of Constantinople; she made this clear
when she despatched a fleet to support the Turks in May 1876, and took

an increasingly firm line once the Turkish atrocities in Bulgaria seized the popular mind. Bismarck's principle (to which he remained constant throughout, in spite of occasional short-lived digressions 'typical of the irritable restlessness which stamped all his policy' at this time[1]) was to avoid committing himself to anyone but so far as possible to ensure that no settlement was made without Germany's foreknowledge and consent, and he was outstandingly successful in doing this when he presided at the Berlin Congress of June and July 1878. The Treaty of San Stefano, which ended the Russo-Turkish War, had weakened Turkey (thus harming British interests) by creating a large Bulgaria, had given Russia territory, and had denied Austria the annexations she sought; at Berlin, Bulgaria was reduced in size, Austria gained Bosnia and Herzegovina, and Turkey was strengthened but ordered to reform.

Vicky feared that war, if it came, would be more horrible than any Prussia had seen before, and that a trained soldier like Fritz would stand no chance against irregulars who stabbed in the back, tortured and took no prisoners. Fritz, on the other hand, was maddeningly calm: he would go to war if ordered to do so, but until then he would carry on as usual. His coolness made the anxious Vicky fly into a rage: if only she were a man, a British minister or the British queen, she would 'settle it all in five minutes'.[2] Her pen ran away with her in hastily written letters to her mother, who got a very bad impression from Vicky's entreaties to 'take Turkey' and 'take Egypt'. Unfortunately the Queen remembered that not long ago Bismarck had urged England to occupy Egypt (an anti-French trick which Lord Salisbury had quickly seen through[3]), and drew the conclusion that Vicky was in the toils of Bismarck, who had lately annoyed her by his abuse of England on the ground that she had seen no enemy on her soil since 1066. It was left to Salisbury to reassure the Queen that Vicky was not under Bismarck's spell; after a stay at the Neue Palais, he reported that Vicky still hated Bismarck like poison but believed that he sincerely wanted peace. Salisbury was right. Since 1871 Vicky had tried hard to convince herself that now that he had apparently achieved all he had set out to do, a period of goodwill to all men and all countries would follow: culture would replace guns, and a united Germany would lead the world in a drive for peace. The fact that the Chancellor spent more and more time on his country estates was proof to Vicky that she must be right about this: had not dearest papa once told her that an urge to till the soil did not go with an urge to make war? Bismarck's ill-health was another factor. Vicky had seen him at a reception soon after the Franco-Prussian war and he had looked in poor shape – he was gouty, with racking toothache and a twitch in his cheek so bad that he had to grow a beard to disguise it, and he was overweight and a bad colour.

Naturally Bismarck did not thank Vicky for championing him – any more than the Queen thanked her for trying to open her eyes. On the contrary, he wanted to get her out of Germany before the Congress of Berlin opened, lest she and Beaconsfield made mischief against Germany together. He went straight to the Emperor and told him in plain terms that if he was to handle the conference it must be 'my way and without interference'.[4]

William thus had to tell Fritz bluntly to take Vicky away while the conference was in session. They did not wait to be told twice. By the end of April 1878 they were in London, staying with the Prince and Princess of Wales at Marlborough House and enjoying matchless spring weather. Every morning Vicky rode in the park; she went the round of the exhibitions and artists' studios by day and to the theatre or opera at night, and felt young and gay again. But she discovered 'reservations' about dearest Alex's happiness.

A series of country-house visits was brought to an abrupt halt at Hatfield by the news of an attempt on the Emperor William's life. As they hurried back to Germany, Vicky desperately hoped that her father-in-law would not die. Hard years in Prussia had not coarsened her finer feelings; she did not want Fritz to come to the throne by the assassin's hand. She had felt the same repugnance when an unemployed youth called Hodel had tried to shoot the Emperor in May 1876. When the old man recovered she was so thankful for his escape that she went with him to the family mausoleum to offer thanks. This time it was more serious. There had been severe loss of blood and William was convinced he was dying. They brought him a Regency Bill to sign, and as he feebly made his mark he whispered that his son was 'only to represent me' and that the government was to be 'as before'.

Bismarck had done his work well.

There are many versions of this bedside scene, all highly coloured and all equally false. Vicky is supposed to have turned away, her face distorted with rage, while Fritz was scarcely more composed. There is no doubt that both were hurt at William's lack of confidence in his son, but they were under no illusions as to who was the real emperor and had expected nothing better. They realised the danger of Fritz's position: to the German people he was responsible for policy during the Regency; that is, for Bismarck's policy. It was an ugly situation, and Fritz did not like it but, like everything else, it had to be borne since no one round Bismarck or the Emperor ever treated him as though he were a human being with feelings to be considered.

William's recovery was remarkably rapid; he emerged after a month, greatly refreshed by the rest. His return put new life into Bismarck, who did not relish Fritz for master yet. His confidence returned overnight, and in June and July he galloped through the business at the Congress with unseemly haste, but not so fast that he lost sight of his objective – 'nothing should be done without Germany, but nothing that was done should commit Germany to any one antagonist against any other'[5] – and his attitude took a bullying turn as he carved up the Balkans with an utter disregard for the feelings of her people. When Vicky heard how he was behaving, she became suspicious. What was the Chancellor up to? Four months later, in November 1878, she knew. In a letter to Fritz (still deputising for the Emperor) Bismarck said: 'It would be a triumph for our statesmanship if we succeeded in keeping the Eastern ulcer open and thus jarred the harmony of the other Great Powers in order to secure our own peace.'[6]

So much for the 'honest broker'.

*

The shock of the attempt on his life was presumably the reason why the old Emperor now got it into his head that Germany had had a poor deal at the Berlin Congress, and that Fritz was to blame for it. Fritz tried to explain to his father that he had not said one word to Bismarck, who was entirely responsible and that he himself had been in England and had had no idea of what was taking place. The Emperor's answer no doubt seemed complete logic to him: 'I was ill and not expected to recover. Prince Bismarck is only human, it was but natural that he should try to make himself pleasant to the Crown Prince.'[7]

William's complete misunderstanding of the true facts shows how infirm he had become, and explains why henceforward he was more in Bismarck's power than ever. When in his father's room one day, Fritz discovered with a shock that he signed everything the Chancellor put before him without reading it first. Fritz remonstrated with him, pointing out the dangers of such blind trust, but the Emperor replied coldly 'Prince Bismarck knows what he is doing'.[8]

There were signs, however, that the German public did not think like the Emperor. They were beginning to be uneasy. Possibly Vicky and Fritz read too much into these signs, but it is true to say that Bismarck was so often in the country, and for such prolonged periods, that a generation was growing up which did not know him and took German unity for granted rather than (as Bismarck supposed) the particular achievement of one man. Memories were short and there was an increasing feeling that Bismarck was no more than a Prussian despot who lived on his rich estates and governed from his armchair.

One thing was certain: Bismarck had made the succession peculiarly difficult. Vicky worried about what would happen. If the Emperor were to die tomorrow, what would Fritz do? He had been deliberately kept back and was a greenhorn in statecraft. Bismarck held the reins tightly and he alone knew how to govern. If the Chancellor were also to die, what a legacy of abuses he would bequeath to Fritz. 'It would impose a hard and ungrateful task on a sovereign who would have to find and appoint the Ministers capable of re-establishing constitutional-ism in Germany.'[9]

In the years following the Franco-Prussian War nothing had been done to prepare Fritz for the throne; he was still jobless. Vicky and Fritz had never given up asking that he be given something useful to do, but Bismarck always avoided the issue and the Emperor would not listen. The Chancellor no longer pretended to care what became of Fritz – the more he effaced himself the better. Vicky sometimes felt that both he and his master were only waiting for a bullet to finish Fritz off, so that Willy could become the next emperor. They both certainly lent substance to this by the fuss they made of the boy and by the casual way in which they sent Fritz into danger-spots without precautions of any kind.

When Czar Alexander II was killed by a Nihilist's bomb in March 1881, Bismarck and the Emperor ordered Fritz to the funeral although they knew that he had received letters threatening his life if he went. Even the Prince of Wales urged him not to go, saying he had heard from the Czarina (his sister-in-law Marie) that things in Russia were in a chaotic state with riots, street-fighting and stone-throwing, and that all the royal family went in fear of their lives. But Fritz had to go. When he returned without a scratch Vicky greeted him as though he had been given back to her from the dead. Nevertheless, the anxiety of those ten days left a permanent mark on her.

*

In the same year a new menace, one Vicky had never taken into account before, appeared on the scene to 'threaten the bonds between England and Germany'. It took the form of Bismarck's elder son Herbert, whom his father had appointed Secretary of Embassy in London 'because he needed to have an agent he could trust in England'.[10] 'The young tiger has the temper of the old one' was less than the truth. Herbert Bismarck was in appearance a paler edition of his father, and he had all the faults of both his parents intensified tenfold. He was vain, cantankerous and humourless, without charm or good manners, and he possessed a tongue so vicious that even his friends found it hard to like him. There was nothing to which he would not stoop; Vicky warned the Queen that, far from London 'not taking to him', he would be loathed on sight, and that his unpopularity would do Germany much harm.

The appointment would have ruined Vicky's enjoyment of the mild autumn weather of 1881 if the Liberals had not had the good fortune to win the October elections with a huge majority. In some ways the good news wiped out the bad. Vicky hoped that Fortune was about to smile at last. But she had been caught too often not to view the Liberals' success with reservations. She knew several of their leaders personally, and her assessment of their character led her to think that they were not yet confident enough to inaugurate a bold policy of their own. Not all the right ideas in the world (and she believed they did have these) could compensate for lack of courage and the strength of will to stick to their principles. 'Much would be different' if they possessed a leader of the force and character of Ludwig Windhorst.[11]

Vicky and Fritz were determined on one thing – the Liberals must stop the disgraceful persecution of the Catholics (the Kulturkampf) which they had helped in some measure to promote, and which was weakening Germany and giving her a shocking reputation abroad. Tentative negotiations with the Vatican had raised their hopes but, since the negotiations were carried on over glasses of sulphur-water at Bad Kissingen between a papal nuncio made mulish with gout and a Chancellor distended with overeating, it was not surprising that they came to nothing. Vicky knew it was no laughing matter, but she saw the funny side all the same, and merrily told Fritz that the conversations would have been more successful if they had taken place at a gourmet's dinner of ten courses, a papal clerk ready with pen and paper behind each chair, the agreement signed over glasses of champagne.

Despite Bismarck's war-cry 'we shall not go to Canossa', the Catholics were far from crushed. With the appointment of Dr Falk as Kultur-Minister, Windhorst was constantly under fire as he vainly tried to stem the mounting hate that Bismarck stirred up against the Jesuits, whom he was threatening to banish from Germany. Behind the scenes, Vicky was striving to prevent such an unwarranted punishment, since many of the Jesuits were old and enfeebled, had never been out of Germany in their lives and could speak no other language. Vicky and Fritz discussed the best way of helping them in whispers in bed at night. The strain of these furtive conversations in their own home would have been unbearable but for Vicky's determination to treat the spying merely as a passing nuisance. With Fritz's tendency to melancholy, Vicky felt responsible for trying to make him look forward hopefully. But she spoke more often than she realised of 'when we are free', as though they were serving a prison sentence.

Fritz had been terribly downcast ever since his court marshal Karl von Norman had been dismissed by the Chancellor for doing Fritz a favour. Von Norman had arranged a secret meeting between Fritz and Eugen Richter, a prominent member of the Progressive Liberals. Vicky felt deeply the humiliation of not being able to protect their friends. If things had been as they should have been, Fritz could openly have seen Richter or anyone else he chose. Von Norman's going left only one man whom Fritz could trust – his secretary Count Götz von Seckendorff. How much longer would he be allowed to remain? Bismarck was constantly attacking him in the press and was patently trying to oust him. Seckendorff's strength lay in the fact that he knew what the Chancellor was about; thus forewarned, he took every care. But it was a cat-and-mouse existence between Seckendorff and Radolinski – the man whom Bismarck wanted to put in his place – with Bismarck playing the dog. No one defied the Chancellor with impunity. Seckendorff's brother took the rap. He was summarily dismissed from the Foreign Office after twenty years' service. Fritz interceded for him through Lord Ampthill (the former Odo Russell), the British Ambassador in Berlin, but nothing could be done.

Ever since unification Vicky had been trying to see the good that must be hidden somewhere in Bismarck and to make the best of their restricted lives. As time went by this was becoming harder and harder to do. By 1881 Bismarck was showing openly how much he disliked her. On the 28th of November he said bluntly that he had no intention of allowing Germany to be governed 'after the English fashion'. This was a direct warning to Vicky in her future rôle as empress, but she treated it with scorn. On the 7th of January he followed this with a declaration against parliamentary government: there must be one single central authority to deal with the danger that obsessed him – a war on two fronts (in fact, this danger had just been reduced by a secret treaty with Austria which the cynical Prince Gortschakoff called 'a reward for the help Bismarck gave Austria in the Berlin Congress', saying that 'the honest broker acted for a big commission'). So much for the Liberals' hopes! Vicky angrily asked 'Why does not Prince Bismarck say "as long as I live both the constitution and the crown are suspended"?'[12]

Vicky was tormented by Bismarck's lack of flair in domestic matters. The new tariffs on corn made her hot with anger; to her, protection of any sort was short-sighted policy and might drive the workers into socialism, since all it did was to make the poor man's loaf dearer. Vicky was a fervent supporter of the workers, the 'humble people' from whom one could 'learn so much'. If Prince Bismarck was the expert on agriculture he claimed to be, why did he not tax industry, in other words the rich, fast-growing middle class? Vicky knew the answer well – in the next war these were the people to supply Bismarck with the guns and ammunition he would need. Under the new tax the man who owned the cornfields grew fat while the farm labourer grew thin, ate less and so worked less well.[13]

What would happen if they came to the throne overnight and unprepared? The corn laws would have to be swallowed along with a lot of other indigestible material.[14] And their succession was not a remote possibility any more. Baron von Roggenbach ('our dear old friend') was at Ems in July 1883 when the Emperor fainted while taking the waters early one morning. He fainted again the same evening. The incident was hushed up, but the Baron thought it only right that Vicky and Fritz should know, so that if William died suddenly they should 'be prepared and stand on firm ground'.[15] Despondently Fritz asked Vicky where such ground was to be discovered. He had just heard some unfair criticism of himself: 'he does nothing but enjoy himself, travelling all over Europe to every gay function, leaving the poor Emperor to do all the work.'[16] He was deeply hurt, although Vicky implored him to take no notice 'since everybody says things against everybody else in Berlin'.

Yet by now there was perhaps more 'firm ground' than he realised. In the summer of 1882 Bismarck had learned with dismay that a large part of the Reichstag was ready to support the Crown Prince when he came to the throne. This following was composed of the Secessionists (radical Liberals) and the Progressives, who together formed a liberal-radical union which later took the name of Deutsch-Freisinnige Partei and was sometimes known as the Crown Prince's party.[17] Bismarck immediately saw a danger he must meet with speed and determination. He sought for a wedge to drive between Fritz and 'his' party, and believed he had found it in the colonial question; later he was to curse his own stupidity for espousing a cause which was to bring him so many headaches. The Kronprinzen Partei was not in favour of colonies. Bismarck had heard that Fritz thought colonies an absolute necessity, if Germany was to remain great. The Chancellor's naïve idea was that by favouring colonisation he could show that Fritz was in opposition to his own party, so that his following would disappear. Moreover, colonies would provide a pretext for a clash with England at any moment in the next reign, if one were needed.[18]

Bismarck's intelligence and his reading of the situation were for once badly at fault; by 1882 he was no longer the man he had been. It was not Fritz who favoured colonies, but his son Willy, who – now twenty-five and longing for action – was beginning to make his parents' position still more difficult through the close friendship he had struck up with Bismarck during the last few months.

*

Even as a child, during the Franco-Prussian War, Willy had shown traits of character markedly different from those of his parents, but he had grown still more unlike them with the years. When he left school for good in May 1876, Vicky immediately noticed that he had not improved. All the old faults were still there, but they had become greatly intensified, and Vicky feared for the future.

It may have been because she was preoccupied at the time with the Turkish troubles that Vicky did not use the right mixture of firmness and tact towards her difficult eldest son. A quarrel flared up between them at once, unfortunately (since there were bigger issues at stake) on a trivial matter of good manners. Vicky was fond of having friends over for tea and tennis 'English fashion' in the summer, and one afternoon she caught Willy rudely swinging his racquet against the behind of a visiting diplomat (perhaps it was pure chance that he was English) whom he had caught tying his shoe-lace. Afterwards Vicky saw the funny side, but Willy felt he was too old to be reproved and sulked for days. Sulks were not the whole of it. Willy was argumentative and opinionated, contradicted his father rudely and was often insolent to his mother, calling Marx's *Das Kapital* 'drivel' and Vicky a socialist for reading it.* He had no good to say of the school (although Vicky felt certain he had been happy there) criticising the headmaster, the staff, the boys and the curriculum, complaining that the 'tone' had not nearly enough 'Germanism' in it, opinions corroborated by Hinzpeter who encouraged Willy 'to speak out'. The tutor too had only changed for the worse: whenever Vicky and Fritz saw him he pontificated in an arrogant and dictatorial fashion, while Willy listened with deferential respect. Vicky noticed that he treated her as a social equal and an intellectual inferior, and longed to laugh, it was so silly; and yet it made her uneasy too.

Willy was packed off to Windsor in the autumn – without Hinzpeter – to be 'cut down to size' by his grandmother. He returned with an exaggerated admiration for the Eton boys, who had somehow managed to give him the impression that they were 'inspired with the idea of making Britain great'. Willy's occult powers had told him that these boys dreamed of 'new colonial conquests, of exploring unknown regions, of expanding British trade and of acting as pioneers for the Fatherland'.[19]

*Vicky's interest in the book was so great that she wanted to know what the author was like, and persuaded a friend to make his acquaintance and send her a report.

A clash with his grandmother was barely avoided by the Queen's forbearance in trying to 'make allowances', and by Willy's one saving grace: he could 'take hints'. And he got plenty of these. The day before he left, the Queen gave him a piece of sound advice – he must mix more with ordinary people from whom he could 'learn'. For the Queen had learned something from Willy that surprised her very much – that in Prussia a boy in his position never met ordinary people, and that the only time Willy had done so (at the school in Cassel) he had not cared for the experience. Vicky was quite as alarmed as Queen Victoria – where would it all lead to? On the 26th of January 1877 (his eighteenth birthday and coming-of-age) it led to another 'great parade of pride' as Willy, in his Guards' uniform, displayed the highest decorations Russia, Austria and Italy had to offer. Queen Victoria made him only a G.C.B., so Willy sulked and forced his mother to ask the Queen to change the Bath for the Garter with the lame excuse that 'Willy would be satisfied with the Bath but the nation could not'.[20] With the Garter strapped round his shapely leg, Willy drove to the palace to receive the Prussian 'Black Eagle' at a simple family gathering, of which, however, grandfather and grandson made as much as possible. Watching the ceremony, Fritz sent up a silent prayer for 'improvement', that his son should be 'true, upright and honest'.[21]

A short period at Bonn University followed – merely a way of filling in time for Willy until he could become a soldier. He was a bad scholar; his head was too full of dreams of making the army the greatest in the world, to match the throne which Bismarck had made so great since his birth.

Vicky clung to the faint hope of Willy's ultimate redemption: after Bonn, after the army, after marriage – one day he must be better. But Willy was not the only one of the children to give trouble. Princess Charlotte, 'little Ditta', was at seventeen a pretty, pert girl who criticised everything her parents said or did, and was very much under Willy's influence. Her defiance was probably no more than a natural wish to go her own way. She forgot that as the daughter of the Crown Prince she had to pay the price of privilege in discretion and tact, and that because she was always in the public eye every nonsensical word she uttered was taken seriously and repeated. To Vicky's enemies, however, Ditta's nonsense was exactly what they wanted to hear: 'even her own daughter says . . .'. The Empress Augusta indulged Ditta almost as much as she did Willy, and the girl was clever enough to sense that although Augusta did not actively encourage criticism of her parents, she did not rebuke it. In the summer of 1877 Charlotte fell in love with a college friend of Willy's, the hereditary Prince Bernard of Saxe-Meiningen. The romance began on the switch-back railway built on the Pfaueninsel (the 'Isle of

Peacocks') in the Havelsee to amuse Charlotte's aunts and uncles. Bernard had been standing behind Ditta's seat, when Willy – who was working the controls – accelerated for a joke, terrifying Ditta so much that she clung to Bernard for protection. After that she imagined she was in love. She and Bernard were married on the 18th of January 1878. Ditta looked like a 'fresh little rose' in her wedding dress, but Vicky, marvelling at her daughter's cool and almost calculating attitude to marriage, realised that times had changed and that girls were no longer reluctant to leave their mothers but would nowadays walk down the aisle almost brazenly unruffled and leave for the honeymoon without a backward look. Vicky attributed the good temper of all the old aunts and uncles to the tact of the Prince of Wales, who moved amongst the guests at the reception, showering charm like confetti, singling out the sourest old ladies for special attention, complimenting the middle-aged spinsters on their looks and ogling the pretty girls. The Prince even called on Bismarck – too ill (so he said) to attend the ceremony.

The affection between Vicky and her eldest brother had increased with the years. The Prince of Wales's gay and light-hearted attitude did much to keep Vicky's own sense of humour alive. The Prince had made Homburg his special playground, and Vicky would often stay with him there, trying unsuccessfully to keep his penchant for pretty women in check.

Vicky went to stay with the Princess of Wales at Sandringham in March 1879 after attending the wedding at St George's, Windsor, of her brother Arthur, Duke of Connaught to Princess Louise, youngest daughter of Prince Frederick Charles of Prussia and of that Marianne whom she had befriended during her early years in Berlin. Vicky was still suffering from shock following the death of her sister Alice from diphtheria the previous December. Alice's whole family had first contracted the disease, and her youngest child (the four-year-old May) had succumbed to it. Less than three weeks later, Alice herself was dead. Now, no sooner was Arthur's wedding over, than the same dreaded disease suddenly summoned Vicky to the sick-bed of her own eleven-year-old Waldemar in Berlin. Waldie too died in only a few days. He had been the cleverest and most affectionate of her sons, and she had always claimed him to be 'so like dearest papa'. In reality, he was not in the least like the Prince Consort: strong and boisterous, he was full of fun, an extrovert who delighted in harmless practical jokes and whose charm saved him from 'many a skelping'. Now diphtheria claimed him as suddenly as his cousins. Waldie's death opened up a new train of thought – why did everyone accept diphtheria as inevitable? What caused it? What could be done to make others safe from this deadly peril which seemed to have such a special significance for her family? The death-rate was even higher in Germany than in England, and it was an accepted thing that at least one from every household would succumb. Alice's whole family had been affected, yet Waldie was an isolated case. Vicky had held him in her arms to ease his breathing, had kissed him as he died, yet she had not caught it. But Alice had received the 'kiss of death' from her son Ernest and soon she too had gone. Vicky could think of little else: she would not accept things as they were, there must be an explanation, a preventative, a cure. She sent to England for books on chemistry, biology, even on the construction of drains. In the silence of the long nights when grief stopped her from sleeping she devoured book after book, hoping to find a clue which could lead some English scientist to a practical solution. She must do something, otherwise Alice, May and beloved Waldie had died in vain; it was a 'cause' as sacred as her mission, but medical science was not able to solve the mystery for another fifteen years. She was on the right track herself, however, in her conviction that diphtheria was connected with the deplorable condition of the drains in every country. Many years later, when building her house at Kronberg, she lavished so much money on the sewage system that Herr Ihne the architect came to regard it as one of his client's freakish obsessions.

When Vicky had recovered a little from Waldie's death, she went incognito to Rome and wandered forlorn and lonely round the art galleries and churches, empty pursuits when the heart is leaden. For the first time Italy gave her no pleasure; not an hour passed that she did not long to go home, but Fritz insisted on her staying. When she returned to Berlin, she heard that her daughter Charlotte had given birth to a girl – making her a grandmother at thirty-eight and the Queen a great-grandmother at fifty-nine. Birth following so soon after death could not assuage her wound, however, as her friends hoped. She felt only outrage that another human being should be given life when 'my own Waldie has been taken'.

*

After a period of comparative peace Vicky clashed with the Emperor again in the winter of 1879, on behalf of Willy of all people. After a mild flirtation with his cousin Ella of Hesse, Willy had fallen deeply in love with Princess Augusta Victoria of Schleswig-Holstein-Sonder-burg-Augustenburg, known in the family as Dona, daughter of that Fritz Holstein whom Bismarck had ruined and whom he had referred to ever since as 'that idiot of Holstein'. For a haughty prince like Willy, heir to the greatest throne on the continent, the match was a poor one. Dona had nothing except a handicap – Berlin society did not consider the Augustenburgs sufficiently aristocratic (*ebenbürtig*).[22] But the very fact that Willy was determined to marry her in spite of it raised him in his mother's eyes: 'It did him great credit.' She had never thought that with him love could overcome pride, and she was touched.

Despite Queen Victoria's approval of this romantic match, the Emperor would not hear of it at first, nor listen to Vicky's pleadings. However, he soon relented when he heard that Bismarck was indifferent now that Duke Frederick was dead: to Bismarck, one girl was as good as another, so long as she was not an Englishwoman or chosen by that old hag the Empress from Weimar. Fortunately Dona was the type of woman Bismarck approved of and could understand, the epitome of the German *Hausfrau*, all her actions predictable. Bismarck predicted one the moment he set eyes on her – she would soon be eating out of his hand. Indeed Dona was so docile and so adoring that Willy's mother was afraid that she would never keep his 'bad tendencies' in check. But both Queen Victoria and Vicky felt strongly that the marriage was 'a kind of atonement'.[23]

Once the Emperor had given his consent, there was nothing to wait for, so Willy and Dona were married on the 27th of February 1881. The marriage ceremony was so long and so dreary that Vicky was drained of all vitality long before it was over, although the eighty-three-year-old Emperor and the seventy-five-year-old Empress remained fresh throughout.

There was a reason for Vicky's fatigue. Love had not softened Willy, indeed the courtship period had been impossibly difficult. Dona's abject adoration had increased Willy's tendency to show off, and he became ruder and more demanding than ever, without a scrap of that charm which sometimes makes such faults in the young more bearable. Vicky's cry of irritation 'This son has never been really mine'[24] was not strictly true, as she well knew. Before he went to Cassel and came completely under Hinzpeter's influence there, Willy had often been affectionate and good-tempered and had enjoyed his mother's company, holding her hand when they drove together, asking her advice on books and playing peacefully with the younger children whom he now teased unmercifully. There was only one person who mattered to William, someone to whom even Hinzpeter had to take second place: Bismarck. He venerated the Chancellor above every one, while in return for admiration the great man flattered the silly boy shamefully. Ill-health did not keep him from Willy's wedding.

*

Vicky's belief that marriage must strengthen family ties took some hard knocks from Willy and Dona. Charlotte was another whose conduct helped to shatter this illusion. She led the life of a social butterfly, bored, discontented and quite lacking in occupation or purpose, but talked glibly of 'my freedom' and much resented parental rebuke now that she was a married woman. Vicky redoubled her own efforts to bind her family together, trying to see good in them all and hoping that as they got older and had children of their own the married ones would improve, that Willy's heart was in the right place and that Ditta did not mean half she said. Her own silver wedding fell on the 25th of January 1883, and with family union in mind she revived an old Windsor custom, the once popular *tableaux vivants*, in which all the children could take part. They proved disastrous. The rehearsals were marred by quarrels, and the performance itself was a fiasco: Ditta (still looking like a 'fresh little rose' despite motherhood) tried to steal the limelight, Dona missed a vital cue as well as wearing a dress so tight that it made her pregnancy too obvious. Fritz was the only success, and he looked handsomer than ever in a gorgeous costume.

The Prince of Wales was to be present. Vicky had asked him outright if he would speak to Willy about his disrespectful behaviour. Willy had become impossible since his marriage. He treated his parents like strangers, never moved without a large suite – so that Vicky and Fritz had no chance to speak to him alone – and behaved as though he was already Emperor. Vicky attributed this new attitude to an unwise proclamation of Bismarck's in the autumn of 1882, defining Willy's duties ('to secure tuition in the management of the office and the examination of despatches') at the Foreign Office, which he had joined without their knowledge. Fritz had written to Bismarck to say that it was 'unsafe' to allow such an inexperienced young man to see Foreign Office secrets, but Bismarck contemptuously threw the letter into the fire. In his memoirs Willy calls his father's letter 'offensive',[25] forgetting, it would seem, that Bismarck's action in the first place was extremely insulting to the heir to the throne and that in consequence his father was completely justified in what he did.

Every morning Willy walked, 'with a ridiculous air of importance', the short distance from his palace to the Wilhelmstrasse, where Bismarck (flattered by Willy's admiration) treated him like an Emperor and not the callow youth he really was.[26] Soon he was lunching with the great man, who uncorked his finest wines to flatter his young pupil. After they had eaten, Bismarck would stretch out on the sofa, while Willy was 'allowed' to fill and light the Chancellor's pipe.[27] They would then spend a pleasant hour in conversation.

Bismarck had not expected Willy to be so inquisitive, and did not care for some of his pupil's questions at all. Willy had colonies on the brain, and despite any number of hints, he refused to allow the talk to be directed into other channels. Why was Germany's colonial expansion so slow? Why was Germany not taking her place alongside Britain in this field? Secretly Bismarck at this time shared Vicky's view that the colonial sugar-plum might turn into a bitter almond, but he puffed his pipe while Willy rattled on ('speaking out', for Hinzpeter had told him that he must let the Chancellor know his ideas) and his bland expression betrayed nothing of the rage he felt at these first signs of Willy's hot-headedness. For a flash of his old intuition had shown him how to turn the son's awkward new enthusiasm to his own advantage by using it against the father. It was necessary for him to humour Willy, for Willy was an important pawn in the game, 'should the Emperor die to-morrow', and colonies, he suddenly saw, might be used to destroy the unity of the Kronprinzen-Partei. His reasoning was not altogether sound, and the colonial question was to haunt him later, but for immediate purposes what had at first seemed a troublesome new embarrassment might serve to advance his campaign against Vicky and Fritz.

*

Willy and Dona became parents in the spring of 1882 with the birth of a son, another William. Maternity played havoc with Dona's looks. Her confinement over, no good fairy's magic wand restored her pale statuesque beauty. Vicky did her best to encourage her to exercise her shapeless body, to induce her to wear tight corsets and to buy some pretty clothes. Dona merely said sullenly that she saw no point in getting back a figure that was soon to be huge again, since Willy intended to make the succession properly safe.

Vicky strove to hide her disappointment in Dona. The two women did not understand each other at all. Dona was scared of her mother-in-law, who was reputed to be clever and to enjoy managing other people's lives. No one was going to manage Dona's life if she could help it. Soon after she had met Willy's mother she had decided, with the finality of the very stubborn, that she would never allow herself to be patronised by a woman who gave herself such airs. So Dona hardened her heart when she might have done better to accept Vicky's guidance and advice, which were often sound. Vicky noticed that Dona had cooled towards her since marriage and searched for reasons, for she knew that she had shown her daughter-in-law every affection and that she had made a determined effort to be understanding. Unfortunately Vicky was impatient with Dona's slow mind and with her occasional stupidities; Dona saw this and resented it. A barrier rose between them and instead of being a great help to each other, they drifted further and further apart. Before long Vicky could not prevent a critical note creeping into her voice whenever she spoke of her eldest son's wife. Irritated but remorseful, she tried to compensate by being kinder than ever. She had given Dona a beautiful dress for the Venetian ball which was to follow the *tableaux vivants*, because she was sorry for the young bride whom marriage had made so unattractive. Dona decided not to wear it, simply to show her mother-in-law that she would not let her dictate what she should wear, but Vicky's feelings were saved from hurt by the sudden death of Fritz's uncle Charles two days before the ball. The Prince of Wales was furious. He had come to dance and was obliged to stay and sing funeral dirges. As he ruefully told Vicky, Prince Charles was the one member of the Prussian royal family he had never expected to bury.

To her surprise, Vicky missed this sprightly uncle. It was only after he had gone that she realised how his light-hearted banter and good humour had made many a dreary family occasion more bearable for her. She remembered with gratitude and affection his frequent kindnesses when others had not been so well disposed. She was hardly out of mourning for Prince Charles before she was plunged into it again for her haemophiliac brother Leopold, Duke of Albany, who died suddenly at Cannes of a burst blood vessel in the head, leaving a pregnant widow and an eighteen-month-old daughter. Grief at the loss of these two talented men left her in no fit state for a new and embittered conflict with Bismarck; a fight for the happiness of her second daughter Victoria (nick-named Moretta) which was now threatened by the harsh and uncompromising hand of politics.

*

The 1878 treaty of Berlin had created the new state of Bulgaria; though nominally under the Sultan, it was regarded by Russia as belonging to her sphere of influence through ties of blood and religion. The Czar had chosen the twenty-two-year-old Prince Alexander of Battenberg (known in the family as 'Sandro'), one of the four sons of Alexander of Hesse, as Bulgaria's ruler. Sandro seems to have been a sincere and honest young man who intended to do his best for his new country; this did not suit the Czar at all, since he looked on Bulgaria as existing only for Russia's benefit. From the beginning Sandro's task was therefore almost impossible. His uncle, the Czar Alexander II, who had an affection for him, died soon after his accession, and his cousin Alexander III did not like him at all. More to the point, Bismarck loathed him, with that unreasoning personal hatred peculiar to him, and which Vicky found so difficult to understand.

In the spring of 1884 Sandro came to Potsdam while on a tour of the European courts. There, he met and fell in love with the eighteen-year-

Schloss Babelsberg, Potsdam

The Neue Palais, Potsdam

Crown Princess of Prussia and
Prince William

left to right: Princess Charlotte,
Crown Prince Frederick William,
Princesses Margaret and Sophie, the
Crown Princess, Prince Waldemar,
seated in front: Princess Victoria

The Crown Prince with his sons
Prince William and Prince Henry

Prince William of
Prussia and Princess
Augusta Victoria of
Schleswig-Holstein-
Sonderburg-
Augustenburg

Emperor William I
with his son,
grandson and great-
grandson, 1882

seated: Queen Victoria and the Crown Princess
standing: Princesses Victoria of Wales, Victoria of Prussia and Victoria Melita of Edinburgh, 1884

left to right, back: Prince Albert Victor of Wales, Princess Beatrice, Princess Victoria of Wales, Duchess of Edinburgh, Crown Princess of Prussia, Princess Victoria Melita of Edinburgh, Alexandra Princess of Wales, Princess Louise of Wales
left to right, front: Princess Victoria of Prussia, Princess Alexandra of Edinburgh, Queen Victoria, Princess Maud of Wales, Princess Marie of Edinburgh, 1884

old Princess Victoria of Prussia. At first everything was wonderful. Vicky and Fritz were delighted with Sandro, who was good-looking and intelligent and thoroughly taken with their tom-boy daughter. Nothing remained but to fix the wedding day. They had reckoned without Bismarck. He had no use for Sandro and no use for romance, and cynically remarked that one husband was as good as another for Moretta as long as he was manly. What was wrong with the Catholic Crown Prince of Portugal, who had been on the cards before Sandro appeared? Moretta announced what was wrong in no uncertain terms – she wished to remain a Protestant and could not accept the Chancellor's view that her repugnance for a new faith would be overcome by degrees.[28]

In championing her daughter's cause, Vicky did not sufficiently take into account Bismarck's uncompromising attitude in personal relationships. If he could forbid his son Herbert, whom he loved dearly, to marry 'an unsuitable woman' – thereby destroying his happiness without a qualm – how much less important was the happiness of another's child? He feared that the marriage might cause offence to Russia and increase English influence in the Balkans. So he convinced the Emperor that the marriage would not do: Sandro was the 'tool of England', the marriage a 'plot of Queen Victoria to make the young man secure against Russia by an alliance with our court'[29] (he even affected to believe that she might suddenly arrive in Berlin 'with the parson in her travelling-bag and the bridegroom in her trunk', and get the wedding performed on the spot), and that there would be unpleasant repercussions from Russia, since the Czar was bound to view it as a political alliance. Finally, by dwelling on Sandro's humble origin – he was the issue of a morganatic marriage to a 'mere countess' – he won Willy over to his side. Thereafter, Willy was heart and soul against his sister's choice.

It was a blow for Bismarck, however, when Vicky's family 'snapped up' two of the four attractive Battenberg brothers. Early in 1884 her niece Victoria of Hesse married Louis of Battenberg – a wedding that sent the unhappy Moretta to her room in tears over the unfairness that allowed one brother to marry without opposition while the other was banished from love by 'stupid politics' – while Vicky's sister Beatrice married Louis' handsome brother, Henry ('Liko'), at Osborne the same July. Moretta spent another miserable day, and Vicky blamed Willy for breaking his sister's heart.

Willy and Dona had become so sure of themselves that they cold-shouldered Beatrice and her Liko when they stayed in Potsdam with Vicky and Fritz on their way back to England after their honeymoon, saying that Beatrice's marriage had made her 'unacceptable'. Queen

Victoria was furious: 'extraordinary impertinence and insolence and I must add great unkindness of Willy and that foolish Dona . . . poor little insignificant Princess raised entirely by your kindness to the position she is in. Lord Granville very truly said . . . that if the Queen of England thinks a person good enough for her daughter, what have other people got to say.'[30]

Queen Victoria was in favour of Moretta's marrying Sandro. Bismarck's explanations that 'the old Queen is fond of match-making . . . but obviously her main objects are political – a permanent estrangement between ourselves and Russia'[31] were wrong. To use her grandchildren's marriages to make political alliances would have been abhorrent to her nature, and the simple truth was that Sandro had established himself firmly in the Queen's favour when he stayed at Windsor because 'there is something about him which reminds me of dearest papa'.[32] Thus encouraged, Vicky fought still harder for her daughter's happiness, and saw a strength and sagacity in Sandro far greater than one so young could possibly have possessed. She hoped that Bulgaria would emerge victorious from the war with Serbia in 1885.[33] Instead, Sandro lost his throne: kidnapped, tortured and forced to abdicate, he left Bulgaria in September, permanently broken in health.

Russia had got her way, Bismarck and Willy had got theirs, only Moretta and Sandro were beaten and bereft. Stiffened by the two conspirators, the Emperor refused to allow his grand-daughter to follow her prince into exile; her tears and pleadings were in vain. Vicky heard with horror that the Czar was laughing at the extent of Sandro's injuries and disparaging England which, he said, counted for nothing in European politics and had only 'imitation steel guns'.[34] Queen Victoria dipped into the 'black past', and hit back by recalling that the Empress Augusta (who was opposed to the match) had even allowed her daughter Louise to marry the grandson of a mere commoner, and no one had objected. Without new blood, the royal line would become degenerate morally and physically. In England, if a king chose to marry a peasant she would be Queen just as much as any princess. If any one inquired into the history of all the royal and princely families 'many black spots' would be found.[35]

Queen Victoria and Vicky were helpless, however, against Bismarck's implacable will, and for three years more the lovers' fate remained in suspense.

*

Something must be said briefly of the insinuations made by Berlin society that Vicky was more than half in love with Sandro herself. The only evidence for this is the glowing terms she used when talking of him (which were thought far too extravagant for a mere prospective mother-in-law) and her fierceness in his defence. One of the reasons for this was that Sandro's mother had recently died and Vicky tried to take her place, a position that would be easy and natural once Moretta and Sandro were married. Righteous indignation for another's misfortunes was not understood in fashionable Prussian society and in consequence, when Vicky spoke publicly and with the warmest admiration of Sandro, glances were exchanged and it was felt that there must be 'more than met the eye' in her words. Nobody accused Queen Victoria, however, of being in love with the prince, although she referred to him frequently in the most affectionate way, often invited him to stay at Windsor[36] and had likened him to her adored dead Albert – the highest compliment. Moreover, the Prussians simply could not understand that Vicky always used highly-coloured expressions ('barefaced audacity' – 'treacherous and abominable conspirators' – 'shameful dastardly plot') whenever she was deeply moved, and quite forgot that she had used them earlier to describe Russia's treatment of the Poles, Bismarck's treachery to the Austrians, and countless other wrongs which she had tried to put right.

Vicky herself often talked of her whole-hearted defence of a cause as 'the Englishwoman coming out in me'. By this she meant her inability to tolerate injustice and her passionate love of liberty, without which life was not worth living.

*

Sandro went to England to convalesce with his brother Henry. Restored in some measure by the peace of the country and the loving care of his family, he had been able to talk about his sufferings, and had told his brother and sister-in-law everything. The case against Bismarck was black indeed. As Vicky had suspected from the first, it was Bismarck who had urged Sandro to accept the Bulgarian throne but, when trouble began, had folded his arms and looked the other way: 'the Prince of Bulgaria was old enough to know his own mind.'[37]

Bismarck had not been slow to turn the affair to further advantage. With cool deliberation, he lied in order to implicate Robert Morier, now British Ambassador in St Petersburg, in what he continued to call 'the plot', in order to discredit him. He let it be known that Morier had said that he was delighted that Sandro had been expelled from Bulgaria, and that he was a liar and a charlatan (Bismarck's own words for Sandro).[38]

Vicky refused to believe a word of these stories – she had heard their like too often before. But Queen Victoria fell for them and wanted

Lord Salisbury to recall Morier, 'since he does awful mischief'.[39] Fortunately the Foreign Office refused to act in a hurry, although Morier was suspended while enquiries were made. Temporarily unemployed, he went to London, where he waited while the Foreign Office tried to induce that devoted Bismarckian Signor Crespi, the Italian Foreign Secretary, to receive him as Ambassador in Rome.[40] Morier was appointed to Rome, but before he had been there many months Bismarck hounded him out of this post as well. As Vicky said bitterly, human beings had no soul when they were on Bismarck's black list.

CHAPTER 19

'Learn to Suffer without Complaining'

THE Emperor William was ill. He said bitterly that the fuss about Sandro, the tears of his grand-daughter, Vicky's entreaties and Bismarck's irritability were killing him fast. Fritz tried to explain that he had brought it on himself: if he had been strong and allowed Moretta her way, he might have saved himself and others much discomfort and pain. The old man refused to see this, and kept muttering that he was going to die. The arrival of Czar Alexander III in November 1887 for a brief visit proved the last straw. William found no sympathy in that quarter and the moment Alexander left, he took to his bed.

The Czar had reached Berlin in a vile mood. He was haughty, disdainful and rude. Indeed, to everyone's surprise – since her views on Russia's treatment of Sandro were well known – the only person he was at all agreeable to was Vicky, whom he invested with the mantle of his wronged mother. Willy was the reason for this. The Czar had disliked the behaviour of this 'arrogant young man' at the Czarevitch's coming-of-age in the autumn of 1885, and by a natural reaction now held Vicky in high favour. In his opinionated way Willy had tried to ingratiate himself with his host by speaking bitingly of his mother without bothering to find out first what Alexander thought. Willy had hardly arrived before he gave Alexander the unsolicited information that his mother ruled his father 'with a rod of iron', that her family were 'all rotten' and his English uncles 'untrustworthy' – especially the Prince of Wales who had 'as much truth in him as he [Willy] had in his little finger'.[1] Alexander was shocked and disgusted to hear such talk. Willy had not realised that the Czar was filial to a fault, particularly devoted to his mother and that he prized family life as highly as Vicky did. Willy's disparaging remarks were badly received and never forgotten.

While in Berlin Alexander talked loudly of a universal conflagration, involving France, Germany and perhaps England, talk that did not deceive Vicky for a moment since she knew he had nothing with which to back it up. But the Emperor shook in his shoes and was so prostrated that the family felt certain that the end was near and began to look over their mourning clothes.

Lying on the truckle bed on which he had slept for over eighty years, covered with a tattered cotton sheet and threadbare army blankets, in a room quite bare of all the appurtenances of a King, the old man understood perfectly why his relations were gathering and the sight made him determined to disappoint them. Their expectant faces, their crocodile tears, worked like a charm. He began to improve at once, and when Queen Victoria's birthday dinner came round in May he was in his usual place at the head of the table and in excellent spirits.

The Emperor had celebrated his own birthday on the 22nd of March 1887. He was ninety years old, and a huge dinner had been given in his honour at which Fritz had made a speech. Fritz had caught a cold in the New Year which had settled in his throat and he could not shake it off. As he stood in his Field Marshal's uniform, tall and handsome at fifty-five, it was noticed that his usually clear and resonant voice was hoarse and that he had difficulty in speaking. These frequent colds of Fritz's had been the cause of recurring disagreements between the Emperor and Vicky. She argued that prevention was better than cure, and insisted that Fritz should wear his great-coat in the bitterly cold Berlin winters. William had never worn an overcoat in his life and ridiculed his son for what he called 'coddling' and nothing but a 'feminine habit'. Fritz did not want to be different, Vicky insisted, the Emperor scoffed and all the princes tittered; before the matter was settled Fritz caught another cold. This time it was more severe than usual and instead of a mere day or two in bed, he was confined to his room for a fortnight. He emerged weak, depressed and with his voice gone. The low spirits Vicky put down to worry about Willy, who never came to the Neue Palais without making a scene. Bismarck and his uncharitable friends attributed Fritz's depression to his father's almost frightening longevity, and were saying that Fritz despaired of ever becoming Emperor himself and that he would like to see the old man dead – talk which Vicky did her best to keep from Fritz's ears.

At this stage Dr Wegner was confident that he could treat the throat himself; but when it did not improve he called in Dr Gerhardt, Professor of Medicine at the University of Berlin, who diagnosed a small growth on the left vocal cord which he tried to remove surgically. Gerhardt was unsuccessful, and so without more ado (and before consulting a throat specialist) he burned it with a galvanic cautery – drastic treatment and most unwise (even by nineteenth-century standards) without thorough exploratory examination. For the moment, however, Fritz seemed better and at Ems where Vicky took him to convalesce he improved rapidly in the warm April sunshine.

They returned to Berlin with high hopes, and it was therefore a great disappointment to be told after the next examination that the growth was not only still there but if anything larger than before. Dr Gerhardt's almost casual remark that the wound made by the cautery had not healed sounded most ominous to Vicky. Suddenly she felt very frightened. Dr Gerhardt told her gravely that it was not a 'granule', as he had at first supposed, but an 'epithelian' with roots that might be sunk deep into the larynx. A surgeon, Dr Ernst von Bergmann, Professor of Surgery in Berlin, was consulted next. Not unnaturally – since it was his job – he advised an immediate operation from the outside. Dr Gerhardt expressed doubts about this, but did not produce a better idea to take its place. The doctors' conclusion was a terrible shock. Vicky's fright turned to horror of the knife, and she was 'more dead than alive with distress'.[2]

This was a problem she could not share with Fritz. 'Fritz is not to know anything about it', she wrote in anguish to the Queen, to whom she was to turn increasingly during the months that followed. But already Fritz suspected that something must be wrong and miserably predicted that he would die before his father, blaming himself bitterly for bringing Vicky to such a pass. She was at her wits' end to keep him cheerful, no easy matter when she felt apprehensive and nervous herself. Fritz's purgatory – the cauterising of the swelling with red-hot wires – was performed daily from the beginning of May and although he endured the torture without uttering a word ('learn to suffer without complaining', he was to tell Willy in March 1888,[3] when the latter was making a fuss about the discomfort of a sore ear), each treatment left him exhausted and low for hours.

Not knowing quite what to do for the best, Vicky went to Berlin to interview the doctors secretly. They told her plainly that it might be cancer and that because of Fritz's position (and to safeguard themselves – though they did not mention this) they would like an outside opinion, preferably from a man of international reputation, and suggested three names, all foreign, which they thereupon wrote down and handed to Vicky. They told her that they were agreed that a British laryngologist would be best, and that Dr Morell Mackenzie was the top specialist in this field.[4] Vicky had never heard the name before, but she was to hear it again a few days later during a christening luncheon at the British Embassy in Berlin. She asked the Ambassador, Sir Edward Malet, if he could suggest a specialist for Fritz, adding ruefully that this was a subject she had never taken an interest in before.[5] The Ambassador then mentioned Morell Mackenzie and advised Vicky to urge the doctors to send for him.

Next day Bismarck called at the Embassy. He was in an agitated state. He had only just heard that Fritz was to have a serious operation (the splitting of the larynx and the removal of the growth) and that the doctors were behaving unethically in not informing the Emperor, the Chancellor or indeed even the patient himself. He became very intense and accused the doctors of acting irresponsibly by withholding vital information.[6] He describes what happened in his *Recollections and Reminiscences*: 'The doctors were determined to make him unconscious and to carry out the removal of the larynx without having informed him of their intention. I raised objections and required that they should not proceed without the consent of the Prince and as they were dealing with the successor to the throne, that the approval of the head of the family would also be required. The Emperor, after being informed by me, forbade them to carry out the operation without the consent of his son.'[7]

Vicky learned much later that the doctors had decided from the beginning 'not to tell the Crown Prince and Princess all the dangers', infamous conduct they attempted to excuse by saying that if the family had been 'told all, they would not have got them to submit to it'.[8]

A short summary of the different stages of Fritz's illness from this time onwards is needed here as the basis for a proper understanding of what happened later.* Up to the first week in May, Fritz had already been examined by three doctors, of whom the two most important (Professors Gerhardt and Bergmann) were not specialists in diseases of the throat. On the 8th of May Bismarck called in three more doctors known to him to examine Fritz. They were Professor Tobold, a senior Berlin laryngologist – the first real specialist in the case – Dr Schrader, Surgeon-in-Ordinary to the Crown Prince, and Dr Lauer, the Emperor's own physician (who was no doubt chosen only to report to Bismarck).

On the 18th of May all six doctors met for consultation and came to the conclusion that Fritz had cancer. Four of them decided that an immediate operation was essential; Dr Gerhardt would not agree to this, giving as his reasons the very high mortality rate from this kind of surgery and the grave risks involved even should the patient survive.

---

*The latest account is Michael Freund: *Das Drama der 99 Tage* (1966). It is excessively critical of Mackenzie (whose chief faults were probably indecision and the fear that an operation meant death—hence *any* other treatment was preferable) and repeats Bismarck's later wild talk of a conspiracy between Vicky and Mackenzie against the German doctors: a theory which is pushed to absurd lengths when the visit to England for the Jubilee is represented as 'a flight from Germany . . . from the Prussian system . . . desertion by a Prussian general for which any other Prussian officer would have been court-martialled' (Freund 118). It does, however, support the view taken here that all of Virchow's four reports evaded a clear opinion for or against cancer.

Dr Schrader agreed with him. They sent a report to Bismarck, who refused to allow the operation before an independent specialist had examined Fritz. He even condescended to tell Vicky personally what he had done. He was 'very nice', almost sympathetic, and brought a message from his wife – the Princess 'must not allow the operation under any conditions'. He told Vicky with some emphasis that 'it was better to fall into the hands of God than of man'.

Bismarck's veto came as a welcome relief to the doctors. All of them, and Bergmann in particular, had talked loudly of operations and different treatment, but none was willing to take responsibility for the operation, which they later asserted to be 'almost harmless' and one 'undertaken without hesitation in the case of children and old people'.[9] They clutched eagerly at the proposal for an outside opinion.[10] If anything should go wrong (and the chances were that it would), someone other than themselves must be there to take the blame. The choice of a foreign specialist was therefore deliberate, and of an English one, diabolical – what a handle it would give them to have the German Crown Prince killed off by an English specialist! Bismarck was beside himself with worry, and this anxiety for the heir to the throne struck many people as most strange.

What had happened to make Bismarck suddenly so solicitous for the health of a man whom he had constantly opposed and affected to despise? Why did he not welcome the prospect that disease might remove Fritz from the succession and leave him as Chancellor to serve his young admirer Willy? It was simply this: Bismarck thought his career to be in jeopardy. Some time during the previous year the Chancellor had begun to have second thoughts about Willy, who was turning out to be a very different proposition from what he had at first imagined. The young Prince was no longer eating out of his hand with quite the same eager appetite. Bismarck had encouraged Willy to talk about his plans for his own reign, and had got more than he bargained for. Willy's wild colonial schemes took his breath away, and he saw that if Willy became Emperor before his impetuosity had cooled, he himself might be the chief sufferer. He had disturbing visions of his power disappearing overnight. Fritz's illness came at a most inconvenient (not to say inconsiderate) time and filled him with alarm. If he was to be safe he must take good care to preserve the life that he had once despised, ridiculed and boasted that Germany did not need, for now it had suddenly become essential to him.

*

Fritz's operation was provisionally fixed to take place on the 20th of May 1887. On the 14th of May Vicky was told that the doctors had chosen Dr Morell Mackenzie as the best outside opinion, with the full consent of Bismarck. He was said to have 'wonderful manual dexterity and was rapid in his diagnosis'.[11] When Vicky heard this her heart felt lighter, and once again she was filled with hope as she added her plea for urgency to that of the doctors in a cipher telegram to the Queen, begging her to use her influence to ensure that Mackenzie left for Germany at once.

The Queen was somewhat alarmed at such haste, but nevertheless acted quickly. She knew nothing of Mackenzie, but on the 18th of May she thought it best to send her own doctor, Dr Reid, to see him and send him off: 'Sir William* said Dr Mackenzie certainly is very clever in that particular line about throats, but that he is greedy and grasping about money and tries to make profit out of his attendance, and that the profession dislike him for that. I only mention this that you may know whom you are dealing with.'[12]

At five o'clock on the 20th of May 1887 Dr Morell Mackenzie was in the Neue Palais, the operation having meanwhile been postponed. Tall, good-looking, suave and a man of the world, Mackenzie was the kind of person Vicky felt at ease with and whose language she understood. He took charge at once. Relief flowed over her as she looked at 'this interesting man's long lean face, clever eyes, quick movements and elegant manners'.[13] His confidence was infectious. For the first time since Fritz's illness began Vicky felt he was in 'safe hands'. This feeling was reinforced by Mackenzie's methods. Half an hour after his arrival he examined Fritz's throat with forceps (a borrowed pair, since strangely enough the doctor had not brought his own instruments with him – a lapse that does not make posterity love him more). He anointed the tumour with cocaine and painlessly removed a tiny fragment, which he sent to Professor Rudolf Virchow, the celebrated pathologist, for microscopic examination. This was something the German doctors had never done,[14] and Vicky was impressed.

Virchow reported that the piece of mucus was 'too superficial for a proper diagnosis'. On the 23rd of May Mackenzie dug deeper and this specimen was also sent off to the pathologist. According to Dr Bergmann, Mackenzie had inadvertently injured the healthy right vocal cord, which had begun to bleed profusely. A quarrel at once broke out which involved the British doctor. There had been sordid disagreements among the German doctors over the treatment to be adopted before Mackenzie arrived. Unfortunately Mackenzie's manner did nothing to smooth matters over. Vicky had been given a crumb of comfort when the German doctors had assured her that the disease was in an early stage and had not yet done much damage. Mackenzie went

*Sir William Jenner, Queen Victoria's physician.

further on little more evidence and promised a complete cure in a few weeks. When Dr Gerhardt asked him to explain what he meant, Mackenzie icily replied that for the moment he would continue the present treatment – daily cauterising with hot wires. Dr Bergmann challenged Mackenzie on this and said forcibly that the Crown Prince was in grave danger – he would die if they did not operate. Mackenzie briskly replied that he would certainly die if they did.* While they argued, Fritz languished, suffering great pain and distress of mind; Vicky wept and Bismarck thunderously reminded the physicians that they were dealing with the heir to the throne and that his life was 'too precious to be considered like that of an ordinary man'.[15]

Vicky was the helpless victim of the doctors' quarrels; it was dreadful for her to have Dr Mackenzie hold out hope one moment, only to have it dashed by the German doctors the next.[16] Queen Victoria could not make out what was happening. She had received a telegram from Dr Mackenzie to say all was 'satisfactory', followed by a letter from Vicky to say it was not.

By the end of the month the doctors were not merely disagreeing, but quarrelling openly and fighting bitterly for their rights. It was like a nightmare, and Vicky did all she could to keep up Fritz's spirits and to maintain her own courage. In a long letter to the Queen on the 2nd of June she tried to say that she had not lost heart, but her despair was very evident to her mother: 'I fancy it will all come right somehow, but it is pure anguish to see Fritz suffer so.'[17]

Rumour was rife in Berlin and the word 'cancer' was furtively whispered, for no one dared talk about it openly. Still worse, someone had revived an old legend, no truer than Grimms' fairy tales, that a dumb sovereign could not rule, and when the old Emperor died Willy would be the new Kaiser. This led to much adulation of Willy and Dona, who were fêted everywhere; their heads were quite turned by all those who wanted favours in the new reign, and what a large number did! They quickly became grander, haughtier and generally more insufferable than ever. They even ventured to patronise Bismarck, who exploded with wrath and cut such nonsense short by proclaiming all over Berlin that there was no such family law, and that the Crown Prince could never hand the succession over to his son. Vicky heard the story too and also its sequel – Bismarck's emphatic defence of

*In the prevailing conditions of medical knowledge and skill, Mackenzie was probably right. Two years later, at the height of his controversy with Mackenzie, Bergmann announced that he was about to vindicate German science by performing upon another patient, with exactly the same symptoms, the operation which he had not been allowed to perform on Fritz. The operation failed, and the patient died at once (Corti, 307-8).

Fritz's rights. She thought sadly what a difference it would have made to their lives if Bismarck had done this before.

The Chancellor's protestations soon took a personal turn. He made sure that nobody should be left in any doubt that when the Crown Prince succeeded his own position was secure. He enlarges on this in his *Recollections*.[18] Apparently after the Emperor's fainting fits at Ems he had been called to the Neue Palais and asked if he would be willing to remain in office when the Emperor died. According to his own account Bismarck replied that he was ready to do so on two conditions – no parliamentary government and no foreign influence in politics. To this the Crown Prince at once agreed: 'I have not a thought of that.'[19]

Unfortunately Bismarck's reminiscences are full of inaccuracies; incidents are twisted, conversations distorted and often invented, either by Bismarck or by Lothar Bucher to whom he dictated his life story. There seems little doubt that Bucher sometimes filled in gaps in the story from his own imagination. Probably only the first part of the above account is true (the offer to retain Bismarck). After the tension and uncertainty, the promise that he should remain Chancellor was quite enough to make him purr like a cat when he boasted to Moritz Busch after the interview 'they are most anxious to retain me, she also. They wrap me up in cotton wool and velvet'.[20] Mr A. J. P. Taylor believes, however, that Bismarck was speaking the truth and that Fritz accepted these conditions without reserve.[21] Against Mr Taylor's theory it must be remembered that in 1885, the date Bismarck gave for the interview, Fritz was hale and hearty. He had known for some time that he would not be able to govern without Bismarck at any rate at first. It would be more in character if Bismarck had said he would remain, had made no conditions, and had lied about it afterwards. He was safe, since he knew Fritz would never go back on his word. Indeed, by his very trust in the heir to the throne Bismarck unconsciously demonstrated to posterity exactly the kind of man he really knew Fritz to be. In any case, from that moment it was in his own interests to keep the rightful heir to the throne alive.

*

Dr Mackenzie wanted to treat Fritz in his clinic in England 'like an ordinary mortal'.[22] Vicky was willing, but would the other doctors agree? Prudently she decided against saying anything to influence them. But on the evening of the 1st of June she impulsively sought out Professor Gerhardt and beseeched him to tell her the truth, which he did with great brutality. According to Gerhardt, Fritz was deteriorating fast, the tumour was growing and had begun to suppurate – a very bad sign. He said he hoped to Heaven he was wrong and Dr Mackenzie right – 'for we have nothing else to suggest'.[23] At these words Vicky covered her face with her hands. She was utterly forlorn, but she thanked God Fritz did not guess how close he was to death.

Vicky now made a brave and selfless decision. Fiercely protective in her love, she vowed Fritz should not know the 'cruel truth'. She would pretend he was in no danger, and that he was getting better; she would be cheerful and unconcerned, if she could manage it – no mean feat in her strained and nervous condition. Fritz had written on the pad he used as his mouthpiece that he longed to go to Queen Victoria's Jubilee celebrations in London on the 21st of June. Vicky assured him confidently that he would be well enough to go. They would stay in an hotel outside London where the air was pure, and would combine daily visits to Dr Mackenzie's clinic with the festivities. At once Fritz's face broke into a smile, and he looked so happy that tears sprang into Vicky's eyes and she had to turn away.[24]

Willy had taken it for granted that his grandfather would want to be represented by his eldest grandson at the Queen's Jubilee. In fact he had been so sure of his own importance and of his father's lack of it that without consulting anybody he had already written to tell Queen Victoria to expect him. He was disconcerted when, having gone to the Neue Palais to announce his departure for London, he was quietly told by Vicky that he was mistaken: if the Emperor had 'ordered' him, as Willy loudly asserted, it was an order that must be rescinded. Vicky had been misled by a similar story in August 1885 when Willy had gone, over his father's head, to represent the Emperor at the Conference at Gastein. The Emperor had 'ordered' him to go and he could not disobey the imperial command.[25] But it was not an order he obeyed unwillingly, despite the protestations in his memoirs. Willy had learned the habit of 'an eye for an eye' from Bismarck: he was so furious that he could not move his mother about the Jubilee that he cruelly twisted the knife in her heart – Dr Mackenzie was 'holding out false hopes'.[26]

It appeared that no one wanted Fritz to go to England. Wherever she turned, Vicky heard glib arguments why Fritz should be denied even this small pleasure. Suppose the Emperor were to die while they were away and the Crown Prince be too unwell to return? Suppose the Crown Prince were to die on foreign soil? Dr Wegner (he was to accompany them) fussed about the 'responsibility'. Suppose a tracheotomy had to be performed in a hurry – he knew he would be blamed if anything went wrong. Vicky tried to keep her head while those around her lost theirs. 'All these things are always possible', Vicky wrote to the Queen as calmly as she could on the 3rd of June, 'and one cannot be kept a prisoner here and be prevented from following a useful course by the fear of what might happen.'[27]

As the news of Fritz's illness leaked out, there was consternation when the German people learned that their handsome Crown Prince might never be their Emperor. His many good points were remembered, his courage in the Franco-Prussian War, his humanity, his popularity with his troops (Bismarck had never been able to cloud this), even his youthful Danzig speech, considered so foolhardy at the time but recalled after the passage of years as a brave act 'without thought of self'. The alternative – Willy – was not to everyone's taste; indeed many felt that a hot-headed arrogant young prince was a poor exchange for an older and more experienced man with wisdom and judgement. To those who thought this way, the future looked black for Germany.

On the 7th of June Mackenzie returned to Potsdam and removed another fragment from Fritz's throat without telling the German doctors, and sent it to Virchow. The report which came back in a few days was a model of non-committal verbiage. Professor Virchow has emerged almost unscathed from this sorry business. Yet here was a man who could have put an end to the torture Fritz had to endure from the unseemly quarrels of the doctors, and from the harmful and painful daily cauterising. One decisive word might have made Fritz's last months more bearable. But he did not say it, and continued to sit on the fence until the bitter end. Did he really see nothing? Or did Mackenzie again take his specimen from the healthy side, as the German doctors said he did the first time? – a blunder presumably inconceivable in a man as practised in examination of the throat as Mackenzie.

In the *British Medical Journal* for the 4th of June 1887 Henry Butlin, a former pupil of Mackenzie's, sounded a grave warning against the optimistic view of pathological examinations. No notice was taken of this, however, possibly because Butlin was a struggling young doctor, while Virchow was a man of international fame. Virchow's many other interests (he was a member of the Reichstag as well as being Director of the Institute of Pathology in Berlin) do not strike one as a good combination, even for the nineteenth century when it was not unusual for men to hold diverse jobs at the same time. Nevertheless, Vicky read Virchow's report with something approaching happiness: 'Virchow's report bears out completely all he [Dr Mackenzie] has said.'[28]

On the 12th of June 1887 Vicky and Fritz left for England taking Dr Wegner and Dr Landgraf, Professor Gerhardt's assistant, with them. Fritz stood the journey well. He did not attend the magnificent state dinner Queen Victoria gave the next night at Windsor Castle, but Vicky left his bedroom door open, so that he should hear the Grenadier Guards' band play some of his favourite tunes which the

Queen had specially commanded. Vicky sat near her mother among the reigning monarchs with whom the horseshoe table was crammed. She made a determined effort to be gay. Willy, on the other hand, found himself sitting very low down, an African princess as his neighbour. He was so outraged and fuming that he left early and went to bed in a towering rage.

CHAPTER 20

'Worthy to be your Child'

THEY moved to Buckingham Palace on the 18th of June so that Fritz could rest before the long and tedious ride to Westminster Abbey three days later. Vicky was given the bedroom she and Alice had shared as young girls. Unlike herself it was untouched by the passing years. But she was nervous and restless, and she slept badly. She could not take her mind off the procession – would it prove too much of an ordeal for Fritz? No sooner had she put out the light on the night before the thanksgiving service than fears of all kinds came to torment her and drive sleep away. She dozed fitfully until daybreak and lay quietly listening to the sound of London awakening to celebrate fifty prosperous years. It was not easy to count her blessings, but Vicky knew there were some still left to her. Fritz already seemed a little better, the pain was less, the swelling no larger nor so tender when he touched it with the tip of his finger. He told her that here in the familiar room where he had slept before his marriage he was much more hopeful than he had been at Potsdam. Each night Vicky sat with him and they talked while she stroked his hands to help him relax. She had learned to read his lips and he surprised her with the many practical plans he had worked out in his mind for the good of Germany, if he ever became emperor. She did not dare think about the future herself, but it gladdened her heart that Fritz was able to do so, for surely it must be a hopeful sign?

When Vicky went to see how Fritz had slept, he greeted her with a smile and holding out his hand he drew her to him. For a moment they clung together in speechless anguish and it took all Vicky's self-control not to break down completely, but she resolutely forced a smile when Fritz told her he had slept well and felt much more comfortable. To please him, she had chosen a dress in his favourite cornflower blue, cornflowers and roses in her bonnet. Dressed and ready but nervous, as she always was now when parted for long from Fritz, she went down alone into the court-yard to watch while he mounted. It hurt her to see how wonderful he still looked in his white uniform with its silver breast-plate and eagle-crested helmet. As he rode slowly to his place in front of the Queen's carriage she prayed that he would see the day through without mishap; then, suddenly trembling with apprehension, she took her place in the open landau next to the Princess of Wales and opposite the Queen. At exactly eleven o'clock the carriage drawn by six of the 'creams' and escorted by Indian cavalry began to move slowly out into the Mall.

Londoners knew the Crown Prince's tragedy and showed their sympathy by cheering him loudly. He towered above the others, and to them he seemed a romantic figure, a Lohengrin, a Charlemagne, a King Arthur, as handsome, erect and riding alone he acknowledged their greeting with a salute. But one observer in the crowd that day said he was more like a living statue than a man of flesh and blood, his dignity and reserve 'a kind of farewell'.

Dr Felix Semon thought the same as he watched the procession from a window in Sir Ernest Cassel's house in Bennet Street. He had a special interest in the Crown Prince, whose sad story poignantly called to mind the Commendatore from Don Giovanni.[1] Semon, a German Jew and naturalised British subject, had been a pupil of Mackenzie's, and he cursed the medical etiquette that stopped him from uttering one word of warning against the specialist whose skill long experience of his methods had led him to distrust.[2]

Vicky watched Fritz all the way to the Abbey, expecting some catastrophe every minute. Yet, if she had not known the true facts she would not have guessed from his appearance that Fritz was seriously ill. Queen Victoria seemed to read Vicky's thoughts; she leaned forward and whispered 'how well', but Vicky shook her head, her eyes suddenly filled with tears. Inside the Abbey the Prince Consort's 'Te Deum' and his anthem 'Gotha' brought comfort to a heart that Vicky thought was beyond all solace. By the time she led the other princesses to kiss the Queen's hand and receive their mother's embrace she no longer felt afraid, for she knew beyond doubt that Fritz would be given this one day.

A week later Vicky and Fritz went to Osborne. A great peace descended on them both. Every morning they walked together in the plantations laid out by the Prince Consort and when the sun shone, which it did almost all the time, they sat on the sea-shore and Fritz watched Vicky bathe. They were happy, because Fritz's voice was a little stronger, he felt better, ate more and looked fatter. Far away from Berlin society, Willy's sarcastic tongue, the Emperor's capricious moods and Bismarck's iron tyranny, life was peaceful and sweet and Vicky's hopes for Fritz's ultimate recovery were revived.

Faith and hope burned fiercely in Vicky's heart; they had to if she was to sustain Fritz, to help him ignore the newspapers' cruel reports – 'the Crown Prince has a fatal illness'. Shortly before leaving Germany Fritz had read such an account of his condition and had been terribly upset. Vicky had been horrified to see him roughly thrust the paper aside, put his head in his hands, and weep bitterly, whispering as she held him tightly in her arms, 'Why do they take every ray of hope away'.[3] Queen Victoria in her turn sustained Vicky: 'one should never for an instant give up hope.'[4]

From Osborne they went to Braemar and drove to Balmoral daily. In the pure air of the Scottish Highlands Fritz's voice became even stronger and his spirits higher. Dr Mackenzie came to Scotland to see his patient, and Vicky and Fritz begged the Queen to knight him, which she did somewhat reluctantly in the drawing room at Balmoral – the Queen could refuse Fritz nothing. Afterwards, when Vicky and Fritz had returned to Braemar, the Queen asked Mackenzie searching questions about Fritz's illness. She was surprised that he could enlighten her so little.[5]

The climate of the Highlands was too damp for a long stay, so they moved to Toblach in the Austrian Tyrol where the air was milder and drier. Scotland had not been an unqualified success. A horrible quarrel had broken out one night between Vicky's secretary Count Seckendorff and Fritz's court marshal Count Radolinski, who had replaced von Normann. Radolinski was an out-and-out Bismarckian and a thoroughly dishonest man who had ingratiated himself into Vicky's good graces and had deceived her so completely that she never had the slightest suspicion that he was not 'sincerely attached to us'. She did not understand that he was attentive from duty and not from devotion; a detailed report on her went weekly to the Chancellor, together with a verbatim account of her conversation. This, taken out of context, made very strange reading and Vicky herself would not have recognised her own words. Seckendorff had been told that Radolinski was doing all he could to get rid of him and that he was spreading rumours that Seckendorff was the Crown Princess's lover and dropping hints to the English court of infamous conduct between them. The court naturally saw that this was nonsense, cold-shouldered Radolinski and warned Seckendorff.[6] Unfortunately the quarrel between the two men did nothing to stop this hateful gossip. The reports circulating in Berlin were even more vicious. If Fritz Holstein is to be believed, Bismarck's spies in the Crown Princess's entourage were not only saying that Seckendorff was Vicky's lover but were inventing specific incidents to add verisimilitude to their stories – of mountain climbs together and nights spent in Alpine huts alone, not to mention the exchange of meaningful glances between the guilty pair.[7] With her usual philosophy Vicky dismissed 'such rubbish' as not worth a thought. She had far too many things on her mind to care.

*

Toblach was colder than Vicky had expected, the air too sharp. Fritz began to cough more, especially at night, and he soon looked pale from loss of sleep, his spirits drooped and he could not eat. Quite suddenly one night he worsened. Vicky was woken by his rasping cough, which nothing could ease; by morning he was so spent that Vicky thought he might die. As soon as he had recovered sufficiently to stand the journey they moved to Baveno where it was warmer and the sun shone all day. Sir Morell Mackenzie hurried out (taking good care to remind Vicky that the Tyrol had not been his choice), and brought his assistant Dr Mark Hovell with him. Hovell was senior surgeon at the London Throat Hospital, a man of resource and skill and by no means lacking in tact. There is evidence that he was the cleverest of all the doctors attending Fritz, but overshadowed by Mackenzie and unfortunately brought in too late. When Mackenzie asked him to examine Fritz's throat he saw at once it was cancer and far gone. 'Dr Hovell is very clever and inspires me with confidence', Vicky wrote hopefully to the Queen on the 17th of October 1887. Vicky's own confidence was sometimes very low and needed a great deal of boosting.

Fritz spent his fifty-sixth birthday at Baveno. It was a very happy day. With the exception of Willy and Charlotte, all the children came to see him. They played the piano, sang duets, and acted a short play and a charade just as they used to do when they were young. But Vicky's gaiety was very forced. Only that morning a letter had come from a well-intentioned friend who had heard of a plot 'to set aside the Crown Prince' and put Willy in his place; she urged Vicky to bring Fritz back to Berlin at once. Sadly Vicky tore up the letter before Fritz could see it. Intrigues were nothing new; they were going on all the time, with their eldest son in the thick of each one, siding with the enemy and helping them all he could. What did it matter any more? Vicky knew that certain sections of the German people were clamouring for Fritz to return to Germany. Their anger might have turned to sympathy if there had been better public relations and they had been given the facts. They were told very little until the end was near – just as in Prince Albert's last illness, but with more devastating results. Bismarck was well aware of this, but he did nothing to put it right. On the other hand he allowed Moritz Busch (indeed he even suggested it to him, Busch says) to publish an article in the *Grenzboten* timed to coincide with the Jubilee, intimating that Fritz was 'in the hands of the

English Queen and her daughter would not allow him to return, and that Vicky had only called in Mackenzie because he was her lover'.[8] Shocking attacks on Vicky followed in the other papers, and when she refused to answer them, Queen Victoria wrote herself to ask Sir Edward Malet to contradict these calumnies and to impress on the public that it was the German doctors alone who had called in the English specialist.[9]

Vicky asked nothing more than to be left alone to nurse Fritz in peace. But peace was the one thing she could not find. Well-meaning friends sent her these articles, and Count Radolinski (still smarting from a rebuke she had given him in Scotland) revengefully retailed every disgusting detail which the gutter-press printed.[10]

Vicky noticed that Fritz was not improving, and wildly looked for the reasons. Could his increased lassitude be due to the haze that sometimes hung about the little town? Perhaps Baveno was too humid, their hotel in too much of a hollow? Another place must be found. By November they were in San Remo on the Italian Riviera, where the climate was mild and sunny, and where they rented a cheerful villa in a beautiful garden within sight of the sea. Vicky loved the house at once and had a strange feeling that it was here that Fritz would be cured. They left Baveno with high hopes and settled amid the olive trees and exotic plants of the Villa Zirio. For the next few months, Vicky's life was bounded by the four brick walls of this Italian home. Nothing in the world outside mattered. She still took all the newspapers, reading to Fritz only those items that would amuse him, for his interest in politics had dwindled to nothing. When in December 1887 Bismarck produced a new bill to provide a huge increase in the armed forces, he merely remarked laconically to Vicky that perhaps the Chancellor was contemplating war.

The change of air did not suit Fritz, and he did not improve at San Remo as much as Vicky had expected. He felt the heat and once again went off his food, looked pale and did not want Vicky to read the papers to him. Vicky had a bed put in a sheltered part of the terrace where it was warmed by the sun but shady and where the scent of the mimosa was strongest. There he lay pale and panting while she fanned him, trying her utmost to keep the panic out of her face, for she had noticed in terror that Fritz had changed, that his vitality was being sapped and that he had suddenly become more detached from the world, even from her. One morning she was tenderly removing the ice bags on his throat when she saw that new swellings had appeared and that Fritz seemed too ill to sit up. Sir Morell Mackenzie was sent for in a hurry. He came out at once, followed by several more doctors who had not been asked for. The Emperor had heard of the relapse and had

promptly sent Dr Moritz Schmidt of Frankfurt to San Remo, while
Willy went one better and sent two doctors, Professor Schrotte of
Vienna and Dr Kreuse of Berlin. These extra doctors did no good,
took up precious space and harassed Fritz almost beyond endurance.
Vicky was frantic. Fritz asked Morell Mackenzie a direct question 'Is it
cancer?' When the reply came he did not flinch: 'Sir, it looks very much
like.'[11] But later when alone with Vicky he shed bitter tears: 'To think
that I should have such a horrid disgusting illness that I shall be an
object of disgust to everyone and a burden to you all.'[12] Vicky did
everything she could to quieten and pacify him, telling him in a comforting and reassuring way, yet consistent with the truth, that they
must not trouble about the future, but remain cheerful and hopeful.
But she wrote to Queen Victoria'. . . as long as there is breath in me,
I shall see that the right thing is done for Fritz for the prolongation of
his life, for his comfort and happiness. They are (many of them) angry
with me for appearing cheerful and unconcerned before Fritz, and for
trying to make the time pass pleasantly and keep his mind free from
care and from dwelling on painful things. They say I try to hide the
gravity of the situation from him, that he ought to feel more what
danger he is in . . . they say I buoy him up with false hopes, which is
also not true, as I carefully avoid speaking of the future in order not to
be obliged to say what I do not think.'[13]

*

On the 9th of November all the doctors held a consultation. Cancer was
confirmed. Vicky waited with Fritz when they were out of the room
and insisted on staying and hearing the verdict. When Fritz wrote on
his pad 'I want the truth', Vicky quietly answered 'you shall have it'.
As the doctors came in Fritz stood up and greeted them with a smile,
facing them calmly, with Vicky white but composed by his side.
Professor Schrotte, who had been chosen as spokesman, stepped
forward and gave Fritz his death-sentence, never once mentioning the
word 'cancer' but making himself perfectly understood. Fritz was given
the choice of total removal of the larynx or the palliative operation of
tracheotomy. He chose the latter. 'When the cruel facts of one's doom
are read to one, it gives one an awful blow . . . my darling has a fate
before him which I hardly dare think of.'[14]

Mackenzie may have been a bad doctor, but he had tact and knew
how to treat severely shocked patients. For two whole days he never
left Fritz's side. His bedside manner was impeccable and he was everything Fritz needed – 'calm, collected, wise and deliberate'. His sympathy and understanding were soothing, especially when seen against
the 'blunt, uncouth and arrogant manners' of the German doctors, who

were at their worst in a crisis that needed delicate handling. Mackenzie hid his ignorance under a cloak of immense self-confidence which affected everyone except the other doctors. But were they any less ignorant and less culpable? It must be remembered that Mackenzie had been called in as much for their sake as for Fritz's, and that their ranks were riddled with dissension before Mackenzie's arrival lowered the temperature considerably by ensuring that at any rate the quarrels did not take place in the sick-room. Moreover the German doctors were dishonest. When the Emperor asked why an operation abandoned in May was brought up again in November they replied that 'the responsibility for its non-performance until too late had been incurred by the physician [i.e. Mackenzie] who had overlooked and even denied the increase of the growth'.[15]

Now she knew the truth, Vicky spent all her time with Fritz. She preferred to renew the ice-bags on his throat herself, she ate her meals with him, read to him, talked to him when he could not sleep, and sat holding his hand while he dozed at short intervals throughout the day. Panic was never far from the surface now, but she forced herself to be calm. It was only when she let her mind dwell on how much worse Fritz's sufferings might become that she could not prevent herself becoming 'half mad'. One morning Willy appeared unexpectedly at the Villa Zirio, bringing a Dr Schmidt with him, and made a frightful scene. He had come to 'take matters into my own hands' and rudely ordered the doctors to his hotel for consultation, without his mother's permission. He told her to get his father up and dressed ready to return with him to Berlin and an operation. But Vicky stood her ground, barring the way to Fritz's room and 'pitching into him with considerable violence'. Yet when she came to describe this sordid quarrel to Queen Victoria she somehow managed to find excuses for her son: 'someone had put him up to it'.[16] But Queen Victoria quickly disposed of Willy and Dona: she advised Vicky to send them abroad 'to find their level'.

*

Someone had indeed put Willy up to it. Like a great number of people of weak character, he was easily swayed by bad influences. There was no one bold enough to warn him – except his mother (and this only made her more unpopular than ever with him) – that it was dangerous to allow his head to be turned by adulation. Thus he allowed himself to be influenced by a most pernicious man, Adolf von Stöcker, the court chaplain, and his Christian Socialist Movement,[17] an organisation whose anti-Semitic objectives were not unlike those pursued by another Adolf in this century. Vicky had never got on with court clergy, whom she found abhorrent and the very antithesis of good Christians. When she had come in contact with them first in 1858, she had seen at once that they were 'false, ambitious, narrow-minded, servile and much disliked by the educated middle class'. They disliked her in return when she said openly that she was opposed to violent sectarianism and that she condemned those who showed by their lack of toleration that they were 'anti-Jew and anti-Roman Catholic'. Fritz had supported her, saying that they were in perfect agreement on this important point,[18] and thereby earned for himself the Stöcker party's contemptuous nickname 'Cohen I, King of the Jews'.[19] Willy, of course, took the opposite line and loved to talk pompously of keeping the German race 'pure'.

Early in November 1887, Willy had presided over a meeting held in Berlin for the 'Development of Evangelistic Church Life and Christian Charity'. Vicky read with considerable distaste the account of a very foolish speech Willy had made at this meeting, exalting national splendour and military glory. He had earned a snub from Bismarck for doing so. In his anger Willy let his tongue run away with him and he was heard to say that the present power of the Chancellor would not last: 'he must not be allowed to forget that I am master.'[20]

*

Willy's unkindness to his mother at this time is hard to understand. He had nothing to gain by not contradicting the falsehoods about Vicky that were spreading like wildfire through Berlin. He knew very well that she had not prevented the operation in May and that Sir Morell Mackenzie had not been called in on her authority, indeed that she had never even heard his name before the German doctors mentioned it. Yet when he returned to Berlin after his stormy visit to San Remo, he made no attempt to stop the self-important Dr Moritz Schmidt from writing a long-winded and false report to the Emperor which was published in full in the State Gazette a little later. It caused a tremendous sensation throughout Germany, as it was meant to do. It seemed for a time as though no one had the sense to see how ridiculous its charges were, and that they would not stand up to investigation for a moment. Vicky and Mackenzie were blamed for Fritz's illness; the English doctor was made out to be a Jew whose real name was Moritz Marko-vitz, and moreover that unforgivable thing, a Jew who had done his work badly. The German doctors behaved no better than the journalists. They wrote letters vindicating themselves here, there and everywhere, and did untold harm. From their reports the German people were led to believe that Fritz could not last above a fortnight, and shops did a roaring trade in mourning. Those who had not given up hope sent Vicky their pet cures, and she received thousands of letters and parcels with bottles of mineral water, tins of ointment and potions of every kind from all corners of the globe. Even magic was recommended. It was a chance for the biggest advertising stunt in history. But Vicky drew comfort from it – it proved that people really cared and so it lightened the load on her heart a little.

Queen Victoria was now Vicky's greatest support, and wrote in her Journal 'May God bless my poor child, who is so good and brave'.[21] She was anxious to know if Fritz had been told 'the alternatives' and whether it really was Fritz who had decided not to have the operation. She had recently heard that splitting the larynx was not particularly dangerous and that there were many instances of success,[22] while Vicky had heard that there had not been one case of a person lasting longer than two or three months – all had died from the after-effects. It was impossible to know what to believe.[23]

In December Fritz was made to suffer unnecessary hurt when the Emperor gave Willy the power to sign all state papers if he should become too feeble to do so himself. On the face of it this was reasonable. Willy was on the spot, eager and ready, Fritz was far away and seriously ill. Fritz would not have minded if it had been arranged with tact and sympathy, indeed in certain circumstances he might have suggested it himself. The hurt lay in the callous manner in which he was allowed to hear of it – after it had taken place, as though he were already dead. A decree came from Bismarck – not even in his own hand – announcing it as an accomplished fact. It was an unfortunate coincidence that the letter arrived on the same day as Professor Bergmann's assistant, who had been sent on the Emperor's orders. It was thoughtless and unnecessary to force another doctor on Fritz and without telling him first; the doctor himself knew very well that he had only come to keep the Emperor – and Berlin – informed of what was happening. With Bismarck's decree in his hand and his father's doctor at his elbow, Fritz became angry and excited and tried to talk – a thing he had been strictly forbidden to do – telling Vicky that he intended going at once to Berlin to confront the Emperor, Bismarck, Willy and the party that was working against him. It was all Vicky could do to calm him down. Vicky had known of 'the party' for some time. It was something similar to the court camarilla of the old days. It was 'the party' who worked behind the scenes, against the heir to the throne, who surrounded him with doctors who were no more than spies behind the plot to force Fritz to sign his own abdication. They wanted to get rid of Vicky too (she was always referred to as 'the Englishwoman' in these circles) because they had been jealous of her for years. Above all they could not forgive her for making them feel inferior. Bismarck had found 'the party' very useful in the old days. To him the untold mischief they did was justified, and if he never actually encouraged them, he did nothing to stop them, but characteristically let matters take their course.[24]

Strangely enough, Bismarck did not hate Vicky in the way 'the party' hated her. He could stand aside and watch them persecute her – she deserved it for being English – but if in 1887 she had appealed to him for help, and done it humbly enough, he might have answered her cry. He would have taken it as a triumphant sign that at last the 'Englishwoman' acknowledged him as master. But such a course never occurred to Vicky.

*

Vicky encouraged friends to visit them at San Remo and help her to keep Fritz occupied. The Queen sent the Prince of Wales to find out exactly what was happening and to be 'a comfort' to Vicky. Baron von Roggenbach came for short periods several times. He played chess and backgammon with Fritz and read to him, but above all he let in some much-needed fresh air, with his sane and balanced views and his optimism. He did not care for Mackenzie, but saw no point in saying so to Vicky or Fritz. Prince Rudolf of Austria came – 'so filial, so kind and such a contrast to Willy', whom he made it plain he did not care for. In December Lady Ponsonby (the former Mary Bulteel) arrived for a first visit to the Villa Zirio. She had not expected to find Fritz so tanned by the sun, and mistook his deceptive high colour for improved health. When Fritz had gone to bed, she was delighted to hear Vicky talk so cheerfully, and to learn that Fritz was getting on so well. Disarmed by genuine sympathy and concern, Vicky suddenly faltered, put her hand in Lady Ponsonby's and broke down completely.[25]

Queen Victoria was always stressing the need to keep Fritz busy, and was furiously angry when Vicky told her Fritz might as well be dead for all the notice his father and Bismarck took of him. Sir Edward Malet had asked Bismarck outright if the Crown Prince was being kept informed of all that was going on, so that he might have things to interest him at San Remo. Bismarck assured him that a special messenger was sent to the Villa Zirio every ten days with summaries of passing events and reports – he omitted to add, however, that these had already been dealt with.

Willy was earning great praise in Berlin for his filial duty. He had let it be known that his visits to San Remo were primarily concerned with politics – his father must be kept up to date. Because Vicky kept these family quarrels to herself, few knew the real truth. Even her second son Henry, who had such an easy-going reputation, imitated his eldest brother and tried to throw his weight about on his first appearance at the Villa. He had hardly entered the door before he was telling his mother ('in a ridiculously pompous way he had copied from Willy') that his father should hand everything over to Willy now he was 'past business'. Although he was as obstinate as a mule Henry was rather weak and easily led, and could usually be managed; as soon as Vicky talked severely to him, he calmed down and became as agreeable as he always was 'when he has been with us for some time, but not when he has been set up by others and his head stuffed full of rubbish at Berlin'.[26]

It is possible to learn from Lady Ponsonby's letters something of the tremendous strain Vicky was enduring quite alone at this time. She lived in daily contact with people whom she knew to be on Bismarck's pay-roll; there was not a single lady-in-waiting in whom she could confide. Countess Brühl was a naturally kind and considerate woman and 'felt very much' for her mistress, but Vicky had to remember that she was on the 'other side'. Mademoiselle de Perpignon was kind and even just in her own strange way, but her kindnesses could not be accepted any more than those of Countess Brühl. It was the same with the others and with those in Fritz's entourage – Seckendorff was the only one either of them could trust, but his position was precarious, so they had to be careful. Vicky must always be on her guard. This was not only a terrible burden on top of everything else, but it also meant that she had no woman with whom she could talk freely, or even pass a few minutes in friendly relaxed conversation. She was very lonely indeed; Lady Ponsonby says 'This is the saddest part of the dear Crown Princess's position'.[27]

Fritz's disease now had a name: 'perichondritis'. On the 9th of February 1888 tracheotomy became necessary and was performed by Bergmann's assistant, Dr Bramann, who inserted a canula in Fritz's throat. Vicky remained in the next room while it was being done and was in an agony of apprehension. When the operation was over and she went into the bedroom, she was surprised and glad to find Fritz pale but otherwise much the same. Thankfully she fell on her knees by the bed and covered his hands with kisses. The doctors told her he had been given a little chloroform and had made no fuss. Bravely Vicky tried her best not to make a fuss either, but she had sunk so low with alarm for Fritz that she could hardly stop trembling. When she took her usual place by his bed she made a great effort to be calm as she held Fritz's hand while he slept a little. It was then she heard the noise made by the air flowing through the canula: 'it was very horrid.'[28]

All Vicky's hopes for peace and quiet were now quite gone. It had even become a struggle to keep the sick-room free from visitors, reporters and indeed anybody who managed to get into the Villa Zirio. The day after the tracheotomy another doctor arrived, sent by the Emperor and Bismarck, so he said. He was Professor Kussmaul from Strasburg, and close on his heels a most unwelcome guest turned up – Count Radolinski. Before the day was done Professor Bergmann was among them again, cowing the other doctors and picking a quarrel with Mackenzie over the type of canula to be used. Then suddenly Bergmann announced that he had finished with the case, since he could no longer keep 'this abominable colleague within the bounds of decency'.[29] A short interview with Vicky followed. It was most unpleasant. Bergmann was as cruel and bullying as ever, telling Vicky repeatedly not to hope for there was none. This made her cling all the more to Sir Morell Mackenzie's assurance that he was 'even more satisfied than he was before'. Radolinski too demanded an interview; he was 'in a state of wild excitement, shrieking in his high-pitched voice that Germany considered the Crown Prince as good as gone'.

Vicky longed to lash out at them all, though she scarcely had the energy. She had hardly dismissed Radolinski when Willy came in, bringing news which increased her agitation still further: the latest bulletins from Berlin made him certain that the Emperor was dying.

CHAPTER 21

'Mere Passing Shadows'

THE Emperor was dying. He lay on his back on his narrow soldier's bed, wearing a white jacket, a red scarf wound round his neck – the same one that he had worn in winter, year in year out on his many campaigns. He had become very still, staring at the ceiling with wide unseeing eyes as though he had already entered eternity. His two valets, Kurt and Franck, old soldiers like their master, knelt one each side of the bed, chafing his hands and feet in an attempt to bring him back to life.

William had seemed to be on the verge of death many times during the last few months. It had become quite common to find him stretched out on the floor unable to get up by himself, and everyone was equipped with smelling-salts and brandy. Each attack left him just that bit feebler than before, although so far his iron constitution had always won in the end. Then one morning early in March they found him as usual on the floor, but could not revive him. The Empress Augusta was summoned. She was a wreck of what she had once been, crippled with rheumatism, far gone with Parkinson's disease (and some said with dropsy as well). She could no longer do anything for herself, but had to be carried about by attendants who dared not leave her for a moment. Her mind was quite unaffected, however, and this made her disabilities harder to bear, yet to everyone's surprise she did manage to do so with philosophical calm and courage.

The Emperor's relations gathered like busy black ants, speculating on the old man's chance of survival and on his son's lack of it, brightening at the thought of all that William II had in store for them, for they did not believe for a moment that Fritz would reign. They did not go into the bedroom until the end was near; after what happened in 1886 they were reluctant to be made fools of a second time two years later. So they stayed out of sight and grumbled at the inconsiderate way William kept them waiting.

Augusta sat near the bed in the bath-chair she had been forced to use for the last four years, her face cold and expressionless as she watched the man who had been her husband for nearly fifty years slip into unconsciousness. Not one word of love had ever passed between them, not even a single endearment, and if this had once made Augusta bitter it was now too late for her to change. Duty had become her strongest emotion: it was her duty to stay with her dying husband, so she stayed. Yet something else must have stirred in her cold heart, some feeling of pity perhaps for the man who had been forced to marry her. While William was still semi-conscious she sent her daughter Louise to fetch the miniature of the woman who had ruined her marriage – Elise Radziwill – which for more than half a century had occupied a place of honour on William's desk, and herself put it into her husband's weakening hands.[1]

Despite the fact that illness had forced her to retire from public life, Augusta was still a subject for gossip. It was now being said that her greatest wish was to live long enough to see her grandson Willy become Emperor so that she could be the power behind the throne.[2] But this was no more than one of those stories without foundation with which Berlin society was riddled. Augusta undoubtedly loved Fritz, and his illness was a great grief to her; it was only unfortunate that she could not bring herself to say so to him or to Vicky. She had lost the art of communicating her real feelings long ago, and her children seldom had any idea what their mother thought or felt.

Bismarck called to see his master. He stood at the bedside for a long time looking down on the man who had made everything possible for him, whose weaknesses had been his good fortune, and wondered whether his actions would have been different if he had known in 1862 that a man of sixty-three would reign for twenty-seven years. When Bismarck had come the previous day, the dying man had been lucid enough to say a few words to him and as Bismarck was leaving he had raised himself on his elbow and called out quite strongly 'I shall see you again'; but this time William rambled, mistook his Chancellor for Fritz and murmured of military matters as though he were on the battlefield.

Like his brother before him William was slow to die. On the 8th of March, just as dusk was falling, the bells in the Berlin churches had begun to toll when he regained consciousness and it was not until the following morning that he passed away in his sleep.

Just as in December 1861 Fritz had tried to prepare Vicky for her father's death, so now it was her turn to break the news gently to him that the Emperor was sinking. For a long time there had been little left for Vicky to love in this harsh parent who had tyrannised over them all. Yet stern as he had been, William had never killed Fritz's affection or respect and if this had hindered him in his dealings with his father, the knowledge that he had always been dutiful consoled him now. There were no regrets as he wept that he could not receive his father's last blessing nor bestow on his withered old cheek a last kiss.[3] Nor could Vicky condemn her father-in-law entirely. Her sense of fair play compelled her to defend him when her friends criticised the Emperor for showing so little concern for Fritz, since she felt that his great age blunted his feelings and dimmed his understanding of the tragedies of others, even that of his only son. William's rejoinder to a friend who dared to mention Fritz's troubles – 'I have no son now'[4] – depends to some extent for its meaning on the tone of voice in which it was said. Fritz Holstein interpreted it as heartless rejection; Vicky believed it was uttered in sorrow. Her interpretation is given more weight when it is remembered that many times during the last year of William's life his mind became so muddled that he believed Fritz to be already dead.[5]

*

Vicky was walking in the garden of the Villa Zirio on the morning of the 9th of March when the telegram arrived announcing the Emperor's death. With a beating heart she ran to Fritz who took her in his arms and kissed her tenderly. Together they walked into the drawing room to meet the household who were waiting, uncomfortable and disconsolate, not knowing whether to congratulate or cry. Fritz went at once to a small table and wrote out the announcement of his accession as Frederick III. Then, taking off the order of the Black Eagle, he laid it lovingly round Vicky's shoulders. Vicky immediately burst into tears. Fritz seized his pad and wrote a message on it for Sir Morell Mackenzie: 'I thank you for having made me live long enough to recompense the valiant courage of my wife.'[6] So he had not been altogether deceived by the smiles, the cheerful words and the optimism she had created around him. Impulsively she knelt down, seized his hand and kissed it, and laid it for a moment against her cheek as she struggled for self-control. The upright figure of the fifty-seven-year-old Emperor, and Vicky's natural dignity, gave this simple domestic scene in the drawing room of a rented Italian villa such nobility that even Bismarck's hirelings had tears in their eyes and were deeply moved.

Vicky's mind was in a turmoil. She hated to leave San Remo, 'this sweet place' that she imagined was doing Fritz so much good. It was torture to know that he would never again be able to lie on his day-bed in a sheltered part of the terrace and draw life and energy from the healing sun. She trembled too when she remembered what awaited them in Berlin, where they would be surrounded by spies and enemies on every hand. As she hurried away to complete arrangements for the journey to Germany she would not have been human if she had not thought what this day would have meant to them twenty years earlier: 'How much good we might have done, how much benefit Germany –

which he loved so dearly – could have had from his benevolent and humane reign. Will time be given him is a question only God can answer.'[7] In the entry in his diary for the 9th of March 1888 Fritz made a brave attempt at self-deception that did not really deceive, although the pretence gave him courage to face the coming days: 'so now I have ascended the throne of my fathers and of the German Emperors, God grant me his help in fulfilling my duties conscientiously and for the benefit of my native Prussia and the whole of Germany.'[8]

Fritz wanted to do everything properly. Among his first duties was a telegram to Queen Victoria, reminding her of his devoted affection and of his 'sincere and earnest desire for a close and lasting friendship between our two nations'.[9] Vicky too wrote a hurried message to the Queen and for the first time allowed herself to use the dreaded word 'stricken': 'To think of my poor Fritz succeeding his father as a sick and stricken man.'[10]

They left San Remo on a day of glorious sunshine. Sir Morell Mackenzie travelled in the royal suite and was the soul of tact and consideration. To Vicky's intense relief the journey over the Alps was both swift and comfortable. They stopped only once, at Leipzig, to allow Bismarck to join the train. When he entered the royal compartment he bowed low over the hand of his new master to give him the kiss of homage. Fritz would not let the old man kneel, but drew him up towards himself.* For the first time the two men faced each other on equal terms. For Vicky it was a poignant moment and one she was never to forget.

It had been arranged that they should go straight to Charlottenburg, which in those days was in the country. The palace was icy cold, the bedroom not prepared for an invalid: it smelled of damp and mildew and was full of draughts as though it had not been lived in for years. It reminded Vicky unpleasantly of the Berlin Schloss in 1858, but then they had been young and strong and it had not mattered, whereas now the cold air in the canula made Fritz cough and choke. Two months before, Fritz had brought up a piece of growth and Mackenzie had sent it to Virchow, who even now did not diagnose cancer. Yet Fritz was slowly but surely getting worse. Two months earlier he had written in his diary that he had a 'wretched feeling generally'. In the freezing conditions of Charlottenburg Vicky was terrified that he would not last a week, yet somehow a fire had been lit and kept going all night and Fritz had not suffered harm. On the 11th of March he was even well enough to receive all the important people and deputations who

---

*Richter (*Bismarck*, p. 324) uses this incident to point out the contrast between father and son: a few months later William II allowed Bismarck to kneel publicly to kiss his hand at the opening of the Reichstag.

had come to his father's funeral. Dignified and upright in full uniform, he went with quick steps to greet everyone, but of course he could not speak and had to write on the pad in his hand. People were astonished to see him like this after what they had heard, and wondered if perhaps he might recover after all.

Fritz had prepared two manifestos: one to 'my people' and the other to 'my Chancellor'. In both he clearly stated his aims for Germany, not as a dying man, but as though he were a strong and healthy monarch at the start of a long reign. Among his chief aims was his determination to make Germany 'a protector of peace'. Mindful of the distress of the poor, the unemployed and the sick and of the general distress in the country, he proclaimed that he intended to give the improvement of education and public welfare the highest priority. He ended on a note of vigour and hope which momentarily lifted the shadow which had hung over the whole country since his accession: 'not caring for the splendours of great deeds, not striving for glory, I shall be satisfied if it be one day said of my reign that it was beneficent to my people, useful to my country and a blessing to the Empire.'[11] Perhaps it was significant that there was not one word in these two manifestos to which Bismarck could object, even had Fritz many years before him.

There was talk of an amnesty to mark the new reign; Fritz very much wanted this to include all political prisoners, but Bismarck would not hear of it. In the end the lawyer Heinrich von Friedberg managed to force the Chancellor into a compromise. Fritz longed to leave the stamp of a 'new era' on his short reign, to bequeath to the German people something they could point to as belonging specially to him. It had been a surprise and an encouragement to find that there were so many good and faithful men ready to support him, although alas, there were also many like the cynical Count Alfred von Waldersee (who had been made chief of the army general staff shortly before the death of William I) who showed their indifference to the opinions of Frederick III – 'everyone who is overthrown now will rise again soon'.[12]

Fritz would have liked to get rid of many of the worst abuses of the last reign and to replace corrupt ministers with at least one or two trustworthy men of his own choosing, Forckenbeck, Schrader and Bamberger in particular. But Bismarck flatly refused to include them, and Fritz was too ill to insist. There were others who would have followed a fit and strong Emperor, but Fritz had one foot in the grave while his son Willy had one on the throne. Because of this Vicky and Fritz were enclosed inside a wall, where no independent voices could reach them, prisoners of circumstances over which they had no control. No one could approach them without a pass from Bismarck 'if they did not belong to the right clique, that is those who were heart and soul sold to the Chancellor'.[13] Many too were afraid that if they supported Frederick III they would be made to pay for it under William II, so they ranged themselves on the new Crown Prince's side. Such are the frailties of human nature. From afar, Queen Victoria did what she could to give Vicky and Fritz a proper sense of their own position: 'I know how good and kind and forgiving you are, but I beg you both to be firm and to put your foot down and especially to make those of your children who were always speaking of the "Emperor and Empress" to remember who they are now.'[14]

On the 14th of March 1888 Vicky drove alone to the cathedral in Berlin where the Emperor was lying in state. The sight of death at that particular moment, when so many fears filled her heart, was agony.[15] Two days later, towards evening, in darkness lit up by flaring torches and to the mournful sound of muffled drums, the hearse with the body of the dead Emperor, drawn by six black-plumed horses, wound its way round the walls of Charlottenburg to the family mausoleum in the park. The cutting east wind made it impossible for Fritz to attend the funeral, so Willy took his father's place as chief mourner, walking alone in front of the other royalties. When the cortège reached the palace, Fritz appeared at a window in full-dress uniform and stood at the salute as his father's coffin moved slowly out of sight; then, deeply moved and pointing to the empty space behind the hearse, Fritz wrote on his pad for Sir Morell Mackenzie 'that is where I ought to be'.

Shortly after the death of the old Emperor, Bismarck had consulted Dr Bergmann; in answer to the question 'How long?' Bergmann had replied 'Not beyond the summer'. Bismarck had found an ally, death, and he could not keep the good news to himself; he told the French Ambassador 'We are just beginning the rule of a woman, or rather the interim rule of a woman for a few months'.[16] But the moment he knew exactly where he stood the situation became much easier – the summer was not far off, after all, and Bismarck could be patient when it suited him.

One of Bismarck's biographers says that the Chancellor noticed that upon his accession Fritz's liberal views began to cool and that he preferred to be a 'hammer and not an anvil', indeed that there were signs that he might become the most reactionary of all the Hohenzollerns.[17] If so, Bismarck was never more mistaken. With so little time left Fritz had to decide what was important and what was possible. It was not his liberalism that was drying up, but his energy, which the growths sapped increasingly. If Bismarck had worked under a healthy and strong Frederick III he would have had a different tale to tell. How much Fritz had wanted to do, and how cruel it was that he was not given the chance to do even some of it! Amongst his smaller dreams had been the rebuilding of Berlin Cathedral from plans he and Vicky had drawn up while wandering through Italy. One day in April Rudolf von Delbrück asked him about these plans. With a look that cut the historian to the heart, Fritz wrote on his pad 'that is all over and done with'.[18] Vicky too came in the end to accept the sad fact that they were 'mere passing shadows'. What irony it was that when at last they were their own masters they could not do the work 'which we have so long and so carefully been preparing'.[19]

The time-factor in Fritz's illness played a big part in influencing the conduct of the court and fashionable Berlin society, who hardly bothered to be civil. Professor Bergmann was a great society man, very talkative and much sought-after that spring for dinners and receptions; if he could not bring them news hot from the sick-bed, who could? But from other sources too the details of Fritz's illness and his fortitude in bearing his sufferings leaked out; good wishes and flowers, some of them no more than humble bunches from a cottage garden, poured into the Neue Palais daily, and Vicky liked to arrange these herself in his room. Moreover it was not mere curiosity either that caused the people to surge round the royal carriage when Vicky and Fritz drove to Berlin on the 30th of March 1888, the first time as Emperor and Empress. It must not be forgotten that many of these Berliners had had personal contact with Vicky and remembered what she had done for them during the Franco-Prussian War. Vicky was grateful for the affection which had flowered in such unpromising soil, not for herself but for Fritz. She noticed on that first drive together that at the sound of cheering the haunted, drawn expression which had become habitual to Fritz since his illness was for a brief moment quite gone.

*

Vicky and Fritz were anxious to settle the future of their daughter Moretta, who was now twenty-two years old and still professed to be passionately in love with Alexander of Battenberg. Since Sandro had left Bulgaria and become a private citizen, there seemed nothing to stop the young people from getting married: nothing that is, except one man's iron determination that the marriage must not take place at any cost.

Bismarck had been in one of his intractable moods even before Fritz brought the matter up. When Fritz invited the Prince to Berlin, the Chancellor promptly exploded, shouting that he had worked himself to the bone to conciliate Russia (who was 'only too ready to stick a knife into Germany's back') and that if the marriage took place everything that he had slaved for would be lost. Fritz knew that the real reason had nothing to do with St Petersburg. Bismarck's spies reported that there was a growing party in Bulgaria which wanted Alexander back. Yet if Sandro were to return with a princess of Prussia as his bride, the position of the anti-Russian party would be greatly strengthened, and that would never do. But there was more to it than that. Bismarck had been maddened by a rumour that Fritz intended bestowing a high Order on Sandro and reinstating him in the German army, possibly as a general, a position for which he was well qualified. All this Fritz did not deny when Bismarck confronted him with it. Sandro had been made almost penniless through no fault of his own, and badly needed a job. As for the Order, 'pour le Mérite' was one of several in the Emperor's gift and was intended as a public mark of Fritz's personal feelings for this much-wronged young man. But it was preposterous to imagine that Vicky had a plan not only to make Sandro Chancellor (as Bismarck believed when the marriage was mooted), but also to dissolve the Reichstag, to hold a new election and so bring back the old majority of Freisinnige, Centre and Socialists who would support Sandro against Bismarck. None of this had the slightest foundation in fact but, as Erich Eyck has said, whenever the Chancellor thought his personal power in question he was inclined to see ghosts.[20]

Once again Bismarck used the old threat of resignation. Too ill to argue, Fritz gave in and sent a telegram to Alexander cancelling the visit. Bismarck had won, but he demanded revenge as well. He whipped up national fury in the press against Vicky and Fritz (and Queen Victoria as well), arguing that Germany would lose Russia's friendship if she was seen to be cordial to Prince Alexander (as Queen Victoria remarked to Lord Salisbury 'What a humiliating position for Germany to be in'.[21]) The public was made to believe this, but the truth was very different. The Czar snubbed Bismarck, and the Russian Foreign Minister Count Giers sent a carefully formulated note to Schweinitz, German Ambassador in St Petersburg, to say that the Czar would not draw any political conclusions if Alexander visited Berlin. The Czar had in fact approved highly of Fritz's proclamation, and had never been so satisfied with his relations with Germany as he had since the accession of Frederick III.[22] Bismarck's 'insufferable affront to the Czar' had no truth in it whatsoever!

If Bismarck's account of this interview with his Emperor on the 31st of March to his henchman Busch makes strange reading, it is as nothing to the report Count Radolinski sent to his friend Fritz Holstein a day or two later. It purports to be an eye-witness account of a conversation between Vicky and Fritz, but there is not a word of truth in it from start to finish. Radolinski poured out his hatred of the Empress to Holstein with spiteful and melodramatic inventiveness. According to his story, Vicky and Fritz had a terrible quarrel about the Battenberg marriage. The moment Vicky heard Fritz tell Radolinski that Sandro's visit had been cancelled, he said, she rushed into the room in a rage (she had been listening at the key-hole) and the sparks flew. 'The poor helpless Kaiser wrote down "I cannot plunge this country into a war with Russia on account of her marriage." She [Vicky] became more and more violent. Radolinski said to her "But, Your Majesty, I implore you to think of the Kaiser's health." She did not even hear him, she kept talking. The Kaiser rent his clothes, wept, tore his hair, gasped for breath, but stood firm about the Battenberg visit.'[23]

Everything that Vicky and Fritz are supposed to have said is so totally out of character that the story is almost self-evidently false. But this is not all. His ignorance of facts betrays Radolinski's fiction. He did not know that Fritz had been told before the 31st of March – the date when Fritz discussed the Battenberg marriage and Sandro's visit to Berlin with Bismarck – that the Czar no longer objected (now that Sandro had abdicated) to his marriage with the Emperor's daughter. So therefore the reason for the supposed 'quarrel' ('it will be the death of my poor child') falls, like Bismarck's 'insufferable affront', to the ground. There was no truth in it at all.

Shortly before this, Queen Victoria had learned that Sandro had fallen in love with an opera-singer, and had warned Vicky to do nothing in a hurry about the marriage: 'above all do not contemplate such a step without the perfect acquiescence of William. You must reckon with him as he is Crown Prince and it would never do to contract a marriage which he could not agree to.'[24] The Queen deliberately (and, as it turned out, unwisely) refrained, however, from telling Vicky about the opera-singer. Vicky disregarded her mother's warning and was overjoyed to learn that the Queen would break her journey to Florence in April and would come to Charlottenburg to see Fritz: with mama's support, Moretta might yet marry her Sandro. Bismarck reacted to this new danger at once. He stalked off to the British Embassy and, using the same tactics as he had done with Fritz, thundered that he would resign if Queen Victoria so much as set foot in Berlin. It was a pity for Vicky that Sir Edward Malet had never got over his early fear of the Chancellor and that Bismarck knew exactly how to handle him and sensed that the last thing the ambassador wanted at this stage of Fritz's illness was a new chancellor. Agitated by Bismarck's violence (which he feared far more than the Queen's displeasure) Malet cabled to Lord Salisbury that the Queen would not be welcome in Berlin and that if the Battenberg marriage question was reopened the Chancellor would not answer for the consequences with Russia. Lord Salisbury would not answer for the consequences with his Queen if he told her this, and coldly informed Malet that 'if German co-operation can only be had at this price we must do without it'.[25] The Queen could not make head or tail of what was going on in Berlin and was even more puzzled when on the 5th of April she received a telegram from Vicky to say that the storm was an invention of the press, and that Fritz and Bismarck had never been on better terms.[26]

The innocent Vicky, so devoid of cunning herself and with her common sense blunted by anxiety, was anxious to grasp at anything that might renew her child's chances of happiness. Unfortunately the Queen's warning had been too general to mean much and she did not know that Bismarck had discovered that Queen Victoria had heard about Sandro's opera-singer[27] and was prepared to use his knowledge ruthlessly for his own ends: Vicky and Sandro could now be finished off at one stroke. He was very sober, almost respectful when he asked Vicky for an interview and when they met he was 'so sincere and sensible' that she was impressed. He told her confidentially that although he must still appear to oppose the marriage, if the two young people were to marry in such a way that he would not have to recognise it officially he would raise no objection.[28] Faint with relief, Vicky fell headlong into the trap. Moretta and Sandro able to marry at last – it seemed too good to be true. It was. When Queen Victoria at last revealed the cruel truth that Sandro now no longer loved Moretta, she saw how she had been taken in, and blamed herself bitterly for giving Moretta false hopes.

The old Emperor William's culpable neglect in not insisting from the start that his Chancellor should treat the heir to the throne properly was having its predictable result. Even as Emperor and Empress, Vicky and Fritz had no one to guard them against private as well as public humiliation. As Vicky remarked bitterly, one had to ask the Chancellor's permission to fall in love – it was not enough that they thought a young man suitable for their daughter.

Perhaps Vicky's chief handicap throughout this whole incident was the lack of somebody to consult. She needed a man of old Baron Stockmar's calibre, someone always close at hand whom she could trust and whom the court and officials would respect and fear. Providentially, such a man had been found only recently, but he lived at a distance and had to be consulted in secret. Vicky's chief help and prop in this dangerous underground work was Baroness Stockmar, widow of Ernest Stockmar, who acted as go-between. The Baroness knew the Liberal Radical deputy Dr Ludwig Bamberger who lived near her.

Bamberger was a thoroughly honest and upright man with the highest principles, and was a devoted admirer of Fritz. He made it his business to know exactly what was going on, and in this way was of valuable service to his Emperor. Baroness Stockmar brought Vicky's and Fritz's problems to him and carried his replies back, sometimes in a letter but more often – and more safely – in her head. In this way Fritz got unbiased advice from one of the most experienced parliamentarians, who knew Bismarck and his ways better than any one else and who would warn them at once of the Chancellor's artful manoeuvres.[29] But it was not possible to obtain Bamberger's advice on everything. Without it, Vicky was acting in the dark and could make mistakes, especially if one of her family was involved and therefore her emotions.

*

Completely undeterred by Bismarck's bluff about resignation, Queen Victoria arrived at Charlottenburg on the 24th of April, bringing a sense of perspective to the over-excited scene. She was welcomed in royal fashion (which proved to her that it was not the people who were hostile to England, only a 'certain person' and his followers) very different from her semi-official, semi-private visit in 1858, 'neither one thing nor the other', that had caused offence in many quarters and had left the youthful Vicky a legacy of jealousy and spite.

The sun shone, the people cheered and waved the Union Jack along a route lined by the magnificent Gardes du Corps, all chosen for their great height. When the carriage stopped at the entrance to the palace gates, two huge soldiers stood sentry with drawn swords 'which is only done for a Sovereign'. After the Queen had tidied up, Vicky came to take her to Fritz. It was an anxious moment which went better than expected. Fritz was in bed propped up with pillows, and at the sight of his mother-in-law his face lit up, he raised both hands in welcome, and gave her a bouquet of forget-me-nots and french fern. The Queen was deeply moved at seeing him so ill. She sat for a short time by the bed, holding his hand and chatting about family gossip while Fritz gave her his pad to read every now and again. After luncheon Sir Morell Mackenzie was fetched and the Queen was surprised to hear him say that his patient was better. But it was clear Vicky did not think so when she went to the Queen's sitting-room in the evening and cried heart-brokenly. The Queen was quite horrified at all Vicky had to bear, not only cruel anxiety about Fritz but 'many unnecessary, unpleasant scenes besides'.

Next day Vicky took her mother to visit the Empress Augusta. The Queen was aghast to see such a change in the woman who had once been her closest friend. One side of her body was paralysed, while the other shook continually and her voice was so weak that it was scarcely audible. She gave the Queen a macabre photograph of the old Emperor taken after death and seemed quite relieved when the meeting came to an end. Vicky had arranged for her mother to see Baroness Stockmar, wisely not alone but together with Frau von Bülow. Nothing was even hinted at, the conversation was mostly harmless nostalgic reminiscences of the old happy days, but there is no doubt from fleeting references in letters that the Queen knew that the Baroness was rendering Vicky services in the best tradition of the old Baron.

On the 25th of April a meeting took place between Queen Victoria and Bismarck. Before the Chancellor was summoned to the Queen's presence he had to wait for a short time in an ante-room with Lord Stamfordham and Sir Henry Ponsonby, both secretly delighted at the highly excitable and nervous state of the illustrious Chancellor, who bombarded them with questions – would the Queen be sitting or standing? How would he know when to retire?

The Queen and Bismarck got on very well. Bismarck, using all his charm, said he had seen her first at Versailles thirty-three years ago and could describe her as she was then. Everyone likes to be remembered, even a great Queen, and Queen Victoria was no exception; she was 'very gratified'. Foreign affairs were touched on, and Bismarck said he thought Austria was over-afraid of Russia, which the Queen thought most odd since only a few days before the Emperor of Austria had made exactly the same remark to her about Bismarck. The Queen mentioned Willy's inexperience, and the Chancellor assured her he was not thinking of a regency: 'It would be cruelty'. The Queen begged him to 'stand by poor Vicky',[30] but the Battenberg marriage was not mentioned between them.

Later on Bismarck redeemed the shame of his nerves by adopting a patronising tone whenever the meeting was mentioned: Grandmama was a 'jolly little body',[31] and had 'behaved quite sensibly at Charlottenburg'.[32] If the Queen kept off the subject of Sandro's marriage with Bismarck, she discussed it from joyous beginning to inglorious end with Vicky, who bravely faced the fact that the affair was drawing to a close and that 'it could never be'. It had already dragged on too long, anyway long enough for her to see that Sandro had changed. But who could blame him if after all the fuss he wanted to marry the singer with whom he had now fallen in love, and retire into private life? The Queen advised Vicky to 'forget the whole business'. She did this, not because since his abdication Sandro had no political significance,* but because, on one side at least, love had vanished. To think otherwise is to misunderstand the Queen's romantic attitude to marriage.

*As N. B. Rich: *Friedrich von Holstein*, i. 131 incorrectly states.

The Queen left Charlottenburg on the 28th of April. Saying good-bye to Fritz was an ordeal, but once again it passed off extremely well. The Queen gave him her photograph, which he kissed: 'and I kissed him as I did every day and said I hoped he could come to us when he was stronger'. And with a perfectly natural smile and a wave of her hand she took leave of this beloved son-in-law for ever.

It was dreadful for Vicky to part with her mother. At the station she was suddenly overcome and struggled hard to control herself, but when the Queen entered her carriage she broke down completely. 'It was terrible to see her standing there in tears while the train moved slowly off and to think of all she was suffering and might have to go through. My poor child, what would I do to help her in her hard lot.'[33]

CHAPTER 22

'I will take Care of Her'

FRITZ had to have a new canula at the end of April. Dr Bergmann, who had been brought back on to the case by Bismarck, insisted on fitting it himself, but did the job so clumsily – using brute force instead of delicate manipulation – that there was heavy bleeding and Fritz was in great pain. In his book *The Fatal Illness of Frederick the Noble* Sir Morell Mackenzie asserts categorically that in mistakenly making a new passage Bergmann signed Fritz's death warrant.[1] The description of this operation makes hideous reading.[2] Bergmann hotly denied he had done any damage, but he was not noted for his manual dexterity and only insisted on inserting the tube in the first place through pique and jealousy of Mackenzie. Vicky describes what took place in a letter to Queen Victoria written after Fritz's death: apparently Bergmann snatched the canula out of Mackenzie's hands and proceeded to insert it in the most awkward and bungling way.[3]

From that moment Fritz began to sink steadily.

With an eye to the future Mackenzie carefully preserved the piece of paper on which Fritz had written 'I hope you will not allow Professor von Bergmann to do any more operations on me'. After this there was nothing for Bergmann to do but retire from the case for a second time, which he did in high dudgeon and an air of injured innocence. But he had not finished with his royal patient. With Willy's acquiescence he arranged for vitriolic attacks to be made on Vicky and on Sir Morell Mackenzie in the papers. Nor did he leave it at that, for he seems to have had time to prepare some strange evidence* to fight the charges he expected the English doctor to make against him after Fritz's death.

Fritz would not give up. He worked at his desk, signing documents, writing letters, making entries in his diary, and reading all the newspapers from cover to cover, showing Vicky with his finger or a pencil any item that struck him particularly. He kept all Renan's works close at hand to dip into whenever he had a moment, because he knew how much Vicky admired him. Just as Vicky did, he felt an urge to be well informed on many subjects.[4] His mind had lost none of its edge, it was only his body that was deteriorating rapidly. He was mere skin and

*Scurrilous hints of intimacy between Vicky and Mackenzie.

bone, drawing strength only from his tremendous will-power and a refusal to admit that he was failing fast. Vicky too was using all her will-power to hold him back from the grave, but it was a losing battle. Yet it seemed that for some he was not dying quickly enough to make room for the rising sun.[5] She had been furious when she had heard that Herbert Bismarck had the impertinence to go out of his way to tell distinguished foreigners, without the slightest compunction, that Fritz was only an encumbrance, that his mind was gone and that he understood nothing.[6]

But it was Vicky who was the chief target of this man and others like him. After all, she was not mortally sick but would be living on, a widowed Empress, still young, still clever and with a voice that knew how to make itself heard. Herbert Bismarck, Radolinski and Fritz Holstein all spread it about that Vicky did not care in the least what happened to Fritz, as long as she got her own way; the first two of these men certainly knew that she lived in daily dread of losing him. She was his devoted watch-dog and guarded him with all her might against everything, especially the kind of scenes he now found hard to endure – Willy's irrational temper and Bismarck's hysterics. 'My only anxiety is to shield the Crown Prince',[7] she had told Countess Bruhl after a stormy set-to in January with Willy at San Remo. Because of the strong wills and total lack of compassion of these two in particular, Vicky suffered continually from nervous headaches. After taking the brunt of their displeasure she had to find energy from somewhere to control the doctors and so prevent almost daily quarrels in the sick-room. Yet Fritz never once heard her complain or saw her other than cheerful. She lavished all her loving care on him, giving him hope and courage to endure his sufferings. Far from wanting power, she would have done anything to preserve the old Emperor's life, if only Fritz could have been allowed to stay in the sun; 'I pray fervently every day to let the Emperor live a little longer, at least until spring when my darling could stand the fatigue of a long journey better than would be the case today',[8] she had written to Princess Catherine Radziwill in February 1888. Indeed all Vicky's letters from San Remo during the winter of 1887–8 are filled with terror at Fritz having to return as a sick man to the rigours of a Berlin winter.

Despite abundant and irrefutable evidence to the contrary there were, and still continue to be, extraordinary accounts written of Vicky's lust for power and her joy on becoming Empress at last. Emil Ludwig describes the first court or mourning reception of the new reign held to receive condolences on the death of the old Emperor. Vicky had to conduct this alone, Ludwig says, 'thus savouring for once in her life the homage of the first men and women in the kingdom'.[9]

The truth is, of course, that to an Empress and the eldest daughter of the Queen of England mere German princelings were nothing. Count Alfred von Waldersee, Willy's close friend and admirer, takes up the tale in his memoirs. He says that he was standing close to the throne as Vicky approached it. The new Empress 'tried to assume a regal bearing, flung her head back and took the two steps up to the throne at a leap',[10] revelling in being the centre of attention. The Count forgot to mention however that every woman present wore a veil of such thickness that not a single feature could be seen. Indeed it was so thick that no one could have known if the Empress had been really Vicky or a substitute. Moreover even an acrobat would have found difficulty in taking the steps up to the throne 'at a leap', encumbered by several yards of heavy material. On the other hand two reliable witnesses who were also present that day – Princess Catherine Radziwill and Frau von Albedyll – say that it was so difficult to see through the opaque darkness of the mourning veil that they had to grope their way along and that it was not possible to recognise the woman in front or behind. Yet Alfred von Waldersee swore that he saw Vicky doing the impossible.

On the 13th of April 1888 the British Military Attaché in Berlin, Colonel Leopold Swaine, sent the Prince of Wales a moving description of Vicky's devotion to her dying husband which does something to lighten the darkness: 'We are living in sad times here in Berlin. Not sad alone because we have an Emperor at death's door, nor sad only because there are family disagreements, but sad, doubly sad, because almost all officials – perhaps with exceptions, but I know them not – are behaving in a way as if the last spark of honour and faithful duty had gone; they are all trimming their sails. It seems as if a curse has come over this country, leaving but one bright spot and that is where stands a solitary woman, doing her duty faithfully and tenderly by her sick husband against all odds. It is one of the most, if not the most, tragic episodes in a country and a life recorded in history.'[11]

*

By the 15th of April Fritz was only able to spend short periods out of bed, and one evening when Vicky was sitting with him as usual he wrote on his pad that he wanted to go back to the Neue Palais.

On a day full of sunshine and the songs of birds Fritz was put into a little river-steamer specially fitted out to make him comfortable, and was taken across the lakes of the Havel to Potsdam. Despite Bismarck's efforts to suppress news of what was happening, Fritz's courageous fight for life had leaked out and had not left the people unmoved. Eager crowds lined the river banks to wish him well, many with garlands of flowers which they threw into the water in an endeavour to show their affection. As the steamer approached Spandau all the workers rushed to the water's edge, eager to cheer the sick Emperor, and as it passed the Pfaueninsel, where Fritz had enjoyed so many family picnics in the old days, he raised himself on his elbow and waved his hand while tears trickled down his cheeks.

When they reached Gleinicke Fritz asked the stretcher-bearers to wait a moment while he looked across the river to Babelsberg. A quarter of a century ago he had brought his young bride to this palace of towers and creepers. There his first child had been born, and there too he came near to losing all his happiness. But he had not done so, and how thankful he had been to have Vicky given back to him. Not long afterwards the chance had come to be king. He would have acted very differently if he could have looked into the future then. The thought that he had been timid and indecisive and that Vicky had paid for his lack of maturity made him unhappy still, and a look of infinite sadness came over his face.[12]

Once again, just before he entered the Neue Palais, Fritz signalled that he wished to stop; taking his pad he wrote that he wanted the Neue Palais to be known in future as 'Friedrichskron'. A suite of rooms had been prepared on the ground floor for him so that if the weather was good the doors could be opened and he would be able to see the garden from his bed. Looking round at everything Vicky had done for his comfort, Fritz was suddenly overwhelmed and putting his head in his hands, he wept silently, while Vicky held him fiercely in her arms. Then pulling himself together he wrote that he wished to work, and still streaked with tears his face took on that awful look of resignation that it had worn ever since he knew he was going to die.

There were still things he could do in the short time left to him. One of these was to dismiss the dishonest Minister of the Interior, Robert Puttkamer, a devoted Bismarckian who had been found guilty of electoral fraud and whom Bamberger had advised him to get rid of.[13] Fritz made Puttkamer's resignation a condition for signing the bill prolonging the life of the Reichstag for three years. On the 7th of June it was announced that Puttkamer would go. This let loose a torrent of abuse against Vicky from the Bismarckians, who accused her of forcing Fritz to get rid of him. But Vicky was beyond caring. What did it signify? They were always abusing her. She wrote to Queen Victoria that 'if Fritz goes, I do not in the least care what becomes of me. I do not want these people's love and I scorn their hatred. Fritz and I will be more than avenged some day by the course events will take when these people come to power.'[14]

After Puttkamer's dismissal Bismarck sent for Bergmann. He wanted to know 'how much longer I have to endure this?' The doctor stood by his former statement: 'He will not see the summer out.'[15] Even a dying Emperor could not go unpunished if he was unwise enough to cross Germany's Chancellor. Two days after Puttkamer's resignation, Bismarck gave an enormous dinner-party, with the ex-Minister as guest of honour. With flamboyant ostentation Bismarck rose and lifting his glass high he proposed Puttkamer's health. It was a petty triumph over Fritz that he loved to savour in the years ahead.*

*

At the beginning of June Fritz's old friend the King of Sweden travelled to Potsdam to see him. He was to be the last visitor from the world outside. Despite Vicky's pleadings not to exhaust himself, Fritz was determined not to receive him in bed like an invalid. He was now terribly wasted and his uniform hung on him, but he still managed to walk upright, only leaning a little on the stick Vicky had given him for Henry's wedding to his cousin Irene of Hesse (which he had insisted on attending a week earlier), and carrying his helmet in his hand. When the greetings were over, without in any way showing that he was ill he sat down in his bath-chair and talked of the King's recent travels in Spain. But it was all King Oscar could do to be cheerful, and the moment he left the room he broke down, telling Sir Edward Malet (who had come with him) that Germany would never see Fritz's like again.[16]

On the last Sunday of his life the great choir of the Twelve Apostles' church in Berlin asked permission to sing some choral music to Fritz. It was arranged that they should use the Muschelsaal while Fritz sat in his bath-chair and listened in the Tamerlan room next door. But when the 'Salve fac Regem' began, Sir Morell Mackenzie called Vicky (who was in the same room as the choir), to come back and sit with Fritz because he was in tears. The words and the music had affected him deeply. 'It is the first time that I hear it as Emperor', he explained to Vicky, ashamed of his emotion; then wiping his eyes he got out of the bath-chair and walked alone with the help of his stick into the Muschelsaal. There was a rush towards him and at once he was surrounded by the whole choir.[17]

On the 13th of June Bismarck came to the Neue Palais, looking remarkably well and spry. Fritz greeted him with a fleeting smile. He was now so weak that he could hardly grasp the pen. Pushing his pad aside, he motioned to Vicky to come and stand beside Bismarck. Then,

---

*William II played a similar trick on Bismarck several years later. Shortly before his own dismissal, Bismarck had dismissed his deputy, Boetticher, because he suspected that Boetticher was intriguing against him with William II. Soon after Bismarck's fall, William gave Boetticher the Order of the Black Eagle.

taking her hand he put it into the Chancellor's with an imploring look. Bismarck understood and leaning over the dying Emperor he said 'I will take care of her'.[18]

That night some food went down the wrong way and Fritz could not get it back into the right channel, so that it slipped through the canula and lodged in the lung. A few hours later pneumonia set in and Sir Morell had to feed Fritz through a rubber tube. During these last hours the English doctor cared for his patient with gentleness and skill, and in this way made up a great deal for his many mistakes. He hardly left Fritz for a moment, was on call day and night and did all he could to keep Vicky from utter despair, which now for the first time threatened to overwhelm her. She had given up hope, in her own words she was 'a sinking ship, so wounded and struck down'.[19] If Fritz was a 'perfect skeleton', Vicky was not much more than skin and bone herself. Anxiety and strain had brought on insomnia and when she did manage to fall asleep she would wake again at the slightest sound. She could not eat and often went for hours without food, but hardly noticed since she never felt hungry. She had aged considerably and her hair, once so soft and shining, was lifeless and greying; she wore it drawn back from her face and wound round in a bun – a style that did not suit her, but was easy to do in a hurry without a maid. Her eyes were as big and blue as ever, but now did not sparkle and were too often filled with tears. The energy and purpose that had shone out of them had gone with her hope; she was 'bleeding from a thousand wounds' as she sat by the bedside of the dying husband whom she had loved passionately for thirty years. She held his hands, which used to be so strong and were now so thin and weak, and covered them with kisses as tears poured down her cheeks. Sir Morell Mackenzie assured Vicky that Fritz's restlessness did not mean that he was in pain, and for that she was thankful.

The next day, the 14th of June, dawned bright and clear and gave promise of one of those days Fritz loved best of all. On mornings like these they had gone riding together, getting up very early to have the world to themselves. Now Vicky could not look on the sunshine without pain. Soon after six she opened the door into the garden so that Fritz could smell the scent of the roses they had chosen together twenty-eight years ago and which this year bloomed more profusely than ever, then she took up her vigil by the bedside she had only left for a few hours' rest. The day passed fairly quietly and towards evening Fritz's pulse was stronger and he slept a little.

That night Vicky lay fully dressed on a sofa close to the open door leading into Fritz's room, but out of sight so as not to frighten him, while Fräulein Fuhrmann (matron of the Victoria Sisters in Berlin) kept watch with Sir Morell Mackenzie. Fritz was quite conscious and hardly slept at all, constantly changing his position and coughing a great deal. After dozing fitfully, Vicky again opened the door at six on the morning of the 15th of June: the birds were singing and the whole garden was bathed in a golden glow from the rising sun. Vicky took Fräulein Fuhrmann's place at the bedside and held one of Fritz's hands in hers. She noticed that it was limp and slightly damp, but when she kissed it Fritz opened his eyes, recognised her and tried to smile. At first he seemed to rally but from ten o'clock on there was a change – his breathing seemed shallower and his colour worse, but he was still conscious and indicated that he wanted to write something on his pad, though he was too weak to do so. His lips moved and Vicky understood him to ask if the doctors were satisfied with his condition and she nodded. At eleven o'clock Willy and Dona came, bringing Charlotte and Bernard who had been summoned by telegram. The three youngest girls crept in and clung to each other weeping. The day before had been Sophie's birthday and her father had ordered a large bouquet of flowers which he had given to her himself. He had looked so cheerful that the poor child had been deceived into thinking he was better.

The servants came to take leave of their Emperor whom they had known and loved and who had been so kind to them. Wetterling, his valet for many years, broke down as he knelt and kissed his master's hand.

In Professor Bergmann's absence Bramann led the doctors silently past their patient; each inclined his head in a stiff gesture of farewell, before joining the others to form an uncomfortable group at the foot of the bed.

Vicky longed to have these last precious minutes alone with Fritz, but she knew it was impossible. Dry-eyed and turned to stone, she did all she could to make Fritz comfortable. She gave him white wine on a sponge which he sucked eagerly and when she asked him if he was tired his lips formed 'very, very' and she told him gently to close his eyes and go to sleep. Gradually his expression changed and he no longer seemed conscious. He coughed, took two or three deep breaths, gave an involuntary jerk, closed his eyes tight and convulsively as though something was hurting him and suddenly was still. Frederick III's purgatory was over.

Vicky kissed Fritz's hands and put them by his side. She got up and took down from the wall a withered laurel wreath that she had given him when he came home from the Franco-Prussian War and laid it on the 'hero who had overcome all'. She fetched his service sword and rested it on his arm. On his heart she placed 'the picture he loved best,

a medallion with my hair in it' which he always wore, and on his
fingers his wedding ring and another ring she had given him: with
one last loving look, Vicky said good-bye to the 'best husband in the
world': 'I have laid everything in the coffin and I his wife lie there too.'[20]

*

Half an hour later a detachment of soldiers from Willy's Hussar
regiment surrounded the Neue Palais and sealed it off from the outside
world. Vicky saw the men when she went into the garden to cut roses
to put on Fritz's bed. She did not understand what was happening and
stared at them bewildered when they appeared with rifles in their
hands from behind every tree and every statue. An officer approached,
took her by the arm and led her back into the house. It was a sign of
her stricken state that she went meekly and without a word. She was
silent when she was told that this was done on the orders of the new
Emperor, who wished to prevent all important papers from leaving
the palace. To show what he meant, the officer there and then proceeded to go through Fritz's desk, throwing the contents all over the
floor. He found nothing. Fritz had feared something of the sort might
happen, and when he and Vicky had gone to England for the Jubilee
he had taken three boxes of papers with him and left them safely in the
archives at Windsor. It was fortunate for Vicky that he had been so
far-seeing. Before Fritz had been dead more than a few hours soldiers
were tramping all over the Neue Palais, entering bedrooms and
emptying drawers and cupboards. But when asked what they were
looking for, they hardly knew. Willy appeared in full-dress uniform
and refused to give his mother an explanation of his infamous conduct.
He was very full of himself, very much the Emperor, playing the bully
right and left; Queen Victoria wondered if he was right in the head
when she heard this story – in a modified form – from Vicky.

Willy (henceforth referred to as William) wanted to have Sir Morell
Mackenzie arrested at once, but was prevented from making such a
blunder by the lawyer Heinrich Friedberg who had come to the palace
on Fritz's business and was horrified to find soldiers everywhere, even
in the telegraph office so that no messages could be sent out. They
would not even allow the servants to order black crape from Berlin.

By the middle of the afternoon high-ranking officers arrived to take
over, among them General von Winterfeld, who at once flung himself
on Fritz's desk for a second raid. Seeing it empty, he said officiously
that he knew it had secret drawers, something must have been overlooked. When he found no hidden springs and no secret hideaway, he
screamed that someone had got there before him and taken everything.
Kessel, Fritz's former aide, who had abandoned the sinking ship and

climbed on to the new one, rushed to William and talked wildly of papers he must confiscate and of others which had disappeared and must be found.[21] Vicky's privacy was not respected, nor a thought spared for her grief. With her arms round her three daughters she sat dry-eyed and silent in the bedroom next to the room where Fritz lay.

Many years later when a cold world had shown him up for what he was, William, then an exile in Doorn, wrote an account of this poignant day: it is very different from what really happened. He describes in some detail the scene in the bedroom, particularly his father's 'last loving look',[22] which included this unaffectionate and undutiful son, who had wronged him and whom he could not trust to look after his mother.

And what of Bismarck's promise to his dying Emperor? Two days later he had forgotten it. He knew that soldiers were in the Neue Palais, he still had considerable influence over William and had it in his power to call them off. Instead he slipped away to Friedrichsruh, leaving his son Herbert to represent him at the funeral. His crops needed attention – Frederick III was beyond needing anything and Bismarck was a practical man.

Fritz had left instructions that he did not wish to lie in state, so the coffin was closed at once and taken to the Jaspersaal. Before it was nailed down Vicky and her daughters, Moretta, Sophie and Mossy came for a last look. Vicky gazed for a long time at the face of her dead husband 'so good, so kind, so tender, brave, patient, noble, so cruelly tried'. She was thankful that for him all suffering was over. How was she going to be able to live on alone? It had fallen to her lot to remain, to remember 'how he went from me'. In 1861, her mother had found strength from somewhere, 'and I will too'.[23]

Fritz had told her, after Waldemar's death, that he wanted to be buried next to this favourite son, and that when his turn came he would like a simple funeral without the pomp and ceremony given to former kings. Vicky arranged that everything should be done just as he would have wished. But she would not attend the funeral herself. Soldiers were still in the Neue Palais; it had become a prison and not a home, and she longed to escape from it. The night before Fritz was to be buried, when it was quite dark, she fled with her daughters from the palace that had been hers for thirty years (she was to return to it only twice) and that she had restored with taste and her own money to its former magnificence, creeping out like a fugitive through the secret side-entrance Prince Charles Anton had used many years ago. Two devoted women, Baroness Stockmar and Frau Schrader (wife of Karl Schrader, the National Liberal) were waiting with a carriage to take them to the Bornstädt farm, where they would be safe.

The decision to leave the Neue Palais had been taken in a hurry. Frau Schrader had come to see Vicky and had found her in a desperate state. William had promised her faithfully there would be no autopsy on his father, but a few hours later he had callously broken that promise, persuaded into it by Dr Bergmann. It is difficult to understand what the German doctors hoped to discover from this pointless operation. If it was done to make Vicky suffer, it succeeded. It drove her mad with 'sorrow, anger and agitation that they dared to touch his dear face, his sacred mortal remains'.[24] Her misery reopened old memories and old wounds, the many sorrows she had borne came flooding back. Even the gentle breeze of that beautiful summer's day reminded her painfully of Sigi's death. Twenty-two years ago on such another perfect June morning she had rushed into the garden frantic with despair, and had been amazed to see the sun still shining and the birds still singing and nothing changed but herself.

The birds were singing on the Bornstädt farm, but she could not hear them; she only heard the tolling of the mourning bell carried on the still summer air. 'Is it really for him?' she asked herself brokenly, 'Why should such men die? They have no right to be taken, for this sad world needs them. Now another has taken his place.'[25] This, Queen Victoria ungrudgingly admitted, was more than she ever had to bear: 'this misfortune is terrible, far worse than mine in '61.'[26]

All that day Vicky lay on the bed in the 'English' bedroom she had shared with Fritz, longing for sleep but too exhausted to rest. She cried out in despair as her mother had before her 'Why was I not allowed to go with him? Why oh why this separation?' Making a valiant attempt to be brave she wrote to the Queen 'you bore it and I must bear it, it would not be right or grateful to mourn against God's decree, but more cruel suffering was never laid on human soul than on mine at this moment'.[27] She thanked God she had been given the power to keep up Fritz's courage and confidence to the very end, so that he 'did not think about the parting'. She thanked God too that she had been given the strength to hide her sorrow, and that she had been able to 'show him a cheerful and contented face' although she could neither eat nor sleep: 'My one thought to help him over the inevitable end, gently, softly, contentedly and quietly.'[28]

And when it was all over her own son had come and driven her away. 'Why does pain not kill immediately?' Vicky wrote in Fritz's diary under the entry for the 15th of June, only one hour after his death.

CHAPTER 23

A Generation Skipped

As a wife Vicky had felt herself capable of anything. As a widow she was lost, floundering, a ship without a rudder. She had never been self-sufficient, and the loss of her husband left her defenceless and exposed. Like many impulsive and passionate women, she only functioned properly with a strong male arm to lean on and an affectionate home life to sustain her. Now both had gone.

To William, the three months of his father's reign had been little more than an interlude that was best forgotten. His mother's face gazing out of the heavy folds of her widow's weeds irritated him, and in consequence he often said more than he meant from an irrational wish to hurt. During one angry outburst he called his father's ideals 'a lot of nonsense' – an expression he used far too often. Vicky had not, for once, sufficient control over her temper to let it pass; white with anger, she defended Fritz fiercely, said too much and she and William parted on the worst possible terms. William went straight to his grandmother Augusta for sympathy and complained bitterly that his mother forgot he was now head of the family and treated him as a son without remembering that he was also Emperor[1] (an idea dismissed by Queen Victoria as 'perfect madness'). He failed to see that this could be taken as a compliment and that it would be a good thing if he now and again emulated his mother's loyalty.

Father and son had been at opposite poles – Bismarck had seen to that. Like the Chancellor, William poured scorn on everything his father esteemed: closer ties with England, the encouragement of culture and progress generally, and improvement in the worker's lot – sunk to such a deplorably low standard under Bismarck. Above all, Fritz had wanted to free Germany from the chains of despotism, and to this end he had prepared himself, by hard work and a devotion seldom equalled among the Hohenzollerns, for the onerous duties of kingship that he had never had a chance to fulfil. But he could have done more than he did in the short time allowed him if he had enjoyed the support of a son who shared his outlook, thoughts and principles. If William had been on his side, he would have risked accepting Bismarck's resignation – nothing would have pleased him more. But as things were he had feared to bring about a crisis and so had to steer a middle course, which annoyed him intensely.[2]

On the 25th of July William made his first speech from the throne; he did not mention his father's name, but spoke of his late grandfather, whose policy he said he was determined to follow. Vicky read every word of this deceptively humble speech and it showed her, with a fresh stab, that she and Fritz had been nothing. A generation had been skipped.

A fortnight after Fritz's death William drove out to see his mother at the Bornstädt farm, bringing such a large suite that the house could not hold them all. Vicky was listlessly making butter in the dairy at the time, and William had to be kept waiting while she was found. It was not a good start to a discussion between them about a date for Vicky to leave the Neue Palais. William was polite and distant; Vicky took her cue from him and did her best to hide her agitation and be polite and distant too. But his request to remove her things and those of his father as soon as possible was an unexpected blow. Of course she had always known that the Neue Palais was Crown property, but she also knew that nobody had cared two straws about it until she and Fritz went to live there and spent their own money on restoring it. It was now desirable and comfortable, the gardens the finest in Germany, but she had not realised that William had his eye on it for himself.

Where was she to go? Queen Victoria had written to tell William how worried she was about 'Mama's future home'. The Prince of Wales was behind this letter. He had returned from the funeral in a fury, longing to kick both William and Herbert Bismarck. His presence had not prevented Herbert Bismarck from using language even more violent than his father's: he talked loudly and contemptuously of the late Emperor, and the Prince noticed with disgust that his nephew allowed it. He had asked William outright what palace he was giving his mother, and had been told that she could have the Villa Liegnitz. The Queen was indignant. It was a poky little place and she had to tell William firmly that it 'would not do for your mother who is the first after you and who is the first Princess after Aunt Alix in Great Britain'.[3] There were of course plenty of empty castles in Germany, but all were inconvenient and in need of repair. There was the Schloss at Homburg (gloomy and with no modern conveniences), another at Wiesbaden in the same condition, and two or three perfect wrecks in Berlin. Vicky ought to have been in a position to buy one of her own if she saw what she liked, perhaps in some pleasant spot along the Rhine, but she had no money for such an expensive purchase and Fritz had left her almost nothing, so it was out of the question.

However, Queen Victoria's letter had some good effect. She was the one person William was still a little afraid of, and although he would have liked to tell her to mind her own business he did not dare. In his reply he misrepresented things just enough to put himself in a better light. He told the Queen that he had offered his mother the Homburg and Wiesbaden castles 'as her own'.[4] But all he had actually done was to offer her the 'use' of these castles, which was not the same at all. The last thing Vicky wanted was to live in a place from which William could turn her out at a moment's notice. She desperately needed a safe roof over her head for her 'three sweet girls', who were suffering from being pushed from pillar to post and had no settled home.

Unfortunately this was not their only trial. The soldiers in the garden on the 15th of June, and the expulsion from the Neue Palais in July, were only the first signs of the persecution Vicky and her daughters were to suffer for several years at the hand of William II and his friends. The scurrilous attacks the press now launched on Vicky were instigated by Bismarck. Her daughters could not bear to read these vile calumnies on their mother, yet they screwed themselves up to read every word though their nerves suffered in consequence. The most absurd of them was the story that Vicky was intriguing to put Ernest of Cumberland back on his father's throne of Hanover – surely no one could believe such rubbish for a moment? But the pamphlet that Professor Bergmann was preparing to publish on Fritz's illness was anything but rubbish. It was a very serious matter, and Vicky did not know how she could bear to have the intimate details of Fritz's sufferings laid bare to the world in order to satisfy the vanity and spite of four doctors who had attended him: Bergmann, Gerhardt, Bramann and Landgraf. Instinctively Vicky turned to her eldest son, but William had no time to answer her cry for help. Yet Vicky could do nothing without him. Who but the Emperor had the right to prohibit the publication of the pamphlet?

Such a prejudiced account could do irreparable harm, especially if William remained silent. Vicky worried day and night about the effect on the German people when they heard of the quarrels between these men and Mackenzie, embellished as the story would be by barbed shots at herself. 'It is an outrage to all my feelings',[5] she wrote in anguish to the Queen. It was more than that. It was a deliberate and diabolical form of torture practised upon a defenceless woman who had already had to bear more than her share of misfortune. An old and well-worn legend was revived, that a dumb Emperor could not rule (Bismarck himself had categorically denied this), but with a new addition: that Sir Morell Mackenzie had known this and had therefore refused to admit that the Crown Prince had cancer. Herbert Bismarck, who of course also knew the story to be totally untrue, thought he saw a chance here to improve his standing with those who would not give him quite the same adulation as his father. He wrote an article which was published in all Bismarck's newspapers and began with the words: 'We now know that an English doctor of no particular account with radical political tendencies took it upon himself to play the part of Privy Councillor and to seek to intervene in directing the destiny of the German nation.'[6]

Everybody understood that this was another outburst against Vicky. Most had been indoctrinated with the belief that it was she who had brought in Mackenzie in the first place. Why then were there fresh attacks made on Vicky? Did Bismarck consider her to be a political danger still? Did he fear that his power was menaced by her in some way, at least enough to make it worth allowing his son Herbert to spread stories about her which he knew to be false? Did he imagine she had a following as ex-Empress? There is no knowing what he thought, for his mind never worked logically and he was quite capable of taking back without a qualm today everything which he had said yesterday. Moreover, everybody must have remembered that in November 1887 a bulletin[7] had been issued from San Remo, with Mackenzie as one of the signatories, stating that the Crown Prince was suffering from cancer of the larynx. This completely disposes of the fabrication which Bismarck was now trying to build up with Herbert's help, to the effect that no one was told the nature of the disease until after the accession.

There seems little doubt that Mackenzie saw from the beginning that it was cancer, but that he did not believe an operation could cure or even relieve it (and medical opinion was very much divided at the time over the success of such an operation). In his standard work *Diseases of the throat and nose*, Mackenzie asserts that in the case of cancer of the larynx the best that could be done was to postpone the inevitable end and make the patient as comfortable as possible. Critics of Mackenzie have to remember that in those days surgery was to be avoided since nothing could be done to prevent the sepsis which always followed and killed faster than cancer. Even the historian Werner Richter – no lover of Mackenzie – called this operation 'cruel and useless' and said that if it could be prevented by a lie, the lie was justified.[8] This opinion was backed up by Baron von Roggenbach, Vicky's and Fritz's great friend, who did not like Mackenzie either. He said that the English doctor had behaved honourably and straight-forwardly in refusing to operate, and that it had not been wrong for him to say that the tumour was not at first malignant: 'Never once did he disguise from the Crown Prince that it might become so.'[9] Nor indeed did Vicky ever say anything to Fritz that was not consistent with the truth.

Bismarck felt no shame in denying after Fritz's death that he had had anything to do with calling in 'that quack', and before the autumn he was putting it about that Vicky was 'at the bottom of all the mischief and it was she who had refused to allow the operation in May [1887]',[10] which he now brazenly said should have been performed. According to the Chancellor, Vicky had 'forced' Sir Morell Mackenzie on the Crown Prince, and she had been 'under the Englishman's influence and authority' ever since.[11]

Bismarck's fellow-conspirator in these lies was the great Bergmann himself. This man was the Chancellor's equal in intrigue and callousness, and his pride made him determined on revenge for the treatment which he complained he had received at the hands of the late Emperor and his wife. He made sure that Vicky's three eldest children – whom he knew to be at odds with her – learned that the operation was a 'mere nothing' and would have saved their father's life, while he told everybody else that the operation had been a matter of 'life and death'. Bergmann was a thoroughly evil man whose great name in surgery was far above his abilities. Unhappily the doctors under him, although more skilful, were far too frightened of him to utter a contrary opinion since he was powerful enough to destroy them and would not hesitate to do it.

Mackenzie would have emerged from this sorry business better than any of them if he had not now written a book on Frederick's illness, partly in answer to Bergmann's pamphlet but even more as a mistaken 'duty to the exalted persons who honoured me with their fullest confidence'[12] – a duty he would have done better to forget, since the book hurt and damaged Vicky without silencing the German doctors.

*

William's first proclamation was very different from his father's, and was all about military and naval affairs. The German people were not mentioned, a tactical mistake he had to pay for with the labour of a second speech to make amends. Even this did not meet with universal approval: 'it is with eyes raised to the King of Kings that I assume the sceptre and I vow before God to be to my people a just and merciful Prince.'[13] Some of his subjects looked in vain for any promise of fuller stomachs, better houses, education or good and steady employment. All this talk of ships and guns and now of justice and mercy smacked more of war than of peace, and many began to wonder what was coming.

Three weeks after Fritz's death, William set off on a round of state visits accompanied by an enormous suite.* This public display of disrespect shocked both Vicky and Queen Victoria, and the latter did

*His first visit was to Russia, and he boasted of his success with Alexander III. Yet the Czar called him 'un garçon mal élevé et de mauvaise foi'.

not hesitate to write her grandson an acid letter: she had expected a year's mourning, followed by his first state visit – of course to Windsor. William had his answer ready: 'State interests go before private feelings.'[14]

Vicky's views on mourning had changed, just as Queen Victoria had once predicted they would. She had forgotten the brushes she had had with her mother years ago, when she had insisted that outward signs of mourning meant very little. Now she could not forgive William's longing to be received as Emperor as soon as possible after only a short period of court mourning, and criticised him for being altogether too gay. If he had been a dutiful and loving son she would easily have been persuaded that it was necessary to get back to normal for the good of the country. As it was she was deeply offended at what she considered the levity of William's first reception, which to her was both unseemly and frivolous. It was held in the Weissersaal only a few weeks after Fritz's death, and was on an exceptionally grandiose scale; the guard in uniforms of Frederick the Great's time, the knights of the Black Eagle in their golden cloaks, the young Emperor entering to a fanfare of trumpets and the only concession to Fritz's memory the bows of black crape at the pages' knees. When this was followed by huge dinner-parties at the Marmor Palais (all, of course, at once faithfully reported to Vicky at Bornstädt by well-meaning friends who did not spare her the details – hundreds of carriages, bright lights and dancing), Vicky wondered if William had one spark of decent feeling left.

William loved the limelight too well to stay out of it longer than was absolutely necessary. At twenty-nine he was too young to realise the risk he thus ran, but there was less harm in entertaining on the grand scale than in many other things he did. He was photogenic and made headlines. His clothes and general air of flamboyance attracted attention in the foreign as well as the German press, and much was made of his good looks (he was shorter than his father and grand-father, but well proportioned and slim) and of the style with which he wore his clothes. All this fed his vanity, but it also fed his mother's anger. She forgot that William's theatrical appearance (for instance he wore his moustaches standing out against his cheeks in a carefully trained semi-circle and encased his supple body in skin-tight uniforms) made news, whereas Fritz's kindly face and solid worth had not. The versatility that he had inherited from the Coburgs was too often mistaken for sagacity, and when he talked of honour and glory and his burning desire to make the Fatherland the greatest country in the world, everyone was deceived except his mother. Above all, he was neither self-critical nor kind, and before very long he had trodden on many sensitive toes, the Prince of Wales's among them.

The quarrel with his uncle began immediately after his father's funeral. The Prince was convinced that if Fritz had lived he would have righted many wrongs, perhaps returned Alsace-Lorraine to France, Schleswig to Denmark and Hanover to the Duke of Cumberland (who was now married to the youngest sister of the Princess of Wales). A little unwisely he asked Herbert Bismarck if Fritz had ever mentioned this.[15] Herbert rushed to William and repeated the conversation, with one or two subtle changes; just as he expected, there was an explosion. A few days later in an angry speech at Frankfurt-an-der-Oder William vehemently denied that his father had any such intentions. He ended his speech with a threat that he 'would not tolerate such an insult to his father's memory'.[16] Coming from a son who not only tolerated insults to his parents, but improved on some and invented others, this made many of the older generation shake their heads at the hot-headed young Emperor who opened his mouth too wide and too often. But a delighted Bismarck was very willing to give the cauldron a stir and he made the emphatic but groundless assertion that the Empress Frederick had 'put the Prince of Wales up to asking such a question'.[17] As it happened Vicky had never heard of the conversation and could not understand what the fuss was about or why her brother was so incensed. Bertie had said it was a 'positive lie' that he had suggested to his nephew that he 'ought' to do these things and added that he had never discussed it with the Empress Frederick at any time.[18] Nevertheless, to his amazement Bismarck took no notice of this denial and attacked him relentlessly in the papers until his popularity in Germany dropped to nothing and he had to forgo a much-needed holiday in Homburg. Baffled and put out by the outburst his innocent question had evoked, Bertie had not understood how deeply he had offended his nephew. When he had cooled down himself he took it for granted that William had done so too and that the quarrel was over and done with. He had forgotten that the Emperor had been (and to some extent still was) under the tutelage of a man whose creed was an eye for an eye. William's chance to get his own back came in September 1888 when the Prince of Wales was on his way to stay with Franz Joseph in Vienna. William, who had also been invited, made a point of arriving first in order to tell the Austrian Emperor that he would not meet his uncle and that he had expected to be the only royal guest during his stay at the Viennese court. An embarrassed Franz Joseph had to ask the Prince not to stop in Vienna or his nephew might cut him in public, an insult that could have dangerous repercussions. So the Prince stayed with friends a few miles away and was rewarded for his good nature by reading in the papers that he had gone to Vienna to stir up trouble before the coming conference of Emperors.

Vicky was furious with William, and mortified that her brother had 'turned the other cheek so readily'. It was not the way to treat one of William's nature. Bertie should have responded with 'sharp decisive actions' that would have shown William that he had gone too far. Queen Victoria was of the same opinion. She refused to swallow such an affront to her heir, and said so without hesitation. William did not care for his grandmother's attitude at all. If he had dared, he would have liked to tell her that she was lacking in respect. Never able to foresee the consequences of his actions, he was already angry at the Queen's cold reception of his envoy General von Winterfeld. Warned by Vicky – 'I hope, dear mama, that you will not forget how he has behaved. Not one confidential word must be said to him'[19] – the Queen treated him with icy reserve. She had last seen von Winterfeld as her son-in-law's A.D.C., but at Windsor he never uttered one word of sorrow for his late master's death and only referred with great delight to the accession of the new one.[20] As the Queen aptly put it to Sir Henry Ponsonby, von Winterfeld was 'a traitor to his beloved master'.[21] Rather naturally, he returned to Berlin with a long tale of 'shocking treatment' that made William boil all the more because he could not bring himself to say a word to his grandmother about it.

*

Vicky left Germany in November with her three daughters for a long holiday in England. At one point the Prince of Wales had tried to stop his sister coming. William's bullying had so intimidated him that he had asked Lord Salisbury to dissuade the Queen from allowing the visit while the quarrel lasted, a display of weakness the Queen soon stopped. The unfortunate Lord Salisbury had to take the brunt of her cutting pen: 'everyone expects her to come to Windsor, wonders she has not come before. It would be of no use and only encourage the Emperor and the Bismarcks still more against us. You all seem frightened of them, which is not the way to make them better. Please let no one mention this again. It would be false and must not be.'[22]

A chastened Bertie went to Flushing in the royal yacht to bring Vicky over, after promising the Queen – who had told him that her 'blood boiled' at Bismarck's monstrous treatment of her daughter – to do everything in his power to lighten the burdens of 'poor persecuted Vicky'. Brother and sister greeted each other affectionately, and Vicky was 'deeply moved to see that dear ship again and all the friendly faces'. Yet there were painful memories, too, of last year when Fritz had been with her and she was still full of hope. When the *Victoria and Albert* docked at Gravesend a little after mid-day, the Queen went on board and the 'sad reunion' took place in private. Fifteen minutes later Vicky appeared, a tiny black-clad figure lost in the folds of her widow's weeds, leaning on the arm of the Prince of Wales. The Queen followed, escorted by her nephew George, and then the three Prussian princesses, all in deepest black.

London greeted Vicky like a reigning Empress. She was overwhelmed. She had expected nothing like it despite the Queen's letter telling her that 'every heart beats in loving sympathy for you here. The people want to show their feelings, love and respect.'[23] Thousands turned out to greet her. Because of court mourning there were no decorations, no cheers, but the silence was more effective than any sound and Vicky was deeply touched. In London a Sovereign's Escort waited to accompany them to Windsor Castle, where a guard of honour was drawn up in the quadrangle. As Vicky stepped down from the carriage the trumpets of the escort sounded a greeting. For a moment she was overcome, but her tears were hidden by her veil and she appeared quite calm as she shook hands with the Queen's household standing in two lines each side of the door to welcome her. These were the first tears for many months not shed in bitterness and sorrow. The sight of Windsor brought back memories of Fritz, but happy memories that Vicky wanted to remember: 'Here in my beloved Windsor Castle I feel the peace of protection and love, I am safe like a storm-wracked ship – at last in a safe harbour. Dearly beloved home of my childhood, my native country, my home. With broken wings, impoverished, bowed down with sorrow I return home . . .'[24]

Tired out in mind and body, Vicky wanted to see no one but her mother and brothers and sisters. Her forty-eighth birthday was spent quietly at Windsor. All the family had remembered her on this first birthday for thirty years without Fritz. There were present-tables in the oak room loaded with parcels and flowers – the Queen's present was a contribution towards the mausoleum. Vicky's nerves felt better and less strained than for months. The affectionate family atmosphere with its sympathy and understanding and the feeling Windsor Castle always held for her of the 'closeness of dearest papa', even the comforts peculiar to 'home' all worked their magic. The bad dreams began to fade and better ones to take their place. She even accepted quite calmly the news that Sandro had married Fräulein Loisinger and wished to be known in future as Count Hastenau. But the finality of it was sad for Moretta especially since her sister Sophie had fallen in love with Crown Prince Constantine of Greece and was going to marry him, a match to which the snobbish William made no objection.

But Sophie dreaded leaving her mother. Because they had all been through so much together, Vicky's three young daughters were pathetically protective towards her. They tried to shield her whenever they could, even from the Morier scandal which burst before she had been three weeks at Windsor.

The vulture had to find new prey. The moment Vicky had left Germany Bismarck had gone tooth and nail for Sir Robert Morier, at that time British Ambassador in Rome. The Chancellor made shocking allegations against him, announcing publicly that when Morier was *chargé d'affaires* at Darmstadt in 1870, during the Franco-Prussian War, he had communicated important military secrets he had learned from the Crown Princess to Marshal Bazaine and that these communications enabled the French to engage the Prussians by surprise at Vionville and inflict heavy losses on them.[25] Herbert Bismarck had been among those wounded and this his father could never forget.

Morier had not wasted a minute before protesting vigorously that he was innocent of such base charges, and had written to Herbert Bismarck enclosing a letter of denial from Marshal Bazaine and asking for an apology to be published in the North German Gazette. Feeling that he was on safe ground, with his father's controlled press at his beck and call, and that no one would ever be able to call his bluff, Herbert took a haughty line; Morier's request was 'an astonishing demand'.[26]

Morier had no effective support from the British Ambassador in Berlin. Sir Edward Malet was slow in refuting the charges, and his indecisive and hesitant behaviour made it seem that he believed Herbert Bismarck. Morier was angry, and wrote that had he been in the Ambassador's place 'I should have flown at the Foreign Minister's throat if he had been ten Herbert Bismarcks rolled into one'.[27]

Queen Victoria saw at once that the attack on Morier was only a roundabout way of getting at Vicky and Fritz, and she wrote very firmly to Lord Salisbury: 'it will do this country and yourself harm if you remain entirely silent. It looks as though we disbelieve the word of our Ambassador . . . it is most important that my Ambassador should not be left unsupported by his own government.'[28] But unsupported Morier remained. If Malet had been 'got at' by the father, the son had worked on Lord Salisbury. Moreover, a certain amount of personal feeling came into it; Salisbury did not like what he called Morier's 'unorthodox methods'. In December 1886 he had told the Queen that he had warned Morier 'to keep his unorthodox opinions to himself and to support the view of the Foreign Office in every society'.[29]

Now that the moment had come to speak out Salisbury was silent. That silence was the end of Morier.

Vicky's distress was great. No one knew better than she – from bitter experience – the horror of the victim's helplessness in this kind of situation. Morier had no one to speak up for him any more than she had. Their friends were all Bismarck's sworn enemies and he would discredit their evidence and crush them one and all the moment they raised their voices against him. It was not that they did not want to help the Ambassador, only that they had no way of making themselves heard. Bismarck knew that Bazaine's letter was genuine, yet he allowed a verbose and muddled article to be printed in the *Berliner Post* saying that the French statesman's defence of Morier was a forgery. The Chancellor had not spent years suppressing the truth to no purpose. But he could not get away with it in England. The *Daily Telegraph* boldly asked if all the late Emperor's friends were 'to be dragged in the mud and stigmatised as traitors?'[30] *The Times* had never liked Bismarck and said emphatically that it was all part and parcel of a 'system that must be called persecution directed against all those who were intimately connected with the Emperor Frederick and not sparing those nearest and dearest to him'.[31]

Feeling in England was very high and a good many stories of Vicky's trials began to leak out, as well as much that Morier had endured at Bismarck's hands. Yet William chose this moment to let the Queen know that she could expect a state visit shortly, while Bismarck made contact with Lord Salisbury (whom he not unnaturally looked on as a friend) with a view to talks on a German-British alliance – in order no doubt to put a spoke in the wheel of his old enemy, France.[32] At the same time as these overtures, Bismarck made a speech in the Reichstag, soft-soaping Lord Salisbury for all he was worth ('England – an old and traditional ally'), so that Vicky, who read every word in the safety of Windsor Castle, wondered whose skin was thickest, the Emperor's or his servant's? She was not surprised when she heard that her mother's Government would not play. 'Germany's friend' – Lord Salisbury – had no backers, and Herbert Bismarck had to go home empty-handed when he came to London for talks. Nor did William come off any better. The quarrel with the Prince of Wales was still not patched up, and with this and the Morier affair to his discredit the Queen had no alternative: 'William must not come this year . . . he would not meet with a very cordial reception, I am sure.'[33]

On the 26th of February, a grey cold winter's day, Vicky and her daughters returned to Germany. The Queen had urged them to stay on until spring at least and Vicky desperately wanted to remain, yet she knew, as she had known years ago, that duty cannot be shirked. She had chosen her lot, she could not turn her back on it now because it had become distasteful. Delaying the evil day solved nothing. Besides there were her three girls to think of, Prussian princesses, who belonged – as she too felt she did – to Germany. The decision was all the harder to make since her girls did not want to return any more than she did. Because they were young and unhappy, they cried bitterly and clung to their grandmother and the safe comfort of Windsor Castle where 'mama could laugh again', a sound they had not heard for many a long day. But Vicky was accustomed to assuming a public face, and she at least looked quite cheerful when she got into an open carriage to drive to the station. Hardened by years of rigid Prussian court etiquette, she braved the biting wind without a second thought – if the people were kind enough to wish to see her, despite the weather, then it would never do to hide herself in the warmth of one of the Queen's closed carriages.

All the royal family were at the station and when the moment came to step into the train, Vicky suddenly faltered as she clung to Alexandra, her favourite sister-in-law, in a last embrace. In a curious way she was experiencing over again the same feeling of lost homesickness that had overwhelmed her when she had left England over thirty years earlier. But then Fritz had been by her side.

CHAPTER 24

'Time will show that Fritz was right'

VICKY and her party crossed the border into Germany in a blizzard; when they reached Wildpark station the snow was inches deep and still falling so heavily that the road to Bornstädt was impassable. There was a hasty change of plan, and Vicky had no alternative but to take the girls to the palace in Berlin, which had not been prepared to receive them; unheated and covered in dust-sheets, it had the unwelcoming air of a temporary shelter. She was still there four days later when the Geffken affair suddenly exploded.

At the end of the Franco-Prussian War, Fritz had shown parts of his diary for those years to his friend Heinrich Geffken, whom he had known at Bonn and who was now Professor of Political Science at Strassburg. With Fritz's complete concurrence, Geffken had copied for his own use parts of this diary, mainly those concerning the events leading up to the proclamation of the Empire at Versailles. Infuriated that Bismarck's repeated attacks on Fritz had not ceased with his death, he published certain extracts anonymously in the October number of the *Deutsche Rundschau*. These told something of the struggle that had gone on in the German headquarters at Versailles over the creation of the Empire. They showed Fritz as the ardent supporter and advocate of the national idea and as a staunch believer in the Liberal organisation of the Reich.[1] They also revealed that Bismarck had been hesitant about the plans for unification and that at one time Fritz had to push him into it, while it uncovered Bismarck's little ruse with the King of Bavaria, and showed how his letter of invitation to William I to accept the imperial crown was no more than a word-for-word copy of a draft by the Chancellor himself. Yet no one who read these extracts impartially could possibly think that they detracted in the least from Bismarck's part in unification.[2] Bismarck did think so, however, and the extracts sent him into a frenzy.* Without hesitation and certainly without a shred of evidence he announced that it was 'all the

*One of the extracts which most annoyed Bismarck was Fritz's account of how Bismarck had refused to allow him to award the Iron Cross to non-Prussians. He shrieked to Busch that it was not he but Moltke who was against it.

work of the Empress Frederick'. When this made little impact, he said the entries were all forgeries. Two days afterwards he took this back and said instead that they were part of a memorandum he himself had kept for William I, containing his most secret ideas and schemes, but that Queen Victoria had stolen it and would not give it up. Busch got yet another version: Bismarck coolly confided to him that the diary extracts were 'quite genuine, but insignificant, superficial stuff without any true conception of the situation and a medley of sentimental politics and self-conceit'.[3] Bismarck knew he was talking absolute rubbish, Busch knew it too, but it helped to poultice his injured pride to play out this farce. But that was not the end of the matter. Geffken's whereabouts were discovered, he was arrested and tried for treason, but no case could be brought against him and he was released. From a legal point of view, therefore, Bismarck's campaign against Fritz's diary ended in defeat.[4] Despite this the witch-hunt continued. Von Roggenbach's house was entered and his papers seized, and so were the houses of other members of Vicky's and Fritz's small circle. Vicky could hardly bear to read the list of victims – Morier, Roggenbach, Keudall, Stosch, Von Loë, Geffken and many others dismissed and discredited, while she had to stand by, helpless to protect friends who had lost everything but their honour because they had been loyal.

Bismarck's conduct at this period is not easy to understand. Fritz was dead, Vicky was powerless, yet he still hated them both with an intensity that was so alarming that remarks were passed about his reason. One likely explanation is that he was suffering from years of over-indulgence, for he complained of irritation in the stomach, liver and bladder, and of blinding headaches which affected his eye-sight. He could not chew properly because his teeth were decayed, and his nerves were constantly on edge. Poison seeping into his blood from abscesses in his gums made him constantly unwell. He was not deranged in the ordinary sense – he cannot be excused by the plea that he was not responsible for his actions – but his naturally robust constitution was unbalanced through ill-health and his enemies suffered the consequences. He could no longer control his malevolent feelings towards the late Emperor and his wife, so that he lost all sense of decency and shame as he spread one untruth after another, each so ridiculous that even his admirers were perturbed: Vicky had stolen the Foreign Office cipher* (he knew quite well, in fact, that it had never been out of the Minister Kessel's hands); Fritz had wanted to use force against the Bavarians in the Franco-Prussian War and to shoot down

*This was the cipher which the Emperor kept for his correspondence with high state officials. It was in Kessel's custody at the time of Fritz's death.

the two army corps if necessary, for lack of discipline, while he himself had to 'rebuke the Crown Prince sternly for this, warning him that if he did so it would be an act of unheard-of treachery which a prince might decide on but which no gentleman could perform'.[5]

The origin of this latter falsehood lay in Bismarck's jealous anger of the Bavarians' open affection for Fritz, an affection which Fritz returned – he had told Bismarck early in the war that he was bound to them by so many close ties that he could 'never again look upon them as foreigners'.[6] The Chancellor had always been jealous, too, whenever he saw signs of love for their gentle afflicted Emperor in the German people, since he claimed that this should, by rights, be his alone. With his totally unforgiving nature Bismarck felt no qualms at hounding Fritz beyond the grave, in the hope that it would besmirch his name for ever and hurt the wife he had left behind. Death did not close the chapter of the sad ninety-nine days reign for him, and he continued to take every opportunity to show his contempt for a man who had never hurt him in any way. The Emperor Frederick's name only had to be mentioned for Bismarck to become instantly as red as a turkey-cock with fury; no matter what the occasion (and often to the embarrassment of foreigners), he would reel off a list of Fritz's short-comings, calling him 'a man with narrow views and small brain'.[7] These shortcomings were excellent conversational topics to revive a flagging dinner-party on one or other of Bismarck's country estates, even the ladies joining in the laughter. Sandro's fate stirred no pity in them either. His marriage to an actress and Vicky's admiration for him were particularly diverting. The Chancellor's conversation had never been hampered by a regard for truth, and his meeting in Charlottenburg with Queen Victoria had become one of his best after-dinner stories – he had suggested the 'line she should take about the marriage and she had followed it'.[8] To curry favour, Busch and Bucher, his constant companions at Varzin and Friedrichsruh, told their master how glad they were to be 'relieved of this incubus' and that the timely death of the Emperor Frederick 'had saved Germany from an evil future'.[9] This sort of talk was the breath of life to Bismarck, as these two sycophants well knew, and indeed this was the main reason why the Chancellor always preferred companions of inferior rank and education – their toadying could be relied on in return for food and drink and a comfortable bed.

These calumnies against Fritz came near to ruining Vicky's health completely. At the time of Geffken's arrest she became so distraught that she was in despair. She wrote to Queen Victoria 'I am quite beside myself with agitation about the diary. Bismarck's official answer is as insulting as it is untrue . . . yesterday I felt very near putting an end to myself.'[10] So much had, what Queen Victoria called, Bismarck's 'shameful conduct'[11] undermined Vicky.

*

The pressures on her during this first year of widowhood were almost overwhelming. Not the least of them was the haste she had to make to clear the Neue Palais, since it held so many treasured memories of Fritz: it was 'where his cradle and his coffin stood', and was the one place 'where I hear my darling's voice everywhere and see him and feel as if he were so near or coming soon'.[12] It held the accumulation of thirty years of marriage, and there was no one but Vicky to supervise its removal. During the next few months she had to perform many heart-rending acts. Fritz's 'dear Highland dress' was packed up and sent to Balmoral, his uniforms and medals stored and other clothes given away. Photographs had to be sorted and those in which Fritz figured sent to special friends. It was one of the most painful tasks of her life to touch and fold clothes that showed the very shape of a beloved husband who would never return, to come across reminders of Sigi and Waldie and to experience again the anguish of their deaths. It did not help her nerves to be distracted all the time by Bismarck's cruel threats that it would go badly with her friends if she did not see that certain documents were brought back to Germany at once.

In terror for their friends and her young daughters (now completely dependent on her) and with her spirits at their lowest after the strain of nursing Fritz, Vicky was so frightened that she begged Queen Victoria to return the boxes of Fritz's papers. She was not allowed to keep them but was forced to hand over everything, the diary included, to Ministers of the Crown, who went through them and placed what they thought important in the archives in Berlin. No sooner had she done this than Vicky was seized with a dreadful feeling that she had made a mistake in giving up the manuscript of the diary. For some reason, possibly because the diary held so many personal allusions, Vicky was afraid that William would order the 'precious manuscript' to be burned. If he did so she would never forgive him[13] – a remark which shows that despite everything and because he was her son, she could still talk of forgiveness.

The Villa Liegnitz was taken from her as well as the Neue Palais: William needed it for 'one of my gentlemen', so she had to give it up before she had set foot in it. In exchange William offered her a room in the Stadt Schloss in Potsdam if she ever wanted to spend a night or two there – but she must ask permission first! It looked as though she would only have the Bornstädt farm, but it was much too small to live in permanently and had only been bought in the first place as an occasional refuge from Berlin.

By the end of October nothing had been settled and Vicky was suffering dreadfully from nerves caused by insecurity. She told her daughter that she was the reincarnation of the Wandering Jew, with nowhere to lay her head. Queen Victoria was aghast at her grandson's inhumanity. She wrote to Vicky at the beginning of October 'If I do not speak of William's shameful and undignified conduct it is because I feel too furious, too indignant, too savage also to trust myself'.[14]

*

In the intervals between worrying about her own future and that of her girls, Vicky was anxious that relations between England and Germany should not suffer because of Bismarck's wickedness and William's folly. She did all she could to persuade Queen Victoria to allow William to pay her a state visit in the summer of 1889 – she knew he was longing for it, and besides 'it might do him good'. Apart from his conduct towards his mother, the Queen could not forget that William had never apologised to the Prince of Wales for the Vienna incident, which (as always happened in Germany) had become distorted out of recognition: the Prince of Wales had insulted the Emperor by refusing to meet him in Vienna. The Queen, however, would not stand for this. No apology, no visit. William took refuge in astonished innocence – how could he apologise for something he had not done? Very subtly he hinted that Uncle Bertie had invented the whole thing 'in a sort of way'.[15] Queen Victoria knew he was lying, and so did Vicky, but Lord Salisbury was quite prepared to sacrifice the Prince of Wales to political expediency – England was the only country which had not received the new ruler, so 'the Emperor should come this year'. The Queen was far from satisfied, but after her minister had worked on her she reluctantly gave way. Vicky had a touching faith in her mother's power to influence William for the better. For some reason best known to himself, so had Lord Salisbury. Both expected too much from the visit and were afraid that some unpleasantness might crop up to prevent William from coming, and both breathed sighs of relief when the Emperor sailed into Spithead on the 2nd of August 1889, childishly excited by the splendour of his uniform as Admiral of the Fleet, which made him 'quite giddy' with delight.

*

The first anniversary of Fritz's death had come and gone, and somehow Vicky had got through one whole year without him and was still alive. Bismarck had been on his country estates all that summer, so his persecution of Vicky had died down for a time. It was renewed with great savagery after the 15th of October 1889 when Sir Morell Mackenzie's book *The Fatal Illness of Frederick the Noble* was published. This book unleashed Bismarck's fury to such an extent that Vicky wondered if his game was to drive her out of Germany altogether. She became distracted beyond endurance and suicide was again in her mind. What had she to live for? Whom could she turn to? There was still a handful of loyal friends left, but their names were on Bismarck's black-list and they had lost everything for her and Fritz. Older men like Geffken and von Roggenbach could never recover their health after the treatment they had received and since she could not recompense them in any way how could she involve them further? 'War to the knife is waged against them all, with the most unheard of and un-justifiable means.'[16] And Vicky shared their fate.

Her friends implored her to let Bismarck and William know that she had nothing to do with the diary or Sir Morell Mackenzie's book, but she refused to say a word. She could not grovel to them; let them think what they liked. All too well she knew what would happen: Bismarck would laugh and answer her civilly enough – civility cost him nothing, especially when he had no intention of mending his ways – but the moment her back was turned there would be a fresh pack of lies in the official press. Writing to William was useless too, since he was too grand to read letters, even those from his mother.

Vicky's trio – Moretta, Sophie and Mossy – kept her from sinking completely. They needed her now more than ever and this knowledge gave her strength, but there was a pressing need to find them good husbands. If anything happened to her, they would be entirely at William's mercy without a man to protect them. Sophie was soon to be married to the Duke of Sparta; she would sail away to Greece where William's opinions did not matter. Mossy was still too young to think of marriage, but Moretta's difficult position weighed on her mind. Moretta was not inconsolable for Sandro – Bismarck had callously said at the time that Princess Victoria would love any husband if he were manly enough. Be that as it may, the 'Battenberg affair' had left its mark. Moretta had taken to saying in a despairing way 'I am so ugly no one will have me'. It was unfortunate that wherever she looked there were happy couples. During a holiday at Windsor and Balmoral in June 1889 her much younger cousin Princess Louise of Wales became engaged to Lord Fife, and the Princess of Wales' nephew, the Grand Duke Paul of Russia, announced his forthcoming marriage to the sister of Sophie's fiancé, not to mention all the fuss for Sophie's own wedding. Vicky felt Moretta's unhappiness keenly, and frantically looked round for a suitable husband – too frantically, Queen Victoria thought. She warned Vicky not to allow Moretta to marry in haste and repent at leisure. She was unsympathetic because she did not quite understand that Vicky sensed that William did not like his sister. Vicky herself was half afraid that Moretta's life was already soured. What would happen to Moretta if she were to become an old maid, and a poor old maid at that?

In August 1889 Vicky's spirits were raised a little by a visit from her sister Princess Christian ('Lenchen'). Instructed by Queen Victoria, the Princess did all she could to help Vicky get on better with William. Could not Vicky ask William's advice on trifles that would flatter and please him? Vicky had already indignantly told her sister how the Empress Augusta played up to her grandson's little foibles shamelessly and never moved from one palace to another without the Emperor's permission, but she herself would never pander to William's tyranny like this, even if she were exhausted in mind and body.

Her English friends meant well, but they only showed their complete ignorance of the situation when they told her to 'take no notice of the Emperor'. Lady Ponsonby, who thought she knew what was best, strongly urged this as 'the most sensible course'.[17] It only proved to Vicky that no one had any idea what they were talking about, and it made her feel sadder and lonelier than ever. If the will to fight for her family left her, she might as well be dead. The fierce fighting spirit which had kept her going through Fritz's illness, Bismarck's machinations and William's wounding behaviour, and which had enabled her to transcend all the sordid intrigues, insults and falsehoods of her detractors, had burned very low, but it was not really extinguished. Queen Victoria had once told her that everybody must have something to live for. Vicky had Moretta, Sophie and Mossy. They looked to her for guidance and protection, and this was the one thing that kept her alive.

*

After Princess Christian's visit, Vicky made many good resolutions to try and get on better with William, if only for the girls' sake. It was another matter to put these good intentions into practice when William himself did so many appalling things.

In the summer of 1889 William honoured the one man Fritz had been able to bring to justice during his short reign. Vicky felt it was going too far even for William when she read he had given Puttkamer the Black Eagle. Two days later it was announced that Bergmann and Gerhardt were both to receive decorations. As though this was not enough, William's new favourite was his father's fiercest opponent Count von Waldersee, whom Fritz had known as far back as the

Franco-Prussian War. He had observed Waldersee closely and had told Vicky that although he was a good soldier he was shifty and changed with the wind. There was another reason why Vicky did not trust him: it was through this man's wife that William and Dona had come under Stöcker's evil influence. By 1889 the disreputable court chaplain had become leader of the Kreuzzeitung Party and was using his position to bait and harry the underprivileged Jews. It was Stöcker who had so bitterly opposed Fritz's championship of the Jews, and who did everything to stop him trying to ease their lives, so impossibly difficult in Germany. With William's connivance Stöcker had begun his campaign in earnest against those he called 'second class citizens' the moment Fritz was dead. An article in the *Jewish World* for the 22nd of June 1888 had sparked this off. It was in the nature of an obituary notice and extolled the virtues of the Emperor Frederick III who had 'personally endeared himself to his Jewish subjects by his scorn of scorn and his hate of hate'. They applied to Fritz the words of the Talmud 'The breath of our life, the anointed of the Lord of whom he said, under his shadow we shall live'.[18]

William and Dona treated Stöcker as a god and worshipped him. Most Bismarckians were also followers of Stöcker, but Bismarck himself was shrewd enough to guess that to admire the man openly would harm his relationship with the German people, who loathed and feared the chaplain. It was a pity Bismarck did not warn William of his subjects' dislike for their Emperor's friendship with this undesirable man.

When she was not feeling provoked, Vicky could find it in her heart to be sorry for William. Everybody was terrified to tell him the truth, for if the Emperor did not like what he was told punishment was swift – instant dismissal. Vicky saw that Bismarck's hold on her fiery and impetuous son was slackening, despite a certain amount of toadying to the young master in a way that would have astonished William I were he still alive to see it. It was plain to her that the Chancellor did not like William's speeches, although he was quick with excuses for the sentiments they contained – 'youthful vivacity which time will correct. Better too much than too little fire'.[19] Vicky followed William's antics closely in the newspapers and never ceased to be astonished that a child of hers and of Fritz's could be so foolish. William I had imbued him with the concept of the Divine Right of Kings – a notion Bismarck (mainly to annoy Fritz, who had repeatedly told William that the idea was ridiculous) had done nothing to dispel.

William I and Frederick III had been hard-working monarchs well aware of their deficiencies, but William II was under the delusion that he had the world wrapped up. Professor von Geest (chosen to instruct him when he first joined the Foreign Office) complained to the French Ambassador that William was unteachable. Yet Bismarck had found him an apt pupil – indeed he learned all too quickly the things Bismarck had to teach. The Chancellor had given his pupil such a puffed-up idea of himself that he did not think it necessary to read his Minister's reports – he found them boring, and Bismarck's advice usually bored him too. (He was glad to accept the advice to pay a series of State visits very soon after his father's death because, like Bismarck, he knew that this would hurt Vicky.) Everything he was, Bismarck had made him: the Chancellor had taken over where Hinzpeter left off and had moulded the young heir in a way calculated to annoy and irritate his parents. William had been Bismarck's chief weapon. Now Bismarck's own career was running to its doom. Vicky could see it happening, and was amazed that he did not. She thought it short-sighted of him to stay on his country estates for such long periods. He had always seen the need to keep William I in his sights; with William II the need was even greater, but this the ageing Chancellor did not seem to understand. Shut away from politics with his horses, his cows and his pigs he was not aware of the dawn of a new independence in the Emperor. When he wanted advice, William did not rush to Varzin or Friedrichsruh but looked for it from those close at hand.

Bismarck did not foresee trouble since he had left Herbert to keep an eye on his sovereign. Unhappily for him, however, the son did not possess the all-seeing eye of his father. Arrogant, tactless, self-assertive to the point of rudeness, vain and conceited, Herbert had no knowledge of men and could not handle people. During the whole of his manhood his father's name had been great and it never occurred to him that it could be otherwise. So he missed much that would have warned him, principally the simple axiom 'out of sight, out of mind'. Herbert saw nothing until it was too late.

*

It made Vicky smile when William returned from his state visit to England full of goodwill and talking of an Anglo-German alliance as though the idea was new. 'Two countries united by the most ancient bonds of race and kindred have marched together in unbroken alliance from the earliest period of their natural existence.'[20] So ran one of his speeches soon after his return. How quickly he had forgotten that not long before he had denounced his father and mother for attempting to create this very bond, made so tenuous by Bismarck! William came to see his mother straight from England, bringing messages from Queen Victoria. He talked of nothing but his wonderful reception, the extent of the cheers and the vigour with which the German National Anthem had been sung at the opera.[21] Vicky saw with some amusement that William had not realised for one moment that the cheers in London had been lukewarm and that the English papers (which he never read) had been critical, referring to abuse of the dowager Empress as 'abuse of England'.[22] He did not know how unsympathetic *The Times* had been towards him during her own visit to Windsor in the autumn, nor how kindly-disposed the press had been towards her, speaking of a 'protracted rest in England for a tired and mourning Empress'.[23] It never occurred to William that to the British his mother was still their Princess Royal and that his own and Bismarck's insults to her were well known and bitterly resented. However, William did read the controlled German press, which told him that 'no Sovereign was ever so fêted before' and that it was an 'invention' that England was on the side of the dowager Empress.[24]

It was a slow process – because of her honesty and lack of guile – but Vicky was gradually learning to manage her vain and difficult son. She had not understood at first why William had consented so readily to Sophie's marriage to the heir to the Greek throne. Then it had suddenly dawned on her that William, who fancied himself as a diplomat, imagined he had arranged the match all by himself, for 'reasons of State'. Vicky was careful not to disabuse him. One day, while discussing the marriage plans with his mother, William had let slip how he thought such a match would open up endless opportunities for those secret treaties whose importance he had learned all about as a fledgling at Bismarck's knee. The bride was not only the grand-daughter of the Queen of England, but a niece of her future King, while the bridegroom was a nephew of both the Princess of Wales and the Czarina and through them he had connections with Denmark. William thought he had made a very clever move indeed.

Vicky looked on Sophie's marriage as a mixed blessing. The Greek throne was not secure and the country itself underdeveloped and primitive. Sophie was a clinging girl and like her father quickly cast down. But she really loved the young Duke of Sparta, who was all Vicky could wish as a son-in-law. Although she did not at the time rate this aspect of it highly, the marriage brought her into contact with the jolly Danish royal family with their carefree outlook on life that had such a salutary effect on her own strained nerves. There had been a happy holiday in Scandinavia before the wedding, when Vicky had laughed at the ridiculous antics of Alix (the Princess of Wales) and her brothers and sisters, and her daughters had romped with the other young people, played charades again and practical jokes without end.[25]

By October 1889 they were in Greece. But Vicky's joy at Sophie's happiness was marred by Moretta's glum face and by her refusal to speak to William whom she accused of ruining her life. She had taken this line when she had learned that it had been her father's dying wish that she and Sandro should marry.

Vicky had designed Sophie's wedding dress herself; in the fashion of the day it was an elaborate confection of silver tulle over white satin trimmed with lilies cut out of lace and garlands of orange blossom and myrtle, with a long hand-embroidered train carried by eight young girls all in white. But Sophie was in tears, the bridal veil was missing, left behind in Berlin, and Sophie had to go to the altar in a substitute, a very plain affair in white tulle which was all the local shop could supply. The story leaked out and some of the older more superstitious guests shook their heads – Tino and Sophie would never come to the throne.

The Greek marriage ceremony was too much of a pantomime for Vicky; it made her uneasy with its lighted candles, golden crowns and all that marching round the altar. More to her taste was the short service afterwards in the little Protestant chapel in Athens. But Vicky's 'Kleeblatt' (trio) was broken up, and she and her two remaining girls felt it keenly. To give themselves time to get over it they did not go straight home but broke their journey in Naples, where they stayed a month. In this friendly town Vicky began to make great efforts to live again through her daughters. She ate and slept better, and tried not to think of her own loss and heartache. Once she had made the initial effort she found it was fun to take the girls in a charabanc for a picnic, to walk on the beach looking for shells – Moretta and Mossy running ahead like children – to go sight-seeing like ordinary tourists, and to eat in the open air even though it was November.

From Naples they went to Rome, where the same pattern was repeated. They were there when the Empress Augusta died on the 7th of January 1890. The sense of freedom Vicky always found in Italy, and the kindness of King Humbert and Queen Margharita had all helped to make up her mind to stay in Rome for the rest of the winter. No sooner had she decided this than the news came. Wryly she remembered how during the Franco-Prussian War she had written in exasperation to her mother that she never made a plan that was not upset by the King or the Queen. But there was a certain pathos in knowing that this was the last time.

Augusta had not behaved well in the Battenberg marriage dispute. She had sided with William, and Vicky had not been able to make her see how her open opposition played into Bismarck's hands. The year before, Fräulein Neuerndorff, Augusta's maid and confidante, the woman who had brought her all the gossip, had fallen down dead while dressing her mistress. Augusta had been really fond of this jealous and devoted old servant, and she never recovered from the loss. Now she too had gone. Vicky went to see her lying in state in the Schloss chapel. They had wrapped her palsied body in her ermine and gold cloak, and arranged her wedding veil on her head. She looked calm and peaceful, even young: 'there seemed not a wrinkle,' Vicky wrote to the Queen, 'the eyes that used to stare so and look one through and through were closed, which gave her a gentle expression I never saw in life.'[26]

The Empress had only left her daughter-in-law one thing – a rebuff. During her life-time Augusta had been the nominal head of the German Red Cross and the Vaterländische Frauenverein; these were really under Vicky's orders, especially during a war, and therefore she had every reason to expect William to ask her to take the Empress's place. It was an excellent chance too for William to fulfil a promise he had made to Queen Victoria during his State visit to England – to 'do something to please mama'. But the Empress had offered Dona the headship of these organisations as far back as the previous year and had not told Vicky. She tried hard not to mind, but she did mind very much and with cause. Dona knew nothing at all about the work and would not do it well, whereas she herself already had years of experience and was brimming over with new ideas which she had never had a chance to put into practice. Moreover, it was an opportunity to 'do good' which would take her out of herself. The disappointment was great, but like many other things it would have to be borne.

After the funeral she had no energy to return to Italy, although Berlin seemed very dismal after Rome. Above all she missed the invigorating walks. There was nowhere to go in Berlin, and Vicky took her exercise marching up and down the Sugnitz gardens as she had done every winter since coming to Prussia. It bored her to distraction. There had been only one change in the little garden since 1858: a square mound in the centre where Fritz's old horse 'Wörth' was buried.

It all had a very bad effect on her spirits.

*

Before the winter was over Vicky had another cross to bear – the treachery of a man she and Fritz had looked on as a friend; Gustav Freytag the novelist. This man (who had been with Fritz as chronicler in the Franco-Prussian War) published a volume of reminiscences *Der Kronprinz und die deutsche Kaiserkrone* 'to show the world that Fritz was overrated and a danger to Germany'[27] as Vicky wrote to the Queen. During the time they had been together in the war, Fritz had talked freely to Freytag, who now repaid these confidences by showing Fritz and his ideals in a totally false light – even going so far as to make him out a traitor to his country.

Freytag's story was not new. It was merely the old one of Bismarck's hatching, that 'through indiscretions to his wife and her English relations' certain German military secrets had reached the French commanders during the Franco-Prussian War. This was a monstrous charge and almost identical to those made against Robert Morier – the 'enemy', Vicky noticed with scorn, had very little originality. But they were persistent. Vicky was very cast down all that winter and spring when she remembered that Freytag, who had once been so pleasant, had sold his honour for a cut from the 'Welfen-Fonds'. Financial difficulties had been his downfall, and the book was the price Bismarck demanded for paying his debts.

To Vicky's consternation her uncle Duke Ernest of Saxe-Coburg made a great point of congratulating the novelist on the excellence of his memoirs, publicly telling the author that it quite delighted him.[28] As though he had not already done enough damage, the following week, without even bothering to find a pretext, he dismissed the Liberal Dr Aldenhoven, who had for a number of years been the director of the Gotha museum. Vicky knew that old age and licentious living had made Ernest stupid – had he gone completely out of his mind at last? Loyalty to 'dearest papa's only brother' made Vicky want to find excuses for him when he followed this scandalous conduct with an even more scandalous pamphlet, published anonymously, but which he proudly said he had written. The pamphlet's main theme was a panegyric on Bismarck, followed by a diatribe against Fritz, and it faithfully repeated the Chancellor's own words – that it would have been fatal for Germany had Fritz lived.

A new champion suddenly appeared to defend the dead Emperor: Dr Harmening, a man Vicky had never heard of before. He was promptly arrested on a charge of libelling Duke Ernest, sent to prison for six months, and ordered to pay his own costs. There was much sympathy for him, and he showed up well in court in marked contrast to Duke Ernest, who now swore that he had not written the pamphlet. But Ernest had clever lawyers and Harmening had not.

Unfortunately Vicky had no proof of authorship. If she had had it, would she have given evidence against her uncle? It is doubtful if it would have helped, and it would have been distasteful to expose her own flesh and blood: 'I could not do such a thing against papa's own brother and also for Alfred's sake – besides the disgust at creating such a scandal.'[29] A few years before she could not have lived with herself if she had not spoken out. The incident gives an insight into the extent of her fatigue and lack of vitality. She was too drained to be able to do battle. But the close blood ties Vicky was so aware of did not inhibit Duke Ernest in the least.

The whole sorry business proved to Vicky that all Germany was not lost. The insults flung at Fritz were beginning to be resented, and Bismarck's lack of magnanimity to be criticised; even his admirers felt that he had over-played his hand.

A lead for the future was given by Prince Henry Carolath, an old friend of Fritz, when he made a speech in the Reichstag in January 1890 objecting to the muzzling of the press although free rein was allowed to those who 'wished to stone the late Emperor Frederick III, his wife and Queen Victoria'. The speech was heard in silence but when Carolath sat down he was loudly cheered and many of the braver members agreed that the calumnies had gone too far and must cease. Vicky was given a complete account of the scene in the Reichstag by Baroness Stockmar, who had got it from Bamberger. Was there to be a change of heart at last?

The virulence of the attacks on Fritz did in fact soon diminish a little. The pressure never eased enough to satisfy Vicky's sense of justice, but she retained throughout an unshakeable faith that time would eventually prove Fritz to have been right. Shortly after Carolath's speech, she wrote to her mother 'One must have patience and keep quite quiet and say nothing. The day will come perhaps when the truth will come to light, and to attempt to hurry on that day would be to spoil all',[30] and three years later in reflective mood she told her chamberlain, Reischach, 'The Emperor Frederick's hopes and what he worked for may some day be realised, but not for a long time. Maybe they will come after hard times, but I shall not live to see them.'[31]

CHAPTER 25

The Chance to do Good

VICKY was only forty-seven when Fritz died and William succeeded, yet she had no alternative but to submit to being 'buried alive', never consulted, hardly visited, pushed into the back-ground, given no more importance in family functions than an old aunt or cousin, of no account to anyone except her three girls. After the death of the Prince Consort, Queen Victoria went into self-imposed seclusion: Vicky had seclusion thrust upon her when she would have preferred to be of use.

Even so, no amount of neglect could suppress her intense interest in politics. Perhaps because she had to watch from the sidelines, she saw the way things were going with great clarity: how von Waldersee and Stöcker were doing their utmost to drive a wedge between William and Bismarck and were succeeding, and how the Chancellor made it easy for them by refusing to face the truth – that he was no longer indispensable. Vicky guessed that he was counting on the callow Emperor to get into some dreadful scrape from which only he could extricate him.[1] This proved to her how little Bismarck really knew of William.

William was unpredictable. When a big strike broke out amongst the Westphalian miners in May 1889, to Vicky's consternation William sided with the men, refusing to listen to a word the employers had to say. No one knew better than she that William's flirtation with the working classes had nothing to do with concern about them. For years she and Fritz had been trying to raise the standard of living of the poor, but William had refused to become involved. Vicky had hoped that once he was Emperor he would look at the question more closely, consult more people and go amongst them to see for himself. He had not done so. Now the men had been duped by a mixture of personal ambition, jealousy and Stöcker's intrigues; there was no more behind William's action than this, and it was not, as the workers thought, the dawn of a new day. William had kept in close touch with Hinzpeter; Vicky had heard that the ex-tutor had been haranguing him on Christian Socialism and that it was he who had been urging the Emperor to act in this way, 'because there was a mine of popularity for himself', and that it was the one sure way to 'make him a great man'.[2] While under Hinzpeter's influence William acted impulsively and without prudence, but despite his championship of the miners the troops were called out, shots were fired, there were some fatalities and William lost prestige. To regain this he again took Hinzpeter's advice and summoned representatives from both sides to a council under his chairmanship. Nothing constructive came of it, for he did not listen to a word but dictatorially gave orders for employers to raise wages. When they did this the strike ended.[3]

Vicky saw more danger than ever. She was convinced that William imagined he had gained a great victory. Bismarck had not been recalled to give advice; he had done it alone, he was 'a Kaiser who could stop a strike with a single order'. She shuddered at the outcome and longed to write 'look before you leap' over her impetuous son's desk, though 'it would be very little use, I fear'. She wondered how Bismarck liked watching William take over his rôle of despot. Did he realise that he was to blame and that he had sown the seeds of this autocratic behaviour in the Emperor? Bismarck had many blind spots, and William was one of them. Vicky summed up the whole situation very aptly in a letter to Queen Victoria in March 1890: 'It would be a curious nemesis if, for all his past sins, Prince Bismarck were to fall just the very time he happened to be in the right.'[4]

One day at the beginning of April Vicky was startled to receive a visit from Prince and Princess Bismarck. She had not seen the Chancellor to speak to since Fritz's death. On that day she had asked him to explain why she had to endure the indignity of a cordon of soldiers round her house, but he had sent word to say he was too busy to come. Yet now that he was losing his hold over William he turned for sympathy to the woman whose life he had deliberately ruined. This could have been Vicky's moment of triumph. It is to her everlasting credit that she did not take advantage of it. Her finest gesture, like much that she did, passed unobserved and unremarked. She listened courteously as Bismarck talked. He had plenty to say, especially about William's newest coup, which he dwelt on at great length and which was 'much on his mind'. With compassion she noticed that he looked bowed and old and that he was uncertain of himself and of his position. Princess Bismarck too looked shrivelled and ill. Putting aside personal feelings she tried not to think of the wrongs he had done her and Fritz and the suffering they had endured at his hands – 'the wounds and daggers in my heart' – and to remember only all he had achieved for Germany. She would not add to his humiliation, which was soon to overwhelm him.

Vicky had watched the Chancellor make one mistake after the other with William, who she was sure was bent on getting rid of a man who had become an encumbrance. She had heard that at the beginning of his reign William had remarked to Stöcker that he would 'give the old man six months to recover his breath, then I shall rule myself'.[5] Bismarck's time was running out, and Vicky thought that he knew it. But she could not believe that even William would dismiss him out of hand, although she knew that once he had an excuse he would be merciless.

His chance came in January 1890 when the Reichstag was discussing whether to make permanent Bismarck's anti-Socialist law of 1876. Bismarck was forced to appear at the Prussian Council of State to defend his reason for wanting to retain the law. When driven by the Emperor to avow open opposition to this proposal to abolish it, Bismarck lost control, could not hide his feelings and became shrill and angry, while William remained calm and adroitly out-manoeuvred him. In this way Bismarck was obliged to allow the publication of two proclamations promising labour legislation and another proposing a European conference to standardise industrial regulations in order that German industry should not be placed at a disadvantage.[6] At the next meeting of the Reichstag Bismarck was in truculent mood and would not compromise, even refusing to countersign the Emperor's proclamation. Disregarding warning signs, he went all out to break William's project of an international congress to be held in Berlin, again with the mistaken idea that if William could be convinced that it was a bad idea he might return to the fold. Not unnaturally he produced the contrary effect, and from that moment his power began to ebb. As Bismarck's influence declined, Stöcker's increased, and rather late in the day William remembered that Bismarck's banker, Gerson Bleichröder, was a Jew and that in using his services the Chancellor was encouraging Jews, whom William hated as much as he hated Jesuits 'Jews and Jesuits always hang together' had become one of his favourite remarks. Surprisingly few hung on to Bismarck as the Emperor tore his power to pieces, bit by bit like a thoughtless child with a fly.

The Chancellor's teaching was now being put to the test. He had taught his pupil that it was a sign of weakness to show pity and that pity had nothing to do with politics. 'Be polite up to the steps of the gallows', William had often heard him say, 'but hang all the same'. But the Emperor carried out his execution without bothering to be civil. Early in March he demanded the repeal of the order of 1852 which separated the monarch from his Ministers of State,[7] a request Bismarck refused. There was nothing for it but to offer his resignation, and on the 18th of March he did so. Two days later William accepted it. Bismarck's reign was over. 'Nothing good will come of it',[8] Vicky wrote to the Queen. She knew only too well that William had not got rid of Bismarck because his system was corrupt and rotten, but solely because while Bismarck was in power he felt tied and kept down. All that happened, of course, was the replacement of one despot by another and inferior one. The sweet songs Bismarck had sung about the Emperor very quickly turned into snarls of abuse, and he told everyone who cared to listen that 'this man will certainly ruin the Empire'.[9] Few did care to listen and Bismarck suddenly found himself short of friends. He went to the British Embassy to pour complaints into Sir Edward Malet's sympathetic ears: 'he has no doubts, he thinks he can do all things and he wishes to have all the credit to himself.'[10] He had forgotten that he himself had been consumed with his own power and prestige and that he had gone to any lengths to protect them. Tears of self-pity filled his eyes when he went over the past that for him had been glorious and memorable, but that had brought Vicky and Fritz to dust and ashes.

Discretion went with his power, and Bismarck boasted about anything that bolstered his injured pride. Most of all he seemed anxious to let people know that it was he who brought on the Franco-Prussian War: 'In 1870 I was obliged to have to resort to a stratagem to force on war at that moment.'[11] Too late he saw that it was not Fritz who had been the snake in the grass – not the Crown Prince, whom he had spent much time and energy in hating and misrepresenting in order to bring him down and destroy him, but the petted pupil who had once sat at his feet and worshipped. Unwittingly he had been lulled into a feeling of security as insubstantial as the soft summer breeze that dried his crops after the torrential spring rains in Pomerania. William had been the spring rain, relentless, all destroying, sweeping everything away; indeed the very qualities that Bismarck had fostered in William in order to strengthen himself when Fritz succeeded were those that now helped to overthrow him.[12]

Unblushingly William wrote a letter full of excuses to Queen Victoria: 'I was obliged to part from him to keep him alive.'[13]

To Vicky's surprise Bismarck asked if he might come and see her before he left Berlin. When they met she could not help but be stirred by a deep pity of the kind Bismarck was incapable of feeling for anyone but himself. When he kissed her hand in farewell there were tears in his eyes and Vicky herself felt moved. 'We parted amicably and in peace', she wrote to Queen Victoria, 'which I am glad of, as I should have been sorry – having suffered so much all these long years under the system – that it should appear as if I had any spirit of revenge, which I really have not.'[14]

*

William chose General Leo von Caprivi to replace Bismarck as Chancellor. He was the last person Vicky expected, and she wondered if it was a sign that William had undergone a change of heart. It was the first time that he had shown any interest in someone his father had looked on with favour. Fritz had earmarked Caprivi, an excellent soldier, for his Minister of War in the cabinet he had never had. Vicky knew him to be a conscientious and honest man, and against the tinsel glitter and artificiality of Berlin society this bachelor with his Prussian-Spartan ideals stood out as an unusually austere figure. Very soon he showed the way he intended to go. His politics had a liberalising air; he put an end to the repression of the socialists and allowed the remnants of the Kulturkampf to die away. He had none of Bismarck's Russian sympathies and under him the Reinsurance Treaty due to expire in 1890 was not renewed, even though William had sent for the Russian Ambassador, Shuvalov, one morning soon after Bismarck's dismissal on purpose to tell him he intended to renew the alliance.[15]

Vicky was afraid that Caprivi would not last, because he had been chosen for the wrong reasons. He stood for better relations with Britain. For the present this suited William well since it was a friendship that brought with it a plethora of regimental and naval uniforms – and, he hoped (since he had a poor opinion of British intelligence), Britain's secrets thrown in for good measure. But Vicky knew that William's feelings would soon change, and that Caprivi would have to go the moment they did.

Vicky would have liked very much to discuss politics – especially Germany's foreign policy – with the new Chancellor, but she dared not jeopardise his position by inviting him to come and see her. She had noticed with astonishment that politics in Germany were changing; changes which under Fritz's gentle rule might have taken years to achieve had been quickly brought about by the very brutality of William's nature. Who would believe that Bismarck, 'so high and mighty and all powerful', would disappear overnight? Vicky had come to look on him as a fixed institution that nothing could overthrow, and yet William had got rid of him with one determined stroke. And he knew nothing of politics. It was simply a quirk of fate.

*

The Queen had been cool with her grandson ever since the Viennese affair; William knew it and was anxious to get back into favour, but without bowing the imperial knee to the Prince of Wales. When in April 1890 Queen Victoria went to Darmstadt to see her grandchildren, William rushed over without a second's delay, believing that to get in first was to get in most. It was a shock to find the Queen paying more attention to his mother's views than to his own, and galling to have to listen to her saying repeatedly how well informed she was and to have to pay attention (without answering back) to her pointed remarks that this was all the more surprising since no official person ever came near her.

Shortly after Bismarck's dismissal the Prince of Wales arrived in Germany on a visit to Vicky bringing his sons Eddie and George. Still hoping to make up the quarrel, William went out of his way to make a great fuss of his uncle, but it was now the uncle's turn to be off-hand. He coolly refused to fulfil an engagement his nephew had arranged for him, and instead accepted an invitation to lunch with the ex-Chancellor. William could hardly hide his anger, especially when next day the Prince excused himself again, this time to lunch with Herbert Bismarck – to listen, as William knew very well, to abuse of himself. It made matters worse that William had to swallow the affront without showing too openly that he cared, since the Prince made it plain that it was punishment for Vienna, which still rankled. Privately he told Vicky that although he could never forgive the Bismarcks for their treatment of her, he saw that in some ways he had under-estimated them; their judgement of William was 'very sound'.

*

By the spring of 1890 Vicky was temporarily housed in the Schloss at Homburg, a gloomy inconvenient place filled with furniture not at all to her taste. But it had one redeeming feature: a beautiful garden, with a lake and some attractive weeping willow trees – which reminded Vicky sadly of herself. She put up with Homburg as cheerfully as she could, since she saw more of the Prince of Wales there than she would have done anywhere else. He was continually running over for the cure, and did much that spring and summer to lift her spirits and support her in her battle with William.

Bertie was not the only blessing left her either. The people of Berlin wrote to say they had subscribed for a statue of Fritz to be erected to his memory in the square. They wanted her opinion on the best sculptor for the figure, which was to be of Italian marble and life-size. For four days Vicky happily made a list of names of sculptors whose work she would go and see, when a second letter arrived to say that the Emperor 'would not allow it' and that there was no need for the Berliners to bother, since the State would doubtless erect one 'in due course'.

Vicky was becoming hardened to William's destructive attitude towards his father's short reign. In general she disapproved of statues – so often the money could be put to much better use. But this one meant more to her than a mere inanimate memorial. Fritz would only occupy a very small place in the history books of the future, his reign would not fill many pages. How glad she would be to know that when a child pointed to a statue of Fritz and asked 'who is that?' the answer would be 'that is Frederick the Good'.

*

A new generation was springing up all round her, and she began to understand the pleasure her mother derived from her grand-children. Her three eldest had never asked for her presence when their children were born; with the three youngest it would be different. She looked forward to the prospect of sitting by the bedside reassuring and comforting and to being the first to take the squealing bundle from the nurse's arms. To her sorrow she hardly knew William and Dona's five boys. They were not attractive children; the eldest was pale and did not look strong, and the others had such coarse features that it was difficult to believe they belonged to her family. Sophie, now Duchess of Sparta, was expecting her first child in July and Vicky went to Greece for the confinement. The baby was born at Tatoi near Athens and was a boy called George. Remembering her own terrible first confinement, Vicky had engaged an English housekeeper for Sophie who was really a trained mid-wife from Queen Charlotte's hospital in London particularly skilled at managing difficult cases. Advanced as Vicky was in so many ways, it seems strange to see that she had her full share of Victorian prudery. She thought Sophie too young to be told the real reason this nursing sister was sent to Athens, hence the masquerade.

Sophie had inherited Prince Albert's ability to be 'knocked under' too easily, and she was very dependent on her mother for encouragement and bracing advice. She was too inexperienced to know how to improve her home, begin a garden, choose a nurse for her children or the best way to help the Greek people. Vicky knew, and ideas came pouring out of her, so that one marvels how expert she was about so many different things. She wrote pages of excellent advice on the kind of plants and shrubs that grew best in the soil of that particular part of Greece. She sent out the latest kind of nursery equipment and drew up plans for modernising the little palace Sophie considered so inadequate. The King and Queen, too, sought Vicky's advice for their storm-rocked country and she tried hard to make them see the Macedonian question with her eyes, so that Greece need not always be at loggerheads with 'poor Bulgaria' – as Vicky always called that country. Tactfully she suggested to King George that an international conference might be the answer. One day an ideal but impossible solution occurred to her – if only all the Balkan states could be put under English rule, which was 'so wise, so just'!

She had wonderful ideas for making Greece rich: if only both the Salonika railway and the road through Greece were opened up, so that all the India mail and India passengers could come that way instead of through Brindisi, money would flow into the country: foreign aid should be enlisted for working the marble quarries, growing orange trees, promoting flower-farms for scent and fruit-gardens for preserved fruit – all to help export. With the increased popularity of smoking, tobacco might be profitable, also currants, lemons and oranges, all grown with borrowed foreign capital. Her ideas cannot be dismissed as impracticable; since Vicky's time many of these schemes of hers have been adopted to Greece's great advantage. But in those days they sounded far-fetched and unrealistic, since no one before her had thought of using Greece's natural resources as a commercial proposition.

*

In June 1890 Vicky's problem-child Moretta, now twenty-four, became engaged to Prince Adolf of Schaumburg-Lippe. He was not a catch. Ill-educated and untravelled, he had confessed to Vicky – not without some pride – that he had hardly ever left his native state, that Germany was good enough for him and that he 'never wasted time' reading books. Thoroughly bucolic, he was only happy on a horse or with a gun in his hand, but he was good tempered and easy-going and could be improved. Before they met, Moretta had made up her mind to take the first suitable man who asked her. Love, that had once caused her such heartache, did not enter into it. She was heading – she was certain – for the thankless position of spinster aunt, at everyone's beck and call, pushed about from pillar to post, helping at others' marriages and confinements, but never at her own. Anything was better than that, even Adolf. Queen Victoria was among the first to express doubts that this marriage was right: 'one never knows how it will turn out.'[16] Vicky too had misgivings and over-praised Adolf's few good qualities. His was a 'true, honest, trustworthy nature – which after all is the first thing in life' she wrote revealingly to Sophie. She would not advise Moretta: 'she has to decide for herself.'[17] Moretta had decided and there was no turning back, but the ghost of the handsome Prince Alexander was to haunt this marriage and Vicky for one could never give up regretting the past: 'I think what might have been and ought to have been. It gives me a great pang, especially when I see Sophie and her Tino.'[18]

Fortunately Adolf was the only one who did not know that he was second best. Vicky half hoped William would forbid the match, but he gave his consent readily, so the marriage took place in the Schloss chapel at Homburg on the 19th of November 1890. Sophie travelled from Greece for it and broke her journey at Berlin, where she had a violent quarrel with William. As Greece's future Queen, Sophie had decided to enter the Greek Orthodox church. William got wind of this and before Sophie left Berlin she received a royal command from Dona (then expecting her sixth child) to come and see her at once. Primed by William, Dona recited her piece: that as head of the Lutheran Church William would never agree to Sophie changing her religion and that if she disobeyed him, she would 'end up in hell'.[19]

Sophie had a temper and now did not try to control it. After a sharp retort, she left the room, banging the door behind her. William followed her to Homburg where, booted and spurred, he appeared in his mother's drawing room to deliver an ultimatum: 'If my sister enters the Greek Church I shall forbid her the country.'[20] The gloom that already hung over the marriage was darkened still further by the Emperor's glowering face and Sophie's defiant air. 'He has no heart and Dona no tact', was Vicky's resigned comment to the Queen. Nothing William did surprised her any more, not even his foolish undignified telegram to the King of Greece, announcing his intention to cut his sister off if she defied him. Sophie did defy him, and without a second thought – she had seen too many of William's angry outbursts to fear them. But Vicky dreaded family quarrels and at her suggesting Sophie wrote William an appealing letter, explaining her reasons for adopting the Greek faith. When William would not bend, she sent her mother an open telegram for all the world to read: 'Received answer, keeps to what he said in Berlin, fixes it to three years. Mad. Never mind. Sophie.'[21]

Despite William's ban, Sophie entered the Greek Church in the spring. William did not relish being defied. When his sixth son was born three weeks prematurely he laid the blame on Sophie and wrote hysterically to Queen Victoria: 'If my poor baby dies it is solely Sophie's fault and she has murdered it.'[22] A letter his grandmother ignored. 'Where another person's conscience is concerned,' she wrote to Vicky, 'one must be tolerant and not condemn as one has not the right to do so.'[23]

*

Christmas 1891 was spent quietly at Homburg with Mossy and the newly-married Moretta and Adolf. Although pushed to one side, Vicky was never idle. She wrote long and interesting letters almost daily to Sophie in Greece, to Queen Victoria and many other relations and friends, letters that reveal her affectionate and turbulent nature. Painting – at which she was no mere amateur – was her greatest relaxation,

Paris her source of inspiration. She had visited the French capital three times since Fritz's death, staying incognito at the Hotel Bristol and calling on artists in their studios to discuss painting on equal terms. The simplicity and directness of these men greatly appealed to her and with them she was at her best, talkative, easy, a mine of information yet ready to learn. She was not at any time royalty paying a stiff formal visit but one of themselves, bringing her work to be criticised, asking for advice. The years fell away on these occasions, leaving her vivacious and gay. The antique shops were another source of interest. Vicky went round them all, picking up pieces for the home she was going to build shortly at Kronberg in the Taunus mountains.

The purchase of 350 acres of land and a small villa (which was demolished) had been made in 1889 from a legacy left her by the Duchess of Galliera. The building had been delayed, however, by the fuss over Geffken and the publication of Fritz's war diary; Vicky had lost heart and the whole plan was laid aside for a time: 'somehow or other I feel keen about it no more',[24] she wrote dejectedly to Queen Victoria. The dejection did not last long and the idea of the house soon excited her and made her thoughts fly to that 'cheerful friendly spot' where she was to build a house that was to be also her memorial to Fritz. The name was chosen before one brick was laid – 'Friedrichshof'. It was to be more than a roof over her head, more than a home of her own; building it was a sacred duty created out of a great and lasting love. It brought Fritz back into her life as nothing else could. Moreover, the estate was not isolated, but within easy reach of Frankfurt, Homburg, Wiesbaden and Darmstadt. Vicky did not intend to be lonely. In the spring of 1892 she was about to go to Kronberg to discuss plans with the architect Herr Ihne, when William asked her to go to Paris on a semi-official visit. When questioned by Vicky as to the exact purpose of the trip, he was vague and murmured something about 'showing friendly feelings towards France'.

Vicky was so delighted to be asked to do something for her unfilial son, and so glad to be 'of use', that she was incautious and did not go into the matter as thoroughly as she should have done. Above all, she felt that it was the first sign of a change of heart and she never thought of refusing. The Homburg Schloss hummed with activity as trunks were brought down from the attic, and clothes took on an importance they had not had since Fritz's illness. The sables Fritz had given her when they were in Russia for Affie's wedding, which she had never expected to wear again, were taken out of moth-balls and hung in the fresh air to get rid of the smell, and Vicky ordered a new coat to wear with them. She had not been so happy for years.

On the dark and rain-swept evening of the 9th of February 1892 an excited Vicky jumped off the train at the Gare de l'Est to be greeted by her host, the German Ambassador, who had only just heard she was coming and (stranger still) had no idea why she was coming. The Press had been told nothing and the Ambassador did not know who was in charge of arrangements; he certainly was not. A hasty statement was prepared and given to the newspapers: that as patroness of an art exhibition to be held later in the year in Berlin, to which some well-known French painters were sending work, the Empress had come to Paris to thank them all personally. It sounded rather lame to Vicky, and she could not see how the suspicious Gallic temperament could be induced to swallow it. She herself was suffering badly from a feeling of anti-climax; after she had built up the visit to something of importance, she now found there was nothing to do and nobody wanted her. But she put a brave face on things and for a day or two all went well, and she was beginning to recover and enjoy herself when she was taken to Versailles. Here was a place that had a special meaning for her. It had a special meaning for all Parisians too, and it was not a happy one. The scene of their humiliating defeat in 1870, it was one place where hatred of the Prussians was strongest. How could they know that Vicky looked on Versailles as especially sacred to her because of Fritz, who had always been held in high esteem by those Frenchmen who had come in contact with him in 1870–1? When she walked over the battlefields, on the very earth that Fritz had once trod, her heart was too full for words and she lived again the scenes he had described so vividly in his diary. The French were not told that the Dowager Empress wept when she saw the ruins of St Cloud, where she had stayed when she was young and romantic and had thought the world and all the people in it wonderful. How roughly life had used her since those halcyon days! Only Fritz's affection had remained the same. She could feel it here in the France which he had loved almost as much as his own country. If the Parisians had known this, their hearts might have been touched by the lonely widow. As it was, the visit was mis-understood because it had never been explained and over-sensitive Paris saw patronage in everything she did. They accused her of coming to gloat (an emotion quite foreign to her nature) and – still worse – of doing so in a thoroughly 'Coburg pinch-penny fashion'.[25] The tips Count Seckendorff distributed among the petty officials were considered mean and unroyal. Unknown to Vicky, her thrifty Court Chamberlain saved her hundreds a year by his habit of cutting by half all the tips she ordered him to give. He did it from the highest motives – to save his mistress money she could ill afford to give away. In fact, he did her the greatest disservice, and she never knew the reason for much ill-will she innocently had to bear. Two separate rumbles became one clap of thunder when an official of the Ministry of Fine Arts allowed Vicky to be blamed for the removal of a laurel wreath (which, in fact, he had taken away himself) from the memorial to Henri Regnault,[26] the painter who had been killed in the last desperate sortie from Paris in 1871.* The Press seized on the incident avidly and added other absurd charges. One of the most extraordinary was that she had visited 'Jewish collections'. (In some derision she wrote to Queen Victoria, 'I went to see the great Spitzer collection and he certainly was a Jew when he was alive'.[27]) Such an outcry was created against Vicky that she had to leave not only in a hurry but by stealth; she was bundled out of Paris at midnight on the 26th of February, after the Embassy press-attaché had announced she would be leaving the following day. It was all most undignified and Vicky's distress was very great.

It is not clear how far William was responsible for his mother's humiliation. He certainly was not blameless, if only from neglect. A likely explanation is that he sent Vicky to Paris to test public reaction before he paid France one of his state visits. This was not so unreasonable in itself: what was wrong was his furtive underhand approach. He should have been perfectly frank with her so that she knew what she was in for and could take special care. This he did not do.

Vicky went straight to Sandringham to recover. Walking in the cold Norfolk air did her good, so much so that she almost made up her mind to make England her home. For several days she found comfort in playing with the idea. But it was only an idea and in her heart she never doubted for a moment that she would go back to Fritz's country: 'His aims, his endeavours, his ideals', all were for Prussia and there she must remain.[28] Her destiny had been shaped by the Prince Consort long ago; it was too late to turn her back on it. To Baroness Stockmar Vicky confided that she made the sacrifice willingly, since only in that way could she keep Fritz's memory before the people.

*All the painters who had been invited to Berlin received, every morning until they withdrew their acceptances, the following macabre visiting-card: 'Henri Regnault, 69 bataillon de marche, 4 compagnie, Buzenval.'

CHAPTER 26

A World changing for the Better

BEFORE returning to Germany Vicky spent a few days in London. The Homburg Schloss was very dreary after the comforts of Buckingham Palace, where the well-trained servants never allowed the fires to die down or the writing-paper to run out, and where the food was so good and the beds so comfortable that even an early riser like Vicky was reluctant to get up in the morning. In Berlin there were no daughters to greet her either. Mossy was in Bonn with the newly-married Moretta, and Sophie was in Greece. But letters clamouring for advice awaited her from all three. Moretta was having a hard time with her Adolf, who was thoroughly German and did not take to the English ways his wife favoured, Sophie was pregnant again and demanded her mother's presence, and Mossy had fallen in love. Even Queen Victoria needed support. She wrote indignantly that during a dinner for the French fleet at Osborne she had been forced to stand while the Marseillaise was played; Vicky was rather unsympathetic, for although she could never forget that the blood of kings, aristocrats and priests had flowed to that song, it had to be accepted as part of French national life. If there was much that made her depressed she had to remember that the world was changing for the better in many ways. Everybody was affected. Even Vicky herself had altered, if imperceptibly: no longer was she so quickly roused to indignation, and she counted her blessings more often. On the other hand, she had not become more flexible with age. Because life had treated her roughly she 'gave' a little less easily, now that the injuries to her heart, her pride and her morale had become deep and lasting, and the scars indelible. She was like a tree that has so often been made to bend before storms that it cannot straighten itself again properly when the winds have died down. Even so, the core of her personality remained the same as it had always been: she was affectionate and generous and much in need of love herself. Unselfishness motivated all her actions towards her children. Although it would leave her lonely, she did not dream of standing in the way of Mossy's happiness when she wanted to marry Prince Frederick Charles (known as 'Fischy'), son of the Landgrave Frederick William of Hesse. Nor would she hear of the suggestion, made by well-

meaning friends, that the young couple should live with her – 'to be
a comfort to me in my old age' – and she refused to let Mossy's hopes
for the future be overshadowed by thoughts of her mother's loneliness.

Her daughter's choice of a husband delighted her: of all her sons-in-
law, Fischy was the one most after her own heart. Cultivated, well-read,
serious-minded, yet with a sense of humour, he had an outlook on life
that was capable of developing all Mossy's good qualities. Moreover,
he and Vicky had much in common – what more could she ask? Queen
Victoria, however, did not quite share Vicky's joy, and there was a
certain element of disapproval in her good wishes. Younger children
had a duty to widowed mothers, but Vicky felt Mossy had as much
right to happiness as the others.

On the 25th of January 1893 (the anniversary of Vicky's own
wedding), a dark grey winter's day that in no way dimmed the bride's
radiance, Mossy and Fischy were married in the Friedenskirche in
Potsdam in a ceremony that almost equalled in splendour her own in
1858. But Vicky was saddened by the gaps here and there among the
guests. The young Duke of Clarence had died at Sandringham the year
before, to be followed two months later (the 14th of March 1892) by
the Grand Duke of Hesse-Darmstadt ('dear Louis', the widower of
Princess Alice) who had succumbed to a short illness. There were gaps
too amongst the living: the weather was too cold for Queen Victoria
to travel so far, and King Humbert was kept in Italy by the bedside of
a sick wife. But the Emperor made up for the royal absentees by being
very conspicuous and very majestical, doing the rounds of the guests
as head of the family, patronising a resentful Czarevitch and looking
down his nose at the bridegroom whom he thought 'too thin and
solemn'. William had taken upon himself to tell Queen Victoria (who
had never met Fischy) that it was a 'poor match' for Mossy and that
if she had not been a younger child and of little importance he would
not have been persuaded into giving his consent. But the Queen was
well aware of the truth of the matter: that Fischy knew too much about
William's behaviour to his mother and sisters to wish to be friendly.

Vicky waved the happy pair off with a brave smile. She did not dare
think about the empty house and Mossy's deserted room, but Fischy
had a 'noble character', her child was in 'safe hands'.[1] To avoid anti-
climax she left at once for England. These holidays with the Queen
were becoming more and more necessary to her. The twenty-year gap
between her and her mother had lessened with the years, as Vicky got
older and the Queen seemed to remain the same. Queen Victoria always
did her best to make Vicky accept her hard lot with placidity and calm.
Vicky herself was well aware that the many irritations that drove her

half frantic in Germany always took on a proper perspective in England. It was as though she had two personalities. She hated the woman she seemed to be in Germany, yet try as she could she never managed to remain her quiet, reasonable English self in Potsdam or Berlin. It was not that she was the slightest bit different in England, only that she knew she was liked there and that no one ever dreamed of falsifying and distorting her words and actions. Whenever she was recognised in London there were smiles and courtesies, and crowds gathered to cheer the 'Princess Royal' as they always called her.

Her mother's homes had become more precious to her with the years. Where else in the world was spring so wonderful as it was at Windsor? Or the air so mild as at Osborne, where the trees turned green soon after Christmas and the gardens were full of flowers in March? It was to Osborne that Vicky went in February 1893 to be rejuvenated by friendly faces and a comfortable house where the huge fires lit up the shadows and enveloped the whole place with a warmth that found an answering glow in her heart.

There was a change in the Queen this year that disturbed Vicky: she was more bent and only walked with difficulty after an injury to her ankle. Her eye-sight too was poor, she could not find glasses to suit her and complained that she had trouble in reading – hardly surprising since she was now over seventy. There was a change too in Vicky, but for the better; the Queen noticed it at once. At last she was more resigned, and the tight look about her mouth had softened, giving her whole face a happier expression. Many links with the past had been broken since they last met. They talked of Sir Morell Mackenzie who had died in February 1892 at the early age of fifty-five, a victim of Bismarck's hatred: 'shameful attacks and intrigues, added to the controversy over his book, were too great a strain.' Bismarck had succeeded too in hounding Sir Robert Morier into a premature grave on the 16th of November 1892, his health and nerves quite broken after the Chancellor's treatment: 'the only British diplomat who looked on German affairs as I do. Bismarck never forgave that.'[2]

Not the least affecting part of these holidays was the fun Vicky had with her sister Beatrice's children, to whom she was a favourite aunt. How she wished she knew her Berlin grandchildren 'as I do these'.[3] Since Fritz's death she had leaned more and more on the Queen for help with her family, especially the three eldest. But the fact had to be faced that her mother would not always be there to give it. The signs of old age in the Queen filled Vicky with alarm. When they went for a last drive together an overwhelming sadness crept over her to make the parting doubly hard. It was a glorious afternoon without a cloud in the sky, the Queen was cheerful and well, yet Vicky could not throw off this feeling of depression. 'Living far away from her is very painful,'[4] she wrote to Sophie in a dejected mood on her return to Germany.

Because of her failure with William, Charlotte and Henry, it meant a great deal that her three youngest daughters needed her. At the same time she wished that some of her new-found philosophy would rub off on to them. Moretta's longing for a child was beginning to make her ill, and she dwelt more and more on 'What might have been'. She did what Vicky knew to be most dangerous for her marriage – to look back instead of forward, and with an aching regret. Moretta was too young to understand that it was destructive to fret and grieve for something that has long gone out of reach. With the death of Sandro Battenberg in November 1893 when only thirty-six, old wounds were opened up for both Moretta and her mother. Unwisely perhaps, Vicky had cherished the hope that Sandro would rise again and triumph over his enemies. Sometimes, from wisdom gained by her own bitter experience, she had to remind her girls that 'life is a long sequence of sacrifices, trials and difficulties and one rarely gets what one wants'. But Moretta only wanted children – was that too much to ask? Sophie only wanted Greece to be nearer Prussia so that she could have both her mother and her husband always near her. For the moment the newly-married Mossy found life perfect, but later on she too felt that what she wanted most was not too much to ask.

*

From conversation with von Roggenbach in the autumn of 1893 Vicky learned that there were still too many of Bismarck's followers in active public life for safety, and that they were all working for Caprivi's fall. She felt that it was absolutely necessary for Germany that this sensible unprejudiced man should remain as Chancellor. His chief shortcoming was his failure to understand the intricacies of politics, and his precarious position was not helped by William's constant demands. The high army estimates which he had pressed Caprivi to ask for, despite the Chancellor's misgivings, had given a fillip to Socialism and made master and servant equally unpopular. The Socialists had scandalised German society by refusing to stand for the National Anthem or to rise when three cheers were called for in the Reichstag, saying that they 'could not cheer for a man who exhorted his soldiers in a speech to fire at the rest of the people whenever he ordered it'.[5] With a certain amount of wry amusement, Vicky found herself sympathising with the Socialists, and she saw in William's actions and speeches the red rag that made them so angry. It was a strange world.

But where was it all leading? Vicky told the Queen that her hair stood on end 'at all the things William says and does'. He called

Napoleon a Corsican parvenu in public, he wrote classical tags in visitors' books instead of his name – once, in Munich town hall, 'Suprema Lex Regis Voluntas*'. Because it had suited him at the time he had taken up the workers' cause, but he had not made them any better off. Taxes were high and business bad; the army's demands for money never ceased. The workers came off worst, but they were not the only ones to suffer. Hope of better times was dwindling to nothing and memories too were short. Vicky had been outraged when a section who did not care for Caprivi's moderation and honesty had the audacity to ask for her help in restoring Bismarck to power: 'You may imagine how I laughed.'[6]

With his 'mad colonial expansion policy', Vicky was in no doubt where William was heading – straight for disaster. It went hand in hand with the huge navy he was creating. In an unguarded moment Vicky had said that the British were the only good colonisers: Zanzibar, for instance, had been glad to be out of Germany's clutches and under the protection of the Queen of England. White with rage, William had almost arrested his mother for high treason on the spot.

William's conflicts with England also took more trivial but equally irritating forms. In 1892 he had tasted the delights of Cowes Regatta for the first time and enjoyed it so much that he had returned the following year to win the Queen's Cup. To the Prince of Wales's horror and the Queen's discomfort, he then announced that henceforth he would come to Cowes Week every year. But once back in Germany the gaiety and the excitement faded, to be replaced by jealousy, and he had redoubled his efforts to make his navy greater still. It was to become a burning obsession to beat the British here too.

The Queen thought that William had 'much improved' and with her he was often (but not always) a different person – reasonable, respectful, behaving as grandson to grandmother, not as Emperor to Queen. In April 1894 Queen Victoria made him Colonel-in-Chief of the 'Royals', an honour that delighted him – it meant another red coat to add to his extensive collection of uniforms.[7] The Queen showered these favours on her grandson in the hope that they would make him nicer to his mother. Vicky knew differently. She thought he came by them too easily. Lord Rosebery thought so too. He urged the Queen to reserve them as 'bait' to get something out of the Emperor. The British statesman did not care for William's tone whenever he mentioned England – as though it was no more than one of his own petty states.

Vicky was proved right when in June, despite favours, he was shamelessly accusing England of two-faced conduct because she had signed an Anglo-Congolese treaty right under Germany's nose,[8] beat-

*'The will of the King is the highest law.'

ing William at his own game. In a very frank letter Vicky warned the Queen exactly how much importance William attached to colonies and that he would never allow Britain to gain by treaty or any other means the smallest piece of land in Africa. She begged the Queen to give William 'nothing for nothing': 'A red coat or a Field Marshal's baton would have come in handy over Africa.'[9]

Like his Weimar grandmother before him, William did not equate his feelings for Queen Victoria with those he held for her government. Vicky was flabbergasted to learn that he was arranging to go to Cowes at the same time as he was urging his new Chancellor, Prince Chlodwig von Hohenlohe (who had replaced Caprivi in October 1894), to 'show his teeth' to Britain over the Anglo-Congolese Treaty. The Queen's ministers had to ask Sir Edward Malet to drop hints to the Emperor that he would not be welcome at Cowes that year and that in any case too many visits were a burden. But the timid Sir Edward wrapped his hints in such flowery language that the intention he conveyed was the reverse of that intended. When Vicky was asked to take over the job of speaking plainly to William, she very wisely refused; 'William will think I have some ulterior motive', she protested to the Queen, 'I am only a silent and much distressed spectator.'[10] Criticism, however mild, merely irritated William and made him suspicious; there was nothing for it but to 'shut one's mouth'.

This had been the hardest thing for her to learn. She had made no comment when in the autumn Bismarck appeared on the Berlin scene for the last time. His arrival coincided with Caprivi's resignation. He was dressed just as he had been on the day of his dismissal, in the steel helmet and thick cloak of the cuirassiers. When he called on Vicky she thought he looked in poor shape in spite of his peaceful country life; the black of his cloak intensified the waxen pallor of his skin and he walked more slowly than before. Vicky ran down to him as she wished to save an old man of seventy-nine the steep climb to her sitting-room. By chance she took him instead to the very room where she had received him in 1887 when he had come to ask her not to allow Bergmann to operate on Fritz's throat. She reminded him of this, and he replied with a touch of sadness, 'these are past times. How charming and patient the Emperor was throughout his illness.'[11] It was the only time in her life that Vicky heard Bismarck praise Fritz.

It was plain to her that Bismarck was finished, although William still feared his influence and, for example, prevented the old man from coming to Berlin for his eightieth birthday. Making it look like a favour, William went instead to Friedrichsruh on the 1st of April 1895, paraded some squadrons of cavalry and presented him with a sword of honour. Indeed, the ex-Chancellor was allowed to receive the whole of official

Germany like a king – but a king with his teeth drawn. Vicky noticed with amusement that all the newspapers carried the story of his life as though he were already dead and these were his obituaries. Bismarck had not controlled the press for so long for nothing: digs were made at the Emperor and some papers said outright that the birthday celebrations had taken place in the country to save expense, that William II was as close with money as William I because he discouraged state visits to Germany (in return for those that ruined his neighbours) and only entertained foreign royalty when they were passing through.

Princess Bismarck had died in November 1894. Vicky heard that Bismarck was prostrate with grief and, remembering her own similar experience and her loneliness, she had sent him a 'feeling letter'. She was surprised and glad to know that the 'wicked man' did have a heart after all and that the bitter pangs of separation affected him as deeply as they had affected her. But Princess Bismarck had watched her husband have his day of glory and they had had the satisfaction of looking back together on the things he had accomplished – something she herself could never have, for Fritz's day had come only when he was a stricken man.

*

There was a family reunion in Coburg in the spring of 1894 for the marriage of 'Ernie' of Hesse to his cousin Victoria Melita ('Ducky') of Edinburgh, daughter of Prince Alfred, who had succeeded his uncle Ernest as Duke of Coburg.

After Ernest's scurrilous attack on Fritz, Vicky had vowed never to go to Coburg again while her uncle was alive. But the rake's progress that had given Ernest thirty-two years more than the pure-living Albert had ended in August 1893 in time to save Vicky from putting her threat into practice. Ernest's spite against Vicky and Fritz had helped to enliven his old age: he had died unrepentant to the last, and although Vicky had forgiven him solely because he was 'beloved papa's only brother', she had also put him out of her life for ever.

It was April, the leaves on the trees and hedges were fresh and green and all Coburg looked just as the Prince Consort had loved it best. The peace and beauty of the country round Gotha put Vicky in the mood to be enthusiastic again about the home she was building in Kronberg. Each day her thoughts turned more and more to the Taunus mountains, until suddenly she was excited and eager to get on with it. By the summer of 1894 Friedrichshof was nearly finished. It was very grand, very comfortable and all Vicky's own. Laying out the park gave her particular pleasure. Like her father before her, she paid meticulous attention to the kind of trees and shrubs best suited to the soil, the climate and the general appearance of the grounds.* The fortunate knack of being able to visualise the whole effect before planting saved her much expense and disappointment. Her happiest hours were spent out of doors in all weathers, darting all over the place with pencil and paper, Herr Walther the landscape gardener puffing and panting after her as she chose the exact spot where each tree and plant must go.

There was life everywhere. Cows with bells round their necks grazed in fields while their calves frisked and rolled in the grass, and there were horses, cats and dogs. The meadows were covered in wild flowers, and heather grew in abundance as did the blackberries and mushrooms which Vicky collected in her handkerchief whenever she went for a walk.

With such a large house there were bound to be mistakes. The library had been big enough on paper, but when it came to arranging her books there was not room for a third of them. The electric light was 'too stark' and gave a crude hard look to everything. The ground round the stables was not level so the grass could not be sown, and there were faults in the gardeners' cottages, the porter's lodge and the dairy. 'My head aches with all I have to think of', she told Sophie, loving every minute of it. Indeed, she enjoyed it all so much and was so happy that her household dreaded the day it would come to an end.

If there was happiness there was sadness too. The 'dear little Bornstädt home' had to be given up, since the furniture was needed for her chamberlain's house. The pangs of parting with a place that had meant so much were dreadful, but without Fritz it was nothing but an empty shell. They had been there together for the last time just before Fritz's illness and he had sung to them in the deep rich voice which had been reduced to a whisper so soon afterwards and was now stilled for ever.

On the day she went to Bornstädt to close the house she opened a new wing in the kindergarten she and Fritz had started with a mere handful of ragged children. Since then it had grown until it was now big enough to take eighty-six boys and girls. It was a small thing, she knew, but its success lightened her spirits. She hated saying good-bye to the peasants whose lives they had changed, every one of them known by name and loved. They clung to her hands and her skirts, begging her not to forget them. She had to promise that one day she would return. Before the bend in the road hid the little house from sight, she turned and looked at it and she fancied that she saw Fritz waving to her from the door as he always used to do long ago.

Sometimes she was very lonely like many a widow whose children have married and left home. She felt this much more in Berlin than in

*She planted so much that the tree which Queen Victoria planted to commemorate her visit in April 1895 had no space to grow properly, and still remains stunted.

Empress Frederick with Queen Victoria, 1889

above left: Emperor William I

above right: Empress Augusta

left: Bismarck

Emperor William II with his son Prince William

Empress Frederick

Kronberg, where there was so much to do. It was during one of these lonely periods that she noticed that she was developing the old lady's habit of staring at nothing while her mind roved over the past: 'Sometimes one has not the strength to resist these memories.'[12] The habit alarmed her but it never happened when she was fully occupied and happy.

Before Friedrichshof was finished she had already begun to take an interest in the village of Kronberg. There was no hospital nearer than Frankfurt, so she gave the land for one to be built with a nursery wing which she offered to pay for herself. With the additional outlet this provided for her energies, over and above that of making a home of her own, the worries about her children that used to torment her so much greatly diminished and even resolved themselves without any interference from her. Now that he was no longer under Bismarck's influence, William was nicer to her and everyone, even Charlotte, had improved since getting away from Berlin. She was still too frivolous ('So 19th century') in Vicky's opinion, thinking of nothing but clothes and her appearance, smoking heavily and smelling like a walking cigar shop,[13] but she no longer condemned all her father's and mother's ideals. Irene, too, had done much to make Henry more considerate towards her. But Moretta still preyed on Vicky's mind since every new baby in the family upset her. Sometimes Sophie too was a cause for concern. The climate of Greece did not seem to agree with her and each pregnancy brought on some new complaint. Vicky's pen flew over the pages with warnings, advice and suggestions for remedies. Mossy, usually so good and placid, had given her a bad fright when she produced a premature son on the 24th of November 1893 while on a short visit to her mother-in-law in Frankfurt.

A less contentious life had calmed her nerves and made her more robust and better able to take these ups and downs in her stride. More difficult to accept, because of her experiences in the past, were the childhood ailments of her grandchildren. Medical science was progressing too slowly and her anxious temperament often led her to worry unduly. When a child had chicken-pox or measles Vicky was in a fever in case the illness had been wrongly diagnosed and was really something much worse. In other respects she managed her grandchildren better than their own mothers, and her advice shows a remarkable insight into a child's mind. When little Georgie of Greece showed signs of developing a will of his own, Vicky begged Sophie not to punish him but to direct his energies into the right channels, for a child 'feels bitterly and is profoundly unhappy when misunderstood'. Unconsciously she quoted Lady Lyttelton: 'punishment does no good, perhaps only great harm, for one cannot tell if it is fully understood by the child'.

If a child is afraid of horses he must not be forced to ride, if left alone he would come to it all the quicker later on. To Mossy, now and again inclined to be impatient with her children, she pointed out how soon childhood passes and that there would come a time when Mossy too would be old and long for those happy times with her family that had passed so quickly away.

CHAPTER 27

'The Future has passed into other Hands'

DESPITE Friedrichshof's increasing demands and a growing affection for the inhabitants of Kronberg, Vicky always spent a part of each winter in Berlin, although she heartily disliked it and never felt well there. Her reasons for going were unselfish. The many charitable institutions she had started needed an eye kept on them. Chief of these was the 'Victoria Haus' for British and American governesses whose plight in old age was deplorable before Vicky took a hand. It had all begun through a chance remark of an English friend who was anxious about an old governess who had taken a post in Germany and was dying of poverty and neglect. Vicky had been given an address and in her thoughtful way had followed it up. She had been horrified to discover that when their day of usefulness was done these women were cast adrift with only their small savings to live on, often ending up in garrets and workhouses as friendless paupers. Vicky had quickly changed all that. Then there was the children's hospital and the cookery school – both started from nothing – and many others besides. The list is long and impressive and shows the amazing scope of her energetic mind. No one must think she had forgotten them. 'All the ladies of my different institutions are invited to tea', was a more formidable task than it sounds. Hearts were faint and the difficulties many. Vicky had to brace, encourage, praise and restore self-confidence, and with tact and firmness spur on to greater and greater efforts. It was vital too to show how important she thought their work and to plan for the future.

There were compensations: it was easier to see her friends in Berlin. There were professors, politicians, writers, painters and interesting foreigners passing through – men like von Angeli, Passini, Leighton and Alma Tadema, whose fame she had helped to spread throughout the Continent. Amongst historians, Professor Nippold had become a particular favourite. The more he knew Vicky the more he liked and admired her. He wrote of her 'cheerful temperament and great sense of humour' and that she 'saw everything from the good side and quickly forgave people'.[1] She had plenty to forgive. At the time Nippold said this, many people who had never set eyes on her were

writing very different accounts with great freedom and inventiveness
and no fear of contradiction.

Music had begun to interest her again, brought back into her life by
'strange Alick', Fischy's blind elder brother, who often came to
Vicky's house in Berlin. This lonely man, who was a most talented
pianist, had taken to Vicky as soon as they met, although all he could
judge her by was the warmth of her voice. Sensing that here was someone who really appreciated his performance, he would play to her for
hours while Vicky relaxed on a sofa. She noticed that music brought
the same solace to this afflicted young man as it had once done to her
father.

Because she had Friedrichshof to escape to, Berlin was more endurable. Kronberg had brought her a happiness she had never expected
to experience again. For months after Fritz's death she had been
strained, her nerves on edge, her sleep affected. She had to learn again
how to enjoy life. Sophie and Mossy's children were an important part
of this rehabilitation. Despite William's ban, Vicky had asked Sophie
and Tino to Friedrichshof and, after endless tactful manœuvres by
Vicky, in June 1895 William had invited the Greek pair to the opening
of the Kiel Canal. Before that happened Sophie and her husband had
met William in Potsdam and all 'went beautifully'.

Vicky was trying to learn to handle William. To flatter him he was
her first official guest at Friedrichshof, although the Prince of Wales
had already stayed in her house quietly with only his private secretary.
Since Vicky was no longer surrounded by spies, William never heard
of this breach of faith. When he did come, he had nothing to complain
of; the little town was gay with flags and bunting, all its inhabitants in
the street cheering the Emperor (whom they had never set eyes on
before) during the whole of the short drive from the station to the
Schloss. Out of consideration for his mother he came with only a
'small suite' – a mere handful of eighteen, all of whom expected a set
of rooms to themselves. Full of good resolutions to swallow every
irritation without a word, Vicky struggled to keep a bridle on her
tongue whenever William made some foolish remark. She longed to
tell this egotistical son that often when he imagined he was giving
pleasure, he was acting with lack of consideration for others. Good
intentions were not enough. He turned up unexpectedly one day at
Schloss Rumpenheim – Mossy's and Fischy's house near Frankfurt –
while Vicky was spending her birthday there, and upset the entire
household arrangements. William was the only one to enjoy himself
and he went away in excellent humour, leaving a trail of sick headaches
and twanging nerves. Vicky herself was quite drained and had to go
to bed to recover.

But family matters were improving as William mellowed and Bismarck's influence receded. Although William still never followed his mother's advice, he did at last listen to what she had to say without flying into a temper. Yet this was not altogether an advantage. In the more relaxed atmosphere Vicky had to watch herself even more carefully than before, since a slip of the tongue might damage his relations with a member of the family. It was a strange thing that the moment Vicky became indifferent to his moods and whims, William ceased to blame her for everything. When Prince George of England went to the opening of the Kiel Canal instead of the Prince of Wales (who was shortly to represent the Queen at the Olympic Games in Athens), it was his grandmother who was made to suffer. William was still smarting when he went to Cowes for the regatta in August. He was rude to Lord Salisbury, called his Uncle Bertie names in public and kept the Queen waiting for dinner. Yet it had been Vicky and not the Queen who had persuaded the Prince of Wales to go to Greece. But William did not know this.

Vicky looked on the Olympic Games as a heaven-sent chance for Greece to snatch the tourist trade. Her head was bursting with ideas as to how this could best be done. Could Tino invite Mr Cook to Athens? She had heard that the head of the travel agency was a snob and, nothing loth to turn this human weakness to Greece's advantage, she begged Tino to flatter Mr Cook by seeing the man himself. With the unbeatable combination of the Prince of Wales and Mr Cook, 'poor little Greece would become rich at once'.

The Emperor's arbitrariness increased year by year, and the actions of his whole family were governed by the attempt to guess what William would allow. His commands were not all novelties, however; William allowed much that should have been dead and buried to be kept alive. Every year the whole of Germany celebrated the winning of the Franco-Prussian War. In 1895, greatly daring, Vicky asked him why he 'hurt the feelings of the French' in this way. William, insensitive to the national pride of any but Germans, had said that all he meant to do was to encourage the army with past glories. He was equally insensitive towards the Socialists, with even worse results. When they were angered by anti-Socialist measures, the Berlin Socialists refused to take part in the celebrations out of sympathy with their fellow-Socialists in France. Immediately all the Socialists in Hamburg came out on strike in sympathy. Vicky saw their point – what else could they do? William produced his well-worn formula – he would not allow it, and they must return to work at once. But he was no longer an Emperor who could stop a strike with a single order; the Socialists were showing, what Vicky had been saying for some time, that an absolute monarchy was becoming an anomaly even in Germany.[2] Where William could use his will he did, without rhyme or reason. Vicky thought the moment inopportune for unveiling a statue of Fritz on one of the battlefields of the Franco-Prussian War, especially since Fritz had never wanted to keep enmity alive. In any case, Vicky hated William to use his father's memory as an occasion to make a silly speech (which Fritz would never have approved) about honour and glory. But William refused to postpone it until the spring. Vicky had no more success when she did her best to make William see that in fact he encouraged the Sozialdemokratische Partei Deutschlands (known as S.P.D.) by the continual arrests, imprisonments, fines and injunctions for treason, sedition, libel or agitation with which he harried its members.[3] She was battering her head against a brick wall, and in despair she wrote to Baroness Stockmar, 'The sovereign . . . has lost a great deal and is taking further risks. He should help in building up a strong, firm and sound edifice on a broad foundation if Germany is not to slip down the steep path that leads to a republic or a Socialist state.'[4]

*

The completion of Friedrichshof gave Vicky new leisure, and she used it to develop her long-standing interest in science and education. She corresponded with a scientist who had discovered a serum which might be effective against diphtheria, which had killed Waldie, and she asked William to allow her to raise money to test it properly. Early in 1896 she invited Röntgen to lecture at Friedrichshof on his discovery of X-rays, and she founded the public library at Kronberg in the same year. She urged a reluctant William to take more interest in things of this kind and to divert a part of his huge military budget to the building of much-needed schools. But to William it was a waste of money and effort – the masses did not want to be educated. Vicky knew they did. Her chamberlain, Baron Reischach, had said that her new library at Kronberg would not be used, but the people rushed for the books. It made her impatient that Sophie did not build schools in Athens, since the people could not read or write. Sophie was only interested in her husband and children, and complained of being bored. It made Vicky despair when there was so much to do. She tried to interest Sophie in Crete, which she longed to free from the Turkish yoke. The whole of Europe should feel 'moral obligation' to this poor island and not imitate Bismarck's cynical attitude – he took no interest in Near Eastern politics since they did not affect Germany. Yet in fairness Vicky felt she could not blame a 'mere child' like Sophie, when a mature man like William did not understand the devastating effect of many of his words and actions. In January 1896 Queen Victoria had to give William a 'good skelping' in an angry letter[5] after his telegram to President Kruger. William had praised Kruger for routing the Jameson raid and forcing Cecil Rhodes from the premiership of the Cape because he had gone to the assistance of the Uitlanders who were plotting rebellion against Kruger's archaic rule.

The Queen complained bitterly that William often deliberately stirred up hatred of England and that it was plain he did not care a fig for his grandmother or her country as long as his telegrams made headlines in the newspapers. Vicky knew that he acted impulsively and with lack of thought and that the results often surprised him.

In February 1896 Greece and Turkey were at each other's throats again. Distracted at seeing her husband prepare for war, Sophie sent William a pathetic appeal for help 'in this mass-murder of Christians and Mohammedans'. But William cared more for the Sultan's friendship than for his sister's plight, so poor Sophie's telegram was ignored. Vicky was outraged – were Sophie, Tino and the 'dear chicks' to be annihilated because no one dared to offend an infidel ruler, who was merciless and cruel?

Vicky was at Osborne at the time. It had been a house of mourning since the death of Beatrice's husband, 'Liko' of Battenberg, on the 21st of January 1896, from enteric fever. Liko had chafed at his enforced inactivity in England as the husband of a daughter of the Queen, and had joined the Ashanti expedition as a volunteer. Vicky had been at Schloss Rumpenheim, looking after Mossy (who had given birth to twin boys, Philip and Wolfgang) and Fischy (ill in bed with rheumatic fever) when she received the news of Liko's death. 'Quite stunned', she left for the Isle of Wight in a hurry, leaving a barely-recovered Mossy and Fischy still unwell. Beatrice's loss brought back all the tortured memories of the early days of her own widowhood. But between bouts of grief, Beatrice amazed her by 'quiet resignation' and complete acceptance of her lot, with none of those terrible rebellious feelings that had so racked and torn Vicky herself. Yet Beatrice too had adored her husband; it was simply a question of temperament. The suffering was the same, it only took a different form. 'How like Alice she is', Vicky said to herself, thinking of her dead sister, her heart full of love and admiration for Beatrice.

Affairs in Greece were still in a turmoil and Sophie had written to Osborne to beg her mother to do what she could 'through Grandmama', who willingly put Greece's case before Lord Salisbury. Vicky had just read a speech of Lord Salisbury's and was hopeful. Salisbury had admitted that 'in our Eastern policy we have staked our money on the wrong horse'.[6] However, this did not mean that Parliament was ready to back the right one. All Vicky was able to do was to telegraph to Sophie the doubtful comfort of a promise that a warship would stand by to help evacuate the royal family, should they need to leave Greece in a hurry.[7] More generous than her minister, Queen Victoria gave Vicky money for the Greek wounded and refugees, but her name 'must on no account be mentioned'.

Vicky had the agony of sitting helpless at Osborne when on the 18th of April 1896 Turkey declared war on Greece. Seven days later it was all over. The entire Greek army had melted away before the Turks, who were stopped in their turn by the silent strength of the 'mighty Russian army' threatening their rear. Vicky pleaded with William to spare Greece more humiliation, and found it 'a crying shame' that Greece had to pay an indemnity of four million pounds in the peace settlement.

Suddenly the Greek royal family were out of favour; Tino was especially unpopular and Sophie's courage all but sank. She cried to her mother for help. It came swiftly. This was familiar ground. Unpopularity was something Vicky knew all about and was experienced in handling. Her fighting spirit (so crushed by the worry of the war and the Greek royal family's plight) flared up at once. Sophie must take 'no notice of this rubbish'. In order to help her daughter adopt a more robust attitude, Vicky reopened a painful chapter in her life which she had thought closed for ever. 'In the year 1888 when people talked of my having stolen State papers after the publication of dear papa's journal, they said I should have to leave Germany . . . I said I should do nothing of the kind and quietly settled here. Now people do not remember the calumnies and lies that were spread (though I do).'[8]

*

On the 30th of July 1898 Bismarck died quietly in his sleep at Friedrichsruh. Vicky heard the news without emotion of any sort. The old enemy had ceased to exist for her ten years ago, his wickedness buried in the grave with all Fritz's hopes and aspirations for Germany. Nothing that Bismarck did afterwards could hurt in the same way. All that remained was to send a formal letter of condolence to Herbert Bismarck, now a back number himself.

A death that affected her more deeply was that of Mr Gladstone in April 1896. Vicky had discerned the 'noble man' where Queen Victoria had seen only a nuisance. The ineptitude with women that had hampered his dealings with a female sovereign had not spoilt his relationship with Vicky in the least.[9] They had got on well, and Vicky had always tried to keep his great qualities before the Queen. With sadness she noticed his empty seat when she went to her mother's Diamond

Jubilee in June. Her thoughts had been full of him while she sang the Prince Consort's Te Deum in St George's Chapel, and she wondered whether, if papa had lived, he would have been able to make mama see the 'grand old man' in a different light.

Age did not remove the sting of death as Vicky had been told it would. As one beloved face after another disappeared she never failed to grieve as much as ever. The sudden death of her cousin Mary Teck on the 10th of October 1897 from an illness she had concealed was a pain she carried with her for a long time. A month before she had been mourning her friend the Empress Elisabeth of Austria, tragically murdered in Geneva ('who could have hated her so much? She would not hurt a fly, poor soul'). Just after Fritz's death, when Vicky had not cared whether she lived or died, Elisabeth had confessed that she too was 'tired of life'. Since the suicide of her son Rudolf,* she had been so cut up that she no longer cared how she looked. When she had called on Vicky in Berlin, alone and wearing a shabby old coat, the guards had refused to believe that she was the Empress of Austria and Vicky had been obliged to rescue her.

Her thoughts had been on Elisabeth's terrible death when out riding in the autumn, and she was not paying attention when her horse took fright at a threshing-machine and threw her. Her habit caught in the pommel as she fell, but her head and shoulders were on the ground, almost under the horse's hooves. It was a miraculous escape, for the horse only trod on her hand,[10] but she was badly shaken and had to stay in her room with a swollen arm and a mounting temperature. She was dreadfully restless and kept moving from bed to sofa to ease her aches and pains. In a few days she was better, and in a week she was up and about. Indomitable as ever, she insisted on going to Breslau the following month for the marriage of Charlotte and Bernard's only child Feodora to Prince Reuss. But she was unwell on the journey and developed lumbago in her back. The pain was so intense she could only endure it by continual activity. Before the wedding she nearly wore her ladies out with her sight-seeing, and they drooped as she visited churches, museums, art galleries, indeed anything that was worth seeing. Her back was no better when she went to Balmoral soon afterwards. It was impossible to relax, so she took long walks over the hills with the dogs or accompanied by Bertie, who could not talk of anything but William's rudeness and complained that his nephew was playing off England and Russia against each other, but getting nowhere. William's latest proposal made Vicky burst out laughing – an exchange of colonies between England and Germany, a flea-bite for a lion's share. Preposterous! William's diplomacy was no less outrageous and

*With his mistress, Maria Vetsera, at Mayerling on the 30th of January 1889.

could lead Germany into serious trouble. Vicky knew William's idea of diplomacy was to tell one country that the other had secret plans to ruin it, and when they had fallen out to seize what plums he could for Germany. Sir Frank Lascelles, the new British Ambassador, had grumbled to Vicky about this very thing. It was difficult to know what line to take with a monarch who talked in Russia of England's 'self-interest', at the same time informing the British Ambassador that Russia was preparing to 'ruin England'.[11] Even as she laughed, Vicky wondered if her foolish eldest son would ever stop being so obtuse. When Vicky met him shortly after her return to Berlin, William was in excellent spirits, telling her confidentially that he had brought off a 'coup' and murmuring mysteriously of having 'reached a full agreement with Britain' that would soon be 'signed and sealed, if she behaved herself'.[12] Vicky listened to his boasting with something akin to horror. William was even more stupid than she thought possible – 'where would it all finish?'

As it happened it was to finish in her own drawing-room. Vicky was supervising the closing of Friedrichshof for the winter one day in October when Sir Frank Lascelles arrived from Berlin in a state of agitation. Could the Empress explain her son's conduct, for he could not make head nor tail of it: no English alliance with Germany had ever been under consideration. Five minutes later William appeared in hot pursuit and, like a tidal wave that has arisen without warning on a calm sea, he made a terrible scene, cutting all the corners of civility and throwing dignity to the winds as he accused the innocent Ambassador of 'leading me astray'.

Quarrels like this were bad for her and she could no longer bear them. All night long William's raised voice beat against her brain, setting her nerves on edge and making her back throb. Before the restless night was over she knew she was not strong enough to face a winter in Berlin. Then and there she made up her mind to go to Italy, where the mild climate might cure her lumbago.

CHAPTER 28

'Surely God will bless Her'

By the end of January 1899 Vicky was settled in the Hotel Augst at Bordighera on the Italian Riviera, 'a great big white house' built on the side of a hill covered with Aleppo pines. An olive grove in front had been cleverly converted into a garden by adding palms, aloes, cryptomerias and roses, while the bedrooms opened on to balconies scented with heliotrope and jasmine that grew in abundance on the walls.[1] From her sitting-room Vicky had a wonderful view of Ventimiglia, Menton, Cap Martin and Monaco with its busy traffic of mules and donkeys. The weather was so warm that she was able to set up her easel out of doors straight away and begin a water-colour of the rocks and a little beach with a strip of blue sea and a small church in the distance.

She enjoyed painting in the company of other people; to be one of a crowd of artists at work stimulated her. Her style was changing. After months spent examining the work of modern artists in the galleries of Rome and London, the finickiness and chocolate-box subjects of Alma Tadema and Millais no longer appealed to her. Instead she had become fascinated by the structure of form and the effect of light and shade which, once understood, held devastating possibilities. No longer did she depict what she saw exactly as it was. The household thought this new and bolder work 'very strange'.

Her secretary, Count Seckendorff, was Vicky's regular painting companion, and was far and away the closest to her in skill. Privately he considered himself the best painter of the bunch and technically he probably was, although a little uninspired and too orthodox to be receptive to anything other than the pedestrian. Unlike Vicky he scorned new ideas. As the senior member of the household he guarded his position jealously; it was an unwritten rule that his easel be placed next to Vicky's. In Seckendorff's opinion he and his mistress were the only ones who took their work seriously, the rest were mere dabblers, whose place was in the rear where they could splash the paint about and chatter to their heart's content.

There is no evidence that Vicky was aware of the stories about herself and her private secretary which began to circulate about the

time of Fritz's illness. In his diary for the 20th of May 1887 Fritz
Holstein records that the gossip that the Empress Victoria and Count
Seckendorff were lovers was 'going the rounds'.[2] By September of the
same year, in true Berlin fashion, it had gathered momentum and
Holstein is quoting a scurrilous letter supposed to have been sent to
Count Radolinski by 'a friend', but which bears the unmistakable
stamp of the Machiavellian count himself in yet another attempt to
remove his rival Seckendorff from the royal household. This letter
mentions intimacies in a hut between Vicky and Seckendorff during an
entirely imaginary mountaineering expedition in Austria at a critical
stage in Fritz's illness when Vicky in fact left him no longer than was
needed to take a turn round the garden – the only fresh air and exercise
she allowed herself.

Seckendorff was a born old maid, fussy, set in his ways, a stickler for
tradition and entirely uninterested in women. Tall and thin, he was
handsome in a stiff way, with pronounced bone structure on a long
face covered with tightly-drawn parchment skin. His nose was too
long, his lips somewhat sharp, and he had fine greying hair that set off
a well-shaped head. The cut of his clothes was old-fashioned and never
changed, indeed he was well aware that his impeccable tailcoats
showed off his spare frame to perfection and made him more conspicuous just because they were not up-to-date. No one ever saw
him anything but immaculately dressed, not even in the highlands
of Scotland where Vicky's household liked to sport very bizarre
attire.

His appeal for Vicky and Fritz lay in the sad fact that once Bismarck's
reign began he was the only loyal and trustworthy person in the whole
of their entourage. Surrounded by bribery and corruption at a time
when most others could be bought, Seckendorff sailed through un-
defiled if not wholly unscathed, and this they could never forget. In
those days it had been essential that he should go everywhere with
them, and he very quickly became the 'indispensable one'. Fritz's
death only increased Vicky's need for him as a companion who could
talk about the old days which were now so precious to her. He had been
with Fritz in the Franco-Prussian War, and could recall with great
accuracy all the highlights of his generalship. He knew all the ins-and-
outs of their difficulties with the old Emperor, how they had suffered
from the vagaries of the Empress Augusta's strange temperament, and
he could recall the full story of the embittered quarrels with Bismarck.
He knew the first moment Fritz became ill, the last time Vicky shared
Fritz's room, when she began to lose hope. He saw their last kiss and
Vicky's tears as she held the wasted hand of the one man she had ever
loved. Only Seckendorff understood the full extent of her courage, the

efforts she had made to hide her fears, and her struggles to keep the sick-room free of quarrels.

The gossip changed after Fritz's death: the Empress Victoria and Count Seckendorff were secretly married. For evidence, fingers were pointed at the easy silence between them as they painted together and at their shopping expeditions to buy antiques for Vicky's new home – it was said that she asked his opinion 'like a wife' and that he was sometimes rude to her in a way no one else dared.

If Vicky had been the kind of woman who considered her reputation more than the feelings of others, she might not have taken her private secretary everywhere with her in her widowhood in the same way as when Fritz was alive. Even Queen Victoria, more aware of wagging tongues, criticised her for doing this and thought it unwise. But what had in the past been a necessity had now become a habit that if dropped would hurt Seckendorff more than it would inconvenience Vicky – she would not, for the world, offend an old servant, who had been loyal and had lost so much because of his loyalty. There were simple explanations for all Vicky's actions. They painted together because she enjoyed the competition of someone as skilful as herself. No one cared to remember that many other people painted with her too. She took him with her when she bought antiques, old silver and pictures because of his expert knowledge. His skilful advice saved much disappointment, while his sharp eye secured her many a bargain. Indeed, since her purse was limited, his advice was invaluable when it came to assessing the worth of a particular piece. He was doing little more than fulfilling his rôle as private secretary. The rudeness was Seckendorff's way of asserting his independence, an exercise Vicky knew to be very necessary to his self-esteem.

Her ladies had heard the stories and looked for signs – an unguarded endearment, Seckendorff coming out of her room – but there was nothing. Dry as dust, all Seckendorff loved were inanimate objects like his excellent collection of rare books and pictures. He was married to royal service, enslaved when he was young, and he could not free himself from it even if he wanted. Deep ties bound him to Vicky; they were cold and artificial perhaps, but nevertheless took all the warmth he was capable of towards another human being.

One further point must be taken into account. Vicky's views on remarriage were as rigid as those of Queen Victoria. Even had she not loved Fritz so passionately, she would have thought it wrong to take a second husband. Seckendorff was no more to Vicky than an old friend and loyal servant of whom she was fond. One day while discussing the gossip about Baron Roggenbach and the Princess of Wied with her maid-of-honour Marie de Bunsen, Vicky unconsciously vindicated herself. She treated the story that these two old friends were secretly married with contempt. 'I don't for one moment believe in her secret marriage, that would not be like the woman she is in the least. If she were to marry she would do it openly. I am firmly convinced that it is an unusually beautiful friendship, but of course people can't be induced to believe it.'[3]

*

Vicky returned to Friedrichshof at the end of May 1899, her back as painful as ever. It was the coldest spring she ever remembered. Cold weather had always upset her system – she had never enjoyed the severe winters in Berlin – but this year the late frosts and bitter winds were made harder to bear by a growing stiffness in her joints and swellings in her hands and ankles. Walking in the hills one afternoon in Italy she had told Marie de Bunsen that she was suffering from inoperable cancer of the spine, but that she would 'fight it to the end'.[4] How long she had known about it is uncertain, but it cannot have been earlier than the previous winter that her doctor had diagnosed cancer: her letters contain no mention of it at all until some time afterwards. For the moment no one knew, she told Marie, except her chamberlain Baron Reischach whom she had told in order that he should understand why he must cut down her engagements. Reischach had pressed her to consult the Berlin specialist, Professor Renvers, whose opinion, so he told Reischach, was that she could have been saved if she had disclosed her symptoms six months earlier, but that her condition had become incurable by the summer of 1899. Soon she began to prepare for the days when her illness must worsen. Immediately on her return to Kronberg she appointed a new young doctor, Dr Spielhagen, out of consideration for her old physician who was past night calls. But Sophie, who had come for a long holiday with her children and her dogs, was not to be worried yet. To her, Moretta and Mossy, for a time at least, it was nothing more serious than lumbago. Outwardly her life continued much as before. From now on, however, as though her three loving daughters did perhaps suspect it might be something more serious, Vicky was never alone. When Sophie left in September, Mossy and her family took her place, while Moretta kept running over from Bonn. Whatever Vicky had to bear it was not neglect.

The summer of 1899 was over much too quickly, and soon it was time for Sophie and her children to return to Greece. It was painful for Vicky to part with them – would she be spared to see them again? Scarcely had the carriage that was to take them to the station in Frankfurt disappeared from sight, than her longing for this daughter drew her like a magnet to her desk. For the first time in her life she was at a loss for words. Almost overcome with anguish, all that came into her head was a benediction from the Bible: 'The Lord bless thee and keep thee, the Lord let the light of his countenance shine upon thee and give thee His peace.'[5]

*

Life was complicated by a new habit of William's. He often called to let off steam about someone who happened to be in his black books at the moment. In the autumn 1899 it was Queen Victoria with whom he was at loggerheads over the Samoa Islands. William was in a rage, telling his mother that England had behaved disgracefully in greedily grabbing the best for herself, while Germany had been fobbed off with a 'twopenny-ha'penny island'. Vicky saw the 'insult' had gone deep. William marched unceremoniously into her sitting-room where she was resting on a sofa and launched at once into a storm of abuse of his grandmother and Lord Salisbury, indeed the 'whole gang of robbers' whose only offence appeared to be that they were English and more astute than he was. Not for the first time, Vicky noticed how he showed remarkable affinity to the dead Bismarck in his jealousy of her country.

When the Boer War broke out in October 1899 Vicky put the blame on William for German attacks on England in the press. William had pointed the way by his support of Kruger. When things began to go badly for Britain, William did not bother to hide his satisfaction, even taking the trouble to drive from Homburg with daily bulletins of England's appalling losses. It needed all Vicky's newly-learned patience to listen silently while William retailed the 'advice' he was giving his Uncle Bertie in those letters of sympathy it was his duty to send: 'The sight of white man killing white is not good for the blacks to look on for too long.'[6] Vicky wanted to hit him as with stiff and swollen fingers she furiously knitted comforts for the troops. How she hated the very thought of England at war! Yet on reflection the war could be of immense use in revealing the weak points in Britain's armour. It would force people to 'show their hand and weld the Empire together' as well, so that when a greater conflict came (and she was sure it would), England would be prepared. These thoughts were summed up in a letter Vicky sent Queen Victoria in January 1900: 'The experience gained will be a blessing hereafter.'[7]

Vicky often practised her new-found philosophy on herself, not always with the desired result. It was difficult to take life calmly when death struck at her own family. Her sister Princess Christian's son 'Christle' had gone to fight the Boers, full of patriotic duty and hope, only to die of typhoid in Pretoria. Many other friends' sons had perished as well, so that German gloating at British defeat was hard to put up with: 'Oh, if I were a man I should like to knock a few people down.' Indeed, she almost did when some German ships were seized and found to contain contraband for the Boers.

Against German spite, Greece's sympathy was balm. Many Greeks had volunteered for the British navy, and Sophie was busy organising parcels for the army to which every one of King George's subjects had subscribed. Vicky herself was so occupied with doing all she could to further the British cause that she was able to push her own stricken state to the back of her mind, at least most of the time. Then suddenly the Duke of Edinburgh ('Affie') died in Coburg on the 30th of July 1900 after a brief illness. The illness turned out to be cancer, its brevity a blessing. But Affie's swift end brought a new and frightening thought to Vicky – she too could go just as quickly. She began to look over her will and to put her house in order, for she had noticed a change in herself. She was losing weight rapidly, there was more pain and she had difficulty in sleeping. By Christmas she had declined even further. Her limbs were too stiff to bend and she had to be carried up and down stairs like a baby. She was not the only one to see the deterioration. The Prince of Wales, who had been to Coburg for his brother's funeral, spent a week or two in Homburg afterwards and drove daily the short distance to Kronberg. He too noticed a difference in Vicky.

The affection between brother and sister had deepened with the years. For a long time now Bertie had understood Vicky's difficulties in a way no one else could. He had been in Germany far more often than any other member of his family and had witnessed Bismarck's spite, heard William's hurtful remarks and seen the effect they had had on his sister. These were things he could not forgive, and whenever Vicky was in England he did everything in his power to make it up to her in a hundred thoughtful ways. Vicky noticed this and was grateful. During the Diamond Jubilee state banquet in Buckingham Palace, Vicky had been startled and delighted to see her brother rise and propose 'the health of the Empress Frederick'. Indeed, he went out of his way to give her every consideration as a sister and honour as a queen. When he saw her slowly die before his eyes he found it difficult to show a cheerful face.

By the New Year 1900, Vicky could no longer hide the truth from her three girls, but she begged them to keep it an 'absolute secret'. Sadly she explained that such subterfuges were still necessary: 'To have all the world know it would be to make my life utterly wretched and deprive me of all peace and independence. You know how indiscreet people in Berlin are. I am not much loved, so I should not like to have people most likely rejoicing over my misfortune and speculating on my coming decease before it is necessary.'[8]

There no longer seemed time for all she had to do. Now that Sophie was in the secret, without a trace of morbidness, Vicky reminded her that the Greek king had once promised that she should have a block of marble from the Pentelikon quarries for her tomb in the Friedenskirche – would Sophie tell her father-in-law that she would like to have the marble?

Her 'secret' could not be hidden much longer. She looked so ill that it was not difficult for people to guess that something was drastically wrong. When in Italy in March, she had met the Empress Eugénie, who had seen at once that Vicky was dying. But neither woman alluded to her state of health. Instead Eugénie offered Vicky her villa at Cap Martin for the winter, a sympathetic gesture that warmed Vicky's heart. 'It is just like her,' she wrote to Sophie, 'she does not stop to ask whether it will do her good or harm in the eyes of her party in France.'[9]

Vicky and Eugénie met again in April when Queen Victoria was at Cimiez for her annual spring holiday. The three widows were a striking sight; the two empresses walking one on each side of the little carriage drawn by a white donkey, in which sat an old lady in a black padded silk jacket and round straw hat – the greatest Queen Empress of them all. Eugénie was beautiful still, and it amused and delighted Vicky to see the effect the ex-Empress had on her ladies – just the same as on Vicky herself when she was young.[10]

Vicky had always had an excellent memory, a gift she had inherited from her mother, but the effect of her disease was to make her forgetful even of things that had happened quite recently. That is why in January 1900 she began to keep a diary of day-to-day events however trivial. It went on unbroken (although not always in her own hand) until the 31st of July 1901; it is not only a chronicle of her martyrdom, but also shows her amazing courage in managing to live an almost normal life up to the last two months, despite increasing pain and weakness. To get outside herself, she concentrated on her children's and grandchildren's activities. Tino's new motor car struck terror into her heart (there are entries about hair-raising speeds of 25–30 miles an hour on rough Greek roads), as did Moretta's cycling expeditions and Mossy's babies' daring exploits. Henry and Irene, shadowy figures up to now, appear more frequently as kindly and considerate towards her. William and Dona too have become nicer with the years. Dona's looks had not improved. She was fatter than ever and irritatingly vague, but she no longer looked for hidden meanings in Vicky's every innocent remark and was more at ease with her mother-in-law. Sometimes she would call in her carriage with one or other of her sons and take Vicky for a drive. Vicky guessed that she was lonely, for although he was a faithful husband, William was not averse to a rest now and again from Dona's cloying adoration. Moretta and Mossy ran over to Friedrichshof more and more frequently, and soon Mossy, Fischy and their children moved into their mother's house altogether.

Vicky's world was shrinking. It was soon to become very small and very full of suffering. After the bad summer of 1900, when the damp weather gave her rheumatism and cramp in her legs, the pain steadily increased, despite poultices, ice-bags and injections of morphia. On the night of the 18th of October (the anniversary of Fritz's birthday, as she noted in her diary) she was frightened by a sharp attack and thought that she was dying.[11] As dawn broke the crisis passed, and by morning she was weak but no longer in danger. 'I am so thankful to be alive,' she wrote two days later to Sophie. For those two days Mossy had hardly left her mother's side. She did everything possible for her: read to her, fed her with a spoon, administered drops of brandy and water, filled in the two blank entries in her diary and encouraged her as bravely as she could with a breaking heart. Vicky had far more friends than she ever knew, and now they came to see her and to help her by their devotion: Baroness Stockmar, who had rendered her such service and whom she loved, the Prince and Princess of Wales – 'dearest Alix the soul of tenderness' – their children, the Darmstadt nephews and nieces, her own sisters, Lady Ponsonby and her daughter Maggie, and many others. Anniversaries were not forgotten. On the 27th of March her thoughts were with 'my most precious Waldie' all day, and on the 18th of June the cruel pain of Sigi's loss came flooding back. Wakeful at night, with no hope of sleep, her mind would rove over the past. In an attempt to forget her sufferings she would think of something that had once given her great pleasure. Greece was a favourite subject, and she would try to recall the things she had loved most about that country – the reflection of the rocks on the sea, the eerie hooting of the owls in the stillness of the night, the stars in the sky 'which have a colour they have nowhere else', the smell of myrtle and of thyme.

Her sixtieth birthday was spent in bed, where she had been for over six weeks. Summer had turned into autumn, and winter had come almost without her noticing it. Her legs were shrunken, the flesh fallen away to nothing, her whole body no more than skin and bone, a mere skeleton, yet alive because of her unquenchable spirit. At times, frantic with pain, she could not stop herself screaming aloud, and when that happened she longed to die and be 'safe in my grave'.

Count Seckendorff was of the opinion that his mistress's sufferings were not lessened by the hordes of children and relations that filled the Schloss, which he described as half hotel, half hospital. But Vicky's letters and diary express only pleasure at the kindnesses of her family and friends in sitting with her, reading to her, holding her hands and wiping the tears away when she lost control. She loved the 'merry laughter of the little people' and said it did her good.

Christmas 1900, her last, passed quietly with Mossy, Fischy and the children round her. Presents had been bought for everyone and money sent to all her charities. President Kruger arrived in Berlin in the New Year after a triumphal tour through Europe. But since 'a little talk' with Queen Victoria, in the autumn,[12] William refused to meet the man whom Vicky called 'that nasty common old thief'. William had come to see his mother's usefulness as a go-between. Early in January he had confided to her that he had set his heart on celebrating the two-hundredth anniversary of the Prussian monarchy and that he wanted his mother to persuade the Prince of Wales to come. But Bertie told Vicky he wanted no part in his nephew's 'self-glorification'.

The autumn before, Vicky had been bitterly disappointed that the Queen had been forced to abandon her usual holiday at Cimiez because of Europe's hostile attitude to England over the Boer War. She went instead to Ireland, and Vicky never saw her mother again. The Queen's health was failing and Vicky became alarmed. But with a telegram for her birthday on the 21st of November her fears lessened. The Queen had prayed that 'darling Vicky may suffer less', her thoughts with her child all day as Vicky's were with her. On the 20th of December Vicky heard that the Queen had travelled to Osborne and that she was feeling better. She took it for a good sign when two days later she heard that her mother had received Lord Roberts and Mr Chamberlain and (immediately after Christmas) the new German Ambassador, Baron von Eckhardstein. But on the 18th of January William came to Friedrichshof to tell his mother that the Queen was dying.

William's Prussian monarchy celebrations were in full swing, but he dramatically announced that, important as they were, he had to go at once to his dying grandmother (as Vicky told Mossy, 'he will bury grandmama before she is dead'). But when William reached Osborne the Queen's mind was wandering and she mistook him for his father.

On the 23rd of January Mossy broke the news to her mother that the Queen was dead. Vicky had been expecting it, but paradoxically it was a shock. The Queen had lived so long into Vicky's adult life that existence without her seemed too desolate and bleak to contemplate. With tears pouring down her cheeks, blotching the ink and blurring her sight, Vicky wrote in her diary, 'Oh, how can my pen write it, my sweet darling beloved mama; the best of mothers and greatest of

Queens, our centre and help and support – all seems a blank, a terrible awful dream. Realise it one cannot.'[13]

At Easter, Bertie – now King of England – travelled to Kronberg to see his dying sister. He brought with him a well-known doctor, Sir Francis Laking, who he hoped might mitigate Vicky's sufferings. Her godson, Frederick Ponsonby, the King's equerry, completed the small party (unlike his nephew, King Edward liked to travel inconspicuously). To him Vicky secretly entrusted all her private letters and papers (two large black boxes) to be taken to Windsor for safe keeping. The following month the new Queen arrived for a second visit, 'so kind and dear and gentle and quite touching in her goodness to me – no other would I have liked to see at the head of our dear old home and bearing the name so sacred to us'.[14] Princess Beatrice followed, accompanied by the sad-faced Princess Christian, still mourning for her son. The sisters clustered together in the invalid's bedroom or on Vicky's better days round the couch in her sitting-room, and hugged their sorrows, weeping for their mother and for their eldest sister who must be the next to go, comforting each other and doing everything in their power to alleviate Vicky's hell.

As the days got warmer Vicky was carried on a stretcher into the garden and laid on a special bed, her head and arms supported by a sling. There was always a little table by her side with a vase of freshly-cut flowers placed so that she could smell their scent. Since the autumn she had been sleeping less and less, snatching an odd five minutes here and there whenever the pain allowed. Her diary is full of the sight of Kronberg at night as she saw it from her bed: sheet lightning or beautiful moonlight that gave an ethereal appearance to the trees in the park, the gentle tap of the wild cherry against her window whenever there was a slight breeze, the smell of the new-mown grass and the rich sweet scent of the roses.

As May turned into June it got hotter and sleep became impossible, so they carried her bed to her studio on the north side of the house where it was cooler. She still would not allow anyone to sit up with her at night. She dreaded them hearing her moans and her beseeching cries to Fritz as she held out her crippled arms for him to take her where there was no more pain, only calm and peace and infinite love. At other times, when the cruel spasms had passed and she could breathe more easily, she would stare into the darkness, willing the end to come, repeating over and over again, 'God shall wipe away all tears from my eyes, and behold there shall be no more suffering, only peace and joy that shall last for ever more'.[15] Her former maid-of-honour, Marie de Bunsen, travelled from England to see her. She was so overcome by the change in her beloved mistress that she fell on her knees and covered Vicky's swollen hand with kisses. Vicky tried to smile through her own tears as she said without self-pity, 'If I had known of the horrors lying in wait for me, I should have put an end to my life'.[16]

*

Nothing but Vicky's amazing spirit enabled her to go on living. By the middle of June she could neither eat nor sleep, but between bouts of pain she still liked to talk and could take an interest in what was going on. The great clock on the tower needed repainting. Vicky had strips of paper of different shades of blue held up against the face before she could decide on the exact colour. The Bishop of Ripon, who had called to see her, was amazed that the dying woman could still concentrate on such a practical matter. With the enhanced sensitivity of the very ill, she guessed his thoughts and said sadly, 'I feel like Moses on Pisgah looking at the Promised Land which I must not enter'.[17]

Friedrichshof was to know birth as well as death that summer. In July Mossy's second set of twins was born; they were brought down at once for their grandmother to see. It was a poignant moment. Vicky knew that she would never have the happiness of seeing these children running about like the other 'little people' who had brought her such joy. Two weeks later Sophie arrived from Greece to share the nursing with her sisters. All three hardly ever left the house. On the 21st of July Vicky wrote her last entry in her diary, '. . . pain in arm and back very bad. Moretta a great help – one of my worst days'.[18]

Remembering how difficult it had been to keep the air in Fritz's room sweet and fresh, Vicky insisted on staying in the garden until almost the very end. Then one evening – it was the 3rd of August – when they carried her in, she knew she would never come out again. When her attendants reached the door she asked them to stop so that she could take one last look at the garden she had made in memory of a great and undying love.

That night she drifted into unconsciousness. When William and Dona arrived next day she did not know them, but her heart still showed a feeble flicker for twenty-four more hours. Just before the end, Sophie and Mossy went into the garden for a breath of air. When they returned to the bedroom a minute or two later their mother had gone.

Vicky had left instructions for a very simple funeral. No post mortem, no enbalming, no photographs and no lying in state. The coffin was to be closed at once and taken to the town church at Kronberg and kept there until it could be placed next to Fritz in Potsdam: 'any one who pleases may visit the church'. The court chaplain was to say a short prayer at her funeral but 'on no account to make a speech'.

Her will carefully disposed of everything she possessed. Friedrichshof and most of its contents to Mossy; jewellery, silver and the pictures she had collected were left to individual members of her family whom she named. Every servant was remembered. As tidy in death as she was in life, she left no tangles for others to unravel.

Just as Fritz had died in the same year as his father, so Vicky died in the same year as her mother. She was just sixty years and nine months old.

*

The German people's reaction to Vicky's death was swift, and showed how deep their affection for her had become. It had been demonstrated often enough already: by the gratitude shown for her visits to the victims of the frequent floods in eastern Germany, for instance, by the love of the slum-dwellers of Berlin whose wretched lives she had tried to relieve, by her work during three wars for the military hospitals – and perhaps most of all by her immediate recall from them when her work made her too popular for Bismarck's comfort. This affection had long been clear, but the universal mourning in August 1901 put it beyond doubt. Bismarck had tried to keep Vicky and the German people apart. With his disappearance the mists that had obscured her were dispersed by the warmth of her own rich personality, and the one thing that Bismarck had done his best to prevent came to pass after all: Vicky was beloved in Germany.

The bells that tolled for the Empress's death on the 5th of August were the signal for people to flock into Kronberg from miles around. They came by train, in carriages, on horseback and on foot to pay tribute to a woman they had learned to know as simple, unaffected and kind, whose chief concern was for their well-being. Yet little significance has been attached to this. 'The Crown Princess knew that she was detested in Germany,' says Mr N. B. Rich.[19] In fact, the people had never disliked her, indeed whenever she was able to make contact with them the result was the very opposite. This was what Bismarck had feared. Unfortunately, for most of Vicky's life in Prussia all power was in the hands of Bismarck and his followers. It was in their interest to distort her image.

Ironically Bismarck's own death had created no stir. Yet crowds stood tightly packed in the streets when twelve N.C.O.s of Vicky's own regiment (the Royal Prussian Fusiliers),* preceded by torchbearers, carried the coffin down the hill to the parish church. The day

*The arrival of troops for the funeral gave rise to the legend that Friedrichshof was surrounded in 1901, just as the Neue Palais had been in 1888, to prevent the removal of private papers.

had been hot and oppressive. As night fell, lightning flashed across the mountains (a sleepless Vicky had often watched it from her bed that summer), and the distant roll of thunder could be heard mingling with the melancholy sound of muffled drums. But not even the threat of a storm could deter the people from queueing all night to pay their last respects. At seven o'clock next morning – as Vicky had requested – the doors were opened to the public who throughout the day filed past the coffin as it stood on a catafalque before the altar, covered with a purple ermine-trimmed pall, the imperial crown upon it. Four officers from the Bockenheimer Hussars stood guard.

Vicky had always disliked long and lugubrious funeral services. Gloom was banished as much as possible from her own. One observer[20] described the colourful uniforms, the massed flowers, the sun streaming through the windows (suffusing everything with those 'magic tinges' that had so affected the young Vicky at the coronation of William I) as dazzling in their brilliance. At the suggestion of the Emperor, the Berlin Cathedral choir closed the service with a favourite poem, sent anonymously to Vicky after Fritz's death, set to music for the occasion and sung in English.

> A voice is calling from a brighter world,
> 'Be of good courage, love, and struggle on.
> Though wrong and falsehood all around be hurled,
> There shall be victory when the day is done'.

That evening the coffin was taken to the station for its last journey to Potsdam. As the train began to move, drums rolled, and Vicky's standard was lowered. William was trying to make amends by burying his mother like an Empress.*

---

*Vicky now lies next to Fritz in the Friedenskirche, Potsdam, in a mausoleum she had designed herself. With them are their two sons, Sigismund and Waldemar. Her effigy, executed by Begas, is of finest Pentelikon marble: the King of Greece remembered his promise.

CHAPTER 29

'*Men are perishable but Ideas live*'

In 1871, not long after the end of the Franco-Prussian War, when Vicky was worried by the ever-widening gulf between Britain and Germany, she wrote to Queen Victoria in terms she tried hard to believe were reassuring: 'Count Bismarck is not eternal, he will be forgotten as the Emperor Napoleon who is now scarcely remembered.'[1]

Less than five years later she was reeling from the effects of Bismarck's diabolical plan to fashion her own son in opposition; a plan he carried out with his customary care and thoroughness. Bismarck's object was to ensure that the pattern of misrepresentation, already well under way, should be continued. Before the tyranny of the master was removed, the tyranny of the pupil had begun and was infinitely more painful – 'the fact that my son's soul was alienated from me is the wilful and purposeful work of one man'.[2] Bismarck taught Willy to trample on his parents' ideals and beliefs, so that all point of contact was lost and Vicky's warm and affectionate heart was wounded. As she told her mother with infinite pathos, 'If he had been a stranger one could have got over it'.[3] Yet she did in some measure get over it, and even learned to manage her difficult son with tact and humour, thus leaving a way open for reconciliation. She could not forget, but she could forgive. Here she was totally magnanimous. The past was too black with re-criminations, disloyalty, heartbreak and tears to think of without emotion, but she did manage to be unbiased and unrevengeful, prevented herself from being swayed by what had happened, and even began to look at events with detachment. This lack of destructive personal involvement proved in the end to be her strength and salvation in her dealings with Bismarck. He seems, of course, never to have understood this, since his own feelings were egotistical to the point of megalomania. Everything he did had a personal slant and was all the more unpredictable and dangerous for that. With commendable generosity Vicky never hesitated to give Bismarck his due – what could they not accomplish together for Prussia, she once wrote, 'if only Bismarck were a good man'. She acknowledged that he was a great man who had led Prussia to 'dizzy heights', and she praised him as a 'great opportunist, a master in creation of situations; his perception was rapid and the means he employed were clever; his courage was great, but his example was a wrong one to copy, and bad for the training of others. I am speaking without rancour, and bear him no grudge.'[4] She would gladly have put up with everything she and Fritz had to endure if it had been for Germany's ultimate good. But she believed that they had suffered for nothing and that 'internal soundness, intrinsic solidarity and real worth' cannot emerge from a corrupt system, however brilliant the triumph might seem at the time.

Great credit must be given her for trying to penetrate the many strange recesses of Bismarck's mind: she did not condemn without first trying to understand and to justify. Bismarck's methods were the exact opposite, and he dismissed everything she said and did as bad and pro-English. In her love for England he saw only disloyalty to Prussia; in her longing to serve the German people only a craving for power. He mocked what he called her 'slavish veneration' for Britain because to him it smacked of something he could not endure – criticism of Prussia. When he said 'I will not have the influence of British ideas in Germany', he revealed a stubborn short-sightedness which does not do him the honour he supposed, despite the plaudits of his supporters. He failed to grasp the fact that Vicky's reason for wishing to emulate English habits and customs was purely in order to benefit Germany. To take the best from her old country to improve her new one – this was to her no more than common sense. She knew that no country was at that time more advanced than her own and that it was 'the only one that understands liberty, the only one that understands true progress, the only happy, the only really free and above all the only really humane country'.[5]

Unfortunately Bismarck did not hesitate to use Vicky's English proclivities to drive a wedge between her and the German people. Yet hard as he tried, he never completely succeeded in distorting her image, and those who knew her personally or whose lives had crossed hers were drawn to her because they sensed that here was someone who really cared about them and wanted to improve their lives. It is important not to forget that Fritz Holstein's vicious comments were all second-hand, gathered from most dubious sources. There is no record that he and Vicky ever met. Bismarck feared that Vicky's warm personality might catch public imagination and hold it for herself, and his fear was well founded. He recognised her charm, intelligence and integrity at once and realised as quickly that these qualities were formidable when allied to boundless energy and a burning zeal for reform. It made things worse that she used her gifts to promote the Liberal cause, which he distrusted, and that she propagated it by her constant search for ways and means of relieving the wretched conditions of the poor in Germany – a class looked on by Bismarck as useful for cannon-fodder and little else. Her ideas were all sound and practical, and most of her objectives had been achieved by the end of her life.

Vicky's honesty and open nature played into Bismarck's hands. The truth had only to be tilted a little to give a very different impression from the one she intended. A wrong emphasis on a word, a sentence taken out of context or a slight human error of judgment were all used against her. Very little was enough. Bismarck had no more than this to draw upon when he devised the ugly picture of a weak husband bullied by a strong-willed wife. How much truth was there in the repeated accusation that Vicky dominated Fritz? It has often been said that she did. It became the fashion to denigrate Vicky as soon as Bismarck gave the lead, and directly this happened nobody hesitated to accept invention as if it were fact. But a willingness to spread falsehoods does not make them true. It is worth noting that the charge that she dominated Fritz was not mentioned until after Bismarck came to power in 1862, although all Vicky's words and actions were discussed with great freedom during her first four years in Germany – the family were not the sort of people to allow what to them would amount to a monstrous infringement of masculine rights to go unremarked. The charge was not made for the simple reason that there was no evidence for it. That it flowered so freely after 1862 was due solely to Bismarck, who had no difficulty in convincing himself that it was essential for the preservation of his power to keep such stories circulating. This was a simple matter in the artificial atmosphere of Berlin court life, where no name was too sacred to blacken – a curious paradox in such an aristocratic society.

Fritz did not deny that Vicky influenced him. She strengthened his liberal ideas (already formed before they met), his resolution when his father tried to pick a quarrel, and even his belief in himself. Conversely, he certainly modified many of Vicky's opinions and altered others. If he did not teach her to suffer fools gladly at least he persuaded her to see the necessity of hiding her impatience with those whose minds were less agile than her own. The greater tolerance of the short-comings of others, which became very evident in her widowhood, was entirely due to his admonitions and to his example. All in all, their influence on each other was no more than in most successful marriages. Since Vicky was vivacious and talkative and Fritz was quiet and self-effacing, it was assumed – even by some of those who did not wish her ill – that Vicky was always the one to take the lead. Moreover, each of them unconsciously encouraged this idea. Scornful of the German conception of the rôle of a wife, they went out of their way to demonstrate that in their own marriage husband and wife were equal. It was unwise of Fritz to refer to Vicky in public and to be heard asking for her opinion, and short-sighted of Vicky to let everyone know that she at least was mistress of her home, that she had rearranged the Neue Palais just as she liked and had planned the gardens, that she had a full share in the upbringing of the children, even of the boys, including the heir to the throne. In his life of Fritz Holstein, Mr N. B. Rich says 'that the Crown Princess dominated her husband was the opinion of all who came in contact with the royal household'.[6] But what weight can be attached to the opinion of the household – a pack of Bismarckian spies, brain-washed to belittle the Crown Prince and Princess? 'All my entourage are his creatures,' Vicky told Lady Ponsonby almost matter-of-factly in 1887, and Lady Ponsonby knew that such a state of affairs had prevailed for a long time. To support his statement Mr Rich quotes an unpleasant character sketch of Vicky, written by Archduke Albrecht in 1875, which he has taken from Corti's *The English Empress*. 'So many indications of real womanly feeling, a good mother, and then again such contrariness and eccentricities, a great desire for undisturbed domesticity and an inordinate lust for power: spoiled in England as Princess Royal, she needed an iron hand to control her, instead she entirely dominated her husband, has remained completely English and her parents-in-law have no idea how to deal with her.'[7] The aged Habsburg Archduke who wrote this was, however, a diehard reaction-ary to whom Vicky's liberalism was anathema; like his friend Bismarck (whom he greatly admired), Albrecht felt himself threatened by her personality. Further, it may well be that he had heard the stories current in Berlin four years earlier, to the effect that Vicky had Fritz so much under her thumb that even from a distance she was able to keep him from bombarding Paris – whereas, in fact, Fritz lumped Vicky and Bismarck together as mere civilians who did not under-stand war, and delayed the bombardment for quite different and purely military reasons.

Perhaps if she had been aware of what was happening at the time, Vicky might have been more circumspect, although she was never one to count the cost to herself: she would have thought it cowardly to remain silent even if speaking out would have harmed her.

*

Vicky was not in the least like other Prussian princesses. They cannot be blamed for looking on her as a creature from another world, with her forthright manner, her fearless opinions and the air of authority which birth and education gave her. They had never seen a woman like her before. Brought up to speak her mind and with an almost exaggerated regard for the truth, she never quite understood the devastating effect of such outspokenness in a country where women were second-class citizens and where subterfuge was the rule. Before she had been many weeks in Prussia she had earned the reputation for tactlessness which has stuck to her ever since, little though she deserved it. It made no difference that her bluntness held no malice, that her strictures were often followed by the kindest and most considerate actions, and that she never had the slightest intention of inflicting wounds. William II's defence of his constant quarrels with his mother – that they were too much alike to agree – was true in only one respect: neither understood the effect of their words on other people – although William was by far the worse offender because he lacked his mother's goodness of heart.

Even had Vicky's nationality been different, she would have clashed with Bismarck on other issues. The Chancellor was in many ways unusually old-fashioned, while Vicky was unusually advanced ('everything modern interests me far too much, but I learn from it') and made it her business to involve herself in matters that had never concerned a woman before – certainly never a royal princess. Politics was strictly a man's province when Vicky came to Prussia, while social welfare was an orphan child – nobody felt it their responsibility. Vicky's eagerness to solve these problems by tackling them in a practical way (more schools, better homes, wholesale slum-clearance) caused a stir she could not begin to understand. Her explosive remarks on the bondage of Prussian women and the immediate need to emancipate them were repeated everywhere; not unnaturally they brought her into conflict with Bismarck, who distorted her humanity until it seemed a power-complex. He took care that people remembered Prince Albert's schemes for unity and his unwise remarks on constitutional government before the marriage, and Vicky's own views on the English parliamentary system, presenting them all in the guise of calculated interference.

It was not among the princesses that Vicky looked for adherents in her fight for equal rights (the brisk advice 'not to put up with it for a moment' which she gave her friend Marianne, who had been boxed on the ears by her husband for producing a third daughter, was met with incredulity even by the sufferer herself) but among the daughters of the new middle class. Vicky found the material for running her hospitals, her schools and her homes and craft centres in these women who were looking for scope for their energies and education. Her appeal for them was all the greater when they discovered that she was neither strait-laced nor haughty in an age when prudery abounded and snobbery was considered a virtue. Vicky was one of the very few who did not ostracise Count Hatzfeldt and his wife when they were divorced, and she was the first to praise their courage and unselfishness

when they remarried for the sake of their daughter. Although she held
strict views on adultery, she could not understand why Russian society,
corrupt in so many ways, was shocked when Alexander II married his
mistress, Countess Dolgoroukova, the mother of four of his children,
six weeks after the death of his wife. Vicky saw in Alexander's action
only an attempt 'to do his duty as a man of honour by a lady and his
children whom he had placed in so painful a position'.[8] It was incom-
prehensible to her that those who were shocked were the very people
who did not utter one word of disgust at the awful treatment of the
Poles or lift a finger to ease the 'no less cruel' misery of the Russian
poor. Unlike many of her contemporaries, Vicky seldom got her
priorities wrong. She was very well able to distinguish between what
really mattered and what was only a pity.

*

It never ceased to surprise Vicky that she evoked strong feelings in
everyone: with her, neutrality was impossible and indifference something she never had to endure. For much too long only one side – that
of her enemies – has been allowed to make itself heard. Indeed, the
abuse hurled at her by Bismarck and his devotees has been so overwhelming that it has successfully drowned the praise that she earned
for her many attractive qualities. Scarcely two people were drawn to
her for the same reasons – a tribute to the many-sidedness of her
character. Her sensitivity to the troubles and sorrows of others was
the quality the Empress Eugénie rated highest. Eugénie had reason to
know, for it was the genuine grief and sympathy in Vicky's letter that
gave her most comfort on the death of her only child, the Prince
Imperial. During Fritz's illness Vicky's courage and devotion was plain
to everyone who cared to look; Ranke pointed this out at the time,
when Vicky was short of people to defend her. But only the shocking
innuendoes of Radolinski, Holstein and others were recorded, and
only they are still given prominence.

Friendship was a word that held a special meaning for her; she had
so little of it in Prussia, yet what she had she held for life, as Bamberger
– who was also attracted by her humanity – often pointed out. Ludwig
Windhorst, one of her most ardent admirers, was struck by the
generosity of her nature and the breadth of her vision, and he earned
Bismarck's wrath for saying so. For Heinrich von Angeli, who knew
her well, Vicky had 'every quality of heart and mind'. Over and over
again there is evidence that people in all walks of life felt her charm.
Even dour Scottish Lord Rectors were known to succumb. When
Vicky was painting Dr Story one day at Balmoral, Marie Adeane, a
young maid-of-honour of the Queen's, noticed with amusement that

341

despite his initial trepidation – he had expected the session to be stiff and awkward – he was soon talking animatedly on a variety of subjects: 'The Empress has a talent for putting everyone at their ease and drawing clever people out.'[9]

Vicky's charm was so endearing because at heart she was a simple and uncomplicated person, as George Eliot discovered when she was presented to Vicky at a reception. The novelist was startled that an empress could turn to her with an engaging smile and the words 'I think you know my sister Louise'. The quality of her conversation is lost to posterity, and what can be gleaned from reported speech lacks the fire that undoubtedly characterised everything she said. But the sparkle in her personality comes through in her letters, and it was this vitality in the ten-year-old girl that Fritz remembered four years later when he was looking for a wife. Vicky enjoyed a companionship with Fritz that was unique between husband and wife in Prussia and was thus bound to be misunderstood. She was far from being the tyrant so many have called her. Heinrich von Angeli, who spent many months in the Neue Palais, painting portraits of the family and giving Vicky painting lessons, says he was struck by the harmony in the home, by the fun the parents had with their children, and by the fact that the children were not repressed in any way. This is a very different picture from that of Georg Hinzpeter, who asserted that neither Vicky nor Fritz understood their children and that they demanded strict and unnecessary obedience – a strange accusation to come from a man who prided himself on his discipline. As it happens, Vicky has left us in no doubt about her views on this subject in a letter to her daughter Sophie: 'I always think we grown-up people ought to be so careful how we exact obedience from our children. Obedience that is not cheerful or willing only ruins the character. All that nonsense of "breaking the will" is now recognised as making children vicious and false and sly.'[10]

After the move to Kronberg, Vicky saw that being out of affairs had its compensations. In her village in the Taunus she could enjoy a freedom she had never known before. It was a freedom that was respected by the villagers, who soon got used to seeing her come and go as she pleased, accompanied only by a lady-in-waiting. Whenever she was at Friedrichshof she would walk down the hill two or three times a week to the house of the artist Norbert Schrödl to join a group who had become known as the 'Kronberg painters', and she did this not as dowager Empress but simply as another painter to work and exchange ideas. And Vicky's ideas were always worth hearing. Her new house excited curiosity just because it was full of them; Friedrichshof became known far and wide as the most 'modern' house in

Germany. It was characteristic of Vicky that she paid as much attention to the servants' rooms as to her own. It was the first house to have a kitchen on the ground floor, next to the dining-room, instead of in the usual dark and dismal basement. Skylights were done away with; all the servants had windows to their bedrooms, which overlooked the park. There were other innovations that now have become commonplace, but they caused endless comment then – such as central heating under the windows instead of against the walls, and a drive with a one-way system for carriages. The sophistication of her taste could be seen in the furniture with which she filled her home. Vicky was buying Roentgen chests, Chippendale desks and Hepplewhite chairs when her friends (and Queen Victoria too) were enthusing over machine-made monstrosities.

*

Despite the unbelievable hardships which were the direct result of her life in Prussia, Vicky never had any doubt that marriage to Fritz was the best thing that ever happened to her – it was 'my golden lot'. Fritz felt the same, and the words he wrote to the fifteen-year-old Vicky remained true to the end of his life: 'You are everything in the world to me.'

But the fits of melancholy that were an integral part of Fritz's nature, and which Vicky's cheerful outlook did much to lessen, turned to sheer despondency at moments towards the end of his life when he remembered that it was marriage to him that had brought her to such a pass. At these times he cursed his early immature conduct and felt that he had done wrong in 1862 by not calling the King's bluff and accepting his offer to abdicate.

Yet had he been so wrong to refuse? Could a king with his known constitutional views, so different from Prussian tradition, have ruled without difficulties? How many people would have understood him? There were few men with Liberal and parliamentary experience in Prussia, too few then who would have supported his plans or wanted to put them into effect. Besides, he would have taken over at a time of crisis (the question of the army estimates was at its height) when the Liberals and progressives – whose numbers greatly increased at the two general elections of 1862 – were in opposition to the monarchy, so that it would not merely have been a conflict of interests but of conviction.[11] There were other hazards too. Fritz might have had to face the dilemma of angering the generals by abandoning the army estimates, and since he had no political experience himself this might have led to calling in another 'strong man' – perhaps with the result we know. Apart from these disadvantages, Fritz knew that with

Vicky's support they might have had the chance to achieve some of the social legislation which would have meant so much to them. They both longed to see religious toleration in Prussia, and with their views on racial discrimination they would have done everything in their power to ease the life of the Jews.

To some extent they deluded themselves when they believed that they had missed a chance to work for the good of Prussia in 1862. It was not a political opportunity that was missed, but an opportunity for personal happiness – with trials, no doubt, but also with the satisfaction that comes with steady progress.

One more hypothesis must be examined briefly. What would have happened if Fritz had been well and strong in 1888? Although already fifty-six years old, in some respects Fritz was still politically uneducated, and the politics of a united Germany were far more complicated than Prussian politics in 1862. Yet a glance at the list of names Fritz had prepared for his first Cabinet shows that he had a gift of picking able men to help him in his work, and the fact that so many of them willingly suffered for him demonstrates that he had a capacity for inspiring devotion which was never allowed to develop fully. Against this, however, there would have been a new menace to contend with – Socialism – that 'Wild and poisonous nonsense',[12] although under a more liberal régime it would perhaps not have developed so rapidly as it did under William II. With the disappearance of Bismarck from the scene, either by dismissal or death, Fritz would have modified the autocratic system, and in Vicky's words 'would have finished and complemented Bismarck's great work'.[13] It is certain that William II's sabre-rattling would have been replaced by the alliance with England which Vicky longed for, a move that would have been welcomed in London, where Vicky and Fritz were popular, and which would have put war out of the question. Above all, they would have managed to apply a brake to Germany's headlong race to ruin, which fortunately Vicky did not live to see.

And what of the Prince Consort's dream – unity by intellectual forces? Did Vicky ever come to admit that it had no more substance than a dream, that unity could only have come by the sword? Politically acute though she was in so many ways, Vicky clung all her life to the conviction that her father was right – anything else would have been the grossest disloyalty to an adored parent who was an oracle to her. Vicky could not have lived with that on her conscience. Besides, her belief in the ultimate reasonableness of human nature blinded her to the difficulty of ejecting Austria from the leadership of Germany which she had held for centuries as of right and of inducing the other states to accept Prussian dominance except by military means. Something in Vicky, as in her father, always shrank from the idea of war. To have accepted it, however worthy the end it served, would have been a betrayal of her father's trust in her ability to accomplish 'my mission', and this she could never have done.

By 1893 she had begun to draw comfort from the belief that William II and his followers were only a phase in the development of Germany and would pass away like black clouds after a storm. With the dawn of a new day Fritz's 'hopes and what he worked for may some day be realised, but not for a long time . . . for sometimes things turn out better than one thinks'.[14]

*

Vicky swept through Prussia like a fresh breeze, blowing away the cobwebs of years and breaking down the barriers of prejudice and class. She brought with her a message of hope for all who cared to listen, in her humanity, her energy and the imaginative qualities of her mind, all of which she longed to use to 'do good' and to bring the greatest gift of all – freedom, 'without which man's life is worth nothing'.

Notes, Bibliography, Index

Notes on the Empress Frederick's children

William II abdicated at the close of the First World War in November 1918 and went into exile at Doorn in Holland. After the death of his first wife, Augusta Victoria (Dona), Princess of Schleswig-Holstein, in 1921 he married Hermine, daughter of Prince Henry of Reuss. He died in 1941.

Charlotte (Ditta) married Bernard, Duke of Saxe-Meiningen in 1878 and died in 1919.

Henry married Irene, daughter of the Grand Duke Louis of Hesse in 1888 and died in 1929.

Sigismund (1864–6) and Waldemar (1868–79) both died as children.

Victoria (Moretta) married Prince Adolf of Schaumburg-Lippe in 1890. He died in 1916. She married Alexander Zoubkoff, a Russian adventurer, in 1927 and died in 1929. He disappeared with her fortune.

Sophie married, in 1889, Constantine (Tino), Duke of Sparta who in 1913 became King of Greece. In 1922 he was forced to abdicate. He died in 1923 and she in 1932.

Margaret (Mossy) married Frederick (Fischy), Prince (afterwards Landgrave) of Hesse in 1893. She inherited Friedrichshof from her mother and died there in 1954. The mansion itself was for a time a club for American officers after 1945, and thereafter an hotel.

Reference Notes

1 'Albert, Father of a Daughter'

1. Bolitho, 34, Prince Albert to his brother Ernest, 21 Nov 1840
2. *Letters*, I. i. 249, Baron Stockmar to Viscount Melbourne, 21 Nov 1840
3. *Letters*, I. i. 200, Queen Victoria to Prince Albert, 20 Nov 1839
4. *Letters*, I. i. 214, King of Belgians to Queen Victoria, 31 Jan 1840
5. *Sophie*, 200
6. Martin, i. 55; Fulford *The Prince Consort*, 49
7. *Letters P.C.*, 69, Prince Consort to Prince William of Löwenstein, May 1840
8. Longford, 130
9. Grey *The Early Years of the Prince Consort*, 8
10. Fulford *The Prince Consort*, 95
11. Ponsonby, 5
12. *Letters*, I. i. 251, Queen Victoria to King of Belgians, 15 Dec 1840
13. *The Times*, 11 Feb 1841
14. *The Times*, 15 Nov 1840
15. Lyttelton, 310
16. *Letters P.C.*, 82, Stockmar to Prince Consort
17. Martin, ii. 2
18. Martin, ii. 182, Memorandum by the Queen
19. Lyttelton, 344
20. *Letters*, I. ii. 3, Queen Victoria to King of Belgians, 9 Jan 1844
21. Martin, i. 34
22. Martin, ii. 183, Memorandum by Queen Victoria
23. Lyttelton, 360
24. *Letters*, I. i. 380, Queen Victoria to King of Belgians, 8 Feb 1842
25. Martin, ii. 232
26. *Letters*, I. ii. 106, Queen Victoria to King of Belgians, 29 Sept 1846

2 'A Child with very strong Feelings'

1. Martin, ii. 24
2. Frank Eyck, 86
3. Saxe-Coburg-Gotha *Memoirs*, i. 48
4. Frank Eyck, 94; Ramm, 178
5. Bunsen, ii. 115
6. Martin, ii. 37; Bunsen, ii. 170
7. Frank Eyck, 75

8. Martin, ii. 111, Prince Albert to King of Belgians, 24 March 1848
9. Martin, ii. 362
10. 30 May 1851
11. *Further Letters*, 25, Queen Victoria to Princess Augusta, 19 June 1851
12. *Further Letters*, 35, Queen Victoria to Princess Augusta, 24 Jan 1853
13. *Letters*, I. iii. 170, Queen Victoria to Miss Florence Nightingale, Jan 1856
14. Stanley *Letters*, 106
15. *Further Letters*, 39, Queen Victoria to Princess Augusta, 28 March 1853
16. *A Memoir*, 29
17. 22 Dec 1857

3   A Sprig of White Heather

1. *Leaves*, 96
2. Martin, iii. 371
3. *Letters*, I. iii. 147, Queen Victoria to King of Belgians, 22 Sept 1855
4. Longford, 260
5. *Letters P.C.*, 239, Prince Consort to Baron Stockmar, Oct 1855
6. Longford, 135
7. *Further Letters*, 59, Queen Victoria to Princess Augusta, 22 Oct 1855
8. Saxe-Coburg-Gotha *Memoirs*, i. 214
9. *The Times*, 3 Oct 1855
10. Martin, iv. 376
11. *The Times*, 4 Oct 1855
12. *Further Letters*, 60, Queen Victoria to Princess Augusta, 23 Oct 1855
13. 22 July 1856
14. *Further Letters*, 62, Queen Victoria to King of Prussia, 4 April 1856
15. *Letters P.C.*, 259, Prince Consort to Prince William, 2 March 1856
16. *Letters*, I. iii. 253, Queen Victoria to Lord Clarendon, 25 Oct 1857
17. *Letters P.C.*, 272, Prince Consort to Baron Stockmar
18. Bolitho, 168, 26 June 1857
19. *Letters*, I. iii. 263, Queen Victoria to King of Belgians, 12 Jan 1858
20. Martin, iii. 157
21. Martin, iii. 160
22. *A Memoir*, 69
23. *Letters P.C.*, 288, Prince Consort to Princess Royal

4   'That Cruel Moment'

1. *Letters P.C.*, 289, Prince Consort to Baron Stockmar, 5 Feb 1858
2. Martin, iii. 386, Prince Consort to Prince Frederick William; *A Memoir*, 78
3. *Dearest Child*, 30, 2 Feb 1858
4. *Dearest Child*, 31, undated
5. 10 March 1858
6. *Letters P.C.*, 290, Prince Consort to Princess Royal, 11 Feb 1858

7. *A Memoir*, 74
8. *A Memoir*, 75
9. 8 Feb 1858
10. *Dearest Child*, 50
11. *Dearest Child*, 42
12. *Dearest Child*, 73
13. *Dearest Child*, 132
14. Paget, 74
15. *Dearest Child*, 60
16. *Dearest Child*, 101
17. *Dearest Child*, 74
18. *A Memoir*, 93

5 'The Pull of Home'

1. 14 March 1858
2. *Dearest Child*, 181
3. *Dearest Child*, 183
4. *Dearest Child*, 133, 27 Sept 1858
5. *Letters P.C.*, 294, Prince Consort to Princess Royal, 17 Feb 1858
6. *Letters P.C.*, 294, Prince Consort to Princess Augusta of Prussia, 20 Feb 1858
7. Undated (but probably in April 1858)
8. *Dearest Child*, 64, 27 Feb 1858
9. *Dearest Child*, 136, 4 Oct 1858
10. *Dearest Child*, 35, 7 Feb 1858
11. *Dearest Child*, 50, 20 Feb 1858
12. *Letters P.C.*, 295, Prince Consort to Princess Augusta, 9 March 1858
13. 10 March 1858
14. 10 March 1858
15. *Dearest Child*, 74, 5 March 1858
16. Bolitho, 183
17. 22 April 1858
18. 18 April 1858
19. Bolitho, 187, 22 April 1858
20. 14 Sept 1858
21. 17 March 1858
22. *Letters P.C.*, 297, Prince Consort to Princess Royal, 10 March 1858
23. 24 March 1858
24. 25 March 1858
25. Martin, iv. 403
26. 18 Sept 1858

6 'Not the Conqueror, perhaps the Great'

1. *Dearest Child*, 93, 16 April 1858
2. *Letters P.C.*, 308, Prince Consort to Queen Victoria, 4 June 1858

3. *Letters P.C.*, 307, Prince Consort to Queen Victoria, 3 June 1858
4. *Dearest Child*, 75, 5 March 1858
5. Martin. iv. 298; Stockmar XXCI
6. Martin. iv. 300
7. 20 Aug 1858
8. 28 May 1858
9. *Dearest Child*, 130, 16 Sept 1858
10. 1 Oct 1858
11. 16 Oct 1858
12. Greville *Memoirs*, 12 Dec 1858; Fulford *The Prince Consort*, 138
13. *Dearest Child*, 136, 4 Oct 1858
14. *Dearest Child*, 137, 9 Oct 1858; Fulford *The Prince Consort*, 138
15. *Dearest Child*, 138, note
16. Lyttelton, 321
17. *Dearest Child*, 159, 28 Jan 1859
18. *Dearest Child*, 119, 128
19. *Dearest Child*, 193
20. *Dearest Child*, 165, 8 March 1858
21. *Letters*, I. iii. 276, Queen Victoria to King of Belgians, 23 March 1859
22. *Dearest Child*, 163, 25 Feb 1859
23. 9 March 1859
24. 25 May 1859
25. 26 May 1859

7 'Between two Fires'

1. *Sophie*, 310
2. *Letters*, I. iii. 331, Queen Victoria to King of Belgians, 3 May 1859
3. 5 June 1859
4. *Dearest Child*, 190
5. 13 June 1859
6. 11 Oct 1859
7. Eyck, 249
8. 15 June 1859
9. *Letters P.C.*, 348, Prince Consort to Princess Royal, 26 June 1860
10. 8 March 1860
11. *Letters P.C.*, 357, Prince Consort to Ernest Stockmar, 13 March 1860
12. Eyck, 173

8 'Goodness can provide a Purpose in Life'

1. Radziwill, 154
2. 16 March 1860
3. 20 March 1860
4. *Dearest Child*, 243, 20 March 1860
5. *Dearest Child*, 222, 10 Dec 1859
6. 10 March 1859

7. 27 May 1860
8. Stockmar XCVII
9. *Letters P.C.*, 256
10. *Letters P.C.*, 357, Prince Consort to Princess Royal, 25 Dec 1860
11. *Letters E.F.*, 29
12. *Letters E.F.*, 29
13. *Dearest Child*, 300, 4 Jan 1861
14. *Letters E.F.*, 31
15. 17 April 1861
16. 20 April 1861
17. 15 March 1861
18. Grant & Temperley, 313
19. 18 Dec 1860
20. 17 Jan 1860
21. 7 April 1861
22. *Letters E.F.*, 31
23. Paget, 72
24. 12 Nov 1861
25. *Letters P.C.*, 538, Prince Consort to Crown Princess, 29 Jan 1861
26. *Dearest Child*, 357, 15 Nov 1861
27. *Letters P.C.*, 370, Prince Consort to Queen Augusta, 22 Nov 1861
28. *Dearest Child*, 372, 7 Dec 1861
29. 12 Dec 1861
30. *Dearest Child*, 375, 15 Dec 1861

9 'How terrible to have to say he was'

1. *Letters P.C.*, 299, Prince Consort to Princess Royal, 28 April 1858
2. 20 Jan 1862
3. 17 Feb 1862
4. *Dearest Mama*, 27
5. *Letters P.C.*, 341–57, Prince Consort to Crown Princess, 11 Jan 1859–26 Dec 1860
6. 6 March 1861
7. 17 Feb 1861
8. 11 March 1862
9. Stockmar XVIII
10. 17 March 1862
11. 21 March 1862
12. 20 March 1862
13. 25 April 1862
14. July 1862
15. 19 Sept 1862
16. 19 Sept 1862
17. 19 Sept 1862
18. Undated; Corti, 89
19. 22 Sept 1862

20. 20 Sept 1862
21. 22 Sept 1862

10 'A certain strong Man'

1. 5 March 1861
2. Corti, 84
3. Corti, 26
4. *Recollections*. i. 163
5. Eyck, 40
6. 28 Sept 1862
7. *Recollections*, i. 165
8. Eyck, 58
9. Corti, 100
10. Corti, 100
11. Eyck, 62
12. Eyck, 62; *Letters E.F.*, 41, 8 June 1863
13. *Letters E.F.*, 42
14. 5 June 1863
15. *Letters*, II. i. 86, Crown Princess to Queen Victoria, 8 June 1863
16. *Dearest Mama*, 231, 15 June 1863
17. *Letters*, II. i. 110, King of Belgians to Queen Victoria, 21 Sept 1863
18. Morier, i. 343
19. *Recollections*, i. 343
20. 22 July 1863
21. Eyck, 65

11 'All the Results that Germany expects'

1. 8 June 1863
2. *Dearest Child*, 244, 5 April 1860
3. Bunsen *In Three Legations*, 276
4. Eyck, 68
5. Eyck, 75
6. *Letters*, II. i. 105-7, Memorandum by Queen Victoria, 31 Aug 1863
7. *Dearest Mama*, 294, 27 Jan 1864
8. 25 Dec 1863
9. *Letters E.F.*, 52
10. *Letters*, II. i. 155, King of Belgians to Queen Victoria, 2 Feb 1864
11. 3 Feb 1864
12. 16 March 1864
13. Undated
14. Lee, i. 256
15. Corti, 136
16. Grant Robertson, 236
17. Grant Robertson, 236
18. *Sophie*, 311

19. *Sophie*, 310
20. *A Memoir*, 113
21. Prussia, Princess Victoria of, *My Memoirs*, 16
22. 28 Feb 1865
23. 25 Jan 1865
24. 12 Dec 1865
25. *Letters E.F.*, 68
26. Morier, i. 90
27. Early Life, 118
28. Morier, ii. 97, Stockmar to Robert Morier, 12 Feb 1866

12   The Waiting Game

1. 22 Nov 1865
2. *Dearest Child*, 229
3. 16 April 1866
4. *Letters E.F.*, 57
5. *Letters*, II. i. 280, King of Belgians to Queen Victoria, 28 Oct 1865
6. Undated
7. Undated
8. Busch, i. 139
9. *Holstein Papers*, ii. 177
10. *Holstein Papers*, i. 139, quoting Stosch *Denkwürdigkeiten*
11. 12 Feb 1866
12. 2 March 1866
13. *Letters E.F.*, 59
14. *Letters*, II. i. 305, Queen's Journal, 19 March 1866
15. *Letters E.F.*, 59
16. *Letters*, II. i. 317, Queen Victoria to King of Prussia, 10 April 1866
17. 25 April 1866
18. *Letters*, II. i. 312, Duchess of Coburg to Queen Victoria, 28 March 1866
19. Ludwig *Bismarck*, 270
20. Busch, i. 258
21. *Letters E.F.*, 59
22. *Letters E.F.*, 60
23. *Letters E.F.*, 61
24. Macdonnell, 125
25. *A Memoir*, 217
26. 4 July 1866
27. 5 July 1866
28. 4 July 1866

13   A Patriotic Duty

1. 24 July 1866
2. 20 July 1866
3. Eyck, 128

4. Eyck, 132
5. Radziwill, 94
6. Eyck, 150
7. Ponsonby, 165
8. Ponsonby, 170
9. *Letters*, II. i. 461, Queen Victoria to Lord Stanley, 26 Sept 1867
10. *Letters*, II. i. 463, Queen Victoria to Lord Derby, 29 Sept 1867
11. Busch, i. 139
12. *Recollections*, i. 164
13. 15 Sept 1867
14. *Letters*, II. i. 358, Alice, Grand Duchess of Hesse to Queen Victoria
15. Hesse *Letters*, 165
16. 11 Nov 1867

14   'Everyone preaches Peace'

1. 17 March 1868
2. Radziwill, 121
3. Morier, ii. 127
4. 17 Dec 1865
5. Morier, ii. 152
6. Bunsen *In Three Legations*, 286
7. Grant Robertson, 263
8. Bonnin, 64
9. Ramm, 309
10. *Letters*, II. ii. 10, Lord Clarendon to Queen Victoria, 14 March 1870
11. 6 July 1870
12. *War Diary*, 4
13. Bonnin, 275
14. *Letters E.F.*, 73
15. *Holstein Papers*, i. 41
16. *Letters*, II. ii. 19, Lord Clarendon to Queen Victoria, 3 May 1870
17. Busch, i. 116; Eyck, 164
18. Bonnin, 278
19. Busch, i. 120
20. Ramm, 313
21. Bonnin, 282
22. *Holstein Papers*, i. 41
23. *Holstein Papers*, i. 41
24. *War Diary*, 7
25. *War Diary*, 6

15   'The Watch on the Rhine'

1. *Letters E.F.*, 77
2. *Letters E.F.*, 81
3. *Letters E.F.*, 92

4. *Letters E.F.*, 94
5. Stockmar, LXXXVIII
6. *Letters E.F.*, 96
7. *Letters E.F.*, 96
8. *War Diary*, 111
9. *War Diary*, 112
10. *War Diary*, 99
11. *Letters*, II. i. 76, Col. Ponsonby to Queen Victoria, 12 Oct 1870
12. *Letters*, II. ii. 71, Queen's Journal, 25 Sept 1870
13. Busch, i. 481–2
14. Busch, i. 476
15. *Letters*, II. ii. 91, Queen Victoria to King of Prussia, undated

16   'Prussia's Finest Hour'

1. *War Diary*, 126
2. *War Diary*, 130
3. Busch, i. 315
4. Richter, 192
5. Busch, i. 213
6. *Letters E.F.*, 100
7. *Letters E.F.*, 77
8. Gower *Reminiscences*, 108
9. Howard, 527
10. Busch, i. 218, 406
11. Busch, i. 332
12. *War Diary*, 253
13. *War Diary*, 247
14. *War Diary*, 224–5, 17 Dec 1870 and 243–4, 1 Jan 1871
15. Howard, 345
16. *War Diary*, 222–3
17. *War Diary*, 224–5
18. *War Diary*, 238–9
19. *War Diary*, 255
20. Eyck, 177
21. *War Diary*, 225, 228; Eyck, 177
22. Eyck, 178
23. *War Diary*, 265
24. *Letters E.F.*, 120
25. *War Diary*, 333

17   'The Representatives of the Empire'

1. *War Diary*, 337
2. *Letters*, II. ii. 154, Queen's Journal, 31 July 1871
3. Busch, i. 138
4. Philippson *Das Leben Kaiser Friedrichs III*, 310

5. 27 July 1873
6. *Dearest Mama*, 128, 8 Nov 1862
7. *Holstein Papers*, i, 59
8. 11 March 1873
9. *Letters E.F.*, 139, Queen Victoria to Crown Princess
10. *Letters*, II. ii. 283, Queen Victoria to Crown Princess; Corti, 189
11. *Letters*, II. ii. 389, Lord Derby to Queen Victoria, 5 May 1874
12. *Letters*, II. ii. 391, Disraeli to Queen Victoria, 10 May 1874
13. *Letters E.F.*, 123, Queen Victoria to Crown Princess, 11 Feb 1871
14. 6 Oct 1874
15. Corti, 194
16. *Letters E.F.*, 136
17. Corti, 194
18. Radziwill, 126–7

18 'If the Emperor died tomorrow'

1. Ramm, 336, cf. 352, 368
2. *Letters E.F.*, 140
3. *Letters*, II. ii. 151, Queen Victoria to Crown Princess, 17 July 1877
4. 1 June 1878
5. Ramm, 339
6. Eyck, 251
7. 15 Jan 1879
8. 18 Jan 1881
9. *Letters*, II. iii. 168, Lady Emily Russell to Queen Victoria, 27 Dec 1880
10. 24 Feb 1881
11. 2 Nov 1881
12. *Letters E.F.*, 191
13. 7 Feb 1881
14. Eyck, 160
15. 29 July 1883
16. Undated
17. Eyck, 274–5
18. Eyck, 275
19. *Early Life*, 109
20. *Further Letters*, 174
21. Undated
22. *Letters E.F.*, 178
23. *Further Letters*, 240, 4 Feb 1880
24. Corti, 213
25. *Holstein Papers*, ii. 317; *Early Life*, 202
26. 12 Oct 1883
27. *Early Life*, 200
28. *Holstein Papers*, ii. 14
29. Busch, iii. 171
30. 10 Oct 1885

31. Busch, iii. 174; Rich. i. 154
32. 15 Oct 1885
33. *Letters E.F.*, 203
34. 2 Oct 1885
35. 20 Oct 1885
36. 18 Sept 1885
37. Radziwill, 165
38. 14 Oct 1887
39. *Letters*, III. i. 384, Queen Victoria to Lord Salisbury, 14 Oct 1887
40. *Letters*, III. i. 385, Lord Salisbury to Queen Victoria, 15 Oct 1887

19 'Learn to Suffer without Complaining'

1. 3 Nov 1885
2. *Letters E.F.*, 226
3. Undated
4. *Early Life*, 295
5. Rennell Rodd, 113
6. *Letters E.F.*, 331
7. *Recollections*, 231
8. *Letters E.F.*, 332
9. Corti, 241
10. *Early Life*, 298
11. Semon, 187
12. 20 May 1887
13. Semon, 82; 22 May 1887
14. *Holstein Papers*, ii. 343
15. Corti, 243
16. *Letters E.F.*, 231
17. *Letters E.F.*, 238
18. *Recollections*, ii. 329
19. *Recollections*, ii. 340
20. Busch, iii. 175
21. Taylor, 232
22. *Letters E.F.*, 236
23. *Letters E.F.*, 235
24. *Letters E.F.*, 237
25. *Early Life*, 269
26. Corti, 244
27. *Letters E.F.*, 239
28. Corti, 245

20 'Worthy to be your Child'

1. Semon, 159
2. Semon, 160
3. Ponsonby, 264

4. *Further Letters*, 265
5. *Letters*, III. i. 350, Queen's Journal, 7 Sept 1887
6. *Letters E.F.*, 242, Crown Princess to Lady Ponsonby
7. *Holstein Papers*, ii. 351
8. Busch, iii. 169
9. Corti, 249
10. *Letters E.F.*, 242, Crown Princess to Lady Ponsonby, 5 Oct 1887
11. Mackenzie, 55
12. *Letters E.F.*, 260
13. *Letters E.F.*, 260
14. *Letters E.F.*, 252; *Letters*, III. i. 359, Queen's Journal, 12 Nov 1887
15. Semon, 157–8
16. *Letters E.F.*, 257
17. 31 March 1888
18. 18 Nov 1862
19. Corti, 270
20. Richter, 310–11
21. *Letters*, III. i. 361, Queen's Journal, 14 Nov 1887
22. *Letters E.F.*, 258, Queen Victoria to Crown Princess
23. *Letters E.F.*, 334
24. *Letters E.F.*, 269
25. Ponsonby, 259
26. *Letters E.F.*, 266
27. *Letters E.F.*, 266, Lady Ponsonby to Queen Victoria, 14 Dec 1887
28. *Letters E.F.*, 275
29. Corti, 262, quoting Arend Buchholz *Ernst von Bergmann*, 182

21 'Mere Passing Shadows'

1. Radziwill, 33
2. Radziwill, 200, 210
3. 13 Nov 1887
4. *Holstein Papers*, ii. 343
5. *Holstein Papers*, ii. 343
6. 9 March 1888
7. *Letters E.F.*, 286
8. 9 March 1888
9. *Letters*, III. i. 390, German Emperor to Queen Victoria, 9 March 1888
10. *Letters E.F.*, 287
11. *Letters E.F.*, 291, Frederick III to Prince Bismarck, 12 March 1888
12. Corti, 268
13. 16 March 1888
14. 10 March 1888
15. *Letters E.F.*, 288
16. Freund, 334–5
17. Richter, 317
18. Richter, 317

19. *Letters E.F.*, 293, 16 March 1888
20. Eyck, 303
21. *Letters E.F.*, 300, Queen Victoria to Lord Salisbury, 21 April 1888
22. Eyck, 302
23. *Holstein Papers*, ii. 366
24. 21 March 1888; Corti, 271
25. Corti, 273; Eyck, 302
26. *Letters E.F.*, 294
27. Richter, 322
28. 6 April 1888
29. Eyck, 304
30. 27 April 1888
31. *Holstein Papers*, ii. 142
32. Busch, iii. 187
33. *Letters*, III. i. 407–8, Queen's Journal, 27 April 1888

22 'I will take Care of Her'

1. Mackenzie, 197
2. *Letters E.F.*, 332
3. *Letters E.F.*, 308
4. 21 March 1888
5. Undated 1888
6. Undated 1888
7. Radziwill, 201
8. Radziwill, 201
9. Ludwig *William II*, 49
10. Waldersee, i. 378
11. *Letters E.F.*, 299, Col. Swaine to Prince of Wales, 13 April 1888
12. 1 June 1888
13. Eyck, 304
14. *Letters E.F.*, 313
15. 9 June 1888
16. Undated 1888
17. 8 June 1888
18. 13 June 1888
19. *Letters E.F.*, 314
20. Corti, 305
21. An account of the memories of the year 1888, by the Empress Frederick
22. *Early Life*, 299
23. *Letters E.F.*, 315
24. Corti, 304
25. 15 June 1888
26. 18 June 1888
27. *Letters E.F.*, 319
28. 16 June 1888

23   A Generation Skipped

1. *Letters E.F.*, 364, Col. Swaine to Sir H. Ponsonby, undated
2. Undated 1888
3. *Letters*, III. i. 423, Queen Victoria to German Emperor, 3 July 1888
4. *Letters*, III. i. 425, German Emperor to Queen Victoria, 6 July 1888
5. *Letters E.F.*, 327
6. Rennell Rodd, 146; *Letters E.F.*, 326
7. Freund, 227–8; *Deutscher Reichsanzeiger*, 15 Nov 1887
8. Richter, 325
9. Ponsonby, 266
10. 18 Aug 1888
11. 14 Oct 1888
12. Mackenzie, 6
13. Ludwig *William II*, 58
14. *Letters*, III. i. 425, German Emperor to Queen Victoria, 6 July 1888
15. *Letters*, III. i. 487–9, Prince of Wales to Prince Christian of Schleswig-Holstein, 3 April 1889
16. Lee, i. 645
17. Lee, i. 646
18. Lee, i. 647
19. Corti, 309
20. *Letters E.F.*, 324, Col. Swaine to Sir Henry Ponsonby, 4 July 1888
21. Corti, 308
22. *Letters*, III. i. 448, Queen Victoria to Marquis of Salisbury, cipher telegram, 24 Oct 1888
23. 17 Nov 1888
24. 19 Nov 1888
25. Ramm, 368
26. Undated
27. Corti, 278, Sir Robert Morier to Sir Edward Malet, 17 May 1888
28. *Letters*, III. i. 466, Queen Victoria to the Marquis of Salisbury, cipher telegram, 18 Jan 1889
29. *Letters*, III. i. 239, Marquis of Salisbury to Queen Victoria, 30 Dec 1886
30. *Daily Telegraph*, 31 Dec 1888
31. *The Times*, 31 Dec 1888
32. Richter, 331
33. *Letters*, III. i. 467, Queen Victoria to Prince of Wales, 7 Feb 1889

24   'Time will show that Fritz was right'

1. Eyck, 304
2. Eyck, 304
3. Busch, iii. 195
4. Eyck, 305
5. Busch, iii. 204

6. *War Diary*, 17
7. Busch, iii. 206
8. 8 May 1890
9. Busch, iii. 189
10. Corti, 315
11. 6 Oct 1888
12. *Letters E.F.*, 344
13. *Letters E.F.*, 349
14. 2 Oct 1888
15. *Letters*, III. i. 501, Sir H. Ponsonby to Prince Christian of Schleswig-Holstein, 1 June 1889
16. *Letters E.F.*, 358
17. 2 Sept 1889
18. 22 June 1888
19. Busch, iii. 202
20. Corti, 327
21. 16 Aug 1889
22. *The Times*, 9 Aug 1889
23. *The Times*, 19 Nov 1888
24. *Letters E.F.*, 389
25. *Letters E.F.*, 392
26. *Letters E.F.*, 399
27. *Letters E.F.*, 386
28. *Letters E.F.*, 396
29. *Letters E.F.*, 398
30. *Letters E.F.*, 403
31. *Letters E.F.*, 444

25 The Chance to do Good

1. *Letters E.F.*, 409
2. *Letters E.F.*, 407
3. Richter, 337
4. *Letters E.F.*, 409
5. Eyck, 309
6. Ramm, 375
7. Ramm, 376
8. *Letters E.F.*, 416
9. Richter, 361
10. *Letters*, III. i. 565, Sir Edward Malet to Lord Salisbury, 10 Feb 1890
11. *Letters*, III. i. 565, Sir Edward Malet to Lord Salisbury, 10 Feb 1890
12. *Letters*, III. i. 591, Lord Salisbury to Queen Victoria, 9 April 1890
13. *Letters*, III. i. 590, German Emperor to Queen Victoria, 27 March 1890
14. *Letters E.F.*, 413
15. Ramm, 378
16. 14 June 1890
17. *Sophie*, 67

18. Pope-Hennessy *Queen Victoria at Windsor and Balmoral,* 98
19. Corti, 337
20. 15 Nov 1890
21. *Sophie,* 86
22. Corti, 339
23. 13 April 1891
24. *Letters E.F.,* 349–50
25. Richter, 319
26. *A Memoir,* 340
27. *Letters E.F.,* 425
28. 17 April 1891

26   A World changing for the Better

1. 8 Dec 1893
2. *Sophie,* 156
3. *Sophie,* 143
4. *Sophie,* 144
5. *Letters E.F.,* 451
6. *Letters E.F.,* 431
7. *Letters,* III. ii. 395, German Emperor to Queen Victoria, 24 April 1894
8. *Letters,* III. ii. 404, Earl of Rosebery to Queen Victoria
9. *Letters E.F.,* 447
10. *Letters E.F.,* 449
11. Corti, 347
12. *Sophie,* 175
13. *Sophie,* 151

27   'The Future has passed into other Hands'

1. *A Memoir,* 353
2. *Letters E.F.,* 425
3. Ramm, 379
4. 10 May 1895
5. *Letters,* III. iii. 8, Queen Victoria to German Emperor, 5 Jan 1896
6. *The Times,* 2 Feb 1896
7. *Letters,* III. iii. 155, Sir Arthur Bigge to Mr Egerton, 27 April 1897
8. *Sophie,* 236
9. Ponsonby, 253
10. Lee, i. 737
11. Lee, i. 738
12. Lee, i. 739

28   'Surely God will bless Her'

1. *Sophie,* 293
2. *Holstein Papers,* ii. 344

3. Bunsen *The World I Used to Know*, 214
4. Bunsen *The World I Used to Know*, 204
5. *Sophie*, 305
6. Lee, ii. 755, William II to Prince of Wales, 21 Dec 1900
7. *Letters*, III. iii. 459, Empress Frederick to Queen Victoria, 10 Jan 1900
8. *Sophie*, 322
9. *Sophie*, 336
10. Bunsen *The World I Used to Know*, 205
11. 18 Oct 1900
12. 6 Feb 1901
13. 23 Jan 1901
14. *Sophie*, 345
15. 8 June 1901
16. Bunsen *The World I Used to Know*, 218
17. *A Memoir*, 370
18. 21 July 1901
19. Rich, i. 130
20. Schrödl *Ein Künstlerleben im Sonnenschein*, 505–7 (Diary of Frau Schrödl, 5–21 August 1901)

29 'Men are perishable but Ideas live'

1. *Letters E.F.*, 126
2. *Letters E.F.*, 444
3. *Letters E.F.*, 446
4. *Letters E.F.*, 443
5. *Letters E.F.*, 447
6. Rich, i. 130
7. Rich, i. 130
8. *Letters E.F.*, 182
9. Mallet, 140
10. *Sophie*, 200
11. Ramm, 284
12. *Letters E.F.*, 442
13. *Letters E.F.*, 443
14. *Letters E.F.*, 444

Bibliography

Manuscript

Letters and papers in private possession. These are cited in the Notes by date alone.

Printed

Note: The left-hand column shows the abbreviations used in the Notes for books frequently cited. The works are listed alphabetically under abbreviations or (when there is no abbreviation) under the author's name.

ALBERT, H. A. *Queen Victoria's sister. The Life and Letters of Princess Feodora* (London 1967)

ALICE, H.R.H. Princess *For My Grandchildren: Some Reminiscences* (London 1966)

ANON *A diary of royal movements . . . in the reign of Queen Victoria*, vol. i. 1819–46, no more published (London 1883)

A Memoir   ANON *The Empress Frederick, a Memoir* (London 1912)

BARKELEY, R. *The Empress Frederick* (London 1956)

BEAL, Erica *Royal Cavalcade* (London 1939)

BENSON, E. F. *As We Were* (London 1930)

BENSON, E. F. *The Kaiser and his English Relations* (London 1936)

BENSON, E. F. *Daughters of Queen Victoria* (London 1939)

BLAKE, Robert *Disraeli* (London 1966)

BLOOMFIELD, Georgiana Baroness *Reminiscences of Court and Diplomatic Life* (London 1883)

BLÜCHER, Evelyn Mary, Countess *An English Wife in Berlin* (London 1920)

Bolitho   BOLITHO, Hector (ed.) *The Prince Consort and his Brother* Letters (London 1933)

Bonnin   BONNIN, Georges *Bismarck and the Hohenzollern Candidature to the Throne of Spain* (London 1957)

BRIGGS, Asa *Victorian People* (London 1954)

BUCHANAN, M. *Queen Victoria's Relations* (London 1954)

BÜLOW, Fürst von   *Memoirs,* trans. F. A. Voigt, 4 vols. (London 1931)

Bunsen   BUNSEN, Chevalier Charles de   *Memoirs,* 2 vols. (London 1868)

BUNSEN, Madame Charles de   *In Three Legations* (London 1909)

BUNSEN, Marie von   *The World I Used to Know, 1860–1912* (London 1930)

Busch   BUSCH, M.   *Bismarck, Some Secret Passages of his History,* 3 vols. (London 1898)

Corti   CORTI, Egon Caesar, Count   *The English Empress.* A Study of the Relations between Queen Victoria and her eldest daughter the Empress Frederick of Germany, trans. by E. M. Hodgson (London 1957)

COWLES, Virginia   *The Kaiser* (London 1963)

Dearest Child   FULFORD, Roger (ed.)   *Dearest Child.* Letters between Queen Victoria and the Princess Royal, 1858–1861. A Selection from the Kronberg Archives (London 1964)

Dearest Mama   FULFORD, Roger (ed.)   *Dearest Mama.* Letters between Queen Victoria and the Crown Princess of Prussia 1861–1864 (London 1968)

DUFF, D.   *Hessian Tapestry* (London 1967)

Early Life   WILLIAM II, Emperor   *My Early Life* (London 1926)

EVANS, Joan   *The Victorians,* Introduced by Joan Evans (Cambridge 1966)

Eyck   EYCK, Erich   *Bismarck and the German Empire* (London 1950)

Frank Eyck   EYCK, Frank   *The Prince Consort: A Political Study* (London 1959)

Freund   FREUND, Michael   *Das Drama der 99 Tage.* Krankheit und Tod Friedrichs III (Köln-Berlin 1966)

FULFORD, Roger   *The Prince Consort* (London 1949)

Further Letters   BOLITHO, Hector (ed.)   *Further Letters of Queen Victoria.* From the Archives of The House of Brandenburg-Prussia (London 1938)

GOWER, Lord Ronald   *Reminiscences* (London 1895)

Grant Robertson   GRANT ROBERTSON, C.   *Bismarck* (London 1918)

Grant and Temperley   GRANT, A. J. and TEMPERLEY, H.   *Europe in the Nineteenth Century* (1789–1914) (London 1931)

GREVILLE, Charles   *Memoirs,* ed. by Roger Fulford (London 1963)

GREY, The Hon. C.   *The Early Years of the Prince Consort* (London 1867)

GREY, of Fallodon, Viscount   *Twenty-Five Years* (London 1925)

HESSE, Alice, Grand Duchess of   *Letters* (London 1884)

HOBHOUSE, Christopher *1851 and the Crystal Palace* (London 1937)

HOHENLOHE-SCHILLINGSFÜRST, Chlodwig Fürst zu *Memoirs*, trans. by G. W. Chrystal (London 1906)

Holstein Papers   RICH, N. B. (ed.) and FISHER, M. R. (ed.) *The Holstein Papers:* The memoirs, diaries and correspondence of Friedrich von Holstein 1837–1909, 3 vols. (Cambridge 1957)

Howard   HOWARD, Michael *The Franco-Prussian War* (London 1961)

Leaves   VICTORIA, Queen *Leaves from a Journal . . . 1855*, ed. R. Mortimer (London 1961)

Lee   LEE, Sir Sidney *King Edward VII*, 2 vols. (London 1925)

LEINHAAS, G. A. *Königin Friedrich* (Berlin 1914)

Letters   VICTORIA, Queen *Letters: A Selection from Her Majesty's Correspondence.* First Series: 1837–1861, ed. by A. C. Benson and Viscount Esher, 3 vols. (London 1907). Second series: 1862–1885, ed. by G. E. Buckle, 3 vols. (London 1926). Third series: 1886–1901, ed. by G. E. Buckle, 3 vols. (London 1930)

Letters E.F.   PONSONBY, Sir Frederick (ed.) *The Letters of the Empress Frederick* (London 1929)

Letters P.C.   JAGOW, K. (ed.) *Letters of the Prince Consort, 1831–1861* (London 1938)

Longford   LONGFORD, Elizabeth *Victoria R.I.* (London 1964)

Ludwig *Bismarck*   LUDWIG, Emil *Bismarck, the Story of a Fighter*, trans. by Eden and Cedar Paul (London 1927)

Ludwig *William II*   LUDWIG, Emil *Kaiser William II*, trans. by Ethel Colburn Mayne (London and New York 1926)

Lyttelton   LYTTELTON, Sarah Lady *Correspondence 1787–1870*, ed. by the Hon. Mrs Hugh Wyndham (London 1912)

Macdonell   MACDONELL, Anne Lady *Reminiscences of Diplomatic Life* (London 1913)

Mackenzie   MACKENZIE, Sir Morell *The Fatal Illness of Frederick the Noble* (London 1888)

Mallet   MALLET, Sir Victor *Life with Queen Victoria.* Mary Mallet's letters from Court 1887–1901 (London 1968)

Martin   MARTIN, Sir Theodore *Life of His Royal Highness The Prince Consort*, 5 vols. (London 1875–80)

MCGUIGAN, D. M. *The Habsburgs* (New York 1966)

MEDLICOTT, W. N. *Bismarck and Modern Germany* (London 1965)

MONTGOMERY of Alamein, Field Marshal Viscount *A History of Warfare* (London 1968)

Morier   MORIER, Sir Robert *Memoirs and Letters 1826–1876*, ed. by his daughter Mrs Rosslyn Wemyss, 2 vols. (London 1911)

BIBLIOGRAPHY

PAGET, Walburga Lady *Embassies of other Days*, 2 vols. (London 1923)

Paget   PAGET, Walburga Lady *Scenes and Memories* (London 1912)

PALMERSTON, Emily Mary, Viscountess *Letters*. Selected and edited from the originals at Broadlands and elsewhere by T. Lever (London 1957)

PASSANT, E. J. *A Short History of Germany 1815–1945* (Cambridge 1962)

PFLANZE, Otto *Bismarck and the Development of Germany* (Princeton 1964)

PHILIPPSON, Martin *Das Leben Kaiser Friedrichs III* (Wiesbaden 1908)

Ponsonby   PONSONBY, Magdalen *Mary Ponsonby: a memoir, some letters and a journal* (London 1927)

POPE-HENNESSY, James *Queen Mary* (London 1959)

POPE-HENNESSY, James *Queen Victoria at Windsor and Balmoral* (London 1959)

PRUSSIA, Princess Frederick Leopold of *Behind the Scenes at the Prussian Court* (London 1939)

PRUSSIA, Princess Victoria of *My Memoirs* (London 1929)

Radziwill   RADZIWILL, Princess Catherine *The Empress Frederick* (London 1934)

Ramm   RAMM, Agatha *Germany 1789–1919* (London 1967)

Recollections   BISMARCK, Prince Otto von *Recollections and Reminiscences*, ed. by A. M. Gibson, 2 vols. (Cambridge 1940)

REISCHACH, Baron Hugo von *Under Three Emperors*, trans. by Prince Blücher (London 1927)

Rennell Rodd   RODD, Sir Rennell *Social and Diplomatic Memories*, 3 vols. (London 1922)

Rich   RICH, N. B. *Friedrich von Holstein: Politics and Diplomacy in the era of Bismarck and Wilhelm II*, 2 vols. (Cambridge 1965)

Richter   RICHTER, Werner *Bismarck*, trans. by B. Battershaw (London 1964)

RUMBOLD, Sir Horace *Final Recollections of a Diplomatist* (London 1905)

SAXE-COBURG-GOTHA, Duke Ernest II of *Memoirs*, trans. by P. Andreae, 4 vols. (London 1888)

SCHRÖDL, Norbert *Ein Künstlerleben im Sonnenschein* (Frankfurt 1922)

SCHWERING, Count Axel von *The Berlin Court under William II* (London 1915)

Semon   SEMON, Sir Felix *Autobiography*, ed. by H. C. Semon and T. A. McIntyre (London 1926)

370

Sophie	LEE, Arthur Gould (ed.) *The Empress Frederick writes to Sophie . . . Letters 1889–1901* (London 1955)
Stanley *Letters*	STANLEY, Lady Augusta *Letters, 1849–1863*, ed. by A. V. Baillie and H. Bolitho (London 1927)
Stanley *Later Letters*	STANLEY, Lady Augusta *Later Letters, 1864–1873*, ed. by A. V. Baillie and H. Bolitho (London 1929)
	STEVENSON, R. Scott *Morell Mackenzie* (London 1946)
	STOCKMAR, Baron Ernest von (ed.) *The Memoirs of Baron Stockmar*, trans. by G. A. Mueller, 2 vols. (London 1872)
	SYKES, Christopher *Troubled Loyalty*. A biography of Adam von Trott (London 1968)
Taylor	TAYLOR, A. J. P. *Bismarck* (London 1955)
	TISDALL, E. F. P. *She made world chaos: the intimate story of the Empress Frederick* (London 1940)
	TRIMMER, Mrs S. K. *Fabulous Histories* (London 1788)
	VICTORIA, Queen *Victoria in the Highlands*. The personal journal of Her Majesty Queen Victoria, ed. by David Duff (London 1968)
Waldersee	WALDERSEE, Count Alfred von *Denkwürdigkeiten des Generalfeldmarschalls Alfred Grafen von Waldersee*, 3 vols. (Berlin 1922)
	WALDERSEE, Count Alfred von *A Field Marshal's Memoirs*, condensed and trans. by F. Whyte (London 1924)
War Diary	FREDERICK III, Emperor *War Diary 1870–1871*, trans. and edited by A. R. Allison (London 1927)
	WILLIAM II, Emperor *My Memoirs, 1878–1918* (London 1922)
	YOUNG, G. M. *Victorian England, Portrait of an Age* (London 1936)

Index